William Charles Maughan

Annals of Garelochside

Being an Account historical and topographical of the Parishes of Row, Rosneath and

Cardross

William Charles Maughan

Annals of Garelochside
Being an Account historical and topographical of the Parishes of Row, Rosneath and Cardross

ISBN/EAN: 9783337130862

Printed in Europe, USA, Canada, Australia, Japan

Cover: Foto ©ninafisch / pixelio.de

More available books at **www.hansebooks.com**

ANNALS OF GARELOCHSIDE

BEING AN ACCOUNT HISTORICAL AND
TOPOGRAPHICAL

OF THE

PARISHES OF ROW, ROSNEATH AND CARDROSS

BY

WILLIAM CHARLES MAUGHAN

AUTHOR OF "ROSNEATH PAST AND PRESENT," "THE ALPS OF ARABIA,"
"JULIAN ORMONDE," ETC., ETC.

WITH ILLUSTRATIONS BY ALEXANDER M'GIBBON, ESQ., ARCHITECT

ALEXANDER GARDNER
Publisher to Her Majesty the Queen
PAISLEY; AND 26 PATERNOSTER SQUARE, LONDON

1897

I Dedicate
This Book
to
My Dear Wife

PREFACE.

THE success which attended his book *Rosneath : Past and Present*, has encouraged the author to attempt a larger work treated in a similar style. There is so much of interest in the whole neighbourhood of the Gareloch, and it is such a favourite resort in summer, that it is hoped that a careful topographical study of the parishes of Row and Cardross, as they existed in the latter part of last century, and coming down to the present day, will secure approval. It is thought desirable to incorporate Rosneath with the other parishes, because the author has gained much additional information upon the subject. Many noble families have owned the lands near the Gareloch, and played their part in the affairs of the nation, although in some instances, they no longer are connected with Dunbartonshire.

The first part of the book treats of the County of Dunbarton as a whole, and gives some details as to the life and pursuits of the inhabitants of that part of Scotland. Particulars regarding the old industries and occupations, as well as about the social habits of the landowners and peasantry, and the many changes in the ownership of the estates, form an interesting and instructive picture.

In discoursing upon the separate parishes of Row, Cardross, and Rosneath, the author wished to point out the ancient holdings of the various families, and to specify what they did to bring out the resources of the soil. The old ecclesiastical divisions are noted, and details given which will be acceptable to the student of Church history.

In various instances the author was fortunate in being able to draw upon the recollections of very aged persons, whose memories happily retained a wonderful vigour, and who could give graphic

pictures of scenes and customs of over eighty years ago.   The
favourite town of Helensburgh demanded a full and careful account,
and its gradual rise, from a single row of thatched houses on the
shore to its present extensive boundaries, cannot but be of interest to
many.

Though some of the family matters given may seem rather
minute, still, as a picture of men and manners, they have a value of
their own.   The ecclesiastical details, taken from authentic sources,
characterise a state of matters now passing away.

The notes and anecdotes as to the agriculture, ornithology, and
natural history of the Gareloch, indicate that much may be gleaned
in this department.   Until within a few years, the district of the
Gareloch was rich in specimens of game, aquatic, and sea-birds, and
some account is given of their various haunts and habits.

The author has to acknowledge his obligation to different works
treating of the West of Scotland, and the County of Dunbarton in
particular.   For many of the details of the ancient families of Row
and Cardross he is indebted to the elaborate and accurate family and
local histories contained in the Dennistoun MS. in the Advocates'
Library.   Irving's laborious *History of Dunbartonshire* has supplied
much valuable information, as has also Dr. David Murray's monograph an *Old Cardross*, and the Rev. Dr. Story's admired life of his
father, from which is condensed the account of the Story family.
Tytler's *History of Scotland* was examined as to the domestic details
and manners of a byegone age, while Sir William Fraser's *Colquhouns
of Luss*, Hew Scott's *Fasti*, *Origines Parochiales*, and the two *Statistical
Accounts of Scotland*, all contributed many facts of interest.   Amongst
other works consulted were *Eminent Scotsmen*, Whyte and M'Farlane's
Agriculture of Dunbartonshire, *Sketches of Clergy of the Gareloch*, *The
Scottish Nation*, *Beauties of Scotland*, *Memorials of John Macleod Camp-
bell*, Macleod's *Lennox Families*, and other works ; *Birds of West of
Scotland*, Morris' *Life of Henry Bell*, Chalmers' *Caledonia*, Glen's
History of Dunbarton, *The Story of Helensburgh*, *Days at the Coast*, etc.

Especial thanks are due to Dr. Murray for extracts from *Old
Cardross*, also to Rev. J. M. Webster of Row, Rev. W. Maxwell of

Cardross, and Rev. Alfred Warr of Rosneath, for useful information afforded and permission to examine church records of their respective parishes. Interesting particulars were kindly given by Mr. James Spy, of Row, upon the topography of that district, by Mr. Duncan M'Kinlay, a venerable native of Shandon, and ferryman there for many long years; and by Mr. Andrew Jardine of Balimenoch, Glenfruin.

For his account of Rosneath the author has to acknowledge his indebtedness to the Marquis of Lorne, K.T., Mr. Peter M'Neilage, Mill of Campsail; Mr. Archibald Stewart, Portkill; Mr. John M'Lean, Clachan of Rosneath; and Mr. Robert Chalmers, Rahane— the two latter natives of the parish having since passed away. Thanks are also due to Sir James Colquhoun, Bart., of Colquhoun; Sir Joseph D. Hooker, K.C.S.I.; Mr. John M'Farlane, Faslane; Mr. John William Burns of Kilmahew; Mr. Adam Miller, Helensburgh; Mr. C. T. Couper, Row; Mr. Michael Honeyman; Mr. John Bell, Dunbarton; Mr. Robert Craig, Sheriff Clerk; Mr. R. Bennett Browne of Bendarroch; Mr. Barrett, Secretary of Mitchell Library; Mr. Donald Maclean, Postmaster, Helensburgh. Also to Mrs. M'Donald, of Belmore; Mrs. Nisbet, Row; Mrs. Bain, Kilcreggan; Mrs. Campbell, Barbour; Mrs. Archd. Marquis, Coulport; Mrs. Macfarlane, Old Ferry House, Kilcreggan. Major John M'Intyre, V.D., Cardross, also obligingly supplied many particulars of special interest.

Mr. Alexander M'Gibbon has furnished the illustrations, with the exception of the Gareloch view, taken by Miss Elma Story from a painting by G. F. Buchanan, of the loch as it appeared in 1846.

KILARDEN.
ROSNEATH, 16th July, 1896.

CONTENTS.

ILLUSTRATIONS.

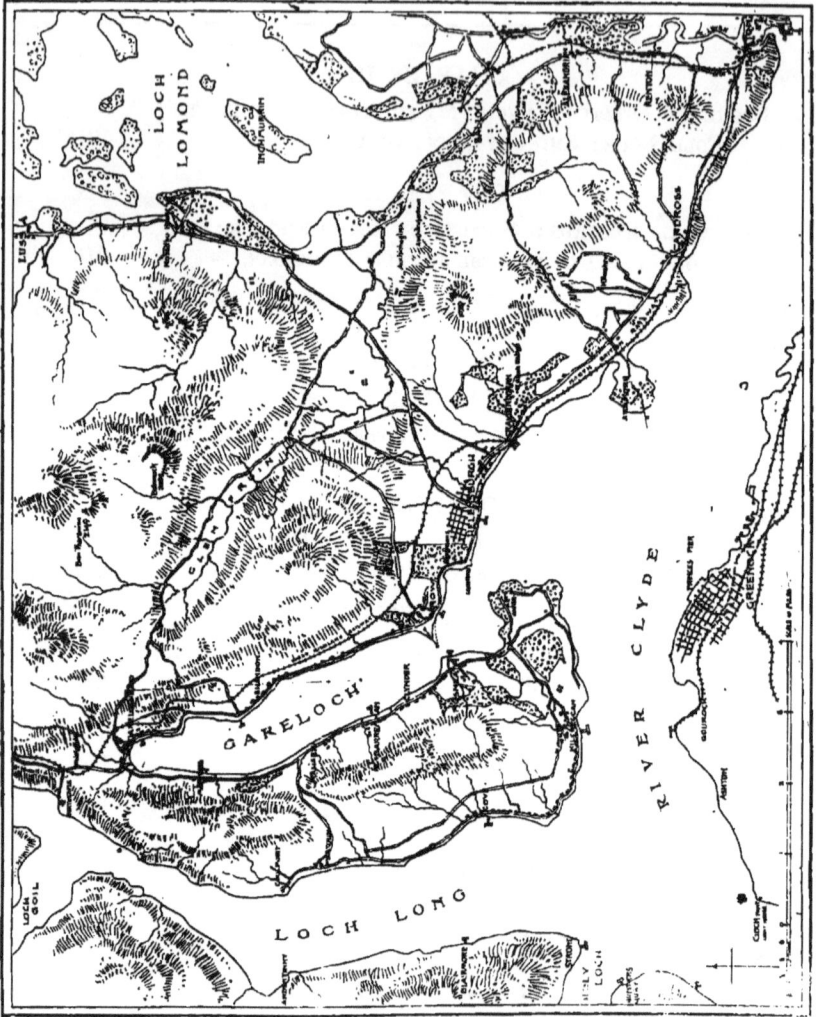

MAP OF THE GARELOCH DISTRICT.

GARELOCHSIDE.

CHAPTER I

The County of Dunbarton Two Centuries Ago.

THE County of Dunbarton, though not one of the largest in Scotland, is certainly one of the most romantic and varied in the beauty of its aspect. It embraces within its limits the most picturesque and striking scenery, sometimes all the wild and savage grandeur of the Alpine fastnesses of the Highlands, mingled with the sweet loveliness and flowery meads of a pastoral landscape. The majestic Ben Voirlich, and the "cloud capt" Ben Lomond, afford to those in search of the sublime in nature, precipices and gorges worthy of the pencil of a Salvator Rosa, while the beautiful Duncroyne completely clad with trees, and the sylvan banks of Loch Lomond, have a charm unequalled in their way. In many a secluded glen, overhung with beetling precipices, in the northern portion of the county, the traveller might well imagine himself to be where it

> " Seems that primeval earthquake's sway
> Hath rent a strange and shattered way
> Through the rude bosom of the hill,
> And that each naked precipice
> Sable ravine and dark abyss
> Tells of the outrage still."

A

Nowhere in Great Britain is there a scene of more exquisite character on a still summer day, in the leafy month of June, than can be beheld from one of the little islands which repose amidst the dark purple waters of Loch Lomond near Luss. On all sides save one, where the gleaming water spreads itself away in silvery reaches to the southern end of the Loch, there arise verdant slopes, decked with umbrageous oak or sombre pine, the purple heather mantling over all, until the crest of the mountain ranges is reached, so clearly defined against the mellow sky. Point and promontory, grey with lichen-covered rocks of sparkling mica or glittering granite, shoot athwart the gazer's eye as it turns upon one after another of the pictures over which the fancy of the artist and the poet loves to dilate. While from the summit of any of the lofty peaks whose shadows slumber in the dark unfathomed depths of the Loch below, there can be gained a panorama of glorious pictures of mountain, crag, leafy dell, and rippling stream, that imprint their features indelibly on the stranger's mind.

The lands of Dunbartonshire were a portion of the ancient territory of Strathclyde, whose capital figured conspicuously in the story of Roman occupation, and throughout the fierce conflicts of the ancient Britons, Picts, and Scots. The name of this capital appears in the old writs and documents under various spellings, sometimes Dunbretane, oftener Dunbertane, and Dunbartan, but latterly chiefly Dumbarton, or Dunbarton, and the town and port, which have given their name to the county, bear the impress of the language spoken by the early inhabitants. By many the derivation of the name is supposed to be Dun-briton, the "fort of the Britons," and it was known at a still earlier period as Alcluid, the capital of the kingdom of the Attacotti. This district of the county, bounded on the west by Loch Long, on the north by Perthshire, on the east by Stirlingshire, and on the south by the broad estuary of the Clyde,—was in former days also known as the *Levenach*, the "field of the Leven." This word, written in the plural, came to be the designation of the powerful lords of the soil, Levenachs, and gradually was corrupted into Lennox. In the thirteenth century the sheriffdom of Dunbarton and the Lennox were co-extensive, but gradually, owing to the jurisdiction of the former being considerably curtailed, their identity ceased.   It would appear from the chartulary of Lennox, and other records, that there had been a judge or justice of Levenax during the reigns of William the Lion and Alexander II.   In the year 1271, as is stated in Hole's *Sutherland*, Walter Stewart, Earl Menteith, the betrayer of Wallace, was sheriff of this county, and constable of the castle of Dunbarton.   In the various Acts of Parliament, published by authority of Government, the county is not once named during the reign of King James I.   During that of his successor, James II., it seems to have come more into notice, and in August 1440, "the castell of Dumbertane, with the lands of Cardross, Rosneathe, the pensione of Cadzowe, with the pensione of the Ferme-Mill of Kilpatrick," appear to have been annexed to the Crown.   In the reign of James IV. many of the western counties of Scotland were much disturbed, and the power of the Crown had to be put forth to stop "thift, reff, and uther ennormities," and for this purpose the Lord of Montgomery is appointed for "Dumbertane, the Leuenax, Bute, and Arran."   Attention was also devoted to the trade of Dunbarton, and, during the reigns of James IV. and V., it was the chief naval station in the west, some of the royal fleet being also anchored in the secluded and picturesque bay of Campsail at Rosneath.

The Danes, who were such sore scourges to both England and Scotland, in the course of their many predatory expeditions, ravaged the shores of the Frith of Clyde, and Dunbarton often saw their hostile ships pass her ramparts.   Readers of History know that Haco, King of Norway, also, in the year 1263, set forth to punish the excesses of those whom he considered his unruly subjects in the Western Isles of Scotland.   That expedition, which was under Magnus, King of the Isle of Man, proceeded up the waters of Loch Long, which are separated from the Gareloch by the beautiful peninsula of Rosneath.   Sailing along its heath-clad mountainous shores to the head of Loch Long, the invaders dragged their boats across the narrow neck of land over to the gravelly strand of the peaceful

Loch Lomond. Here they indulged their savage propensities in
ravaging the country around the Loch, almost reducing it to a solitude, and carried fire and sword far into the confines of Dunbarton
and Stirling shires. Vengeance, however, in the wrath of the elements, overtook the marauders, for, in retiring with their plunder
from Loch Long, a great storm arose and scattered the fleet. Gathering together his forces to the rescue, as well as he could, the Norwegian King subsequently saw his expedition utterly vanquished at the
celebrated battle of Largs.

Generally speaking, the county of Dunbarton was comparatively
little traversed by the broad stream of Scottish warlike history,
although, from time to time, it was the scene of striking episodes.
Part of the adventurous career of Wallace, the hero of Scotland,
was associated with the territory round Dunbarton and the Gareloch,
and, as is well known, the patriot King Robert the Bruce passed
many of his latter days in the parish of Cardross, where he ended
his troubled days in peace. From his castle, not far from the confluence of the Leven with the waters of the Clyde, he could survey
the placid estuary along whose shores he enjoyed sailing his pleasure
boats, and exploring the many lovely inlets and romantic lochs which
allure the voyager by their singular beauty. He died on 7th June,
1329, lamented by the Scottish nation, whose liberties he had
secured, and his pathetic charge, on his death-bed, to Sir James
Douglas, the "brave and gentle knight," is well known, when the
latter was enjoined to take the hero's embalmed heart to Palestine
and deposit it in the Church of the Holy Sepulchre at Jerusalem.
The unfortunate Mary Queen of Scots is associated with the history
of the county, for, shortly after the battle of Pinkie, when but a
child, she took up her residence in the county of Dunbarton, and on
leaving Scotland two years afterwards, she embarked from this
ancient fortress. A small French fleet, consisting of four galleys,
had been sent to transport the youthful Scottish Queen to the shores
of her beloved France, and received their charge on board from the
hands of her mother, the Queen Regent. Accompanied by her
governors, her half brother the Lord James, then in his seventeenth

year, and by her "four Marys," who were children of the same
name and age, chosen as her playmates, from the families of Fleming,
Beaton, Scaton, and Livingstone, the beautiful child Queen, whose
story has been the theme of so many effusions of poetry, set sail for
sunny France.   After but a few stormy, unhappy years of her life
had passed, the Queen lay immured in an English Castle, there to
await the last scene of her strangely chequered career.

> " I was the Queen o' bonny France,
>   Where happy I hae been ;
> Fu' lightly rase I in the morn,
>   As blithe lay down at e'en."

In the troubled times of the Civil War, the county and castle of
Dunbarton were the arena of various sanguinary conflicts, and the
latter was, over and over again, besieged and captured, first by the
Royalist forces, and again by those of the Scottish Estates.   At one
time an order was issued for the destruction of its fortifications, but
eventually it was placed amongst the number of those strongholds
which, at the time of the union of the kingdoms, were decreed always
to be kept in a state of readiness for defence.   Thus we have seen
that the county has had its stirring epochs of history, and in tracing
the changes which have come over that portion of the ancient kingdom of the Lennox, it will be found that many soul-inspiring traditions and poetic legends linger around its heathery braes and frowning mountain heights.

Within the limits of the territory which extends from the corner
of Cardross parish, opposite to the Castle of Dunbarton, along the
shores of the Frith of Clyde, and embracing all the lands on either
side of the Gareloch, there is much to interest the students of secular
and ecclesiastical Scottish history.   It is therefore proposed to
examine into the records which exist in tolerable fulness of the three
parishes of Row, Rosneath, and a portion of Cardross, as the latter
was at one time part of the ancient territory of Rosneath.   With
the exception of the southern division of the latter peninsula, nearly
the whole of the three parishes, at one time formed part of the

great possessions of the noble family of Lennox, and it will therefore
be of interest to trace the history of that distinguished house. Including the historic valley of Glenfruin, with its sorrowful associations of strife and massacre, the district named has been the scene
of many stirring events, and has been the chosen home of a number
of men who have adorned the annals of their time and shed a lustre
upon the scenes amidst which they moved. It is always of importance to trace the gradual environment of a once bare and uncultivated stretch of heath-covered soil within the region of well tilled
and productive farm lands, in which the natural capability of the
surface ground is being fully developed. And the transition from
grassy slopes of natural pasture or luxuriant bracken to the populous
watering places, all adorned with gay gardens and handsome summer
villas, is certainly sufficiently striking to merit careful investigation.
While to unravel the curious details of the family history of those
territorial magnates, who once held sway on the banks of the Gareloch and the classic shores of Cardross, cannot be said to be an un-
profitable task. It will therefore be useful, before actually describing the districts more immediately coming within the scope of this
local history, to give a glance at the general condition of agriculture,
building, archæological remains, and rural economy throughout the
county of Dunbarton, as a whole. To do this properly, it may be
also necessary, here and there, slightly to diverge and take a more
extended survey of the actual state of the whole West of Scotland,
at the period when the great baronial families who owned the broad
domains of the Lennox were in the zenith of their power.

The condition of agriculture and farming throughout the country
in the fifteenth and sixteenth centuries was poor and unproductive.
Lands and property of all descriptions were subject to raids and
spoliation at the hands of rival chiefs, and marauders of various
kinds. The country was in a disturbed state, and the arm of the
civil power was scarcely sufficient to ensure protection for the lieges,
who were fain to place themselves under the guardianship of some
warlike baron. A great deal of the land was covered with dense
and dark forests, or overspread with heather and moss, and little had

been done in the way of tilling and improving the natural capabilities of the soil. Oats, wheat, barley, pease, and beans, were grown in the Lowlands, and in some of the more fruitful straths in the Highlands. The clergy, who had long enjoyed, especially through the liberality of David I. and his successors, great revenues and privileges, were the chief agricultural improvers of the country. They granted leases to their tenants and vassals, and the latter were encouraged in their efforts to clear the forests, and bring the moors and mossy lands under cultivation. All over the southern and western portions of Scotland, there were mills for the grinding of oats into meal, and in the hamlets and villages were numerous malt-kilns and small breweries, where the grain was rendered into malt and ale.

Besides these crops, there were large tracts of rich natural meadow, and the green sward, in the glades of the thick forests, which provided grass that was turned into hay for the use of horses and cattle. The grazings on the mountain braes and glens, and the more open parts of the woods were stocked with ample herds of sheep, cattle, and quantities of swine, whose chief food was the beech mast. Swine, indeed, formed the principal animal food of the humbler denizens of the soil, for certain rights were always reserved to the cottager or village bondman, which ensured him pasturage for his pigs. But the rearing of sheep and cattle was an important element in the farming operations of the period, and these formed not only part of the baron's estate, but were largely consumed as food at his table. It was more in the Lowlands that sheep abounded, for it was not until well on in the eighteenth century, that sheep breeding was intro- duced as a regular business into the Highland counties. In 1747 it was commenced and carried on in Dunbartonshire, by Mr. Campbell of Lagwyne, who then resided in the parish of Luss, before which time Dunbartonshire, generally, was stocked with black cattle, which brought in a poor return. The wool of the sheep formed an impor- tant article of export, or was often manufactured into cloth of a coarse description for the farm servants, the skins being tanned and exported to England or Flanders. Cattle were used as food, their carcasses being sometimes sold in the market of the burgh, while the skins that were not exported were made into shoes, coats, saddles and bridles, or other articles in use, by the rough retainers of the baron or laird of the soil.

The rearing of horses was also an important department in the farming economy, and they were a good deal used in rural work, and great care, as appeared from the various chartularies, was bestowed in ensuring a superior breed of animals. Many of the nobles had breeding studs on their estates, and young brood mares, and their foals, were allowed to run wild through the extensive forests producing hardy and excellent light horses. These domestic horses, however, were quite different from the ponderous war horse, which was itself decked with armour, and had to bear the weight of the knight, armed cap-a-pie with steel mail. In the lighter farming operations such as driving of wood and peats, or taking in corn during harvest, and even in ploughing and harrowing, oxen were used, but carriage of farm produce for distances was performed by horses.

Professor Cosmo Innes, in his *Early Scottish History*, gives some interesting details as to the state of cultivation of the lands in the more Lowland districts of Scotland, which would apply to parts of Dunbartonshire. Strict rules were laid down for the protection of growing corn and hay meadows, and a right of way through a neighbouring territory was sometimes purchased at a considerable price, or made the subject of formal donation. Wheat was cultivated, and even wheaten bread was used on special occasions. Mills driven by water, and even by wind power, were used for grinding corn, although the rude and laborious hand mill or *quern*, still was extensively employed in the preparation of meal. Mention is made of the care exercised in rearing and improving the breed of horses; Roger Avenel, the lord of Eskdale, having a large stud in that pastoral valley, while the Earl of Dunbar, before his departure to the Holy Land in 1247, sold his stud to Melrose Abbey for a large sum. High value was set upon pasturage, whether for cattle or sheep, though this was sometimes found to clash with the rights of game and the forest, for it was necessary to preserve the quiet and solitude which

the red deer especially demanded.   Penalties were exacted for the
trespassing of cattle or sheep upon neighbouring pastures, and the
royal sanction was given to prevent this, while travellers also were
secured, in their rights of pasturage, for one night in passing through
the country.   The word *forest*, as applied to large tracts of land
suitable for game, is early encountered in Scottish history.   Cosmo
Innes says that the right of cutting wood was carefully reserved when
pasturage or arable land was granted ; and if it was for the special
purpose of fuel for a salt work, or for building, its use was mentioned
in explicit terms.   The great lords were jealous of their privileges of
game and forestry, and occasionally resented, or endeavoured to
counteract, the interference with their rights on the part of some of
the religious houses, upon whom their ancestors had bestowed bene-
factions of land.   Game, such as harts and hinds, boars and roe-deer,
even the eyries of hawks and falcons, were all expressly reserved,
when a gift of land was made to some of the abbeys or monasteries,
the very trees in which the hawks built being carefully noted.   The
knights and ladies delighted in the pastime of the chase, and an acquaintance with the mysteries of woodcraft and hunting, was considered essential to the education of those who disdained the more
prosaic occupations of trade, commerce, or the learned professions.
Scottish stag-hounds and wolf-dogs were much prized in foreign
lands, and even in the reign of David II. were an actual article of
export.   On the other hand, the hawks of Norway were considered
the finest for strength and fleetness of flight, and, at one time, were
imported into Scotland in Norwegian merchant vessels.   It will be
remembered that King Robert the Bruce, one of the most accomplished knights of the age, was also an adept in the mysteries of the
chase, and, in particular, could wind his hunting horn in such a
fashion that his devoted follower Sir James Douglas, on one occasion,
pronounced that the blast could be none other than that of the King.

Dunbartonshire being one of the counties bordering both with the
Highlands and Lowlands, the customs of the lords of the soil partook
of the characteristics of each.   Their more peaceful avocations of
farming and hunting were carried on, often for long periods, without

interruption from the savage forays of plundering or vindictive
neighbours.   It was soon after the period of Robert the Bruce and
his successors that, in addition to the baronial hall, the guilds of free
burghers were beginning to be a great civilising power in the land.
The Church also now was asserting itself as a potent factor in the
affairs of Scotland, and no doubt, in times of invasion and internecine
strife, the protection afforded by the monastery and its rulers was
felt of great moment to the afflicted peasantry.   Provided that not
too great enquiry was made into the private lives of the monks, and
the wily schemes of the higher dignitaries of the Church, the ecclesiastical authorities were easy task masters, who were happy to exercise a paternal sway over their humble dependents.   The upper classes
of the people held their own against the encroachments of the sovereign, and the attempted exactions of the priests, and the great middle
body of the people, who now constitute the back-bone of our country,
were, as yet, unendowed with the elements of political power.

Civilisation had not introduced hitherto much of the refinements
or elegancies of modern life.   The dress, no doubt, of the barons and
nobles in the Lowlands at any rate, was, upon certain occasions,
characterised by considerable splendour.   All kind of robes of velvet,
richly adorned with ermine, and a tunic of silk, or brocade, or other
precious material, sometimes fitting close to the figure, or hanging in
loose folds around the person, trunk hose, laced sandals, or shoes,
with a rich head dress, completed the attire of a nobleman of the
period.   Sumptuary laws were enacted by our ancestors, which
rather startle the free and independent Britons of the present day.
In a parliament held in 1455, the following rule was passed.   " All
Earls shall use mantles of brown granit open before, lined with white
fur, and trimmed in front with the same furring, of a handbreadth
down to the belt, with little hoods of the same cloth pendant on the
shoulders.   The other lords of parliament shall have a mantle of red,
open in like manner before, lined with silk or furred with cristic
gray, griece or purray, and a hood of the same, furred as the lining.
All commissioners of burghs shall each have a pair of cloakes of blue
cloth, furred to the feet, open on the right shoulder ; the fur of pro-

portionable value, and a hood of the same. Whatever Earl, Lord, or Commissioner shall enter parliament except dressed as above, shall pay a fine of ten pounds. All men hired as advocates shall wear green habits in the form of a short tunic, the sleeves to be open like those of a tabard." Ordinary burgesses were limited to gowns of silk, trimmed with fur, and, except on holidays, their wives were forbidden to wear long gowns and trains ; short kerchiefs and hoods being deemed sufficient as a rule. The clergy were prohibited from wearing scarlet gowns or "mertrick fur," unless they were dignitaries of some cathedral or collegiate church, or had an income of over 200 merks. In 1471, considering the great poverty which prevailed, and the cost of importing silk, this article was to be worn only by those whose revenue was over one hundred pounds Scots, in landed rent, with the exception of knights, heralds, and minstrels. As for the common order of the people, it was ordained that, at his ordinary work, the labourer or husbandman should wear garments of white or grey colour, although, on holidays, he was graciously permitted to indulge his fancy in the matter of light blue, green, or red attire ; and provided the price was not over forty shillings the elne, his wife might adorn her person with home made kerchiefs of the same prevailing tint.

In the households of the great lords, it was the fashion to keep accurate accounts of the expenditure incurred, and the following details regarding a member of the Argyll family are interesting. "1636. Given to my Lord Lorne's sone, the 28 of March, quhen he went to Rosneth, ane gold ring, set with ane Turkiss stone, pryce xx lib. Spent by my Lordes sone and his company quhen he went to Rosneth the said tyme, iiiixx xi lib. Item the 18 of Junii to be coat and brekis to him x quarteris of fyne skarlet xviii lib. the ell, xlv lib. Item ane pair of silk stockings xxi lib. Item ane black French bever-hat lxxiii lib. 6s. 8d., and ii dusson orange ribband points v lib. xiis. 1st Jany., 1637. To the bairne himself the said day ane Spanish pistolet iiii lib. 6s. 8d. For ane brusche for my Lord of Lorne's sone to brusch his head with xs. Given to my Lord of Lorne's sone to play him with quhen he went to Edinburgh to sie his father x lib. 1638. Mair spent be my Lord of Lorne's sone and his company going out of Balloch to Rosneth, being thrie or four dayes be the way xvi. lib. xiiis."

The residences of the barons and lairds, as may be seen from the ruins of many of these buildings in the county, were of sufficient strength and size to combine the requirements of defence, and accommodation for the family and retainers. Clustering around them were the humble habitations of the armed vassals, who followed their lord to the field, and of the inferior workmen and cultivators, who ministered to his wants and wrought on the soil. At the tables of the nobles a profusion of viands was exhibited, and they groaned under massive joints, cut from "marts," "stirks," and "fed oxen," along with abundance of salmon, all sorts of sea fish, trouts, herrings, fresh and salted, game of all sorts, from great haunches of red deer venison, to the smaller varieties of woodcock and snipe; cheeses and curds, and many sorts of dainty sweetmeats flavoured with all manner of spiceries, ginger, sugar, cinnamon, cloves and saffron. Huge loaves, bannocks, and cakes of oaten and wheaten flour, flanked the more substantial dishes, and the whole was washed down with draughts of Flemish and Spanish wines, along with copious libations of home made spirits, choice Nantz brandy, and the less potent beverages of mead, and home brewed ale. The decorations of the table were by no means splendid, for, although the dresses of the lords and ladies were adorned with costly jewels, diamonds, rubies, topazes, jacinths and emeralds, the dishes of silver plate on the "buffet" were goblets, "chargers," "basins," and "lavers" of silver, sometimes plain, gilt or parcel gilt, and (but rarely) plates for the guests of the same costly material. In place of the tea or coffee of a later period, the breakfast meal consisted of solid and substantial viands, the mighty baron of beef, the tempting venison pasty, the tender sirloin or the spiced ham, along with foaming ale, the milder mead, or generous foreign wines, in flagons of silver, furnished the guests with ample entertainment.

While the foregoing was the style in which the wealthier lords of the soil lived, it must be admitted that the labourers on the estate dwelt often in miserable hovels of clay and stone, thatched with straw or bracken, which succeeded to the wooden structures of the thirteenth century. When stones were so plentiful, and the price of labour so cheap, it is a wonder that wood continued so long to be in use for the humbler classes, both in the burghs and round the mansions of the great. The food of this class consisted greatly of the many varieties of fish which were found in an inexhaustible supply in the seas round the coasts, and in the inland lakes and rivers. Herring and salmon, cod and ling, haddocks, whitings, trouts, eels, perch, pike, and numerous others, along with mussels and oysters, in many localities, were to hand in vast numbers, and proved a staple article of diet, with an occasional surfeit of pork, on holidays and festivals. The waters of the Frith of Clyde, and the innumerable salt water lochs of the western coast of Scotland, were often thronged with fishing boats, some of which had come from a great distance to ply their craft and furnish supplies for the tables of the wealthy and great.

In the work of Cosmo Innes, before mentioned, will be found further interesting particulars, as regards the proceedings of the Barons Courts, which were collected in the year 1621, and gave a picture of the rural economy of the period. There are regulations for "muirburn, summer pasture, peat cutting, mills, smithies, and ale houses," also against poaching on land and water, and even against cutting briars, "but in the waxing of the moon." Curiously enough swine were prescribed, and rooks, hooded crows, magpies, with other birds of evil reputation, are to be destroyed. Regulations are strict for preserving the trees round the cottars' and farmers' houses, and tenants are bound to afford their cottars the comforts of fuel and kailyards, "with corns conform." Encouragement to agriculture is afforded by rules for sowing "uncouth" oats, a species of seed superior to the common black Highland grain, for gathering together manure, and for irrigating, "drawing water through the land," long antecedent to a system of drainage. The greensward on the banks of burns and rivers are not to be dug up or broken, as a precaution against sudden "speats" of water. And tenants are taken bound to make four rude implements of iron, called "crosscuts of iron,"

annually, to be used against wolves, which were not finally extir-
pated from the country till the end of the seventeenth century.

Such, roughly speaking, was something like the condition of affairs
which prevailed over a considerable portion of the more Lowland
districts of Scotland, and it may be taken to apply, as a whole, to
the county of Dunbarton. Although much of the northern portion
of the county bordered on the Highlands, and though the Gaelic
language was largely spoken throughout the whole territory, still it
could hardly be affirmed that Celtic customs and organisation prevailed to any extent. Upon the whole, the influence of the monasteries inclined to the side of law and order, and their inmates, at all
events, showed commendable zeal in spreading a knowledge of agriculture and the improvement of the soil, while they undoubtedly
contributed a good deal to the advancement of mere secular learning.
The rude and warlike barons of an earlier age, cared nothing for
scholastic acquirements, and often gave way to gross superstition in
matters of religion, yet they gladly bestowed money and lands for
pious purposes, and their successors emulated their example to a far
greater extent. Commendable zeal was displayed by the proprietors
of the land in seeing that the parish churches were maintained in
proper order, and that additional chapels were provided in outlying
districts. When the Reformation took place, and the shackles of
Romish superstition were removed, the grand system of education,
established through the influence of John Knox, diffused the boon of
secular knowledge and the priceless benefits of spiritual instruction
throughout the length and breadth of the land.

The three parishes of Row, Rosneath and Cardross, which are the
subject of the present volume, form a very interesting portion of the
county of Dunbarton, and have many features of beauty which will
repay investigation. They all border the Firth of Clyde, and, from
various coigns of vantage in each, a splendid prospect is gained of
these historic waters which once were freighted with the royal navies
of Scotland and France and, in later years, have often seen a portion
of the magnificent squadrons of Great Britain,

" The armaments that thunder strike the walls of mighty cities," slowly steaming up to their allotted station. Any day, from the wooded heights of Cardross, or the heather knowes of the Rosneath peninsula, may be seen those grand specimens of naval architecture, the mighty Atlantic liners, steaming up and down the waters of that Firth, on which once the miniature pleasure vessels of King Robert the Bruce sped along in their panoply of swelling sails and picturesque oarsmen. Vessels of every description of rig and construction are incessantly gliding over the surface of the broad estuary, and transport the produce of the thousand mills and factories of the West of Scotland to distant quarters of the globe. And the rushing locomotives, with their long waving trail of white steam, convey merchandise and passengers over the face of the land with magical celerity,—very unlike the tortoise-like pace of the lumbering vehicles in the olden time.

What a mighty change too has come over the landscape itself, since those early days in the remote period centuries before the Britons of Strathclyde roamed beside the shores of the Clyde. At that time the sea rolled around Dunbarton Rock, its dark blue waves reaching perhaps half-way up the Vale of Leven. The cliffs at the eastern side of the railway between Cardross and the tunnel at Dalreoch clearly show that the sea once laved those fissured rocks. Similarly, at the Gareloch, near Rosneath Castle, the conglomerate cliffs show every indication of there having once been an old sea beach at their base. Dr. Hately Waddell in his work *Ossian and the Clyde*, points out that marine deposits have been discovered all about Cardross and Ardmore Point, and that the acquired lands, near the former place, yearly increasing by the recession of the tide, are full of purest sea channel of all modern tints, and with similar varieties of shells. The Clyde estuary would, in some places, seem to be diminishing in breadth, although as may be witnessed along the shores of the Gareloch, the soil near the beach has been gradually washed away by the tide. Long years ago, says the learned author, there would be great changes in the Clyde estuary, "Erskine submerged, Dunbarton Rock a double-headed islet, and Cardross a tongue-land from Dunbartonshire. Ardmore and Rosneath Points,

now rich with verdure and waving with trees, would then be in-
visible ; Rosneath itself, a mere circular peninsula, tacked like an
emerald by a link of rock to the solid land ; Ardenslate and Hafton
all but separated from Dunoon ; Bute divided by Kilchattan Bay at
Kingarth ; Portincross cut off from the shore, and Arran intersected
by deep and rocky inlets, or scooped into wider bays. Loch-Winnoch
and Loch Lomond, at the date in question, would be inland seas—
the Cart, the Gryffe, and the Leven, as rivers, gone."

The author goes on to speculate upon the changes : "If so, and
we have no reason to doubt it, then there was corresponding breadth
and depth of water in the Gareloch, in the Holy Loch, and Loch
Fyne. Certain it is that, in the glacial period, icebergs with their
load of boulders, like crystal decanters with a cargo of pebbles, were
afloat in the Gareloch. 1 have myself counted not fewer than 90 of
these huge blocks in a mass together, the burden doubtless of some
iceberg which had swung in from the south-east and grounded above
Fernicarie. In those days the ridges between the Gareloch and
Loch Long would be a mere strip, and the moor at Poltalloch,
through which the Crinan Canal now runs, between Lochgilphead
and the Western Ocean would be quiet and deep water. Loch Long,
for example, at no very remote period, must have been deep water a
mile and more beyond the highway at Arrochar ; where an alluvial
deposit of vegetable matter of which the strata can still be counted,
lies plainly extended as a beautiful valley, from 15 to 36 inches deep
of soil on the old bed of the sea."

The geological formation of this part of the county presents specimens of rock from the oldest strata, mica slate, to the limestone.
The mica slate, resting upon the gneiss, is of a uniform character,
composed chiefly of parts adhering together without any intermediate
cement. Mica is everywhere seen, quartz also abounds, but felspar
is scarcely perceptible. Towards the south of Row parish there are
beds of red sandstone and coarse conglomerate. Gypsum and thin
beds of limestone are associated with the sandstone, which is covered
with a whitish constratified clay, full of water. There is a blue
limestone on the top of the slate in Ardenconnal, and in Glenfruin,

in which masses of pyrites are found. In the lower part of the parish there are alluvial beds of gravel, sand, and clay, containing marine shells, shewing that the sea had once covered a great deal of the shore lands. On the opposite side of the Gareloch similar geological features are observed. On the high ground above Clynder there are good examples of chloride slate in the quarries which have been opened up, the direction being from north-west to south-east. Not very far from Knockderry, on the Loch Long side, there appears a large mass of greenstone lying interposed between the strata. The greenstone is like a dyke, from twenty to thirty feet thick, and close to it is more of the chlorite slate rock. The south-western extremity of the parish is pervaded by conglomerate and coarse sandstone rock, which occurs in beds of considerable thickness. This rock is of similar description to the great sandstone formation which extends along the coasts of Renfrew and Ayr, embracing the Cumbraes, and a portion of the southern half of Bute. The line of formation, between the sandstone and primitive rock of the parish, runs along the valley stretching from Campsail Bay to Kilcreggan. In the slate formation on the Loch Long shore, as well as in the quartz, iron pyrites is found in considerable abundance. On the rocks in the neck of land between Loch Long and the Gareloch we see finely bedded strata of mica schist, tilted up at a high angle, and their edges ground and smoothed in a curious way, with long parallel lines, clearly indicating the work of ice. The valley of Loch Long, at one time, must have been completely filled by an immense glacier, part of which extended over this neck of land and down the Gareloch.

Some of the interesting boulder stones which are to be found throughout the West Highlands, still exist on the shores and braes of the Gareloch, and, fifty years ago, more than one hundred fine boulders of grey granite were found in position on the ridges between that Loch and Loch Long. Probably the boulders had their origin in the great granite mountains, such as Ben Cruachan, more than thirty miles distant, as the crow flies ; being transported by the ice across valleys and hills, floating on a sea which may have been over

C

fifteen hundred feet above the present sea level. The conclusion which Mr. Charles M'Laren, the eminent Scotch geologist, came to in 1846 regarding these boulders, was that they have come on the sea at a far higher level than now, brought by currents from the north-west. The most remarkable one in the parish is at Peatoun, on Loch Long, resting in the channel of a burn which runs down to the loch at a height of 226 feet above the sea. It is of gneiss, its dimensions 24 by 18 feet, and probably it was transported across Loch Long to its present site. All along the shore between Kil-creggan and Peatoun numerous large boulders are to be seen, while they also exist in many places on the Gareloch shores. At Shandon there is a large boulder on the shore at the gate of the Hydropathic establishment, about 10 feet by 14. All evidences tend to prove that, at one period, there were extensive glaciers in the valleys of the West Highlands. There is also a huge boulder of mica slate on the farm of Callendown, on the Helensburgh and Luss road, 150 feet above the sea, which may have come from the north, down the valley now occupied by Loch Lomond, and been carried up Glenfruin. The glaciation, however, of this district is, on the whole, from the north-west, so that it is more likely its line of transport was from the west.

The prevailing soils of the county are clay, on a subsoil of till, and gravelly loam. On the banks of the Clyde there is a consider-able extent of deep black loam, but this bears only a small propor-tion to the rest of the surface land. The climate is mild and favour-able to health, but not quite so advantageous for the growth of pasture. The prevailing winds are the west and south-west, but the east wind blows a good deal in March, April, and May. In 1777 the Duke of Argyll made great efforts to introduce a better system of husbandry, and Wright, who visited the county in that year, found the Duke and other proprietors trying to beautify their estates. The progress which he saw was continued gradually; enclosing and plant-ing were carried on, drainage advanced, and the land enhanced in value. On the Duke of Argyll's farm at Rosneath, cultivated by himself, the following rotation of crops prevailed. 1, Oats; 2, pease;

3, barley; 4, potatoes and turnips; 5, wheat and grass seeds; 6, hay; 7 and 8, pasture.   The principal changes were substituting potatoes for fallow land, which was done when the season and soil permitted the ground to be pastured in time, and if enough manure could be got.   Wheat was greatly increased in cultivation, and turnip husbandry generally introduced, and the potato was grown with great success.   Much of the potato crop went for feeding horses, cattle and pigs, and for seed, but a great deal was consumed by the people, as well as exported to Greenock and Glasgow.   The growth of artificial grasses was generally introduced, but rather little attention was given to the management of grass lands and natural pastures. No fruit orchards were grown for profit, but there was a large amount of natural copse woods, and they yielded a handsome return. The introduction of sheep farming over the waste ground had greatly improved the pastures and increased their value.   The sheep were mostly black faced, from breeds which were said to have been introduced from the high lands of Dumfriesshire and Lanarkshire about 1750.   The cattle were chiefly of Highland breed, and were purchased in the various West Highland markets.   Horses used to be bred in the county, but they were of inferior quality, and the Clydesdale breed was recognised as by far the most useful.

Red deer used to be common in certain parts of the county, but now are only found in two of the large islands in Loch Lomond, though roe deer are more numerous.   The introduction of sheep has greatly tended to displace deer, and the gradual restriction of the ground under heather has much diminished the supply of game, although there are some fine grouse moors in various places.   In the Lochs, salmon and sea trout are common, and herring, cod, whiting, haddocks, saithe, and other varieties, abound in Loch Long and the Gareloch.   The king fish had been taken early in the century on the shore near Helensburgh, and about 1830 an enormous tunny, 9 feet long, was captured in the Gareloch.   In this loch, at one time, oysters used to be got, but they were both more numerous and larger in Loch Long.   Mussels are found in great quantities near the Row and Rosneath Points, but no care has been taken for their preserva-

tion, and sometimes several boats at a time may be seen gathering
tons each of fine mussels, to the irreparable injury of the breeding
places.   In the year 1811 an exhaustive "General view of the Agriculture of the County of Dunbarton" was drawn up at the instance
of the Board of Agriculture, from which much valuable information
will be gained as to the state of matters at that date.   Careful descriptions are given of the farms, the soil, mode of husbandry, cottars
houses, implements, pastures, and the entire operations pertaining to
agriculture and forestry.   The farm houses and offices generally,
though of small dimensions, were substantial and commodious, and
the proprietors were beginning to recognise that it was their duty
and interest to see to the comfort of their tenants.   As a rule the
cottages of the labourers were very poor, but an improvement was
observable, windows were being glazed, chimneys constructed in the
gables, and roofed with tiles and slates.   The sheep farms had much
increased in size since 1794, when Mr. Ure estimated them on an
average at 600 acres.   Farms of £20 and £30 rent were to be met
with in various parts, but they were miserably cultivated and ex-
cessively overcropped.   In the Highland districts the small pendicles
were occupied by tenants, who were sometimes artificers, or engaged
in wood cutting, herring fishing, or other occupations; to which, too
often, might be added smuggling.   The farmers were generally of the
old school, of limited education, following implicitly the practices of
their fathers, and had no capital.   In fact the feudal state of society
had scarcely disappeared from the county, and there were still on
some of the estates farms let to three, four, and even more tenants as
conjunct lessees, to be cultivated in common.   The average rent of
arable land in the clay district was about 18s. per Scotch acre, in
gravelly soil 20s., and in rich loam 35s.   In some very favourable
situations fields, and even whole farms, were let at £3 10s. per acre
for a lease.   The rise of rent, particularly in the pasture district, had
been great and, since the introduction of sheep farms, land formerly
let at £20 and £30 had risen to £300 and £400.   The conclusion
which the authors of the report came to was that, in this county,
when judiciously employed, the capital of the arable farmer yielded

about 11⅔ per cent., and that of the sheep grazier 10¾ per cent. ; a
moderate return, when the skill, perseverance, and outlay necessary
are taken into account.

The usual enclosures throughout the county were dry stone dykes,
but hedges and ditches were common. Ploughing was well executed,
a great improvement having taken place in the last few years. The
ploughing was done by a pair of horses driven by a man, but it was
only a short time ago that four horses were used to drive the plough.
In Arrochar, and other Highland parts, the old "Highland spade"
was still used, chiefly for digging very steep ground on the sides of
mountains, and also on boggy ground which would not carry horses.
The wheat grown in the county was, generally, of good quality, and
sold high; the average price per boll in 1808 having been £2 4s.
The quantity of barley raised in 1809 was very small, owing to the
high duties on malt, and the increasing demand for wheat. Oats had
been the grain chiefly cultivated in Dunbartonshire, a second, and
even a third crop often followed the first. The inferior oats were
generally given to the cattle on the farm, or sold to the innkeepers.
The price of oats in 1808 was £1 8s. per boll. Turnips were grown
on nearly every farm in the county, but not to a great extent, and
they were found to thrive best on the gravelly and loam lands.
Justice was not done to the cultivation of turnips in this county, and
the tillage was imperfect, and a strong prejudice existed for potatoes.
They were planted on every variety of soil, and were found to thrive
even on the stiffest clays, where there was sufficient declivity for
carrying off the water. Large quantities of potatoes were sold in
Glasgow and Greenock, and those unsold formed, for eight months
in the year, the chief sustenance of the labouring classes. A little
flax was sown on almost every farm for the use of the family, and
spun by the female servants in the winter evenings.

· The greater part of both cows and oxen in the county were purchased from the West Highlands, the few reared in Dunbartonshire
being of the same breed. The bulk of the cattle wintered were disposed of in April to dealers from the south of Scotland or the north
of England, or else sold in the public markets in May and June.

The number of cattle fattened in the county was much smaller than
that of those wintered.   Oxen were sometimes used in harness, and
were formerly employed at Levenside by Lord Stonefield, and at
Rosneath by the Duke of Argyll, for both ploughing and carting,
but found inferior to horses in every respect.   They were still used
at Ardmore, the seat of General Geils, and were worked both in the
cart and thrashing mill, being managed in the Indian method, by
chains passing over the top of their heads.   The total stock of sheep,
which were all black-faced, in the county was about 28,000.   The
pasture which the hills afforded was their only food, either in winter
or summer.   On the smaller sheep farms, which were far the most
numerous, a breeding stock was generally kept.   Farm servants
were engaged generally for six months, and their wages ran from
£18 to £22 per annum, in addition to their board; the women receiving £8 to £12.   Day labourers earned from 2s. to 2s. 6d. each,
and the day's work was about ten hours.   Provisions were high in
price, the average price of beef being eightpence a pound of 23 oz. ;
mutton ninepence, veal and pork and vegetables still dearer in pro-
portion.   Salmon, which used to be sold at threepence, was seldom
below eighteen pence, and salted herrings were double the price they
were a few years ago.   But the high price of food chiefly affected
the manufacturing population, as the farm servants consumed chiefly
potatoes, oatmeal and cheese.   Coal was the fuel mostly used by all
classes of the people, the price near the pits being upwards of eight
shillings a ton, but double that figure in the more remote parts of
the county.

At the present day, according to an enquiry into the condition of
farm servants held in Dunbarton in December, 1892, there is a considerable change for the better.   It was found that, generally speaking, they worked in summer from 5 a.m. till 6 at night, with an hour
and a half for meals.   They were engaged by the year, and the married men had from 20s. to 22s. per week, a free house, sometimes a
small garden, and coals driven.   There was no allowance for extra
work, except perhaps some refreshment.   Some of the cottages were
very poor and damp, and the drainage was bad.   Ordinary labourers

ranged from 18s. to 20s. per week, and drainers wages were about 3s. 6d. per day. Shepherds wages were £24 a year, with free cottage and garden, ten bolls of meal, a cow and its keep, but he had to feed the lambs out of that. Benefit Societies were not much taken advantage of by the labourers, but some of them were in Assurance Societies. There was no trades unions among them, and the relations between master and servant were very agreeable. The general condition of the farm labourers in this county was better than it was a few years ago. They got few holidays, the only ones being about the term days, or at the new year.

Altogether the writers of the general view of the agriculture of the county in 1811 considered that a great change for the better had occurred in the food and mode of living of the farm labourers. The wretched, damp, and smoky hovels that offended the eye of a stranger were much diminished in number, and the peasants' cottages wore a greater appearance of comfort and cleanliness. The food of the labourers in summer was generally oatmeal porridge and milk for breakfast, bread and cheese with milk for dinner, and porridge for supper. In winter, their dinner for the most part was barley broth, with salt beef or salted herrings. Amongst the peasantry the fondness for ardent spirits, though still too prevalent, had considerably abated, and they were in a healthy condition,—small pox and fever being little known. As regarded the farmers, their general deficiency of capital was one of the most serious obstacles to improvement. The feudal system of land occupation, by which the land was parcelled out amongst a number of occupiers, and cultivated solely by their labour without any expenditure of money in improvements, was totally incompatible with the prosperity of the country. There were still some proprietors who adhered to obsolete notions, such as that their interests were in opposition to those of their tenants, but there were others who encouraged intelligent and enterprising farmers, well knowing that the interests of both were inseparably connected. It was a wrong system to burden tenants with vexatious services, to cripple them with short leases, to compel them to waste their capital in building houses, enclosing fields, and

executing these improvements which, being permanent, ought in all
equity to be done by the landlord. The connection between the
landlord and tenant must be formed on fair and equal terms, and
kept up in the spirit of confidence and liberality.

CHAPTER II.

The Lennox and Colquhoun families. Henry Bell and Robert Napier.

HAVING thus endeavoured to give a general outline of that portion of the county of Dunbarton which is more especially the subject of this volume, it will be well to mention some details regarding the ancient family of Lennox, to whose representatives at one time the whole of Row and Cardross belonged. The name was originally Leven-ach, a Gaelic term signifying the "field of the Leven." In the plural, Levenachs, was the name given to the extensive possessions of the Earls of the district between the river Leven and the Gareloch, and, in process of time, became shortened into Lennox. It is believed that the founder of the family was Arkyll, a Saxon baron of Northumberland, who also owned large estates in Yorkshire, and who rebelled against William the Conqueror. Along with many other Saxon barons in 1070, he fled to Scotland and received from Malcolm Canmore a large tract of land in the counties of Dunbarton and Stirling. Arkyll married for his second wife a Scottish lady, whose son Alwyn was understood to have been first Earl of Lennox, and to have died in 1160. His son Alwyn being very young when his father died, the Earl of Huntington, the brother of William the Lion, was appointed guardian of Alwyn for a long period. His son Aulay got Faslane, at the upper end of the Gareloch, for his patrimony, and he gave to the monastery of Paisley "the church of Rosneath with all its just pertinents in pure and perpetual alms, the charter having been confirmed to Maldouin, Earl of Lennox, his brother, and by King Alexander II. on 12th March, in the twelfth year of his reign. He also made a donation to that monastery of a salt pit in Rosneath, and of wood for repairs. He also gave to it all

D

the tracts of nets through the whole of Gareloch for catching salmon, and other fish, reserving to himself and to his heirs every fourth salmon taken through these tracts." Maldouin, third Earl, succeeded his father in 1225, and was one of the guarantees on the part of King Alexander III. when the differences between him and Henry III. of England were arranged in 1237. Up to this time the castle of Dunbarton had been the principal messuage of the Earls of Lennox, but, after 1238, when he received a new charter of the earldom, neither the castle, territory, and harbour adjacent remained in the Lennox family. Ever since, the castle has been a royal fortress, and the town of Dunbarton was, in 1222, erected into a free royal burgh with extensive privileges.

Malcolm the fifth Earl was, in 1292, one of the nominees on the part of the elder Bruce in his competition for the Crown of Scotland with Baliol, and, in 1296, he assembled his followers, and with other Scottish leaders, invaded Cumberland and assaulted Carlisle. He was slain at the battle of Halidon Hill on 19th July, 1333. His son Donald, sixth Earl, was one of the nobles present in the parliament at Edinburgh in September, 1357, and he became bound for the payment of the ransom of King David II. He was present at the coronation of Robert II. at Scone, 16th March, 1371, and on the following day swore homage and fealty to him. He died in 1373, and, having no male issue, the direct male line ceased with him. The earldom devolved on his only daughter Margaret, who married her cousin, and nearest heir male of the family, Walter, son of Allan de Fasselane who, in her right, in accordance with the territorial nature of feudal dignities at that period, became seventh Earl of Lennox. In 1385 the Countess Margaret and her husband made a resignation of the dignity in favour of their son Duncan who, in consequence, became Earl of Lennox in his father's lifetime. Duncan had no male issue, and was left a widower, with three daughters, the eldest of whom. Isabella, married in 1391, Murdoch, Duke of Albany, who became Regent of Scotland. The contract of marriage, a very curious document, was signed at the old castle in Inchmurrin on Loch Lomond, which was then the principal residence of the Earls of Lennox,

Although his connection with the Duke of Albany made Duncan, Earl of Lennox, one of the most powerful noblemen in the kingdom, yet he thereby incurred the wrath of King James I., who, on his return from his long captivity in England, caused the Earl to be beheaded at Stirling, along with his son-in-law, on 25th May, 1425, when about eighty years of age.   His grandson, Walter of the Levenax, was beheaded at Stirling on the previous day, a cruel and unnecessary act, and his widowed mother spent the remainder of her days on Inchmurrin.   She was a lady of deep piety and benevolence of character, and spent her life in the exercise of an extensive charity, and, about 1450, founded the Collegiate Church at Dunbarton, to which was attached an almshouse for poor beadsmen.

Both of the Duchess Isabella's sisters appear to have predeceased her, and, at her death, took place what is known as the partition or dismemberment of the Lennox.   The celebrated Sir John Stewart, created Lord Darnley about 1460, was served heir to his grandfather, Duncan, Earl of Lennox, in 1473, in the half of the Earldom of Lennox, and in its principal messuage.   In 1489 he took arms against the young King, when his fortresses of Crookston and Dunbarton were besieged, the latter by the Earl of Argyll.   The castle, which was defended by his four sons, had to surrender, after a siege of six weeks, but he succeeded in making his peace with the King, and obtaining a full pardon for himself and his followers.   Owing to a dispute regarding the estates which occurred with the Haldanes of Gleneagles, who claimed to represent the ancient Earls of Lennox, and the arbiters having awarded the former a large part of the property, the territory of the Lennox was now much curtailed of its importance.   Matthew Stewart, Earl of Lennox, succeeded his father in 1494, and in 1503 he obtained a grant from James IV. of the sheriffdom of Dunbartonshire, which was united to the earldom, and made hereditary in the family of Lennox.   Along with the Earl of Argyll, Lennox led the right wing of the Scottish army at the battle of Flodden, the men under their command being almost entirely raised in the western counties.   Both the Earls were slain at that disastrous battle, and John succeeded as Earl of Lennox, playing an

important part during the turbulent minority of James V. In 1524
he warmly supported the Queen-mother when she declared her son
King James of age, though then only in his thirteenth year. He
was a member of the new secret council appointed in 1526, and at
the head of a force of 10,000 men marched from Stirling to Edinburgh for the rescue of the King, who was almost a prisoner in the
hands of the powerful house of Douglas. The Earl of Arran and the
Hamiltons, with a strong army, met Lennox near Linlithgow, and in
the battle which ensued the latter was slain in cold blood after being
taken prisoner by Hamilton of Finnart. Sir Andrew Wood of Largo
found the Earl of Arran weeping over the expiring Lennox, deploring
his loss, and exclaiming "The wisest, the best, the bravest man in
Scotland has fallen this day."

Matthew, his eldest son, spent the early part of his life in the
service of the King of France, and in the wars in Italy, where he
greatly distinguished himself. This nobleman also was a chief actor
in the stirring events which occurred during the early years of Mary
Queen of Scots, and was the rival of Bothwell for the favour of the
Queen-dowager. In 1544, an agreement was entered into at Carlisle
between Lennox, Glencairn, and Henry VIII., in which the latter
promised to Lennox the government of Scotland, and the hand of his
niece, the Lady Margaret Douglas, while the two Earls engaged to
use every effort to seize and deliver the young Queen with the principal Scottish fortresses, into Henry's hands. Soon afterwards he
was married to Lady Margaret, receiving with her lands in England
to the annual value of 6800 merks Scots. In 1544 he resided at
Carlisle, and in 1545, he negotiated with Donald, Lord of the Isles,
and other nobles for an invasion of Scotland, which was however
postponed. In consequence, Lennox was found guilty of treason, at
a Parliament held at Stirling, and his lands forfeited. After a residence of twenty years in England, he was recalled by Queen Mary
in December, 1564, and his forfeiture rescinded. Being the father of
the ill-fated Lord Darnley, Queen Mary's husband, and grandfather
of James VI., he was, in July, 1570, elected Regent of Scotland.
Having called a Parliament to be held at Stirling, in September,

1571, the Queen's party formed a design, planned by Kirkcaldy of Grange, to surprise the Parliament and seize the Regent. The attack, however, failed, but, in the skirmish which ensued, the Earl of Lennox was stabbed in the back by Captain Calder, and died that evening in the Castle of Stirling, where he was interred in the Chapel Royal, and his virtues commemorated in a Latin epitaph by the celebrated George Buchanan.

The Earldom of Lennox, by right of blood relationship, now devolved on King James VI., as heir of his grandfather, and in 1572, this and the Lordship of Darnley, with all the family estates and jurisdictions, were granted to Charles, Lord Darnley's younger brother. He was the father of the unfortunate Lady Arabella Stuart, whose proximity to the throne rendered her the innocent victim of State policy. She died in 1615, aged thirty-eight, and was buried in Westminster Abbey, where most of the subsequent Dukes of Lennox of this family were interred. Robert Stuart, son of John Earl of Lennox, succeeded to the title. He was at one time Provost of the Collegiate Church of Dunbarton, complied with the Reformation, and during his brother's short Regency, was appointed Prior of St. Andrews. The seventh Earl, and first Duke of Lennox of this name, was Esme Stuart, who had been educated in France, and, on his arrival in Scotland in 1579, was made Abbot of Arbroath, besides receiving other honours. He became a special favourite with the King, and was created Duke of Lennox, and appointed Lord High Chamberlain of Scotland. However, the jealousy of the Scottish nobility became so great that the King was constrained to sign an order for the departure of Lennox from Scotland. His son Ludovick, second Duke of Lennox, was distinguished in various ways, and enjoyed the favour of King James, who bestowed on him all the estates and honours held by his father, and, in addition, created him Duke of Richmond in the English Peerage, in 1623. He was one of the noblemen and barons who entered into a bond at Aberdeen, in March, 1592, for the security of religion, and against the Popish Lords. It is unnecessary to pursue any further the fortunes of the Lennox family, for they became merged in the honours of the Dukes of Richmond, and

lost their connection with the important events of Scottish history.
This narrative of an ancient Scottish family, for which the author is
chiefly indebted to the *Scottish Nation*, will, it is believed, interest
those who visit the shores of the Gareloch, where those estates of the
Lords of Lennox were situated, from whence came their early
territorial distinction.

In addition to the large holdings of the Lennox family, details of
which have been given and will follow further on, the following extract from Irving's history of the county will show what a great extent
of territory once was comprised within their estate :—"Leaving the
barony of Colquhoun, and passing the beautiful property of Glenar-
buck, laid out by Gilbert Hamilton, Lord Provost of Glasgow, and
since in the possession of different gentlemen, we enter what may be
termed the church lands of Kilpatrick, gifted by the pious munificence of the early Earls of Lennox to the Abbey of Paisley. Some
time about the end of the twelfth century, Alwyn, the second Earl of
Lennox, confirmed to the Church of Kilpatrick a gift of the lands of
Cochno, Edinbarnet, Cragentulach, Monachkeneran, Dunteglenan,
Cultbuie, and others, and added thereto a grant of his own of the
lands of Cateconon, for the weal of the soul of his sovereign, Alexander II., of his own, and of all his race. In attaching these lands to
the Church of Kilpatrick, the donor seems to have freed them from
all burdens ; for when Earl David, the brother of William the Lion, who
held the superiority of the Earldom during the minority of Alwyn's
successor, attempted to derive aid from them, as from his other
lands, the holders resisted, and he was compelled to depart from
his intention. The various possessions appear at this time to have
been held, on behalf of the church, by a person named Bede Ferdan,
who lived at Monachkeneran, in the great house built of twigs, *domo
magna fabricata de virgis*, and who, with other three individuals, was
bound to receive and entertain all pilgrims repairing to the Church
of St. Patrick. The lands conferred upon the Church of Kilpatrick
formed in after years a fertile subject of dispute, and in one of the
feuds which ensued, Bede Ferdan, above referred to, was slain in de-
fending what he considered the rights of the Church. The dispute

regarding the church lands originated in the following manner. Earl Maldowen, Alwyn's successor, out of the love he entertained for the monks of Paisley, in whose abbey he had chosen his place of sepulture, granted to them the Church of Kilpatrick and all the lands attached thereto. Maldowen's brother, Dugald, was at this time rector of Kilpatrick, and resisted the right of the monks to those lands which they claimed as ancient pertinents of the Church, and as confirmed to them directly by various charters. The case was tried by papal delegates in 1233, and the proceedings, as recorded in the Register of Paisley, give a clear and remarkable insight into our early ecclesiastical polity. Dugald, in the end, was compelled to yield. The Church, as in 1227, was decreed to belong to the Abbey of Paisley, *in propriis usus*, and the vicarage was taxed at twelve merks of the alterage, or the tithe of corn, if the alterage was not sufficient. The procurationes due to the bishop were at that time taxed at one reception *(hospitium)* yearly. The Abbot of Paisley, out of consideration for Dugald, who had thrown himself upon the mercy of the monastery, allowed him to retain the rectorship for his lifetime, and in addition thereto granted him half a carucate of the lands of Cochno. Still the dispute, though decided upon by the papal delegates, was far from being terminated, and the Abbot was more than once obliged to bestow a money equivalent upon those who held land in Kilpatrick, which the monks alleged had been gifted to the monastery. Thus Gilbert, the son of Samuel of Renfrew, obtained sixty silver merks on resigning the lands of Monachkeneran;· and Malcolm, the son of Earl Maldowen, received a similar sum, *pro bona pacis*, on resigning to the monastery the lands of Cochno, Finbelach, and Edinbarnet. About the year 1270, new claimants came forward for the Church lands of Kilpatrick in the person of John de Wardroba, Bernard de Erth, and Norrinus de Monnargand ; and in consideration of their title through their wives, grandnieces and heiresses of Dugald the rector, the Abbot paid them 140 merks, and obtained a charter of resignation from each. Three years afterwards Malcom, Earl of Lennox, " before he received the honour of Knighthood," confirmed to the Abbot and monastery of Paisley all the lands which they held

in Lennox, including not only those which belonged to the Church of
Kilpatrick, but also Drumfower (Duntocher), Renfede, and Drum-
dynanis, which had been given by his predecessors to the monastery
itself.   Yet even before the close of the century Robert, Bishop of
Glasgow, had to inhibit the Earl's steward, Walter Spreull, and at
length the Earl himself, from making a new claim to these lands in a
secular court."

The long-descended race, the Colquhouns of Luss, have held lands
in the county of Dunbarton as far back as the time of Alexander II.,
when Umphredus de Kilpatrick obtained a grant of the barony of
Colquhoun, and in conformity with custom, assumed the name of
his territorial possession.   The barony was in the parish of Kilpatrick, and upon a prominent point, the rock of Dunglas, near
Bowling, the new proprietor erected a stronghold whose ruins still
exist in picturesque decay.   Sir Robert Colquhoun, the grandson of
the above Umphredus, married the heiress of Luss and became the
founder of this ancient family, being succeeded by his son, Sir
Humphrey, whose name appears as witness to charters granted by
the Earls of Lennox in 1390, 1394, and 1395.   His son, Sir John,
was governor of Dunbarton Castle during the minority of James II.,
was slain by a body of Highlanders in 1440, and was succeeded by
his grandson, also Sir John, who was Sheriff of Dunbartonshire in
1471.   In 1474, he was raised to the dignity of Grand Chamberlain,
and was appointed one of the special ambassadors to London, to
treat of a marriage between two young members of the royal family
of England and Scotland.   The King was so much pleased with Sir
John in this delicate mission that he made him governor of Dunbarton Castle for life.   This was in September 1477, and the next
year this brave soldier was killed by a cannon ball at the siege of
the Castle of Dunbar.

Sir Humphrey, who succeeded, received in 1480 a remission from
the Crown for the relief duties of his lands, in consideration of his
father, Sir John, having fallen at Dunbar.   Sir Humphrey, who was
twice married, first to a daughter of Lord Erskine, secondly to a
daughter of Lord Somerville, died in 1493, and was succeeded by his

son Sir John, who married into the family of the Darnley Earls of
Lennox, thus acquiring the life-rent of some lands of Glenfruin.
Sir John also acquired various properties in the Gareloch district,
Lettrowalt and Stuckinduff, Finnart, Portincaple, and Rachane. As
illustrating some of the local feuds of the period it may be told that,
in February 1514, Sir John Colquhoun obtained a summons for
spulzie against Robert Dennistoun of Colgrain for having harried
the Mains of Luss and the mailing of Dumfyn, of certain kye, horses,
and sheep, all duly specified and appraised in the summons. His
son Humphrey succeeded in 1536, and left a family, of whom the
eldest, Sir John, succeeded his father in 1540, and married a daughter
of Lord Boyd. Sir John, in 1568, had a remission from the Regent
Murray for his absence from the muster at Maxwellheugh. Sir
Humphrey succeeded his father in 1575, and left three daughters at
his death. He purchased from Robert Graham of Knockbain the
coronatorship of the county of Dunbarton, to be held blench of the
Crown, for one penny. During one of the feuds which distracted
the Lennox country, he was said to have taken refuge in his old
Castle of Bannachra, where the treachery of a servant in lighting him
up one of the stairs, made him a mark for the arrows of his pursuers,
who had sought him in this retreat, and he was killed.* Sir Alexander Colquhoun succeeded in 1592 on the assassination of his

---

* Dr. Macleay, in his memoirs of Rob Roy, gives a different account of the
death of the laird of Luss, in which, also, he erroneously alludes to him as
having fought the battle of Gleufruin. He says, "Colquhoun of Luss, having
been at a great party in Edinburgh, had grossly insulted the Countess of Mar.
About this same time the laird of Macfarlane, whose lands lay about the north
end of Loch Lomond, had, in a foray to the Leven, killed five gentlemen of the
name of Buchanan, for which he fled and concealed himself in Athol. He there
met Lady Mar, who, anxious to revenge the affront formerly given her by the
laird of Luss, promised to obtain Macfarlane's pardon if he would despatch
Colquhoun. Macfarlane accordingly set off, collected a few of his people, and
went by water to Rossdou. He was noticed by Colquhoun, who fled to
Bannachra, at a short distance, and concealed himself in a vault. Macfarlane
followed, dragging him from his hiding place, and murdered him. It is said his
blood still stains the floor in which the deed was perpetrated."

brother. The principal event in his life was the fatal conflict in Glenfruin between the Colquhouns and the MacGregors in 1603, which will be described elsewhere. He married, in 1595, Helen, daughter of Buchanan of that ilk, and left a large family. Sir John Colquhoun succeeded, and in 1620 he married Lady Lilias, eldest daughter of the fourth Earl of Montrose, and five years afterwards, was created a Nova Scotia baronet. Criminal proceedings were instituted against Sir John for absconding with the sister of his wife, who had taken up her abode at Rossdhu, after her father's death. He therefore fled the country, and after a time his brother completed an arrangement with the numerous creditors against the estate. Charters were taken out, by which Sir John's eldest son was infeft of the lands in 1647. Sir John was excommunicated by the Presbytery of Luss for his crime; and though he made confession and sought to be reponed, still the sentence was not withdrawn.

Sir John Colquhoun, son of the preceding, succeeded, and was a zealous adherent of the Royalist party in Scotland, on whose behalf he endured many hardships. Cromwell inflicted a fine of £2000 upon him, subsequently reduced to £666 13s. 4d. He purchased Balloch in 1652 from James, Duke of Lennox, and, by his marriage with Margaret Baillie, acquired the barony of Lochend in Haddingtonshire. As Sir John died without leaving male issue, the estates devolved upon his eldest brother, Sir James, who married Pennel, daughter of William Cunningham of Ballichen, Ireland. Among the Luss papers there is a "Protection," given to him by General Monk in 1655 "to pass with his traveyling traines to London, or other parts in England, and to repair into Scotland without molestation." His son, Sir Humphrey, was one of the representatives for Dunbartonshire in the last Scottish Parliament, and a determined opponent of the Union between England and Scotland. He married Margaret, daughter of Houston of Houston, and had issue a daughter, Anne. In December 1706 Sir Humphrey executed a deed entailing the estate of Luss on his only daughter, and her husband James, son of Ludovick Grant of Grant, and the heirs of the marriage, whom failing, to the heirs male whatsoever of Sir Humphrey. He died in

1718, and was succeeded by his son-in-law, James Grant, who thereupon assumed the name and arms of Sir James Colquhoun of Luss. On his succeeding to the fine estate of Grant, in terms of Sir Humphrey's will, the estate of Luss devolved upon a younger brother Ludovick, who thereupon assumed the name and arms of Sir Ludovick Colquhoun of Luss. He also˙ succeeded to the Grant estate, when Luss devolved upon the next brother James, who assumed the name and arms of Sir James Colquhoun of Luss. A dispute being likely to arise with the Tullichewan branch of the family regarding the old patent of baronetcy, Sir James was created a baronet of Great Britain in 1786. He married Lady Helen, daughter of William, Lord Strathnaver of the family of Earls of Sutherland. In his lifetime the town of Helensburgh was founded, and so named in honour of his wife Lady Helen. Dying in 1786, he was succeeded by his son Sir James, who was Sheriff-Depute of Dunbartonshire, and a principal Clerk of Session, and dying in 1805 was succeeded by his son James, son of Jane—daughter and co-heiress of James Falconer of Monktown. Sir James was, in 1802, elected member of Parliament for Dunbartonshire, and in 1799 married Janet, only surviving daughter, by his first marriage, of Sir John Sinclair, Bart., of Ulbster, the distinguished Scottish patriot. Lady Colquhoun was a lady of great discernment, and of genuine Christian philanthropy, and lived till October 1846. Sir James died in 1836,—leaving three sons,— James who succeeded, and John who married in 1834 Miss Fuller Maitland, and had a large family, amongst them Colonel Alan John Colquhoun, who is heir presumptive to his cousin, the present Sir James. John Colquhoun was a man of fine character, a single-hearted, God-fearing gentleman, whose works, the *Moor and the Loch*, and the *Rod and the Gun*, have had a wide circulation. He was born in 1805, and entered the army, first joining the 33rd Regiment, and subsequently the 4th Dragoon Guards. When he left the army, John Colquhoun settled in Edinburgh, where his family were educated, and for a great number of years, until his death in 1885, he conducted evangelistic meetings in the Grassmarket. Possessed of a beautiful simplicity of character, gentle and kindly, as a true soldier of the Cross, there was something in the manly bearing and unaffected urbanity of John Colquhoun which gained him affectionate respect. A prayer of his is recorded, in which he dedicated himself to the service of his Heavenly Father, and rested all his hopes on the merits of a crucified Saviour. A keen observer and lover of nature, while following the wild animals and birds, whose ways and haunts he so graphically described in his books, he charms his readers with the picturesqueness of his narrative. His observations upon the habits and ways of both large and small game, and his accuracy of detail, have gained for his writings a lasting popularity. Tenderly loved by an attached and united family, and esteemed by a wide circle of friends, John Colquhoun passed away in all the strong yet humble assurance of a devout Christian. Another of the family, William, was well known and respected, and lived the greater part of his life at Rossdhu, with his brother, the late Sir James Colqu houn.

Sir James Colquhoun of Luss, who succeeded in 1836, was a man of upright character and unswerving integrity, modest and unassum- ing in demeanour, who lived and died among his own people. He was an excellent landlord, and did a great deal for his extensive estates, rebuilding almost every farm steading, and many of the cottages. He planted hundreds of acres, and ornamented the policies of Ross- dhu by transplanting there great numbers of large trees. Many of these trees thus transplanted were from fifty to sixty years growth, and, in nearly every case, they succeeded. Sir James laid out large sums on drainage, land reclamation, and other improvements. He took a keen interest in agricultural matters, and frequently presided at meetings of agricultural societies. He was a strong Liberal in politics, and represented the county for some years in parliament, but he never took much part in parliamentary proceedings. When the rifle volunteer movement first started in 1859, Sir James took it up warmly, and raised a local corps of riflemen from his own estates. He was an ardent supporter of the Church of Scotland, and held firmly to its standards, including strong views upon the Sabbath observance question. In 1859 he resolved to enforce his rights as a landlord in striving to protect the pier at Garelochhead from being made use of by the notorious Sunday steamer, his servants forcibly resisted the landing of passengers, and he carried the case to the Court of Session in Edinburgh. He successfully contended that, as the pier was erected on his own private grounds, and was not a public pier, he had perfect right to make his own regulations for the traffic.

Sir James took a deep interest in Helensburgh, and his measures helped the rising prosperity of the burgh. Any scheme for assisting the water supply, for providing recreation grounds, for municipal improvements, for opening up new roads, was sure of his liberal support. He was a man of sincere and unostentatious piety, but of a most reserved and diffident bearing among strangers, and he cared nothing for the fashionable and social gatherings of the world. Consequently he was rarely seen outside of his own estate, though he was invariably affable and courteous in his circle of familiar friends. His sad death by drowning, in December 1873, caused a great shock in Helensburgh and throughout the Luss estates, where he was well known and beloved. Accompanied by his brother William, Sir James, and four of his servants, had been for some hours deer stalking on Inch Lonaig, one of the islands in Loch Lomond. Returning home with the heavily laden boat, a violent storm arose as they were half way between the island and the shore, and as it was getting dusk, Mr. William Colquhoun, who was rowing in a small boat by himself, suddenly lost sight of the party in a blinding storm. When the gust had blown over, Sir James' boat could not be seen, and, after a long search, it was evident that the stormy waters had engulfed the entire party. The bodies of Sir James and two of his men were found after some days search, and the tragic event was long mourned throughout the neighbourhood of Loch Lomond, for, in the chief of the Colquhouns, the poor lost a generous friend, and his tenantry and dependents a just and liberal landlord.

His son and successor, the present Sir James Colquhoun, inherits his father's character for uprightness, and a desire to forward all measures of usefulness. His singularly modest and retiring disposi-

tion prevents him from entering into public life, but his cultured
mind and natural sagacity well qualify him for fulfilling the duties of
his position.   Owing to the peculiar manner in which the great Luss
estates are now placed, being managed by Trustees, Sir James has
not the power to carry out further improvements, or to spend large
sums in developing the property.   Delicacy of health also obliges
him to live much in the South of England, but being Lord Lieutenant
of Dunbartonshire, he resides part of the year at Rossdhu, and gives
scrupulous attention to the duties of his high office.   Sir James is
characterised by a deep vein of religious fervour, and his published
works testify to the evangelical nature of his views upon sacred
subjects.   Sir James was married in 1875 to Charlotte Mary
Douglas, youngest daughter of the late Major William Munro, of
the 79th Cameron Highlanders, and grand-daughter of Sir Robert
Abercromby, Baronet, of Birkenbog, and has issue two daughters.

The lands and barony of Colquhoun, from which the family derive
their name, have passed into other hands and lay on the south-east
part of the county, mostly in the parish of Old Kilpatrick.   The
woods of Colquhoun were often trodden by Robert the Bruce, and
in these woods in 1313 he, one day, encountered a carpenter of the
name of Roland who, by his timely information, saved the King
from being the victim of a stratagem of Sir John Menteith of Rusky,
who was about to betray him to the English.   On 30th June, 1541,
James V., by letters under the Privy Seal, granted to John Colquhoun of Luss the duties of the lands and barony of Luss, with the
castle, tower and fortalice of Rossdhu, and the lands and "barony of
Culquhone," with the manor-place of Dunglass.   The old ruin of
Dunglass Castle, so picturesquely situated on a headland of the
Clyde near Bowling, was said to have been built in 1380, and was
one of the residences of Sir John Colquhoun, Chamberlain of Scotland in 1439, and long continued to be occupied by the family.   It
used to be of strong military importance, and was garrisoned by the
Covenanters to protect themselves against the Marquis of Montrose.
General David Leslie, commander in chief of the army of the Committee of Estates, issued his orders in December, 1650, for garrison-

ing the "House of Dunglas." In 1735 the Commissioners of Supply "recommended some of the free stones out of the old ruinous house of Dunglas, to be used in repairing the quay." At that time it was possessed by the Edmonstones of Duntreath, but has since formed part of the estate of Buchanan of Auchintorlie. The present mansion house, which immediately adjoins the castle, was built by Sir Humphrey Colquhoun, who was treacherously slain by an arrow at his Castle of Bannachra in 1592.

Henry Bell may almost be said to rank with George Stephenson, as a discoverer of the great capabilities of steam, as a motive power, in propelling ships through the water. He was born at the village of Torphichen, in Linlithgowshire, on 7th April, 1766, and was descended from a race of mechanics who, for generations, were known as practical mill wrights and builders, and had been engaged in many public works. After being educated in the parish school, Henry Bell, in 1780, began to learn the trade of a stone mason. Three years afterwards he became an apprentice to his uncle, who was a mill-wright, and on the termination of his agreement, he went to Borrowstounness to learn ship modelling. In 1787 he worked with Mr. James Inglis, engineer, with the view of completing his knowledge of mechanics. From there he went to London, where he was employed by the celebrated Mr. Rennie, and had opportunity of gaining a practical acquaintance with the higher branches of his art. About the year 1790 he returned to Scotland, and is said to have set up as a house carpenter in Glasgow ; his name appears, in October 1797, as a member of the Corporation of Wrights in that city. He had ambitious designs in Glasgow, and strove to undertake public works but, from a deficiency of means, or from want of steady application, he never succeeded. One who knew Bell at this time wrote thus of him : "The truth is, Bell had many of the features of the enthusiastic prospector ; never calculated means to ends, or looked much farther than the first stages or movements of any scheme. His mind was a chaos of extraordinary projects, the most of which, from his want of accurate, scientific, calculation, he never could carry fully into practice. Owing to an imperfection in even his mechanical skill, he scarcely ever made one part of a model suit the rest, so that many designs, after a great deal of pains and expense were successively abandoned. He was, in short, the hero of a thousand blunders and one success."

The idea of propelling vessels by means of steam early took possession of Henry Bell, and ultimately he brought his ingenious scheme into practice. Towards the close of last century, the *Flyboats*, as they were termed, formed the principal means of communication on the Clyde, between Glasgow and Greenock. These boats were constructed by Mr. William Nicol of Greenock, well known as an excellent builder of ships boats for many years. They were about 28 feet keel, about 8 feet beam, 8 tons burden, and wherry rigged. A slight deck, or awning, was erected abaft the main-mast so as to cover in the passengers, who were accommodated on longitudinal benches. Some of them, on a more improved principle, had a contrivance by which part of the deck or awning might be lifted up on hinges, to allow the passengers in fine weather more freedom in enjoying the voyage. A kind of platform ran along the edge of the deck, outside, to allow those navigating the boat to pass from the bow to the stern, where the steersman sat, without troubling the passengers! The boats generally left Greenock with a flowing tide if possible; if the wind was favourable, a passage of four or five hours to Glasgow was considered a great achievement. When the wind and tide were adverse, then it was toilsome work, and the passengers and crew were glad to get out at Dunglas, and wait there for some hours, enjoying a ramble through the picturesque woods and crags in the neighbourhood.

These boats which, to the present generation, may well seem a slow and wearisome mode of progression, were still an improvement upon the packet boats, or wherries, in vogue till then. One of the owners of the boats was Andrew Rennie, town drummer of Greenock, but a man of considerable ingenuity and speculation, and he proposed to his partners to have one built on a different model to be propelled by wheels. Accordingly he got a boat constructed of a greater breadth of beam, to the sides of which he affixed two paddle wheels, to be worked by manual labour. This boat, which came to be known as "Rennie's wheel boat," after making several trips to the Broomie-law, was sold, as it was not found to be any saving of labour to those who propelled it. Henry Bell heard of this plan of the wheel on the boat's side, and applied to Mr. Nicol to build for him a boat about 15 feet keel, with a well, or opening, in the "run," in which he placed a wheel, to be worked by manual power. Finding this single wheel not to answer the purpose intended, he got Mr. Nicol to close up the well, and tried his boat with two wheels, one on each side. He was convinced, after trial, that this was the true way of distributing the propelling power, though of course being wrought by manual labour no great speed could be attained. Hence it was that, after long consideration, he came to the conclusion that, if he could apply steam power to his wheel, the deficiency in propelling power would be amply made up. Another inventive genius, Symington of Greenock, had caused a canal boat to be fitted up with a steam engine, with a brick funnel, which was actually employed on the Forth and Clyde canal in towing vessels, but he did not suc-ceed in adapting steam to the propulsion of boats in open waters.

Henry Bell now resolved to prosecute his steamboat scheme, and induced Messrs. John & Charles Wood of Port-Glasgow, to lay down the keel of the first STEAMBOAT in their building yard in October, 1811 : this was the celebrated *Comet*, and she was launched in June, 1812, being called after the great meteor of the pre-ceding year. The *Comet* was a wooden boat of 42 feet long, 11 broad, and $5\frac{1}{2}$ deep, and 25 tons burden, and was fitted with the long funnel of the early steamers, which did duty for a mast as well. John Robertson of Glasgow made the engine, which was a conden-sing one of 3 horse power, the crank working below the cylinder, the engine shaft of cast iron, a fly wheel being added to equalise the motion. Originally the vessel was fitted with two pair of paddle wheels, 7 feet in diameter, with spur wheels $3\frac{1}{2}$ feet in diameter ; so that by means of another spur wheel, placed between these, and geared into them, each pair of paddles rotated at the same speed. However, this arrangement was found to be very inefficient, as one

pair of paddles worked in the wash of the other, and there was a
loss of power in working through toothed wheels. Mr. Robertson,
the engineer, tried to dissuade Henry Bell from planning his paddles
in this manner, but the latter insisted on trying the experiment,
which was not successful. The double wheels were then removed,
and Robertson made another engine of 4 horse power, the cylinder
12½ inches in diameter. The workshop where this engine was made
was in Dempster Street, North Frederick Street, Glasgow; it was a
vertical engine. The original model of the *Comet* is in the possession
of Messrs. John Reid & Co. of Port-Glasgow. The boiler of this
historic vessel was made by David Napier of Camlachie.*

Thus was the first steamboat completed, and it was announced in
the *Greenock Advertiser* of 15th August, 1812, that the COMET would
make the passage three times a week between Glasgow, Greenock,
and Helensburgh, by the power of "wind, air, and steam." The
interest this created was widespread and intense, great crowds of
people lined the shores from the Broomielaw downwards to witness
her departure and arrival, but of those who gazed on the novel spectacle few realised to themselves the immense revolution which was
thus being brought about in the annals of maritime enterprise. Few
believed in the ultimate success of the venture, and Bell was looked
upon as an enthusiast, while many were even afraid to set foot in
his vessel. A traveller, in 1815, records that he sailed in the *Comet*

---

* Messrs. Bell and Robertson had seen Symington's boat in the canal, and
had discussed the practicability of propelling vessels by machinery. The latter
had manufactured a small engine on speculation of three horse power, and this
Bell purchased for £165, an additional £27 being promised to other parties for
the boiler and fittings. After the success of the venture was assured, the *Comet*
was beached at Helensburgh and twenty feet added to her length, an engine of
six horse power being substituted. Irving mentions, "the original engine was
first sold to Archibald M'Lellan & Sons, coachbuilders, who applied it to some
of their machinery; it afterwards, by the intervention of the maker Robertson,
passed into the hands of Mr. Alexander, distiller, Greenock; it had several
other owners after this, but ultimately fell into the possession of Messrs. Girdwood & Co., engineers, Glasgow, who exhibited it as a curiosity at one of the
meetings of the British Association in Glasgow."

from Glasgow to Greenock, leaving in the morning, and arriving at Greenock after seven hours passage, three of which, however, had been spent lying on a sandbank at Erskine. Soon after the success of Henry Bell's steamer, the next vessel worked by this novel power was the *Elizabeth*, of 33 tons burden, 58 feet long, and she also was built by John Wood. But so little apprehension was caused by the advent of the steamboats that wherries were regularly announced to sail from Greenock to Helensburgh and the Gareloch *in opposition* to the steamers.

It was years before this successful effort at steam navigation that Bell conceived the idea of propelling vessels by other agency than the power of wind. He thus wrote in 1800, "I applied to Lord Melville on purpose to show his lordship and other members of the Admiralty, the practicability and great utility of applying steam to the propelling of vessels against winds and tides, and every obstruction on rivers and seas where there was depth of water." Disappointed in this application he repeated the attempt in 1803, with the same result, notwithstanding the emphatic declaration of Lord Nelson, who, addressing their lordships on the occasion, said, "My Lords, if you do not adopt Mr. Bell's scheme other nations will, and in the end vex every vein of this empire. It will succeed, and you should encourage Mr. Bell." Failing in this country, Bell tried to induce the naval authorities in Europe as well as the United States government to adopt his plan ; he succeeded with the Americans, who were the first to put his scheme into practice, and were followed by other nations.

After his great achievement in successfully navigating the waters of the Clyde by the power of steam, Bell, who had settled in Helensburgh, continued to prosecute his business of builder and wright. He also embarked upon more speculations in connection with efforts to establish other passenger steamers, but did not make any great success, for he was ever possessed by a restless desire to try new experiments. He originated various improvements in Helensburgh, of which town he was the first Provost, serving from 1807 till 1810. Latterly he had the management of the Baths Hotel, assisted by his

industrious wife, and there he died in November 1830. Efforts were
made by his friends to induce the government to award a sum of
money to one who had done so much to open up the way to our
vast international carrying trade, and whose genius had paved the
road for an entire revolution in the navigation of the ocean. But
all they could succeed in getting was a paltry dole of £200, as will
be seen from the following pathetic letter, written to one who had
interested himself in the matter :

"BATHS, HELENSBURGH, 19th June, 1829.

"MY DEAR FRIEND,—I write these few lines lyeing on my bed
unable to sit up. But the letter you sent me with the remittance of
£200 from the Treasury, a gift ordered by the late Mr. Canning,
will relieve my mind a little, and enable me to get Mrs. Bell's house
finished, and to pay the tradesmen. I was afraid I should not have
got this £200, little as it is. The wounds in my legs are rather
easier during the last few days, owing to my keeping close to my
bed. I will write to you in a day or two more fully.

"I am, your old friend,

"HENRY BELL.

"Mr. E. MORRIS, London."

For a few years he had enjoyed a pension of £100 a year from
the Clyde Trust, for although he had been the pioneer of vast improvements to navigation and commerce, he had reaped none of the
rewards of his inventive genius. His funeral took place on the 19th
November, when a large company of mourners followed the body of
the man who had done so much for steam navigation to its last resting place in the churchyard of Row. In 1839 a stone obelisk in
memory of Henry Bell was erected on the highest point of the rock,
beside the old castle of Dunglass, just overlooking the scene where
his first triumph was gained.

The late Robert Napier of Shandon, who knew well how much his
friend Henry Bell had laboured for the triumph of steam navigation,
placed a fine sitting statue of him in Row Churchyard. The expression of the face is well rendered, and gives a good idea of the man,
as he was in his later years, which were much clouded with dis-

STEAMSHIP "COMET" & DUMBARTON CASTLE.

appointment. A very handsome granite obelisk in memory of Bell also stands in a conspicuous position on the sea esplanade at the foot of James Street, Helensburgh, chiefly erected through the public spirit of the late Sir James Colquhoun and Robert Napier. On the pedestal is the following inscription :—

ERECTED IN 1872

TO THE MEMORY OF

HENRY BELL,

THE FIRST IN GREAT BRITAIN WHO WAS
SUCCESSFUL IN PRACTICALLY APPLYING STEAM
POWER FOR THE PURPOSES OF NAVIGATION.
BORN IN THE COUNTY OF LINLITHGOW IN 1766.
DIED AT HELENSBURGH 1830.

The following is a copy of the advertisement of the first passenger steamboat which plied on the waters of the Clyde :—

"Steam Passage-boat THE COMET, between Glasgow, Greenock, and Helensburgh, for passengers only.

"The Subscriber having, at much expense, fitted up a handsome vessel to ply upon the River Clyde, between Glasgow and Greenock, to sail by the power of wind, air and steam, he intends that the vessel shall leave the Broomielaw on Tuesdays, Thursdays, and Saturdays, about mid-day, or at such hour thereafter as may answer from the state of the tide—and to leave Greenock on Mondays, Wednesdays, and Fridays, in the morning, to suit the tide. The elegance, comfort, safety, and speed of this vessel require only to be proved, to meet the approbation of the public ; and the proprietor is determined to do everything in his power to merit public encouragement. The terms are for the present fixed at 4s. for the best cabin, and 3s. the second ; but beyond these rates nothing is to be allowed to servants or any other person employed about the vessel. The subscriber continues his establishment at Helensburgh Baths, the same as for years past, and a vessel will be in readiness to convey passengers in the *Comet* from Greenock to Helensburgh. Passengers by the *Comet* will receive information of the hours of sailing by applying at Mr. Houston's Office, Broomielaw ; or Mr. Thomas Blackney's, East Quay Head, Greenock.

"HENRY BELL.

"Helensburgh, 5th August, 1812."

For some years the *Comet* continued to ply on her original route, and also for a short period on the Firth of Forth, and subsequently she traded between Glasgow and Fort William, *via* the Crinan Canal. On the 7th of December, 1820, she started on her return journey, but on the 12th, at Salachan, the vessel struck on a rock, and had to be beached to enable the necessary repairs to be made. On the 14th the run to Glasgow was resumed, and on the 15th was at Oban, although by that time water was beginning to enter the vessel. On that day the *Comet* left Oban for Crinan, during a violent snowstorm, and shortly afterwards was driven, near the Dorus Mohr, by the force of the waves and wind on to the rugged point of Craignish, where she parted in two, amidships, at the exact spot where she had been lengthened in 1818. Henry Bell, the owner of the *Comet* was on board, but he, along with all the crew and passengers, were safely landed. After the unhappy striking of the vessel the afterpart drifted out to sea, and the forward part sunk in deep water. The engines, however, were saved, and incorporated in the machinery of the second *Comet* of 94 tons, built by James Lang of the Dockyard, Dunbarton, in 1821, which had one engine of 25 horse power. This vessel also was lost off Kempoch Point, Gourock, on 21st October, 1825, by coming into a collision with a steamer, the *Ayr*, when a lamentable loss of life occurred.

Such was the fate of the little vessel whose success inaugurated a new era in our mercantile marine, with results of wonderful magnitude to all the nations of the world. It is melancholy to reflect how little was done to smooth the closing years of the man to whose ingenuity and perseverance so much of the triumph of steam navigation was due. With almost prophetic foresight Henry Bell thus spoke in 1812, when the little *Comet* first sailed on the Clyde. " Wherever there is a river of four feet in depth of water through the world, there will speedily be a steamboat. They will go over the seas to Egypt, to India, to China, to America, Canada, Australia, everywhere, and they will never be forgotten among the nations." No doubt there were not wanting those who sought to take away from Bell the distinction of having been the first to apply steam to the propelling of vessels, and Fulton, the American, has claimed the honour. Dr. Cleland, the Annalist of Glasgow, writes on this subject. " It was not, however, till the beginning of 1812 that steam was successfully applied to vessels in Europe, as an auxiliary to trade. At that period, Mr. Henry Bell, an ingenious, self-taught engineer, and citizen of Glasgow, fitted up, or it may be said without the hazard of impropriety, invented the steam-propelling system, and applied it to his boat the *Comet*, for, as yet, he knew nothing of the principles which must have been so successfully followed out by Mr. Fulton."

Morris, the friend of Henry Bell, who wrote the only life of the inventor which has ever been published, a brief and unassuming memoir, gives the following memorandum regarding Bell's claims to be the first who introduced steam power, which was drawn up by some of the early Clyde engineers.

" Glasgow, 2nd April, 1825.

" We, the undersigned engineers in Glasgow, having been employed for some time past in making machines for steam vessels on the Clyde, certify that the principles of the machinery and paddles used by Henry Bell in his steamboat the *Comet*, in 1812, have undergone little or no alteration, notwithstanding several attempts of ingenious persons to improve them. Signed by Hugh and Robert Baird, John Neilson, David and Robert Napier, David M'Arthur, Claud Girdwood & Co., Murdoch & Cross, William M'Andrew, William Watson."

The following appreciative sketch of Henry Bell appeared in the modest *Helensburgh Guide*, originally published by the late Mr. William Battrum more than thirty years ago, and now out of print. " In person Mr. Bell was about middle size, a stout built fresh complexioned man, hearty and genial in his manner. His features were regular and expressive, impressing a stranger at a glance with a good opinion of him as a shrewd, pawky Scot, an impression which ten minutes conversation stamped as sound. His general knowledge was extensive, and he had a peculiar aptitude for seizing the salient points of any new invention, and making himself master of the subject. He was a great talker, when excited by any favourite hobby, and nothing delighted him more than an intelligent listener, to whom

he would descant all night on any of his multifarious plans and
schemes. There were always some leading projects in view. The
construction of a canal betwixt east and west Tarbet, in Lochfine,
was a favourite one. He had also a scheme for the partial drainage
of Loch Lomond, and reclamation of the land, about which he had an
extensive correspondence with the Duke of Montrose, who did not
receive it favourably. The introduction of water to Helensburgh
from Glenfruin, he had also in view. The reclamation of waste
lands in Scotland, and even the Suez Canal he discussed, and urged
its practicability, despite the opinion of many eminent engineers.
Of all his plans he was exceedingly sanguine; neither the indifference
of others, the want of resources, partial failure, or any of the thousand
embarrassments that haunt projectors, daunted him. Whatever the
failure or disappointment met, he was always hopeful of ultimate
success. With a large measure of Watt's inventive faculty, he possessed in a good degree the energy and knowledge of men which
Watt's partner, Boulton, enjoyed. To the many doubts and dis-
belief of scientific and unscientific men that steam vessels would
never accomplish much, Bell's reply was always, 'they will yet
traverse the ocean,' and his prophecy, now being fulfilled, living
men who heard it will verify."

Any description of the Gareloch would be incomplete which did
not give some account of the eminent Robert Napier, who so long
resided at his beautiful seat at West Shandon, where his refined
taste displayed itself in the accumulated treasures of art he had
gathered under his roof, and which he delighted to shew to his
friends. He was born at Dunbarton on the 18th June, 1791, being
of a family that, for several generations, had resided in the Vale of
Leven, now so noted for its Turkey Red dye works. His father,
James Napier, was a burgess of the town, and carried on the business of a blacksmith and mill-wright, and his position in the town
enabled him to give his son Robert a good practical education in the
Grammar School of Dunbarton. Here, in addition to Classics,
Mathematics, French, and other branches, he was taught landscape
drawing, and afterwards architectural drawing, by a Mr. Trail, a

man of taste and culture. The latter was on friendly terms with the Napier family, and fostered young Robert's turn for things artistic. At the age of fifteen, his father took him from school to College, but Robert's brain, even at that early age, was full of mechanical ideas. Apprenticed to his father, he was engaged in smith work till he was twenty years of age, when he entered the office of the eminent lighthouse engineer, Robert Stevenson of Edinburgh, who constructed the Bell Rock lighthouse. On returning to his native town, his father wished Robert to enter into partnership, but the young man had ideas of his own, which were much in advance of the humble, though honourable, trade of a blacksmith. Accordingly, in 1815, he started in the Greyfriars Wynd in Glasgow, as engineer and blacksmith, no doubt having in view the future development of marine architecture. At first, orders came in slowly, although he only worked with the aid of two apprentices. In December, 1818, he married his cousin, Isabella Napier, a lifelong and truly happy union it proved. His father-in-law, John Napier, was a clever and prosperous engineer in Dunbarton, carrying on an iron foundry as well, and was among the first to employ steam power to drive machinery, which he used in boring cannon for Government during the Peninsular War.

In 1821 Robert Napier, along with his cousin David, entered upon the occupancy of the Camlachie foundry, and they undertook several large contracts, one of them being the pipes required by the Glasgow Water Company, when bringing the supply from the upper reaches of the Clyde. Mr. Napier's first land engine was, twenty years ago, in use in Mr. Boak's spinning factory in Dundee. The business grew rapidly, and the firm was constantly employed constructing boilers and land engines, until, at last, Robert Napier's cherished dream was realised when, in 1823, he received an order for a marine engine to propel the small paddle steamer *Leven*, plying between Glasgow and Dunbarton. So good was the engine that it wore out no less than three different hulls of the vessel, and may now be viewed at the base of the rock of Dunbarton Castle, where it was erected by his two sons as a memorial of their father. Robert

F

Napier was one of the pioneers of steam engines for marine purposes, and he foresaw the great revolution likely to ensue when the
vast powers of steam should be fully applied to the propulsion of
ships. The idea had occurred to several inventors, Miller of Dal-
swinton, and William Symington, as far back as 1788, had endeavoured to enlist the steam engine as a propeller, and, in 1801,
Symington built the *Charlotte Dundas*, for Lord Dundas, for towing
barges on the Forth and Clyde canal, but the vessel did not prove a
success.   Trevithick, in 1805, was experimenting on the Thames
with his engine for propelling ships, but it was reserved for Henry
Bell, in 1812, to construct the *Comet*, which was successfully driven
through the water by the power of steam. The boiler and engine
castings of this famous little vessel were made by David Napier, the
engines by John Robertson of Glasgow, and were afterwards presented to South Kensington Museum by Robert Napier. Curiously
enough, the cylinder of the *Comet*, on the break up of the vessel, was
placed by Henry Bell on the top of the Baths Hotel at Helensburgh,
where he resided, and it did duty for many a long year as a chimney
can.

In 1828 Mr. Napier's increasing business necessitated his removal
to the famous Vulcan Foundry, and he added to it, in 1835, the
larger engine works of Lancefield. So well known had he become,
that no shipping company of any standing could be started without
first seeking his advice and co-operation. In 1836 he began his connection with the Honourable East India Company, and into one of
their steamers, the *Bernice*, was introduced by his manager, David
Elder, variable expansion valves in the engines. The *British Queen*
followed in 1839, a sister ship to the *President*, for the Atlantic trade.
She was of 420 horse power, and surface condensers for her engines
were introduced after the method of Samuel Hall of Aberdeen.
About this time Mr. Napier built several steam yachts for the well
known sportsman, Mr. Assheton Smith, one of which, the *Fire King*,
of 700 tons, attained to the speed of 15 miles an hour, the greatest
of any vessel then afloat. This rate of speed was due to Mr. Smith's
foresight in building his vessel with fine hollow water lines, instead

of those believed to be the best, namely the "cod's head and the mackerel tail," and it formed a distinct epoch in the formation of steamships. In 1839 was started that great enterprise the Cunard Company, when Mr., afterwards Sir Samuel Cunard, projected his line of steam ships between New York and Liverpool. The first contract was with Robert Napier, who was to furnish four steamers of 900 tons each, and 300 horse power. This size of vessel Mr. Napier considered too small, and pressed Mr. Cunard to increase it to 1200 tons and 400 horse power. Such was the commencement of that remarkable departure in shipping known as the Cunard Company, and of the original subscribers not one now survives. The *Persia* and the *Scotia*, paddle wheel steamers, built by Mr. Napier for the Cunard Company, were famous in their day. The *Scotia* consumed 160 tons of coal in 24 hours, and could make the voyage from New York to Liverpool in 8 days 22 hours, whereas it took the *Britannia*, in 1840, no less than 14 days 8 hours to cross the ocean.

Robert Napier constructed many ships of war for the British Government, famous amongst which was the *Black Prince*, one of the finest war vessels in the navy, besides numerous ironclad warships for others of the great European Powers. From first to last his workmanship elicited the highest encomiums from the naval authorities, and he was the first to throw open his yard to naval officers who sought to gain practical information in the engineering branch of their profession. Foreign governments also took advantage of his liberality in this respect, and his name was an influential and honoured one in naval circles throughout Europe. The last contract which he personally made was in 1865, when he undertook to build the *Pereire* and *Ville de Paris*, of the French Transatlantic Mail Service, which, for speed and economy, surpassed all the vessels then in the Atlantic trade. By this time he had amassed a large fortune, and had many honours bestowed upon him, in recognition of the eminent services which he had rendered to marine architecture. The honours and decorations, crosses and medals, showered upon Mr. Napier had no effect in altering the noble simplicity of character and manner which ever was conspicuous in this distinguished man. He

was practically the father of steamship building, and all his work
was characterised by the highest degree of excellence, often to his
own loss and detriment, for he allowed nothing to leave his yard but
what would bear the closest inspection. It was an absolute guarantee
of the highest order that a ship had been constructed by Mr. Napier's
firm, and his certificates were prized by those who received them, as
certain to lead to future promotion.

In his beautiful residence at West Shandon the latter years of Mr.
Napier's life were passed, after he had retired from active business,
and here he gathered together a very fine collection of all sorts of
objects of art, including paintings, statues, china, and all varieties of
ceramic ware, besides old armour, clocks, watches, glass ornaments,
and other curiosities. It was a great delight to the courteous old
man to go round with his visitors, and point out the rarer gems of
art treasures he possessed, and year by year he had hosts of visitors
of all ranks, for his hospitality was on a lavish scale. The collection
contained many choice specimens, which, at its subsequent dispersal
in London, were acquired for some of the famous galleries and
museums of Europe ; but the pleasure of seeing them at Shandon was
wonderfully enhanced by the presence of the genial but simple
owner. He died on 23rd June, 1876, and his funeral in Dunbarton
Church, a few days afterwards, was attended by a great assemblage
of his friends, neighbours and his workmen, as well as by men
whose names are widely known and honoured in the scientific world.

CHAPTER III.

Parochial Records, Church Minutes, John M'Leod Campbell.

THERE are not many particulars of the ancient state of Row given in *Origines Parochiales*, but the details though meagre are of interest. The modern parish of Row, on the eastern side of the Gareloch, rises from the shore in two ridges of considerable height, one of them skirting the waters of the Gareloch and Loch Long, reaching an elevation of nearly 2000 feet, and the other tending towards Loch Lomond with the secluded pass of Glenfruin between. The latter glen, and the heights above, were not within the boundary of the ancient parish of Rosneath.

The greater part of the Lordship of Lennox, for it was to this noble family that the district belonged, was the property of Amelec, who, in May 1225, received from King Alexander at Cadihow a confirmation of the grant which his brother Maldoven, Earl of Lennox, made to him of the lands of Neved, Glanfrone, Moigliag, Letblaan, Ardereran, Kilmeagdhu, and Doleuchen, to be held of the said Maldoven. In 1351, Donald, Earl of Lennox, confirmed to Walter de Fosselane the donation which Malcolm, Earl of Lennox, granted to Avileth, Lord of Fosselane, of the lands of Keppach, Culgrayne, Camceskanys, Kyrkmychell, Ardengappil, Ardenaconvell, Letdovald, Bullernok, Fosselane, Glenfrone, and Muleig, together with all the lands and offices acquired by Walter within the said earldom, especially the office of forester of the woods of Levenax, and the office of Tossachiorschip of Levenax, both purchased from Patrik Lyndissay. Before long these lands were divided into distinct possessions. The lands of Faslane, and the lands of Ardincaple on the east side of the Gareloch, had each passed into possession of a baronial family, in the 13th century, who resided on the estate. Several of the clan Macfarlane settled in the northern part of the territory of Amelec, while the lands bordering Loch Long and the Gareloch sides were occupied by a colony of the clan Colquhoun. The barons of Ardincapil, who afterwards assumed the name of Macaulay, were the proprietors of that part of the Gareloch side during the wars of the succession.

From the careful sketch of the history, civil and ecclesiastical, contributed to the statistical account of the parishes in Dunbartonshire by the late Rev. John Laurie Fogo, for fifty years minister of Row, we learn many details of importance. It would appear that all the lands at that date, 1839, contained in the parish, constituted part of the original earldom of Lennox. Those which form the eastern shores of the Gareloch, and slope up into Glenfruin, were given by Alwyn, second Earl of Lennox, to his younger son Amelec, in the 12th century. This fine estate descended to Walter, son of Alan, who became the head of the house and married the heiress of the elder branch. Their family mansion was situated at Faslane, a beautiful bay on the upper part of the Gareloch, with well tilled green fields, now rising from its shore. Its site can be distinguished by a small mound near the murmuring burn which flows into the bay. According to Blind Harry, the Scottish hero Wallace was hospitably entertained at Faslane by his friend Earl Malcolm of Lennox, after he had plundered the town of Dunbarton and burnt Rosneath castle. After the succession of the Faslane branch of the family to the honours of Lennox, there is little notice of the castle, and in time the estate became subdivided into small portions or feus. The Macfarlanes acquired part of the northern extremity, and a good many of the Colquhouns settled on the Gareloch shores and largely peopled the peaceful valley of Glenfruin. Also in Glenfruin there resided for a long time a race of petty proprietors of the name of Macwalter, who claimed to be descended from a younger son of Lennox. The Macaulays of Ardencaple, who had assumed the former patronymic surname, gradually gained a considerable holding on the Loch side, which they kept for a long period. This family seems to have settled as landowners in the district in the 13th century. Their estate embraced the whole of the land on which the town of Helensburgh is built, and extended far up the Gareloch. There were two residences on the estate, one, the fine old ivy-clad castle of Ardencaple, part of which, with some modern additions, still stands amidst lofty trees near Cairndhu Point, and the small keep of Faslane. About two hundred years ago the fortunes of the family began to decline, and the then laird, Aulay Macaulay, had to dispose of his estates to the Colquhouns, and the last of the family died at Row in 1767.

The family of the Colquhouns of Luss have gradually gained possession of the whole parish of Row, and hold the extensive lands which once belonged to the Macaulays, Macfarlanes, and Buchanans. About the year 1500 the Colquhouns acquired their first holdings on the Gareloch, and the estate of Faslane was granted to Adam Colquhoun in 1553 by his relative the Earl of Lennox. The last possession in the parish which the Colquhoun family secured was the fine estate of Ardencaple, so long owned by the Macaulays, which only was purchased from the Duke of Argyll by the late Sir James Colquhoun in the year 1862.

The lands in the parish were greatly improved during the last thirty years, chiefly from additional drainage and fencing, and those capable of cultivation were all under crops. But a great deal of the land consisted of the slopes rising from the Garcloch, all the upper part of which was moor and heather. Glenfruin was capable of much more cultivation, as it had abundance of low-lying fertile land, and had once supported a considerable population. Attention had been recently given to the breeding of cattle, and the dairy farms were mostly made up of Ayrshire cows, not of a very pure breed. The cattle, for feeding purposes, were of the West Highland stock, but the recently formed agricultural association was leading to a variety of improvements in the breeding of cattle. The sheep were mostly of the black-faced breed, and a few Cheviots; the average rate of grazing a full-grown one, to the farmer, was about 5s. Male farm

servants living with the farmer received on an average £8 in the half
year, and female servants £4. Masons, carpenters, and other artizans
were usually paid 3s. 6d. per day. The farm buildings mostly were
very inferior; leases usually ran for nineteen years. The lime quarries
in the parish were not constantly worked, as Irish lime was cheap
and easily got, and slate was little in demand. In Glenfruin the
population had greatly decreased, for, almost within the memory of
living persons, there were forty-five families of farmers, besides a
number of cottars, whereas, in 1839, there were only ten farmers and
four families of cottars. Little more grain was grown, with the exception of some barley, than was sufficient for the farmers and their
establishments. About £1000 worth of potatoes and £500 of hay
was sent out of the parish yearly, and the total rental of Row was
stated to be between £4000 and £5000, nine-tenths of which was
drawn by Sir James Colquhoun.

Such was the state of the parish in 1839, and it had not materially
changed since the account given of it in the former statistical record
of 1792, written by the then minister, the Rev. John Allan. At that
time the whole of the upper lands were covered with heath, but, since
the introduction of sheep, a greater expanse of pasture was visible.
There were about sixty-five farmers, but many of the farms then
possessed by one tenant used to be occupied by three or four, in
addition to cottars. There were from 4500 to 5000 sheep altogether,
the average price of white wool being 7s. a stone. At that time the
parish more than supplied itself with provisions for the requirements
of its inhabitants, and potatoes, grain, beef, and mutton were sent to
the markets of Greenock, Paisley, and Glasgow. Beef, veal, and
mutton were 6d. per pound, and even cheaper in summer; butter
cost 9d. and 10d. per pound; a hen cost 1s. to 1s. 3d.; meal 1s. per
peck, oats 16s. per boll. These prices were double what the same
commodities brought forty years before. The farm servants wages
were, for men, £8 and £9, and women, £3 and £4 per annum, and
day labourers on farms 10d. to 1s. per day. Fishing was carried on
in the Gareloch, and salmon, mackerel, and herring were taken in
quantities with nets, and sent to Greenock, the price of salmon being

6d. per pound, and haddocks 1½d. Porpoises and seals were some-times taken, and occasionally a bottle-nose whale would be driven aground. The sea ware was most used for manure, and kelp was burnt in small quantities. The chief fuel used was peat, though coals, which were dear, were sometimes brought from Glasgow.

There were two schools in the parish, one with from thirty to forty scholars in winter, and half that number in summer. The schoolmaster received £80 Scots, but, including his fees as Session Clerk, the total emoluments were barely £18 sterling per annum. Thirty years before that date Mr. Glen, who then owned the estate of Portincaple, mortified a piece of land for the support of another schoolmaster in Glenfruin, and he had more scholars than attended the parish school, and higher emoluments. The poor of the parish were well cared for; in addition to the church-door collections, amounting to £12 a year, there was the interest of £220 of Stock; the number of regular poor on the roll was eight, and a similar number received occasional relief. There were eleven ale, or whiskey houses, and one inn, at what is now known as Cairndhu point, which had been erected as one of the stages for post horses on the road recently made by the Duke of Argyll between Inveraray and Dunbarton. There were eight landowners or heritors, only one of whom, a small pro-prietor, constantly resided in the parish. English was generally spoken, but many used the Gaelic language. The population seemed to be more addicted to seafaring pursuits than to a life on shore, for there were twenty-five or thirty seamen in the navy from Row, but not one soldier. One village existed in the parish, said to contain a hundred people, which had been lately built, and this probably was the now flourishing town of Helensburgh. The account concludes by remarking that "the young people, especially the females, are fond of dress, and more expensive in that way than their circumstances can well afford," which naïve observation may not be considered inapplicable, in many other parishes, even at the present day.

About the middle of the Seventeenth century Row was formed into an independent parish by the separation of land from Rosneath on the one side and Cardross on the other. The portion detached from the former parish lay principally on the east side of the Gareloch, while what was taken from Cardross was chiefly in the valley of Glenfruin.   In 1620 Parliament was petitioned to transfer the church of Rosneath to the opposite lands of Ardenconnell, but in place of this the Church Commissioners erected Row into a distinct parish, though it was not till 1648 that the boundaries of the new parish were finally settled and a deed of erection for the church was procured.   In that year Mr. Archibald M'Lean, the first minister, was translated to it from the parish of Kingarth.   It appeared that the formation of this parish was chiefly owing to the then laird of Ardencaple, who generously built the church at his own expense, besides giving land for it and for the glebe to the extent of ten acres.

The original church was erected near the site of the existing edifice in a fine situation overlooking the beautiful bay of Row, with some old plane trees surrounding the churchyard.   In 1763 a new church was reared just in front of where the present one stands, and an addition to it was made in 1827.   Attached to this church was the burying ground of the Macaulays of Ardencaple, who long owned the lands in the neighbourhood.   The fragment which remains is a stone sculptured with armorial bearings, the shield of irregular shape has emblems or arms of the Macaulays and Drummonds, with the initials V. W. and M. D. and date 1579, which takes us back to the time of Humphrey Macaulay of Ardencaple, and, as he lived before the erection of Row into a parish, the stone must have belonged to some other building.   The church was a very unadorned edifice, with a long sloping roof and a porch in front surmounted with a small bell tower and two rows of windows ; while inside everything was of the plainest description, and even after 1832, there was not even a wooden floor.   This church remained till 1851, when it was replaced by the existing building, with its handsome Gothic tower, a conspicuous object in the landscape, towards the cost of which Sir James Colquhoun and the late Robert Napier of Shandon were large contributors.   There is a costly organ, several stained glass windows, and some good carved work in the church.

Surrounding the churchyard are a number of large plane trees, while the old parish school stood until a few years ago, at the end of the churchyard, and immediately adjoining was the master's dwelling house. There are a good many tombstones and momuments, some of early dates, the most conspicuous of the latter being the sitting figure on a high pedestal erected by Robert Napier of Shandon to his friend Henry Bell, the engineer, famous in steam navigation. One of the old ministers, the Rev. Robert Anderson, who succeeded to the parish in 1684, has a monument to his memory, standing against the wall facing the village green, with the following inscription on the back :

OUT OF LOUE AND RESPEICTE THE PAERISH
HAD TO THERE MINISTER
THEY BULDED THIS TOMBE, 1709.

In front the monument is decorated with the usual devices of an hour glass, a skull and cross bones, below which there is an inscription in Latin, commencing " Hic situs est Mr. Robertus Anderson," and ending, "Anno Domini MDCCVIII." There is also the tombstone of the Rev. John Allan, who was minister, and who died 28th March, 1812, in the 75th year of his age. All the older tombstones are in the portion of the churchyard which lies to the front of the church, and the graves in the upper part only date from the building of the new church. The boundary wall of the old churchyard can be traced from two fragments which are left, and the row of old plane trees on the west side show how the road at one time was inside of what is now the wall round the ground. The most noticeable tomb is the memorial erected by Sir Andrew Buchanan of Craigend to his parents, which consists of part of the gable wall and a small window of the old church ; the mantling ivy giving it a venerable appearance. The stone statue of Henry Bell is a chaste and simple work of art, the sculptor having invested the face of the distinguished inventor with a placid air of repose. Appropriate inscriptions on the pedestal record the dates of birth and death of the builder of the *Comet*, and his memorable triumph in his little vessel. Over twenty years ago his remains were removed from their first resting place in the old part of the ground, and re-interred in front of the statue.

On several of the older stones are to be seen designs indicating the trade followed by the person to whom the tombstone is set up, such as compasses, squares, shoes, implements, cross-bones, hour glasses; on one or two skeletons are engraved, decorations all of the rudest description. Several of them are dated in the early part of last century, and a good number are in memory of inhabitants of Row bearing Highland names, such as M'Farlanes, M'Murrichs, M'Callums, M'Lachlans, M'Kinlays, M'Intyres, Campbells. There is one tomb, made of iron cast at the Shotts Iron Company in 1829, as the massive slab records in large letters, and resting on iron pillars, which was placed there by Henry Bell in memory of Captain Robert Bain of the *Comet*. Captain Bain died in 1827, and the momument narrates how by that vessel a communication was opened up between the Western Islands of Scotland and Glasgow through the Crinan Canal in 1819. This was erected as a tribute of honour for sixteen years' faithful service, by Henry Bell, engineer, Helensburgh.

The old church faced the sea, and its foundations can be faintly traced about the middle of the churchyard. The session house, which closely adjoined, remained for some time after the church was demolished, and was inhabited for a considerable time by a well known native of Row, Jenny M'Auslan, the post runner for Helensburgh. Her humble ruinous dwelling in a grassy hollow beside the Aldonault burn, on the Ardenconnal estate, had been pulled down by orders of the then proprietor, who suspected Jenny of harbouring doubtful wanderers at times. A good many stories are still current regarding Jenny, who was one of the "characters" of the locality, and a well known figure on the Loch side, as she went with her bag from house to house. There are still some in the neighbourhood who can recall the old church, and Dr. M'Leod Campbell preaching in it with his peculiar fervour. The pulpit was next the loch, and at the two ends of the church were galleries, one on the left being Lord John Campbell's pew, and on the right the Ardenconnal pew. The bare earth constituted the floor of the church, and the seats were of rough deal boards, by no means inviting their occupants to repose. On sacramental Sabbaths there were the usual scenes enacted which were so little in keeping with the holy occasion—wooden tents on the green before the church-yard, in which were dispensed liberal supplies of spirituous liquors, along with bread and cheese, and homely bannocks. All the time the devoted Campbell, or Edward Irving, or some other ministers, were addressing the communicants in the adjoining church, almost within hearing of the revelry so little befitting the solemn services. The upper part of the churchyard contains a good many handsome modern monuments, one of them dedicated to a number of boys who died aboard the old *Cumberland* training ship, destroyed by fire in the Gareloch a few years ago, while beside the burying ground of Robert Napier, is the grave of his life-long friend the Rev. John Laurie Fogo.

There seem to have been several other small places of worship scattered about the parish of Row, one in Glenfruin, another on the lands of Kirkmichael, and a third at Kilbride, but there are few remains of them in existence. The proposal to erect Row into a separate parish was strongly opposed by the ministers of the adjoining charges of Rosneath and Cardross. Robert Watson, the minister of Cardross, thinking that the interest of his benefice might suffer, offered to contribute 100 merks towards building a church, or chapel of ease, in Glenfruin, and to surrender 240 pounds Scots out of his stipend for its endowment. The lairds of Luss and of Culcreuch agreed to make a gift of the site of the old chapel of Kilbride, but the General Assembly preferred to erect the new parish. The minister of Rosneath appears to have officiated for about a year in the new church at Row. The following was the succession of ministers of Row parish.

1648. Archibald M'Lean of Kingarth, in Bute, was ordained there, translated to Kilmodan in 1651. Considerable difficulty experienced in getting ministers able to preach in Gaelic, and there being no manse, a long vacancy ensued.

1658. James Glendinning, A.M., formerly of Largs, admitted June, until one having Gaelic should be got. Deprived by Act of Parliament and Privy Council, 1662, continued till June 1663.

1665. Hugh Gordon, A.M. Translated from Comrie; in 1683 transferred to Cardross.

1684. Robert Anderson, succeeded, but demitted the charge at the Revolution. Degree of A.M. from Glasgow University, 1675. Translated to Dunbarton, second charge, before 1689. Returned to Row before 1704, died 1708, aged 53. His son John admitted to bursary, Glasgow, 1718.

1710. Archibald M'Curry. Licensed by Presbytery of Dunoon, December 1708. Died in 1717.

1719. John Allan, native of Kilmadock, became schoolmaster at Campbeltown, and licensed by Presbytery of Kintyre, October, 1713, ordained 1719; died in 1765, in his 81st year. Married Anne, daughter of Archibald Wallace, minister of Cardross, died 1783; an only son who succeeded to the parish, and a daughter, married to Mr. Macfarlane, minister of Drymen.

1761. John Allan, son of preceding minister, licensed 1760, by Presbytery of Dunoon. Got the church rebuilt 1763. Died in 1812 in 75th year. Married 1771 Elizabeth Colquhoun, died 1813, leaving two daughters married to ministers of the Church of Scotland. Wrote Account of Parish in Statistical History.

1812. Alexander M'Arthur, son of the schoolmaster of Inishail. Licensed by Presbytery of Selkirk, April, 1805; became tutor in the family of Thomas Earl of Elgin. Presented to the parish of Row by George William, Duke of Argyll, in 1812, translated to Dairsie in 1825.

1825. John M'Leod Campbell, ordained in 1825, son of Rev. Dr. Campbell, minister of Kilninver, in Argyllshire. In 1831, Mr. Campbell was deposed by sentence of the General Assembly on the ground of holding and teaching doctrines on the assurance of faith and the atonement of our Lord Jesus Christ, which were contrary to the standards of the Church of Scotland. No one disputed the earnest and lofty character of Mr. Campbell, and his ability and originality as a thinker, while his parishioners were devotedly at-tached to their minister. After the sentence of the General Assembly he left the shores of the Gareloch for a number of years, during part of which he preached in a church at Partick. Subsequently he returned to Rosneath, purchased a residence not far from the Clachan village, to which he gave the Gaelic name of Achnasbie, "Field of Peace," and there he died in 1872, and his honoured remains rest in the churchyard of Rosneath, near the old ruined church which had so often resounded to his eloquent voice.

1831. John Laurie Fogo, a native of Sanquhar, born in 1796, student in the University of Edinburgh, presented by George William, Duke of Argyll, and ordained in March. He entered the parish under difficult circumstances, but his courteous and winning way and attractive personality soon gained many friends. He was a careful and accurate observer of men and things, and full of religious enthusiasm and evangelical fervour. In 1835 he married Jane Mathie Fogo, heiress of the small property of Rhu, near Doune, when he assumed her name. Mr. Laurie lived to an advanced age, faithfully discharging his duties as minister to the last, and died in 1882, greatly lamented. Earnest and evangelical as a preacher, he was intimately acquainted with all his parishioners, and spared no labour and knew no fatigue, in ministering to the wants of the aged poor. All along the shores of the Gareloch Mr. Laurie was greatly loved and widely known, both by high and low, he always took part in the school examinations at Row, Rosneath, and Helensburgh, besides frequently officiating at Communion seasons at these places, while, as a physician, at one time his services were much in request and cheerfully rendered. He laboured on though in feeble health, and when he died, in the fulness of years, it was felt that a true Christian and gentleman had been summoned away by that Master for whom he had indeed laboured with his whole heart.

Mr. Laurie was welcomed to the parish by his greatly loved predecessor, who knew his sterling qualities, and urged the Row congregation to give him their warm support. He gratefully alluded to this long afterwards in these words, "In looking forward to Row as my home I expected I should meet with trials and discouragements of a disunited parish, for I came as successor to Dr. M'Leod Campbell, a man much and deservedly loved by all who knew him. Many in the parish were anxious to leave the church with him, but from this source of looked for difficulties I was speedily delivered by Dr. Campbell advising his friends not to leave the church, but to give his successor their support." Feeling that the requirements of the parish were but inadequately met by the church at Row, Mr. Laurie preached alternately on the Sabbath evenings in Helensburgh, Garelochhead, and Glenfruin, occupying the schoolhouses on these occasions. He also diligently endeavoured to raise the funds necessary to provide a place of worship for the adherents of the Church of Scotland both at Helensburgh and Garelochhead. Very soon his labours were crowned with success for, mainly through the great exertions of Mr. James Bennett Browne of Bendarroch, the church at Garelochhead was, in 1839, erected into a parish *quoad sacra*. At Helensburgh Mr. Laurie Fogo, in seeking to endow a similar church, was warmly assisted by a committee of gentlemen, amongst whom may be mentioned the late Sir James Colquhoun, and Mr. Alexander of the Hermitage. The church was opened in May 1847. As showing the appreciation with which Mr. Laurie was held, it may be mentioned that, in the course of his ministry, he received four calls to other churches, all of which he felt constrained to decline, as he preferred to continue with the congregation and friends at Row whom he loved so dearly.

Mr. Laurie Fogo proved himself, during his long ministry of fifty years at Row, to be a worthy representative of those devoted, simple, and hard working men who, for generations, have adorned the ranks of the Scottish clergy. Rarely absent from his pulpit, he delivered his message of salvation through the merits of a Crucified Redeemer with an affecting persuasiveness which moved even callous hearers. His prayers, especially, were fervent and full, as he presented the pleadings of his flock at the Throne of Grace. On the occasion of his Jubilee, in 1881, the sum of £2,500 was raised by his congregation and friends, and a large company of his neighbours and ministerial brethren assembled to do him honour. The venerable minister was greatly affected by this unexpected testimonial, and asked his friend and co-Presbyter the Rev. Mr. Dunn, of Cardross, to express his deep sense of gratitude for so munificent a gift. Soon after the good old minister of Row entered into his rest.

The present minister of Row is the Rev. John M. Webster, son of the Rev. David Webster, of Fetlar, in the Shetland Islands, who was appointed colleague and successor to Mr. Laurie Fogo in December, 1876. Born at Aberdeen, Mr. Webster passed his boyhood in that far off island of the Shetland group where his father was minister for nearly thirty years, and, in due time, was sent to the University of Aberdeen, where he took a high place, especially in the classes of Logic and Moral Philosophy. After passing through his course of Arts, he graduated with honours in the department of Mental Philosophy, and then went to Edinburgh University, where he studied in the Divinity Hall to qualify himself for license. In 1872 he was appointed assistant in Sandyford Church, Glasgow, where then, as now, one of the most evangelical and honoured ministers in the Church of Scotland, the Rev. Dr. Elder Cumming, faithfully preaches the Gospel. Mr. Webster, after his appointment as assistant first, and then as colleague and successor to Mr. Laurie Fogo, soon gained the confidence and esteem of those who worshipped in the parish church. He was a willing worker, and entered into the pleasures as well as the sorrows of the parishioners, and he ever sought to strengthen the kindly ties which united him to the aged minister of Row. In July, 1881, on the death of his father, Mr. Webster received a gratifying and unanimous requisition, in which many members of the Free Church joined, that he should become minister of Fetlar parish, but he felt constrained to decline the call. On the occasion of the jubilee of his friend and colleague, Mr. Laurie Fogo, graceful expression was given by Mr. Webster to the regard which he felt towards the beloved minister in whose honour they were assembled. He also testified to the generous manner in which his aged friend, although not sympathising with some of the changes in the church service, had "never allowed any personal feelings to stand in the way of anything that would promote the welfare of the parish." Courteous and genial in manner, Mr. Webster enjoys much esteem as minister of the parish, and his pulpit discourses evince the preparation of a well cultured mind. He is chaplain to the local corps of Rifle Volunteers, to whom he has frequently addressed words of counsel, while he is ever ready to respond to an invitation to preside at meetings of societies existing for the mutual improvement and strengthening the religious life of the younger members of his own or other churches.

At Garelochhead there are two places of worship, the Established Church, where the Rev. Mr. Calderwood officiates with marked ability since the death of the Rev. John Paisley, who filled the charge for over forty years. The Free Church is represented by the Rev. Walter E. Ireland, M.A., whose grandfather, the Rev. Dr. Ireland, was minister of North Leith in the early part of the present century. Mr. Ireland has laboured to the great satisfaction of his congregation since January, 1880. Shandon Free Church, a neat Gothic building near the pier, which was rebuilt eleven years ago, has for its minister the Rev. Hugh Miller, M.A., who was elected in 1882. He was a distinguished student in the Free Church College, particularly in the department of Natural Philosophy, and his abilities as a preacher are much appreciated in his present sphere of labour.

An account has been given of how the church of Row was originally established, and of its ministers. At one time there were several places of worship within the district now contained in the parish of Row before the year 1648, when it was created. One was at Faslane, the ancient residence of the Lennox family, where a small portion of the chapel remains in a ruinous state. Another was in Glenfruin, with considerable lands attached, and a few fragments of the chapel were built into the adjoining schoolmaster's house. There was also at Kirkmichael, in Helensburgh, a third place for celebrating worship, though no trace of it remains, but religious service is said to have been performed in it in the early part of last century by an indulged Episcopalian minister. At first it was intended that the parish church of Row should be placed in Glenfruin, which, at that time, was the most populous part, but the tenantry succeeded in getting it built in its present situation. The first minister was chosen from his ability to preach in Gaelic, but that language is now only spoken by a very few of the oldest inhabitants, and the last who used it in the pulpit was the Rev. Mr. Allan, who died in 1812.

There is hardly anything of general interest to be gleaned from the Kirk Session records, which do not go back farther than 1719, when the Rev. John Allan was minister, and elders, John Service, John M'Ausland, Humphrey Bane, Archibald M'Ausland, Archibald Taylor, John M'Aulay, Robert Service, and Patrick M'Turner. The handwriting is not easy to decipher, in some places, and there are often gaps of several years. After 1767, there is no entry till 1776, in which year there was one Session meeting as to an Act of General Assembly, anent the age of ruling elders, no one to be ordained until he was twenty-one years old. In 1779 there was one meeting, Mr. Allan, minister, a case of discipline. The next meeting was 1793, another case of discipline. None of these minutes were signed by the moderator. There appears to be no other session records until 8th May, 1832, when Mr. Laurie Fogo was minister of the parish, from which date they are kept with regularity. None of the proceedings of the famous Row heresy case, resulting in the deposition of the Rev. J. M'Leod Campbell, seem to be preserved, at least there is no trace of them in the existing records.

The first minute of 1719 narrates how the minister wishes to be informed of the state of the parish, as to the state of the funds, what were the church "utensils," and as to the poor money. The utensils were a common table, with forms and tablecloth, some towels, and a basin for baptisms, the amount of funds being £16 13s. 4d. Scots, with 22 pounds Scots for "marriage dues." The "Bedell" reports that, whereas the session appoints him yearly 4 pounds Scots, and a pair of shoes valued at 2 merks, payable Martinmas yearly, he wants his shoes for the last year, and is paid 2 merks for them. 11 poor persons are relieved by a small distribution of 1 pound Scots each. Next year a session meeting is held at Garelochhead, and other meetings for discipline cases. In 1720, owing to their being troubled with "groundless and inconsiderable processes of complaint," the session orders that any informer with a complaint must hand in a crown along with it, which is forfeited if the complaint is not found true. In August 1720, there is "collection for Lithuania, 6 pounds Scots." At a meeting in November, 1720, "John Smith, Patt. M'Ghinney, Walter Wilson, and Alexander Thomson, being summarised to ye dyet compeared and being interrogate whyʳ. or not they employed Alexander M'Gormley, the excommunicate person as formerly, they owned they did, but at the same time told that he was again received into ye bosom of the church, then they being removed and the session finding it was through ignorance they did employ him, called them in and admonished them to be warry of it for the future, and so dismissed them."

On 22nd January, 1721, "Dugald Campbell having compeared according to appointment, and being interrogated whiyʳ. (as was reported) he had broken a whin rod at his brother Duncan his marriage, he owned he did, but at ye same time affirmed (tho : deponed) he neither spoke nor thought anything when he did it, nor knew any charm in it, but only did it according to custom, which, when ye session heard, and saw what he did was thro : ignorance, he was interrogate, whiyʳ. he acknowledged he was in ye wrong in so doing, and if he was sorry for what offence he had given to many, he replied he was, and accordingly dismissed."

Several session meetings in 1721 were taken up with the case of a woman who had been heard to utter malignant expressions of hatred, and predictions of evil, against her master, a farmer at Faslane, and was publicly rebuked for her heinous offence. Offences against morality were unhappily too common, and the guilty parties had to submit to rebuke before the congregation. In 1723 complaint was made that Robert M'Aulay in Gareloch had publicly proclaimed that the minister had made false representations to the congregation regarding the charity school at Faslane, and he was censured therefor. In 1724 James Davie chosen elder by "plurality of voices." Regular apportionments of the Poor money made yearly, £3 of the Session Funds loaned to Patrick M'Auslane, Stuckenduff, on good security.

In April, 1733, the elders from Glenfruin report that the schoolmaster complained of the paucity of children attending the school in the glen, and the elders proposed that something should be awarded him out of the funds, and accordingly he was awarded 4s. sterling, and that he should be paid the quarter's wages due from such poor children whose parents could not pay. The Session also appointed 3s. to be paid to Christian Turner for her encouragement in keeping a school at Gareloch-head. In the same year the Presbytery recommends all Sessions in their bounds to have a collection, from house to house, in favour of sufferers by the late fire at Paisley. In 1767, complaints made of the dilatoriness of parties paying their children's fees to the parish school, and it was ordered that no children be admitted without paying their fees at entry, except in the case of paupers. In 1779, two parties rebuked for contracting an irregular marriage, and in acknowledgment of their rebuke they signed the Kirk Session minutes, and agreed to live as Christian spouses. No further meeting of Session seems to have been held till January, 1793, when a couple who had contracted an irregular marriage paid half a guinea to the poor of the parish in acknowledgment of their sin.

In 1832, when the Rev. John Laurie was minister, the minutes again commence to be regularly kept, but they have nothing of general interest. In 1839, a new Session Officer is appointed for £4 sterling per annum. His duties were to ring the bell on Sabbath days, to toll the church bell at funerals, to clean the church, deliver citations from the Kirk Session, and attend their meetings. In April, 1840, Mrs. B——, of Helensburgh, being accused of indecent and unbecoming language towards her sister, was refused a token of admission to the Lord's Supper, but now appeared and expressed sorrow for her conduct, and after being seriously admonished by the moderator, received a token of communion. On 27th August, 1854, the Session agreed to petition the Presbytery to take up the subject of the profanation of the Sabbath by the sailing of the steamer *Emperor* on that day. Nearly all the Session meetings, till the volume ends in 1862, were taken up with breaches of morality and rebukes following thereon.

The case in the Church Courts which attracted great attention, and excited widespread sympathy, was the deposition in 1830 of

the Rev. John M'Leod Campbell, a very faithful and earnest servant
of God. Soon after his appointment as minister of the parish, in
1825, it was seen that he was a man of no ordinary character, and of
deep theological acquirements, although his printed writings were
somewhat involved, and occasionally obscure in style. When he
succeeded to the living, the religious life of the people was at a very
low ebb, there being a great deal of drunkenness and immorality.
Smuggling and other unlawful practices were rife in the neighbourhood, and were regarded in a very indulgent light by the inhabitants.
Though the population of the parish of Row was but little over 2000,
there were no less than thirty public houses scattered over its narrow
bounds, and thus ample facilities were offered for intemperance. All
this Mr. Campbell set himself to reform, and he earnestly and prayer-
fully laboured to this end. He sought to present the gospel of the
Lord Jesus Christ in a solemn and striking manner, pressing home,
as a free and priceless gift, salvation for all who were willing to receive it, through the great atoning sacrifice on Calvary.

The following extract from a letter, prefixed to a collection of his
sermons, gives Mr. Campbell's views of his preaching in his own
words. " I was gradually taught to see that so long as the individual
is uncertain of being the object of love to his God, and is still without
any sure hold of his personal safety, in the prospect of eternity, it is
in vain to attempt to induce him to serve God under the power of
any purer motive than the desire to win God's love for himself, and
so to secure his own happiness; consequently, however high the
standard, correspondence with it was sought under the influence of
unmingled selfishness, making every apparent success only a deeper
deception. And thus I was gradually led to entertain the doctrine
commonly expressed by the words ' Assurance of Faith,' having first
seen that the want of it precluded singleness of heart and eye in the
service of God, and then having found, in studying the Epistles to
the first Christian Churches, that its existence, in those addressed,
was *in them* taken for granted, and in every practical exhortation was
presupposed, I accordingly began to urge on my people that, in order
to their being in a condition to act purely, under the influence of love

to Him, and delight in what He is, their first step in religion would require to be, *resting assured of His love in Christ to them as individuals*, and of their individually having eternal life given to them in Christ.

" I think this was the character of my preaching in the latter part of the year 1826, but I cannot easily fix; and in the summer of 1827, I think, it was first understood that offence was taken with what I taught. This, however, for some time amounted merely to the complaint, ' that I carried my subject too far,' and no one ventured then to advance the charge of heresy. It was at the same time, also, that I first enjoyed the happiness of seeing many awakened from their false security, and not a few to delight themselves in the Lord ; and what my pressing of high attainments as the fruits of faith had been *unable* to accomplish, I now found produced by the earnest demand for the *true faith itself.*"

However, rumours as to the unsoundness of Mr. Campbell's teaching, and to its being in opposition to the standards of the Church of Scotland, grew more definite, and at last, on 30th March, 1830, a memorial libelling their minister was presented, from twelve of his parishioners, to the Presbytery of Dunbarton. In the libel Mr. Campbell was accused of promulgating doctrines contrary to the Word of God, and to the Confession of Faith,—namely, the doctrine of universal atonement by the death of Jesus Christ, of pardon for the whole human race, and that assurance is of the essence of faith and necessary for salvation. In Mr. Campbell's answers to the libel he repelled the charge of teaching doctrines inconsistent with Scripture and the standards of the Church of Scotland, and that, " as to the extent of atonement, I hold and teach that Christ died for all men ; that the propitiation which He made for sin was for the sins of all mankind ; that those for whom He gave Himself an offering and a sacrifice unto God were the children of men, without exception and without distinction ; and this the Scriptures teach." After due examination of witnesses the libel was found "proven," and on appeal to the Synod the judgment of the Presbytery was affirmed, so that the General Assembly, as the ultimate court of decision, was appealed

to by the minister of Row. The case came on for hearing at the
Assembly's meeting in Edinburgh in May, and a petition in favour of
Mr. Campbell was presented by 420 of his individual parishioners,
150 of whom were heads of families, comprising a very large majority
of the population of Row.   Able pleadings on behalf of Mr. Campbell
were advanced by his friends, Rev. Robert Story of Rosneath, Rev.
John Wylie of Carluke, and others, while various well known
ministers were heard on the other side.   The defendant's venerable
father made a touching appeal on behalf of his son, in which he said,
" Moderator, I am the oldest father at present in this house ; I have
been forty years a minister in the Church. . . .   I bow to any
decision to which you may think it right to come.   Moderator, I am
not afraid for my son ; although his brethren cast him out, the
Master whom he serves will not forsake him ; and while I live I will
never be ashamed to be the father of so holy and blameless a son."   In
spite of this affecting address, and the sympathy it evoked, the
General Assembly, by a majority of 119 to 6, adhered to the finding
of the Presbytery, and passed sentence of deposition on John
Macleod Campbell from the office of the ministry of the Church of
Scotland.

ROW & MOUNTAINS OF LOCH LONG.

CHAPTER IV.

Row Estates, Battle of Glenfruin, Ornithology of Row, Topography of Garelochside.

THE lands in the Parish of Row have passed through a number of hands, but are now concentrated in the family of Colquhoun of Luss. Those in proximity to Cardross, namely, the Barony of Malligs, on which the town of Helensburgh stands, were acquired from the Galbraiths by the Macaulays of Ardencaple in the seventeenth century, and in 1705, along with Drumfad and Kirkmichael, were sold by Archibald Macaulay to Sir John Shaw of Greenock. After his death, his daughter sold these, and another portion of the Colgrain estate, to Sir James Colquhoun for 6000 guineas. The old estate of Ardencaple for nearly five centuries was the property of a family who, for several generations, took from the lands the surname of Ardencaple, but afterwards were known in history as the Clan Macaulay. The name of Ardencaple was retained till the time of James V., when Alexander of Ardencaple called himself Macaulay, from an ancestor of the name of Aulay. These lands were the property of barons of that name during the wars caused by the disputed succession to the Crown, and for the independence of the kingdom of Scotland. Enlarging their possessions, the Macaulays of Ardencaple gained the position of a clan, a symbol of power in those days, which depended upon the number of men that could be brought into the field. In Dunbartonshire there were three clans, the Colquhouns, M'Farlanes, and Macaulays. The two latter inhabited the mountainous districts, and often descended on the lands of the Colquhouns in years, gave access to the lonely Glenfruin, the "glen of sorrow," there lies before the traveller some more of the great territorial possessions of the Lennox family now belonging to the Colquhouns. The earliest charter of the lands of Luss mentions the "Freone," which stream took its rise from the narrow green valley at the foot of the lofty hill Maol-na-Fheidh, which is a conspicuous object as you sail up the Gareloch. The lands of Strone, close to the Fruin, were acquired in 1517 by Sir John Colquhoun from the Earl of Lennox, and now present the appearance of fine green pasture, under the improved hill and sheep farming, where once only the purple heather and green bracken flourished. The adjoining lands of Drumlee belonged, in 1545, to David Colquhoun of Drumfad, a younger son of the laird of Luss, and the contiguous farms of Meikle Auchenvennel, Auchengaich, and Stuckindow, were formed at the same time by John Colquhoun, the last of them being an early possession of the Nobles of Ardardan. The first was, over a century ago, held by a family of the M'Farlanes, but all are now part of the great Luss estate.

Auchenvennell-Mouling, comprehending Ballyvouline and Ballyknock, was the patrimony of a race of MacWalter, who claimed to be of the Lennox family. They continued here until the latter part of last century, when the property fell to co-heirs, from whom the greater part was acquired by James Dennistoun of Colgrain, whose grandson conveyed it in 1825 to Sir James Colquhoun, in excambion for Drumfork. The adjoining lands of Blairnairn seem of old to have passed, along with Kirkmichael Striveling, an early possession of the Stirlings of Cadder, through the usurping family of Keir, to Wood of Geilston, to whom they belonged in the seventeenth century. Their history is uncertain from that period till they fell to the Macaulays, from the last of whom they passed to George M'Farlane, a drover, who sold them for £600 to another M'Farlane, who again conveyed them, in 1833, to Sir James Colquhoun, for £8000. This was the last of nine properties once held by the M'Farlanes, and now embraced in the Luss estates. Next to Blairnairn lies Kilbride ; this land seems formerly to have been annexed to Bannachra and Malligs estate. Here there once stood a chapel, because the parish church of Cardross was at so great a distance, and it was dedicated to St. Bride, or Bridget, a virgin saint, whose apron was said to spread a holy influence round many a cottage home in that part of Scotland. The lands of Meikle, West, and Little Kilbride, came into possession of the Colquhouns towards the close of the seventeenth century. In the purchase there was excepted the piece of land called "chapel of Glenfruin," and that acre known as Mackenzies' acre, with the houses and yards belonging thereto. In 1802, Sir James Colquhoun acquired Laigh Kilbride. Wester Kilbride was part of the Ardenconnell estate at one time, and these became detached and consolidated in the Luss property. Across the Fruin is the farm of Durling, which, at the time of the Reformation, belonged to the Galbraiths of Culcreuch, and soon after was held by the house of Ardencaple. At the end of the seventeenth century we find there a family of Macaulay, probably a branch of the main house. In the churchyard of Old Kilpatrick, a gravestone is inscribed to Matthew Colquhoun of Durlin, who died in 1690, aged sixty-nine. Durlin, and the adjoining farm of Blairvattan, were added to the Ardenconnell estate, and have since belonged to it. The barn on this land was burned by the M'Gregors during the raid of 1603, and, indeed, scarcely a spot in this secluded glen but has been the scene of some of the strife and turmoil which had so often devastated the district.

This glen, in the year 1603, was the scene of the memorable conflict between the rival clans of Colquhoun and Macgregor, which had such far-reaching consequences. The entrance to the lower part of the glen is gained about two miles out of Helensburgh from the Luss road, and the clear running, sparkling, stream the Fruin is seen emerging from the glen on its course to Loch Lomond. In former years there were numerous inhabitants in the glen, which contained a number of crofters and small farmers, who were gradually absorbed in the larger holdings, when the land became consolidated into the Colquhoun estates. Vestiges of these crofter residences can be traced, and the lands, which the crofters ploughed to furnish grain

for their use, can even now be identified by the ridges visible far up
the hillside. The few farms scattered throughout the glen are well
cultivated, and their produce indicates that the soil is of varied but
excellent quality for ordinary crops. Glenfruin is a scene over which
an air of peace and calmness seems to brood, and offers many attractions to the wandering pedestrian, who may roam about this secluded
glen gathering inspiration from a spot associated with so many sad
and stirring memories.

   A certain amount of mystery surrounds the origin of the bitter
feud between the clans Colquhoun and Macgregor, and historians
differ as to the degree of blame to be awarded to the rival tribesmen,
and their respective chiefs. In the year 1602 the forays of the Macgregors upon the possessions of the Colquhouns were so fierce and
persistent, that King James VI. issued a royal warrant, in which he
dispensed, in favour of Sir Alexander Colquhoun, with the Act pro-
hibiting the wearing of guns, pistols, and other lethal weapons. The
contiguity of their territories also rendered such feuds more incessant,
and, at length, their mutual dissensions called for the mediation of
their friends. According to the dying declaration of Alexander Macgregor of Glenstrae, the chief of his clan, a great deal of blame rests
upon Archibald, Earl of Argyll, who, in January 1593, obtained a
commission for repressing the violence of "the wicked Clangregour,"
but used his power to stir up the clan against his personal enemies
the Colquhouns of Luss. Sir Walter Scott, in the introduction to
Rob Roy, narrates the story of the origin of the feud between the
Macgregors and Colquhouns, as follows :—"Two of the Macgregors
being benighted asked shelter in a house belonging to a dependent of
the Colquhouns, and were refused. They then retreated to an outhouse, took a wedder from the fold, killed it, and supped off the
carcase, for which (it is said) they offered payment to the proprietor.
The Laird of Luss seized on the offenders and, by the summary process which feudal barons had at their command, had them both con-
demned and executed. The Macgregors verify this account of the
feud by appealing to a proverb current amongst them, execrating the
hour (*Mult dhu an Carbail ghil*) that the black wedder with the white

tail was ever lambed. To avenge this quarrel, the laird of Macgregor assembled his clan, to the number of three or four hundred men, and marched towards Luss from the banks of Loch Long, by a pass called *Raid na Gael*, or the Highlandman's pass."

In his interesting historical memoirs of the unfortunate Clan Macgregor, whose proud motto, in Gaelic, is *S'rioghail mo dream*, or "Royal is my race," Dr. Macleay describes how the chief of the clan, Alexander Macgregor of Glenstrae, went from his country of Rannoch to Lennox, accompanied by two hundred of his friends and kinsmen, for the purpose of endeavouring to extinguish the feud which had lasted so long between his brother and chief of the Colquhouns. The head of the last named clan would seem to have had his own reason for looking forward to an unfavourable result of the interview, and collected a large array of retainers and dependents, along with his neighbours the Buchanans and Grahams, to the number, according to some authorities, of eight hundred men, horse and foot. Macgregor had been made aware of his rival chieftain's insidious purpose, in event of the conference proving abortive, and though he concealed his feelings, yet remained on his guard. In describing the battle, it must be remembered that, in those days, there was no road along the right bank of Loch Lomond, for its banks were so steep and woody that it was not easy to pass along. The road therefore from Dunbarton to Argyllshire passed near the bridge over the Fruin, at the entrance of the glen, and followed the valley to its upper end, along Loch Long to Arrochar, and then turned east to the head of Loch Lomond and Glenfalloch.

The conflict took place not far from the farm of Strone, at the upper end of the glen, where the river Fruin makes a sweeping curve, between the level plain of the valley and the braes beyond. Alexander Macgregor, the chief, had divided his forces into two companies, one of which he commanded himself, and his brother, John Glass Macgregor, the other, which was placed in the ambush, so as to take the Colquhouns in the rear as they proceeded up the glen. For a while the battle was fiercely contested, but the superior valour and tactics of the Macgregors prevailed, and the Colquhouns were forced to beat a disastrous retreat. Emerging from their concealment, the clansmen, under John Macgregor, fell upon their foes, and Alexander, the chief, bore down upon the disorganised fugitives, re-uniting the forces under his own command, when his brother John was slain. The unfortunate Colquhouns were completely vanquished and dispersed, the fugitives being pursued and mercilessly slaughtered, until their scattered remnants gained the shelter of Rossdhu. After the struggle was over, a sanguinary scene of bloodshed and murder ensued, the farm houses were entered and destroyed, their inmates slaughtered, the cattle carried away, and many other atrocities enacted. The language of the subsequent indictment against Macgregor bore that the victors had seized six hundred kye and oxen, eight hundred sheep and goats, fourteen score of horse, that the houses and barn-yards of the tenantry had been destroyed, and enormous damage done to the "haill plenishing, guids, and gear of the fourscore pund land of Luss." The battle cost the Colquhouns a large number of their followers, estimated between one hundred and forty and two hundred, while the victors, it is alleged, lost only two or three men, one of them John Glass, the brother of the chief. Amongst the slain on the Colquhouns' side were Patrick Napier of Kilmahew, Tobias Smollett, bailie of Dunbarton, David Fallisdaill, burgess there, and his two sons Thomas and James, Walter and John Colquhoun, of Barnhill, and Adam and John, sons of Colquhoun of Camstradden.

Another calamitous event resulted from the battle of Glenfruin, namely, the cruel slaughter of a number of boys from the Collegiate School of Dunbarton, whose curiosity had allured them to the scene of the conflict. When these students, a number of whom were Colquhouns, heard of the expected gathering of the two rival clans, where several of their friends were to be present, they started for Glenfruin. Becoming alarmed for their safety, the Colquhouns, as a measure of precaution, locked them up in a barn, but the victorious Macgregors killed the guard in charge of the barn, and set fire to it, whereby the unhappy boys were cruelly burnt to death. Another account states that, after the guards were killed, the boys were placed by Macgregor in charge of one of the clan, Dugald Ciar Mohr, or the "Dun coloured," who is said to have been an ancestor of Rob Roy. As they were the sons of gentlemen, the chief was anxious, after the battle, to restore them to their parents, and returned to the barn for that purpose. Meanwhile the boys having become noisy and impatient at their confinement, the villain in charge, ready to extirpate the whole race, one after another stabbed them with his dirk. Upon the chief enquiring as to the safety of the youths, the savage guardian drew out his blood-stained dirk, at the same time exclaiming in Gaelic, "Ask that, and God save me." Macgregor, who was struck with horror at the inhuman deed, would have cut down the murderer, but he instantly fled, while the unhappy chief exclaimed that his clan would be ruined.*

Some doubt is thrown upon the whole tragic story from the remarkable fact that the massacre is not mentioned in the various indictments against the Clan Gregor. It appears, however, to be referred to in the record of the Privy Council proceedings against Allan Oig M'Intnach, of Glencoe, who, in 1609, was charged with assisting the Clan Gregor, of Glenfruin, and of having with his own hand there, "murdered without pity the number of forty poor persons, who were naked and without armour."

Such was the disastrous issue of the attempt made by the chieftain of the Clan Gregor to effect a reconciliation with his enemies, and he and his followers returned to their own territories lamenting the evil events which had occurred. Great suspicion seems to have arisen against the chief of the Colquhouns that he had formed the plan of exterminating the Macgregors, while they were in his own country and power. A partial statement, also, representing the Macgregors as a set of murderers, who had sought to destroy the Colquhouns, was

---

* In Dr. Macleay's *Rob Roy* the following note is annexed : "This barn stood near the place where the Colquhouns made their first assault, and the site of it is still pointed out. Close by runs a rivulet, the Gaelic name of which signifies 'the burn of the young ghosts;' and in the former superstition of the country it was believed that if a Macgregor crossed the stream alone after sunset, he would be scared by some unhallowed spectre."

H

shortly after the battle transmitted to Stirling, where King James VI. then resided. Soon after the bodies of the slain were stripped, Sir Alexander Colquhoun presented himself before the King, accompanied by the female relatives of those who fell, each clad in deep mourning, and exhibiting the blood-stained raiment of their kinsmen. King James was greatly moved at the sad spectacle, and resolved to decree vengeance against the unfortunate clan. By an act of the Privy Council, dated 3rd April, 1603, it was ordained that the name of Macgregor should for ever be abolished; that all who bore it should forthwith renounce the name; and that none of their posterity should ever afterwards assume the name under penalty of death.

These stirring events have thrown a halo of romance around the peaceful glen, and, of recent years, it has been more visited by wandering tourists in search of the picturesque. The derivation of the name is *Gleann fraoin*, or the "valley of the sheltered places," and the battle which took place is known in the Gaelic as *Ruaig Gleann-fraoin*, or the "rout of Glenfruin," according to Colonel Robertson's *Gaelic Topography*. Flowing from the lower slopes of *Maol-na-Fheidh*, the Fruin winds its way for 12½ miles, until it enters the dark waters of Loch Lomond, passing the lofty *Ben Chaorach*. On the opposite side the Row hills gently rise from the valley, until they attain the height of nearly 1200 feet. From the summit of the road which winds up the side of the hill above Faslane bay, the traveller can look down upon the upper part of the glen, with the trees round Strone farm, near where the battle was fought. A little way from the road side, near the house, is a large grey stone, beside which John Macgregor, the chief's brother, who was one of the few slain on that side, was buried. The river Fruin has gathered strength and volume since leaving the high glen from whence it rises, and curves round the head of the glen, beside the wood—a pure stream of limpid sparkling water. Bounded by the river on one side, and the road along the glen on the other, there is a large level field of fifty acres in extent, now given over to natural pasture, though, thirty years ago, it was waving with the golden grain of autumn. A square mound, measuring about sixty feet on each side, crowned with fine,

rugged, red, old Scotch firs, marks the spot where were buried the
bodies of the gallant clansmen who fell on that bleak morning of early
spring.   An old wall used to environ the mound a number of years
ago, but it has long since mouldered away.   There were a good many
more Scotch firs, also, that have since succumbed to the wintry blasts
rushing along the glen with devastating effect.   It is a lonely and
impressive ravine, and the imagination kindles over the terrible
picture which the now silent glen must have presented that morning
as the snow-clad braes around resounded to the wild slogans of the
contending clans, cheered on by the piercing strains of each martial
pibroch.

> " Ever, as on they bore, more loud
> And louder rung the pibroch proud,
> Then bursting bolder on the ear
> The clans shrill gathering they could hear."

The contending warriors would be dressed in the picturesque cos-
tumes appropriate to their active vocations and martial exercises, while
their arms probably displayed considerable diversity.   While the
chiefs and their more immediate circle of the *Duinhe-wassel*, might be
" plaided and plumed " in the gay colours of their respective tartans ;
the ordinary clansmen would be robed in the belted plaids and kilts
of more sober hue, with a sprig of Scotch fir, the badge of the tribe,
adorning the Macgregors' bonnets.   The former would be flung
aside in the heat of desperate strife, so that the dirk and massive
claymore might be used with greater freedom-   Arrayed in short
Highland coats, doublets and truis, or kilts, their plumed bonnets on
their heads, and armed with silver-mounted dirks, pistols, and broadswords, the leaders would be conspicuous amid the closing ranks of
the combatants.   Possibly some of the leading men might have steel
head pieces, with hauberks and shirts of mail, because the use of
defensive armour was common in the Highlands ; and amongst the
weapons of the men-at-arms would be battle axes, spears, bows and
arrows, dirks, with an occasional " hagbut," or hand gun of ancient
form.   Firearms were common enough, even in the sixteenth century,
and were freely used at the battle of Langside in 1568, and when
Scotch merchants went abroad, they were in the habit of bringing

home "hagbuts." This species of weapon was fired with a match, the balls being carried in a bag, while the powder was in a flask, and the priming in a touch-box. But, in all probability, the grey crags and snow-fringed precipices of Glenfruin that morning would re-echo less with the rattle of firearms than with the clangour of steel broadswords, and the fierce cries and ringing slogans of the combatants as they mingled in deadly strife.*

A solemn look that night would the glen present to the solitary sentinel watching over the spot where fell so many of the children of that romantic country. On the heights above, just faintly illumined by the wan rays of the moon, the untrodden snow now lay like a shroud, while around the field of battle the lustrous mantle was deeply stained with the gore which, from thence, mingled with the mountain stream. Hushed was the night wind amid the dark plantations of fir, whose feathery boughs were lightly frosted with snow, and the querulous cry of the owl, moping to the moon, or the faint scream of the night hawk, fell upon the ear, as though mocking the moans of the wounded. Many a gallant Colquhoun who, that morning, had freely bounded with springing step over his native heath, lay stretched on his lowly bier. The eyes that flashed so fiercely at the sight of their hereditary foes were now glazed with the cold film of death. Arms and feet were locked together with those of opposing hosts, who imbrued their hands with each other's blood, and the savage yells of the victors drowned the despairing

---

* Martin, in his *Western Isles of Scotland* says :—" The ancient way of fighting was by set battles ; and, for arms, some had broad two-handed swords and head-pieces, and others bows and arrows. When all their arrows were spent, they attacked one another with sword in hand. Since the invention of guns, they are very early accustomed to use them, and carry their pieces with them wherever they go ; they likewise learn to handle the broadsword and target. The chief of each tribe advances with his followers within shot of the enemy, having first laid aside their upper garments ; and after one general discharge, they attack them with sword in hand, having their target on their left hand (as they did at Killicrankie), which soon brings the matter to an issue, and verifies the observation made of them by your historians,—

'Aut Mors cito, aut Victoria loeta.' "

shouts of the vanquished, who were sullenly forced to yield to the superior prowess and skill of their enemy. Slowly the night watch rolled away, and the waning moonbeams faded from each splintered crag, or faintly sparkled amid the Fruin as it gently rippled over its slaty bed, and the cold glitter of the stars shed its glimmering rays over that weird scene of death.

Coming down the glen, the pedestrian, as he looks on either side, will see traces of former houses and farm buildings. At the right side, beyond the stream, there was once the holding and steading of Blairvrean, which ran up to the ridge of the hill. The road skirts the foot of the higher range opposite, and you pass the site of the farm house, surrounded with trees, on Auchengeoch. Next comes Auchenvennel, and its old trees, but the house has disappeared, as well as a small hamlet long passed away. Balknock is the next farm, and here, in the middle of a field, is an old burying place, though beyond one or two flat stone slabs, scarcely seen above the turf, there is little to indicate that this was once used as a spot for the purpose of sepulture. Ballyvoulin farm, with some fine spreading trees round it, is now reached, where many years ago there stood an old mansion, with the avenue of trees leading up to it which still exists. Here a glen opens on to Glenfruin, from whence is derived the main supply of water for Helensburgh, a purling clear stream of water, which is stored in the large reservoir on the moor above the town. On the other side of the Fruin are the lands of Stuckidhu and Durling, on the banks of what is now a beautiful stream, with deep pools of water, where many a fine trout will reward the angler. Once more following the left hand of the Fruin, on the way down the valley, Blairnairn and Kilbride farms are passed, both forming part of the Colquhoun estates, with modern farm houses taking the place of the old thatched buildings which stood near the burn. The school in the glen on the small farm of Chapel is now seen; the school house was built in 1840, on the site of a much older building, where the children of the glen received their education. There is no doubt that the old chapel of Kilbride stood close to this, and some of the stones were built into the cottage beside the school, and also into the farm house of Bali-

menoch just beyond. The school is a great boon to the district, and
there are about 15 children in attendance, on an average. Balimenoch
farm house was rebuilt in 1872, by Sir James Colquhoun, for Mr.
Jardine, whose family for about a century have occupied land in the
glen, and who knows its history well. In his young days the road
down the glen was devoid of bridges, you had just to ford the stream,
and there was a public house beside the school. There was excellent
fishing then in the Fruin; he has caught salmon up to 12 pounds
weight in the pool near his farm house, and quantities of fine trout.
He remembers various dwellings and cottages on the farms, where
none are now visible, and has seen far more of the glen under cultivation, and great changes among the tenants of the farms. The old
Walk Mill, as it was called, was on the Fruin opposite his dwelling,
and did a good business in woollen cloth; its foundations can still
be traced, and the narrow stream for turning the wheel still rushes
over the stones where it rejoins the river, above a deep pool sleeping
between natural walls of grey rocks. It is a lonely spot, and the
banks of the stream are piled with a mass of steep rocks forming a
barrier to the naturally calm current. Overhung in many places
with birches, hazel, and rowan trees, the blue grey rocks offer an
obstacle over which the Fruin pursues its rapid course in a series of
small cascades, which fill the warm summer air with their music. All
lovers of the picturesque in nature must appreciate the beauty of the
course of the Fruin as it passes by reaches of mossy and fern clad
sward, grey glistening rocks, and groves of birch and hazel, resonant
with the liquid notes of the mavis and blackbird. In the springtime
primroses, hyacinths, wild violets, celandine, bluebells, and other
varieties of wild flowers give abundance of rich bloom, with a fra-
grance that fills the air, and the glancing stream makes grateful
melody to the ear. Presently the venerable ruin of Bannachra Castle
is seen on the right hand, a little below the old bridge over the Fruin,
and from this point there is a beautiful view of Loch Lomond and
its many islands.*

---

* Dr. Messer, of Helensburgh, in an interesting paper read to the Antiquarian
Society, speaks of a hill or mound stretching across the valley, and he believes

A considerable number of birds will be observed in the wooded glens bordering Glenfruin and the Gareloch, and an ample stock of game is found on the moors. Even in the gardens of the Helensburgh villas in spring, the mavis, blackbird, chaffinch, robin, linnet, and others, will be heard pouring out their carols, and in the fields beyond, the skylark's high and prolonged strain of melody delights the ear. The waters and shores of the Gareloch are frequented by numerous sea birds, the heron being a regular visitor in the shallow bays, perched upon a stone all surrounded by water. This shy bird is rather fond of nocturnal fishing, and can be heard uttering his shrill note as he wings his way across to the heronry on Rosneath point. In a calm night he may be observed standing on a rock in a rigid attitude, when, suddenly, his long bill is darted into the tide, and emerges with a fish which soon disappears down the long sinuous throat. Gulls of different sorts are very familiar objects, both on shore and inland, following the plough and picking up worms from the fresh furrows. Numbers of them congregate at low tide on the muddy shallows in front of Helensburgh, along with curlews, plovers, redshanks, and sandpipers. Cormorants and oyster catchers are often seen, and the beautiful kittiwake gull, as it lightly skims above the crested waves, uttering its cheery cry. Wild ducks, teal, and widgeon are common enough, at certain seasons, more particularly in the shallow bays near Ardmore Point. Of birds of prey there are but few, the merlin, kestrel, sparrow hawk and barn owl, being about the only feathered visitors of that description. The merlin is a most courageous little bird, with a wonderfully rapid flight, and will fly upwards almost out of sight, in striving to surmount some snipe or

---

that at the time of the formation of this rampart of water worn stones, gravel and sand, the Fruin took a different course, and that the water had raised the debris into the shape of a triangular mound. He says, "we find a whole series of such mounds on both sides of the road leading from the Luss road to Dunfin Saw Mill, where the road again crosses the Fruin; while the road from Luss to Balloch cuts through a rampart-like structure, which trends away to Duchlage." He considers the peculiar mounds of ground called "Kames" have been formed when the great glaciers covered this part of Scotland.

lark.   Hooded crows, and an occasional raven, will be met with in
the higher ranges of Glenfruin ; the former is a specially destructive
bird in the way of plundering the nests of grouse and other game
which build on the ground.   Young partridges, chickens, and even
lambs, are not safe from the ravages of this crow, which is particularly obnoxious to gamekeepers.   The raven is only to be met
with among the precipices of the higher ranges of hills above the
Gareloch, and sometimes, of an evening, the harsh croak of a pair of
these destructive birds may be heard far up in the gloom, as they
wing their way to some inaccessible roosting place in the rocks.

Of song birds there are a good many kinds, and any lover of ornithology will find abundant material for investigation and study.   In
all the gardens and plantations beside the Gareloch, thrushes, chaffinches, and blackbirds are found, and their beautiful notes resound
in the warm evenings of spring.   Their nests are known in almost
every garden in Helensburgh, and the wonder is that they escape
the prying eyes of numerous juvenile bird-nesters, on the lookout for
specimens.   Away in Glenfruin they are to be met with, the mellow
mavis pouring forth his music from the fir tree in that retired scene.
The missel thrush is also common enough in the woods and parks,
and its nest is only too conspicuous an object in the bare branches
of a tree, before the covering of foliage affords a screen from observation.   Of the lesser songsters of the grove there are bullfinches and
chaffinches in their gay plumage, and uttering their sweet notes
incessantly, in their quick flight from branch to branch.   The former
bird is only to be seen in some of the more retired woods on the
lower banks of the Fruin, and on the Garelochside.   Linnets and
hedge-sparrows abound, the lovely blue eggs of the familiar inhabi-
tant of our hedges being a great temptation to juvenile collectors,
and, as it builds early in spring, its nest is an easy mark.   The little
wren is at home everywhere, briskly singing its clear, lively note, and
its nest is found in hedges, at roots of trees, in old walls, or sometimes on the face of a rocky bank among the moss.   Golden crested
wrens are uncommon, but are to be seen in the fir plantations, and
it is remarkable how so tiny a bird can make its long annual migra-

tion to our shores from far off climes. Whitethroats and blackcap warblers will be observed where there are sheltering thickets, and they remain later in the season than other warblers, when the rowan berries, which seem to be their favourite food, are plentiful. The siskin and the redpole may be noticed in places where birch trees are numerous, but they are not familiar visitants. Everywhere is to be encountered the robin, so dear to children, and to those who illustrate Christmas cards; he is the first to make his appearance when crumbs of bread are scattered on the window-sills in winter. When all the other songsters have ceased their lays, the simple strain of the redbreast is heard from his perch on some tree, and in late autumn the plaintive melody of the yellow-hammer sounds sweetly among the hedgerows. In early spring, again, the willow-warbler's slender form is seen, darting from tree to tree, uttering its little series of pleasing notes, and telling of approaching summer. And on all the braes near the Gareloch, and in the meadows of Glenfruin, the well known cry of the cuckoo is annually heard.

With the end of April, again, we hail the swallow, paying his welcome visit to our shores, and far away in the lonely glens, wherever the farmhouse or shepherd's hut is situated, there the twittering lively visitor pursues his circling flight. The swift pursues his rapid flight round the church steeples, or in the vicinity of any ruined building, and marvellous is his endurance, incessantly on the wing from "morn till dewy eve," for he never by any chance alights on the ground. No bird has a more rapid flight than the swift, and all the day long their joyous cry is heard high up in the air, for they rarely skim over the ground. On the moors above Helensburgh, and on the upland farms, the friendly peewit, or "peesweep" as it is termed, is heard, uttering his cheery note, generally in small companies, whose motions, as they rapidly circle and wheel round an intruder, have a most pleasing effect. In the fields of long grass, the corncrake may occasionally be seen standing erect, and directing his singular harsh note in all directions, while, in warm summer nights, his peculiar serenade to his mate never ceases till dawn comes. In the upper reaches of the Fruin, and the streamlets which run into it, the beautiful water ouzel, with white spot amidst his black plumage, will often be seen, perched on a mossy stone near some brawling cascade, and his clear piping song is heard above the rushing water. Its nest, under the moist mossy bank, washed by the spray of the fall, is a simple structure, and the eggs are of the purest whiteness. A most interesting bird the dipper is, as he flits to and fro over the stream, sometimes plunging beneath the water, and then lighting on a stone, and shaking the drops off his feathers. In former years, the splendidly plumed kingfisher was was common enough in Glenfruin, and it is now seldom that the goldfinch is encountered, hanging upon some tall thistle, the seed of which in autumn he seems to enjoy. Fieldfares are common, as well as wheatears and sandmartins, whose nests are tunnelled in the sandy faces of old disused quarries. Grey and pied wagtails are to be seen on the burns and marshy fields, flitting gayly from stone to stone in the water, and at other times darting about in the air catching flies; graceful little birds with bright plumage, and long quivering tail. Different kinds of tits are common, the blue headed one, a quick, lively, little bird which, in winter, will be seen creeping all over the leafless trees in search of insects, sometimes hanging on to the outer twigs in curious attitudes. The great tit, with his singular rasping cry, like a file upon a saw, restlessly moves about the fruit trees in gardens, and also in the woods all along the Gareloch. Starlings abound everywhere, their curious chattering notes, sometimes varied by a low whistle, being heard in every street in Helensburgh, and in the fields and farmhouses they are common visitors.*

---

* Birds of Row. In 1838, Mr. George Campbell, Ardencaple, drew up the following list of birds frequenting the parish. Sparrow-hawk, peregrine falcon, kestrel, merlin, common buzzard, hen harrier, kite, short-eared owl, barn owl, tawny owl, goat sucker, chimney swallow, martin, sand martin, swift, spotted fly-catcher, missel-thrush, field-fare, song-thrush, red wing, blackbird, moor blackbird, European dipper, redbreast, redstart, blackcap warbler, whitethroat, wood-wren, gold crested wren, great titmouse, blue tit, cole tit, long-tailed tit, hedge sparrow, pied wagtail, grey wagtail, yellow wagtail, shore pyet, skylark, yellow bunting, corn-bunting, house sparrow, chaffinch, mountain finch, siskin,

Great have been the changes in the appearance of the parish of Row since the year 1830, when the lands began to be feued, and steamers regularly made the voyage from Glasgow to Garelochhead. Starting from the Loch Long end of the parish there was an old farm house, with thatched roof, at Finnart, and a similar one at Arddarroch, both of which have long since been demolished, and the two modern residences, which are seen amidst their surrounding plantations, were built, about the year 1830, by Mr. Burn the architect. Whistlefield, which stands at the brow of the ridge between Loch Long and the Gareloch, was then a small public house, frequented by drovers, who were conducting cattle to Portincaple, whence they were ferried across Loch Long. They had come by the old drove road which led above Finnart, along the high ground at Garelochhead, always keeping well up the sides of the hill, and avoiding the modern impositions of tolls. Here and there, traces of the old road may yet be seen, but it has long been disused. Portincaple is a small cluster of cottages, where a few fishermen prosecute their calling in the dark waters of Loch Long. Returning to the road which runs down from the brow of the hill to Garelochhead, on the left hand, near the burn, are traces of the old meal mill which, long ago, used to stand there, with a few thatched cottages in the vicinity. At the foot of the road, near the shore, is the boundary between Rosneath and Row parish.

The villas which constitute Garelochhead now come into view, for the little cottages tiled or thatched, which in former years sheltered

---

goldfinch, common brown linnet, green grossbeak, bullfinch, crossbill, starling, raven, carrion crow, hooded crow, rook, jackdaw, magpie, jay, common creeper, wren, cuckoo, ringdove, common pheasant, black grouse, red grouse, partridge, heron, curlew, redshank, sandpiper, woodcock, snipe, jack-snipe, dunlin, corncrake, gallinule, coot, oyster catcher, turnstone, water ouzel, green lapwing, golden plover, ringed plover, bernacle goose, sheldrake, wild duck, teal, widgeon, scaup pochard, goosander, horned grebe, red-throated diver, bill auk, common gull, herring gull. The crossbill had only been recently observed in the parish, and it was co-incident with an unusual abundance of fir cones, the peculiar food of this bird.

the inhabitants, have nearly all disappeared. Several of the older
natives can remember when there were no slated houses at the head
of the loch, except Bendarroch, which was built about 1833, and
Fernicarry. Some old cottages used to stand at the entrance to
Bendarroch, and a few others near the Inn, which, fifty years ago,
used to be a three storey house, and, after being burnt down, was
built in its present form. Just beyond the Inn there was formerly
the tollhouse, a small public house, one of the numerous humble
hostelries, where whisky used to be dispensed to all and sundry. On
holidays the *Waverley*,* the *James Oswald* or *Clarence* would bring
numbers of excursionists, who were landed sometimes in the steamer's
own boat, as also by the ferryboat, for there were no piers in those
days, and the steamer was made fast to a buoy.

Walking along the shore you pass the pier, built 1845 on nineteen
years' lease, by Mr. M'Farlane, so long the tenant of Faslane. In
former years there were good large sailing boats, owned by Archibald
Niven, that took passengers and goods both from Garelochhead,
Rosneath, and Row over to Greenock. Faslane bay is soon reached,
and here the sides of the loch are well wooded, with grassy slopes
leading up to the heather hills above, and handsome villas are seen
gleaming amidst their surrounding plantations. Faslane house is a
little way back from the middle of the bay, the former residence of
the Macaulays, and latterly of the Colquhouns of Luss. A good way
down from the house, near the shore, there stands the old oak tree,
under whose boughs, according to tradition, the crowing of a cock
presaged the death of a Macaulay. The name of the spot *Cnoch-na-
Cullah*, or "Knoll of the Cock" seems appropriate to the legend. An
irregular pile Faslane is, the front having been built 1863, the portion behind about 1745, and a still older small structure in the rear.

---

* The children's rhyme in those days ran as follows :—

" The *Waverley*, so cleverly,
Plies on her course with speed ;
Six times a week to Helensburgh,
And three to Gareloch*heed*."

There is a rolling stream, with many a dark eddying pool, and foaming cascade, which runs past the house into the peaceful bay. In former years the Colquhouns of Luss lived at Faslane, for a short time in summer, as a sort of marine residence, occupying the older part of the mansion.

The present tenant of Faslane is Mr. John M'Farlane, who is now at an advanced age, and during his long residence on the Gareloch he has gained the regard of all who know his eminence as an agriculturist, and his worth as a man. His grandfather came to Faslane, in 1785, from Glenfruin, and three generations of the family have tenanted the farm, with other holdings in Glenfruin and Arrochar. Many interesting reminiscences Mr. M'Farlane can give of his life-long connection with the district, and the changes which he has seen on the shores of the Gareloch. When he was a boy, all along the loch, until you came to Ardencaple Castle, there were only, here and there, thatched cottages, with the exception of Ardenconnell, and three or four farm houses. In his early days nearly every farmer grew flax, which went through several processes on the farm, all except heckling, which was done in Greenock. It came back to be spun in the house, and then was sent to the weaver to be made into linen. The "lint dub," as it was called, was a circular pool of water near Faslane house, in which the lint was steeped and afterwards dried on the grass. In those days the wages of the farm servants were less than a half of what they now receive, sticks were gathered in the woods for fuel, and the old fashioned "cruisie" gave a feeble light. Rude candles, with rashes for wicks, were manufactured out of the sheeps' fat; there were no butchers, not even in Helensburgh, and the farmers killed their own beef and mutton. In summer the lambs were killed, and in autumn several families would join together in laying in the supply of salted meat usually provided by the farmers from their cattle. Salt was heavily taxed for common use, but no duty was levied on the salt used for curing herring, and the salt cart regularly appeared in the herring season.

Letters delivered by post were few and far between, and the postman carried his bag between Helensburgh and Garelochhead—a duty

latterly performed by the well-known "Jenny the Post." Shops on
the loch side were almost unknown, but there was one at Shandon,
kept by Mrs. Comrie, for sale of teas, tobacco, and groceries, brought
by the carrier's carts. Bread came from Helensburgh, occasionally,
in vans, and the steamers landed small wares and stores in the ferry-
boats. There was a smith's shop at Helensburgh, and one at Garelochhead for the requirements of the wide district. The schoolmaster
—Bain by name—at Garelochhead, resided in Helensburgh, and
made his perambulations to and fro, and being addicted to botany,
used frequently to diverge from the road, to the detriment of the
expectant children. At Rowmore there was a character known as
"the sodger," who lived in one of the thatched cottages, and the old
toll-house, at the head of what is now Balernock pier, used to sell
spirits, being a favourite "howff" for the aforesaid man of war, and
others in quest of alcoholic conviviality, and libations of "mountain
dew" leading to hilarious uproar.

There is still living in Dunbarton, in his ninety-second year, Mr.
John Bell, who, along with his father, has for many years been a
cattle-salesman in the county, and frequently visited the Gareloch.
The old drove roads in Dunbartonshire and neighbouring counties
were well known to him, though now most of them have been long
since disused, and their grass-grown track can scarcely be distinguished amidst the heather and bracken. Many a time has he been
round the Gareloch, and driven cattle across the Rosneath peninsula,
transacting business with those famed agriculturists, Lorne Campbell
of Portkill, long Chamberlain of Argyll, and Buchanan of Ardenconnell. Eighty years ago it was a work of some difficulty to transport a
large drove of sheep from Argyllshire to Carman market, near Dunbarton, but the drovers had ample time at their disposal, and had
plenty of friends to see. In those days the old Lennox territory on
the Gareloch, most of which is now adorned with handsome villas
and smiling gardens, garlanded with flowers, was a bare stretch of
heath-clad pastures, with an occasional thatched cottage indicating
the presence of inhabitants. About the year 1818 Mr. Bell took
part in one of the old-fashioned conventicles, on a Sabbath day, near

Garelochhead, where there were then a few scattered buildings.   The Cameronian minister of Kilmalcolm, whose name was McLauchlan, had procured the old *Dunbarton* steamer, and a contingent of persons joined at Helensburgh, Dunbarton, and other places, the preaching "tent" being set up on a hill-side commanding a fine view of the loch.   The day turned out very wet, but having been announced several days before, there was a numerous company, though the impression left upon Mr. Bell's mind was that the proceedings partook rather too much of a scene of conviviality and excitement, by no means of a spiritual character.

Smuggling was extensively carried on, many a still was in full swing, and Mr. Bell can recall some of the incidents when the officers of Excise, accompanied by dragoons, proceeded on their mission of investigation.   Even some of the farmers in the county practised this demoralising trade, and, on one occasion, a well-known innkeeper on the loch side liquidated a debt owing by him, by proceeding to his garden and digging in the ground, when a cask of fine old smuggled whisky was disinterred.   In Dunbarton, the smugglers who had been caught in their operations used to be confined, often for weeks at a time, in the old Tolbooth in the High Street, nearly opposite the Elephant Hotel.   Here those awaiting their trial contrived to pass a pleasant enough time, and were divided into messes of five each, one acting in his turn as cook, and excellent broth, beef, and potatoes were prepared in the comfortable room, in which were two large fire-places, one at each end.   Whisky was also procured from the outer world by means of a string, to which a stocking was attached containing an empty bottle, being lowered from the window, and hauled up again with the requisite supply of the national beverage.   With a complaisance only too common, the jailer winked at those proceedings, and was even known, at a time, to leave the door of the prison unlocked, so that the beleaguered inmates could enjoy a short outing by way of relief to the monotony of their enforced sojourn.   All along the shores of the Gareloch there were glens in which smuggling went on, and, under cover of night, the casks of whisky would be stowed safely in small boats, which were able to get up the mouth of the burns, and from thence the contraband article was rowed away and landed under the Castle rock at Dunbarton, or possibly taken to Greenock and distributed amongst the various inns and public-houses. There are still one or two old men living on the Gareloch side who have similar tales to tell, but few have their memories so alert and vivid as the aged tenant of Faslane, who, from his windows, can command a fine view over the loch and the hillside on which his long life has been so happily spent.

Crossing the burn at the back of Faslane House, the old burying place, round the picturesque ruins of the ancient chapel, is seen on the slope of the field, a sequestered and beautiful spot, with oak and ash trees throwing their shade over the mouldering walls, all mantled with wallflower and creepers, and the upper end of the enclosure is rank with long grass. An ash tree of some size has long grown within the crumbling walls, and spread its great boughs over the ruins, while the roofless structure offers free entrance to wintry gales and summer zephyrs alike, with rushing wailing sound. Thorns and briars protrude their encroaching roots from the lower parts of the wall, and a mournful air of forlorn solitude pervades the scene. Here and there, concealed by the long tufted grass, a moss covered stone indicates where repose the remains of those laid at rest, centuries ago, in this lonesome field. Tender memories, doubtless appealing to many, hover round this silent house of the dead, and in the calm summer evening, towards the witching hour of night, the sweet lay of the mavis resounds amid the ruins. The erection of Faslane chapel, apparently of most uncertain antiquity, may probably date from the rise of the family of Lennox, whose piety was undoubted, as was their munificence as donors of property to the early church. Under their auspices, the chapel of St. Michael may have aided in diffusing the light of the Gospel throughout the surrounding country.

A little way beyond, passing by some grey and gnarled beeches, and an old drying kiln, near the murmuring stream, while the field slopes steeply up to the moor, the site of the ancient stronghold or castle of Faslane is reached. It lies in a wooded glen, at the junction of two fern-fringed, mossy banked burns, amidst the oak coppice which clóthes the glen, and conceals its windings, until it is lost in the abrupt declivity of the hills. When you come to the spot, small dark pools of water are seen gathering at the foot of the miniature cascades, which conduct the stream over gleaming facets of slaty rock. Where the two burns meet there is a mound, now thickly clad with trees, which is supposed to be the site of the former abode of the old Lords of Lennox. From this there is a fine view of the Gareloch and its verdant shores, with the leafy promontories at its lower end, and the quiet bay of Faslane in the foreground. Nothing now remains in the vicinity of the once formidable keep to shew that here stood a tower of strength, and place of warlike defence, against the beleaguering foes who might cluster upon the eminences around. It is not easy to conjecture where the large number of retainers, who congregated round the old feudal castles, could well have found their dwellings in the immediate vicinity of Faslane. The bowmen and men at arms would be in the lower part of the building, the rest of the men who turned out, on warlike occasions, would, no doubt, be armed with target and broadsword, for it must be remembered that in those early days there was little wealth in Scotland, and few could indulge in the splendour of a complete suit of armour. The steel bonnet and leathern jacket were common, and the breast-plate would be of armour, while, after the sixteenth century, firearms came into play, and hagbuts, harquebusses, culverins and pistolets, formed part of the defensive covering worn by warriors. This secluded glen must have resounded with the warlike clangour of the mustering followers of the proud Earls of Lennox, and, where now the peaceful swain tends his flocks and herds, there would be seen the armed bands of the chief, gathering round the long silken pennant of war as it fluttered in the breeze.

From the moor above the glen of Faslane there is an easy ascent to the summit of Mhaol-na-Fheidh, which rises to the height of 1934 feet above the loch, and the equivalent of which in English is "round bill of the deer." No doubt the easier and more direct road up to the summit is from the village of Garelochhead, commencing the ascent from beyond the railway station. Very soon you find yourself on the springy heather, after passing some rough grassy stretches, thickly covered in parts with rushes and bog myrtle. Here and there will be noticed some of the ice boulders which are encountered in this locality, one in particular, is deeply grooved with glacial marks on its surface. Birch trees cover the lower glades of the hill, and traces of an old drove road may be seen, while an occasional whirr of the grouse, or cry of the moorcock, falls upon the ear as the birds are startled from their repose. After a time the climb becomes more arduous, and one rounded height succeeds another until, not far from the top, there is a stretch of peat hagg, strewn with shells and white quartzose stones. Then a steep grassy face leads up to the summit, and from its broad eminence there is a grand view over the adjacent valley and surrounding mountains.*

A far reaching and varied prospect is gained both over the Gareloch district and away to the distant confines of Perthshire, in one direction, with the remoter islands beyond Argyllshire in the other, and Loch Long and Glenfruin at your feet. A grand expanse of mountain, moor, loch, and heathery glade, steep corries and boulder strewn glens. Specially striking are the lofty, jagged peaks of Arran and Mull, the former looming dark and shadowy against the sky line, while the rugged outline of Mull seems like a solid mass of dense purple clouds. On some of the distant peaks the sun rays are sleeping, giving a pyramid of light against the encircling shade, while others are scarce seen in their gloomy sublimity amid the haze of the horizon. Gleams of bright lustre indicate the smooth lake with its silvery strand, and waving woods of dark firs clothe the rounded outlines of the lesser heights. Right down below there are the steep pastoral slopes, dotted with sheep, that rise from the winding Glen Macarn, lonely and green, the road leading towards Luss showing

---

* Birds.—Ptarmigan are sometimes seen in this district, but especially in Glenfalloch direction, on Ben Duchray and Ben Oss, and also in Glen Douglas, near Arrochar, peregrine falcons used regularly to build on the summit of a lofty inaccessible crag. The stately and splendid osprey, with his graceful aerial flight, used to frequent the ruined towers on one of the Loch Lomond islands.

like a narrow thread in the quiet valley. It meets the upper reaches of Glenfruin, whose lower part blends with the meadow lands on the banks of the river. Loch Lomond is partly descried, from Luss towards its southern end, and the islands which chequer the calm waters of this beautiful loch. Balmaha, with its craggy sides and rocky heights, shows across the loch, the woods around Buchanan, the great expanse of open country towards Stirling and the Ochills. Casting the eye round by Fintry and the high hills in that direction, the glance rests upon the shores of the Clyde in all their beauty. Ardmore, that dusky headland, stands out, with the fainter outline of Dunbarton rock beyond, and on the opposite point is Rosneath Castle and grounds, with a gleaming stretch of water between. Only the lower part of the Gareloch is visible from the summit, but the long unbroken ridge of the Rosneath peninsula, intervenes between the former loch and Loch Long, with two shining patches of water on the higher ground.

Away towards the Cowal mountains, round the Holy Loch and Dunoon, there is more of shadow, and Bute and the Cumbraes seem blended together in a mass of darkening haze. Through a gap in the ranges of Loch Goil, there emerges the crest of Ben Cruachan, and the grey granite crags of that stern landscape tell of its desolate wildness. Sweeping round by the high peaks, near the head of Glenfalloch, Ben More, Ben Lui, Ben Ledi, and mighty Ben Lawers, are standing in isolated grandeur. There is that sense of freedom and vastness which an extended view, such as this, yields to the lonely spectator, who surveys from his coign of vantage a sight so noble and diversified. The name of this hill shows that, apparently, at one time the deer had ranged up and down these deep glens and wooded straths, but they have long ceased to frequent these heights, and the valleys are given up to sheep and cattle.

Beneath the dark shadows of some of these stately peaks, towering over the undulating country below, strange scenes have been enacted, and the memory kindles at the thought of many moving deeds. What from afar seems a hollow, wreathed in blue mist, placid and undisturbed, long centuries ago witnessed an awful struggle amidst

the din of clan warfare and the riot of predatory foray.   Beneath
these distant precipices there sleeps the dark tarn, over whose coldly
gleaming surface the lambent sunlight rarely plays.   Perchance the
suicide's despairing frame may have sunk to dreary repose beneath
the icy wave, as with desperate resolve he plunged into those depths
that gave not up their dead.   While but a little way down the unfrequented valley, past winding meads bordered by mossy sward,
gay with flowers and spangled with irridescent dewdrops, beneath
ivied towers and vernal groves of clustering trees, there leaps
joyously to the ocean a sparkling, foaming river.   Lightly floating
amid the evening breeze, the airy gossamer flings its filmy tissue
over the quivering tendrils of the tiny harebell and wild sweet briar.
Fine pictorial effects of alternate light and shade are seen on some
of the bracken-circled lochs, as the sunlight falls upon grey streaks
of rocky veins, blended with softer knolls of grass and fern, while
the white sail of a solitary yacht for a moment arrests the eye.

Returning to Faslane bay, the house known as Belmore appears in
the midst of a flourishing plantation, near the road.   There stood
in the early part of the century two thatched houses at the turn of
the bay in front of Rowmore, and others at Chapelton, near the old
church, some of which were inhabited by weavers, and others by
farm-labourers.   One of those at Belmore was the abode of a noted
smuggler, Campbell by name ; indeed, too many of the cottagers
were addicted to this illicit, but fascinating, employment.   There was
a public-house beside an old ash-tree on the shore side of the road,
which was said, at one time, to have been kept by a descendant of the
Macaulays of Ardencaple.   Belmore was originally built, soon after
1830, by a fisherman of the name of M'Farlane, and was a small
two-storeyed house, and some years afterwards was sold to Mr.
Honeyman, who added considerably to the plain structure.   Subsequently it was acquired in 1856 by Mr. M'Donald, who remodelled
the mansion, giving it the handsome appearance which it now has.
In those days the loch side presented a wild scene of nature—whins,
sloes, wild roses, and the indigenous copse woods and shrubs of the
district, abounded on the hillside, with a few older trees and belts of

plantations on the farms.   Meikle and Laigh Balernock, Letrualt, Blairvaddick, and Tor, the farms which succeed one another on the way to Helensburgh, then showed none of the modern villa-residences which now are planted on their lands.   West Shandon, where now the palatial Hydropathic establishment stands, was then a small cottage, added to by the eminent Robert Napier,* who purchased it and reared the fine Gothic mansion, so well known as the residence for many years of that pioneer of the famous Clyde shipbuilders. Shandon House, which lies beyond, fifty years ago was a plain, substantial structure, which had been built as a summer residence, on a three nineteen years lease, by Mr. Ogilvie of Carron, with over forty acres of land attached.   Afterwards the late Walter Buchanan, so genial and popular, and who for a number of years so worthily represented Glasgow in Parliament, lived at Shandon, which had been burnt down, and rebuilt in its present tasteful architectural form.

The earliest of the villas at Shandon was Linburn, built sixty years ago by Samuel M'Call, well known as an honourable Glasgow merchant, and also esteemed a good deal of a "character" by the dwellers on that side of the Gareloch.   His white silk stockings, old-fashioned stock, long-tailed coat, and carefully starched ruffles, bespoke the old beau of bygone years, so dear to the caricaturists of the early Victorian days, and his *cuisine* had gained a reputation which was confirmed by the aristocratic proprietor and guests at Ardencaple Castle.   The old gentleman was very particular in the straight line of his avenue, the formation of his walls, and the symmetry of his garden.   A little previous to this the villa, known as Berriedale, now occupied as a "Home" for poor children, had been built by a Macaulay, and subsequently bought by Mr. Sinclair of the Caithness family, who named it after the title of the eldest son of that ancient house.   It is on the shore, between the road and

---

* West Shandon.   Mr. Napier got permission to alter the road at this point, and at great expense built the high retaining wall, with its ornamental balustrade, concealing the road altogether from the house, and forming a conspicuous feature as seen from the passing steamers on the loch.

the beach, on a narrow strip of ground, and Mr. Sinclair began, though he did not finish, both Croy and Broomfield, now conspicuous amongst the villas on that side of the loch. Above this, on the hillside, is seen the large mansion of Blairvaddick, which at first was an old-fashioned, square, two-storeyed house, with attics, and was enlarged by James Buchanan of Ardenconnell, who resided there; over thirty years ago it was pulled down by the late Sir James Anderson, who reared the existing structure. Fiunnery, where lived the well known family of Macleods, who have given so many eminent scions to the Church of Scotland, is one of the prettily embowered villas on the Shandon shore, and was the loved abode of Dr. Norman Macleod. Broomieknowe, and Altdonaig, near the entrance to the "Whistlers Glen," the former where Sir James Watson resided, an esteemed citizen of Glasgow, and latterly its civic head,—are passed as you approach Row. The two latter houses, at one time, formed the dwelling and part of the extensive buildings of a large company of distillers, and many a cargo of malt liquors has been taken from the little cove which used to be at the mouth of the burn. The existing house of Altdonaig was for a time, when it had ceased to be occupied as a malt house, the place in which the early Free Church congregation assembled for worship, in the stirring "Disruption" days. James Glen, the joiner of that period, who also was a crofter, built the middle portion of Broomieknowe, and the distillery was known as Altdunnalt, and the coals, barrels, stores of malt, and other requisites all used to be landed at the mouth of the burn, which was sufficiently enlarged to admit of boats lying there at high water. At the back of Altdunnalt was a row of workmen's houses, and two other cottages stood near the road a little to the west of Broomieknowe, also the house, shop, and stable of one of the proprietors of the distillery. At the back of the cottages was an old, never-failing, spring of water, and farther on was another well, known familiarly as the "Clash Well," from the fact of its being a place of resort for the gossips of this now bygone hamlet. A little nearer Row was an eminence, a green bank, well clad with grass, above the strand, known as the "shelling hill," from the fact of the farmers and crofters sometimes, in fine weather, winnowing their grain at this point.

From this height easy access is gained to the romantic glen, formerly called Aldonalt, from the Dualt burn, which runs through the glen, a rugged gorge, full of birch, fir, ash, oak and hazel trees.   It is easy to gain the summit of the glen by keeping above its shelving banks, and peering down through the overhanging trees, the silvery stream is seen glancing over its slaty bed frequently gathered in deep pools, overhung with mossy stones, and steep breasts of rock.   Every now and then, a fine peep is gained of the Gareloch, hemmed in with its tree covered slopes, and its background of rounded hills, the long tongue of gravel at Row forming a barrier to the plashing waves.   When you descend into the leafy recesses of the glen, and look upwards and downwards at its sinuous course, its romantic beauties must strike the wanderer in this cool retreat from the hot sunshine of a long summer day.   On all sides its steep, mossy, and grassy banks are gay with the flowers which, in their seasons, adorn the spot ; primroses, violets, bluebells, hyacinths, honeysuckle, and many varieties of ferns, mosses, and ivy. A delightful spot for the artist or lover of nature, for the combination of rippling waterfall, glistening rocks, and long leafy vistas of tender, green undergrowth, offer innumerable subjects for the artist. In addition to the beauties with which the bountiful hand of nature has embellished the glen, it has, for the lovers of the legends of fancy lore, a story of a woman in gray, visible when the moon is at its full, hanging over a dark linn, at the head of the valley, where it emerges from the moor, and sometimes moaning, to the sad accompaniment of the fitful night breeze, over her long lost lover, whose body was found close to the haunted pool.

This glen was, in former days, the scene of a considerable industry of slate quarrying, and the old roads, for carrying away the slates, can be distinctly traced on both sides of the stream.   The refuse from the workings fills many parts of the hollow, and old faces, where the slate was cut, are seen on the slopes of the glen.   One of the last of the workers lived in a sort of natural cavern, which he man-

aged to form into a rude house, or "bourach," the site of which is to
be seen. He was known as Duncan "of the bourach," from his place
of abode, and here he lived and brought up his family. At the spot
known as the "tongue of the glen," where the Ardenconnell and
Succoth glens meet, there is a great heap of debris from the slate
works. Parts of the latter glen are very steep and rocky, and the
unseen stream is heard rippling over its pebbly bed far below. The
visitor is rewarded for his exploring of the Succoth glen by beautiful
bits of scenery, and, if he knows where to look for them, harts tongue, lady fern, and other less common species, will reward his search.
This place was a favourite site for smuggling operations, and before
the railway cutting had interfered with the seclusion of the glen,
there was to be seen one of the complete, built-in stills, and, fire
places, where the illicit work was carried on. The curious thing was
that it was not thought criminal or disreputable to engage in this
contraband trade sixty years ago. It was quite customary for young
men to hire themselves out to smugglers for six months, just like
farm servants at a feeing market. On one occasion when the dragoons
captured a large barrel of whisky, and lodged it in an outhouse at
the Row Inn, while they went inside to enjoy a refresher for the
journey to Dunbarton, the smugglers ran off all the whisky by starting a hoop, and substituted water in the barrel, after which they got
clear away, and the theft was only discovered when the contraband
goods came to be examined.

On the farm of Torr, in a plantation near the Succoth glen, there
is to be seen probably the last remaining smugglers still, *in situ*, all
just as it was left, when used sixty years ago. The place for the
water barrel is surrounded by large stones, where the malt was
steeped beside the still, and the tunnel for the smoke, leading from
the fire-place, is over twelve feet long, the very stones showing traces
of fire,—all are in a wonderful state of preservation considering the
rude and hasty way in which the smugglers erected their plant. Up
above this wood, where the field joins on to the moor, there are some
sweet, secluded spots, hollows carpeted with the finest turf, and
their mossy banks scenting the air with wild thyme and violets,

white saxifrage overspreading the velvety turf, with primroses, bluebells, meadow sweet, and a bright parterre of wild flowers.

On the side of the "Whistler's Glen" nearest Row is the fine old
wood surrounding Ardenconnell house, a solid plain mansion of grey
coloured stone, built more than a century ago by Mr. Andrew
Buchanan. It has a fine commanding position, and, from its front
there is a wide prospect of mountain, moor, and loch. The beech and
oak trees are of great size, and give an air of antiquity and dignity
to the old mansion, which is a conspicuous object in the landscape,
as seen from this point. In former days the Ardenconnell garden
used to run down as far as the field at the back of the church, and the
tracks of the walks of the garden are distinctly marked on the field.
No houses were then built on Row point, which was covered with turf,
and afforded good pasture for cows. Passing by the old church of
Row, and the few red-tiled cottages facing the green, the Inn appears,
with the building known as "Row House" adjoining, which had
been erected by James Buchanan of Ardenconnell, who subsequently
lived in it. The whole row of buildings, as they now face Row bay,
with the exception of the substitution of slates for red tiles, look
much as they did in the early part of the century, but two or three
thatched cottages, which stood where is now Inchalloch gate, have
disappeared. The road was a rough track, thickly bordered with
whins, brambles, and wild roses, and, passing what used to be known
as "Spy's lane," after one of that name whose family has long
occupied a respectable position in the Row district, the view is
opened up of Cairndhu point, with Rosneath bay opposite, and the
promontory of Ardmore in the distance. None of the handsome
villas, now nestling amidst the leafy slopes of Row, were in existence
in 1830, for there was no pier, and the long avenue, with fine beech
trees on either side ending where the pier now stands, led up to
Ardenconnell, the only mansion, until you came to Ardencaple. In
1833 Woodstone was built, and Rowmore, Ardenmore, Dalarne,
Rosslea on the point, and others, followed in rapid succession, until
we have now the modern summer resort of Row.

The geologist will find much to reward his glance over the shore

and rocks at the point of Row, or *Rhue* as it was formerly spelt.
Even when the tide is nearly at its full, there is generally a strong
ripple, sometimes in windy weather a crest of small breakers, showing
where the long tongue of land projects from the bay over the narrow
channel, and giving the Gareloch its placid, inland lake appearance.
In all probability, ages ago, the whole Gareloch was filled with a
glacier, and its "terminal" *moraine* would be where the point now is,
and the clay and gravel, which the glacier discharged from its end,
gradually formed the natural rampart that almost bars the entrance
of the sea.*

While summer throws its mantle of lovely green over the landscape, still the view from the shingly strand of the Row promontories, in early winter, has also a peculiar charm and beauty. The
loch is pervaded by a dull, leaden hue, contrasting with more inten-
sity against the snowy slopes above, and the fitful gleams of sunshine
lying in patches on the hills beyond Glenfruin. Delicate effects of
light and shade are displayed from the sun rays striking upon the
rugged ridges of rock and scaur outlined against the snowy surface
beyond. On a sudden, the sun suffuses the misty cloud on the summit of one of the far off peaks, then glints down into the intervening
valley, and just touches the summits of the mountains above
Arrochar, all arrayed in their snowy garb. Near Loch Goil the hills
are partly illumined, and partly obscured with gathering shade, while
all the lesser heights on the Rosneath shore are lit up by the slanting
sun rays, where the bare and skeleton woods streak the undulating
slopes. Then are noticed the old furrows far up the hillsides, as the
fleecy snow indicates their form, the hedgerows have caught and retained the flakes of snow, and the dark masses of fir are also powdered with the glittering rime. The yellow bracken rises in patches
out of the snow, gleaming in russet beauty in the sun, and the fringe

---

* The tide at Row point is often dangerous, the water is deep, the crossing
risky. A few years ago, one pitch dark night, a gentleman's carriage, horse,
and the unfortunate coachman, in a mysterious way which has never been
cleared up, got into the deep water and were never seen again. A solid, fixed
beacon at the end of the point now shows, at night, a bright revolving light.

of larches and firs on the ridge of the moor, through which the glinting rays of light penetrate, look soft against the background of misty uplands. Some of the fields are bare and destitute of colour, as if the wind had swept them of their wintry covering, while long stretches of sunshine streak the lower part of the hills near Garelochhead, the upper peaks hardly seen in the waning light. In many parts the trunks of trees look gaunt amid the lustrous sheen of the surrounding wintry landscape. Each rough dyke or turf-covered wall seems to stand out in relief against the white surface of the ground around, dark masses of purple heather crown many a swelling height, and a calm pervades the scene. An occasional glint of sunshine rests for a moment on the pale grey boughs of the silver fir and birch, and tips the crests of the topmost trees, and the red withered leaves of the beech rustle at times in the wintry blast. The glistening, green ivy imparts colour to some of the bare stems of older trees, and the mossy mantle, clinging like an emerald velvet robe to the grey wood, gives additional warm tints.

Sometimes, on a winter morning in December, beautiful effects of light and shade will be observed in the sky, and also in the reaches of water about Row bay, and in the opposite bay of Campsail. Towards the high hills beyond Loch Long the background is misty, but a large opening in the cloudy canopy seems to illumine the sky over Glenfruin. This has a delicate pale grey hue, and is bordered with faintly moving fringes of vaporous clouds, and it grows brighter and brighter, with delicate streaks of red gleaming athwart the sky, which now begins to show a lovely silvery grey. The water near the shore is of a leaden colour, the dense dark reflections of the trees sleep in the loch, all along the shore of the Mill bay, and the hulls and masts of the boats are black and motionless. The crossing ferry boat casts a sombre shade against the glassy lambent tide, and there is a wondrous play of glistening sheen on the surface of the water. The white seagull, for an instant, poises with tremulous pinion, and then wheels gracefully away, and in the middle channel the circling eddies of purple water catch the ripple of light. Subtle gradations of silvery lustre, faint violet tints, and subdued greys, all combine to

make a picture of marvellous beauty. Nature seems to be gradually
awakening, and the deepening crimson in the eastern horizon be-
speaks the coming of the rolling orb of day, and the rainbow-tinted
spangles of dew on each spray of fern and ivy glitter as they are suffused with the morning light.

At the corner of what used to be known as "Spy's Lane," there
stood formerly a row of four thatched houses, which were known as
the "shore houses of Laggarie," but were pulled down, and the
existing cottage, belonging to Mr. Watson, Inchalloch,* was built,
and sixty years ago was a public-house. Proceeding up the lane, the
old Ardenconnell Avenue is reached, at the end, forming now the
public road. The road going up the hill leads into what is known
as the "Highlandman's Road," and which passes from the Row
Church over into Glenfruin. In the beginning of the century this
road led directly from the church, past the front of the manse, in a
line which can be still faintly traced, with old trees on either side,
and took a somewhat steeper line than at present through the Laggarie grounds. There were old houses, both at the side of this road,
know as Laigh Laggarie, and further up, not far from where the railway station now stands, called High Laggarie, one of which, a
humble structure, thickly overgrown with ivy, is still to be seen. It
was here that the last of the famous Macaulays of Ardencaple died
in the year 1767. Pursuing his way upwards, the pedestrian has on
his left the upper ranges of the hills on the Row side of Glenfruin,
and on his right the Ardencaple policies and the Torr farm. In the
early spring this is a pleasant stroll, and many varieties of mosses
and ferns, cuckoo flowers, celandine, lilac gentian, woodruff, hearts-
ease, primroses, and hyacinths, well reward the botanist. Coming
down by the hazel and birch clad dell near the Glenan burn, many

---

* Inchalloch. This name seems to have been mentioned in the Report of the
Commissioners for the Valuation of Teinds, in 1630, as a parish, though it long
ago merged into Cardross. It is believed that the confusion was caused by a
portion of the actual parish of Inch-Cailliach, on Loch Lomond, having been at
some remote period attached to the parish of Rosneath, when Inch-Cailliach
was broken up.

ARDENCAPLE CASTLE.

sweet and verdant patches of greensward are passed, as, following the sparkling streamlet, the visitor skirts the end of Ardencaple, and arrives at the Woodend farm in the west of Helensburgh.

Returning to the cluster of houses which constitutes the village of Row, and standing at the end of the narrow strip of land, once known as the "Ferry Acres," now clothed with a plantation of fir trees, in which, a dozen years ago, a colony of rooks established themselves,—the view has many features of interest. Rhu Lodge, built early in the century by Lord John Campbell, has lost the picturesque aspect which it used to present, when covered over with a thatch of heather. The ferry was a busy scene for days when Carman fair was in the era of its glory. Droves of cattle would come across from Argyllshire, by way of Ardentinny and Rosneath, and horses would cross at Row ferry, by the simple process of making them swim over after the ferry boat. On the left hand was the old church and schoolhouse, where amongst other teachers was the unfortunate John Arrol who, in the year 1760, was murdered by a man named Cunningham, who resided in Dunbarton. The murderer afterwards confessed that he had paid Arrol the sum of thirty pounds, a debt which he owed, and, having got a receipt for the money, stabbed his victim to the heart with a knife, and, after hiding the body for some time in a disused chimney, he took it one dark night to the Leven and sunk it in the stream. Cunningham was suspected from the first to have murdered the poor schoolmaster, and, after the body was recovered from the Leven, he was asked to undergo the trial by touch, from the universal belief that if the murderer touched the body of his victim, the wound would bleed afresh. Cunningham, however, declined the ordeal, but his conscience gave him no rest, until he had confessed his guilt. Arrol's grave is in the south-east corner of the parish church yard at Dunbarton, with the inscription, "Here Lyes the body of John Aroll, schoolmaster, at Ye Row, who Died Februar the 2nd, 1760, aged 52 years," followed by a Latin inscription.

On the grassy bank below Woodstone, near the shore, the curious in such matters will find a square stone, with a hole cut in the centre,

and the four sides cut away, to all appearance having once been the
socket of an upright beam of wood. Antiquaries have inspected
it, gravely advancing theories to account for its peculiar shape, but
the most probable and prosaic one is that it was used to support a
flag staff set up when the Queen and Prince Albert anchored off
Helensburgh in 1847. However the local gipsies and tinkers used
the stone as a sort of washing basin, when the exigencies of their
wandering life required such a ceremony. At the head of Row pier,
is the entrance to what, for nearly a century, was the avenue gate of
Ardenconnell. Formerly it was known as the " white yett," from the
fine hewn pillars supporting the gate, and old beech and ash trees on
either side can be followed all the way up to the mansion. It is now
a public road, with villas here and there in the woods adjoining, and
forms a delightful, shady promenade in the heat of summer. Opposite is Row pier, a massive structure, built of huge blocks of stone,
superior in strength and solidity to any similar pier on the Clyde,
and the venerable form of Angus Colquhoun, a splendid specimen of
a highlander, is rarely absent from his post on the arrival of the
steamers. Angus is known far and near, and invests the familiar
operation of catching the ropes with a dignity unattainable by the
minor pier guardians at other Clyde resorts. The " Lagarie Croft "
was the field now occupied by Armadale Villa, and, a little way beyond, on the road side, was the row of thatched houses, known as the
"Shore houses of Torr," in which lived the labourers on that farm.
There used to be a yair opposite Lagarie, and fish have been taken
from it less than sixty years ago, but most of the stones were used
in building the sea wall below the road, and only a few are left. A
little way beyond Lagarie there stands, on the road side, the old
Ardencaple Inn, now a private dwelling house, but, at the beginning
of the century, a place of resort for travellers posting to and from
the Argyllshire Highlands. The Duke of Argyll built it when the
old and humble edifice, which did duty as an inn at Cairndhu point,
was pulled down, and which, for a time, served as the stables for the
new inn.

Ardencaple Castle is certainly the most interesting of the old residences on the Gareloch, and stands on a fine site overlooking the entrance to that beautiful sheet of water. The old castle is an irregular pile of buildings placed on a massive foundation, all covered over with thick ivy. Part of the structure dates back to the fourteenth century, but there is not much in the architecture to attract the notice of the antiquary. There are several vaulted chambers, dark and dismal, in the lowest part of the old castle, which probably go back to a very remote date. The fine old trees around the castle give it an ancient look, in harmony with the wooded landscape and moorland background. In front of the castle is the projecting headland known as Cairndhu,* where the old .inn and outhouses used to stand, but which is now known as Kidston Park, from the fact that it was purchased and presented to the town of Helensburgh by members of the family of that name. Helensburgh owes a deep debt of gratitude to the Kidstons, who have resided there for several generations; the first of the family, Richard Kidston, having filled the office of provost of the Burgh in the year 1836. Of his three sons, William, Richard, and Charles, the first mentioned was, for many years, a well known and prominent figure in ecclesiastical, social, and political circles—a most generous friend to education, a philanthropist of wide sympathies, and one who wrought incessantly for the good of his fellowmen. Only one member of the family still survives, the friend of the friendless, the gentle and devoted promoter of many Christian works.

---

* There were two or three cottages near the shore known as the "shore houses of Ardencaple," in one of which dwelt the Duke's fisherman, from whose name the point was long known as "Neddy's point."

CHAPTER V.

Helensburgh ; its History, Institutions, and Inhabitants.

THE flourishing town of Helensburgh has a fine situation on the undulating slope rising from the shore opposite Greenock, and forms a pleasing object in the landscape as seen from the deck of the steamers sailing up the estuary of the Clyde. It was founded in 1777, by the superior of the land, Sir James Colquhoun, and was named after his wife Helen, daughter of Lord Strathnaver, son of John, Earl of Sutherland. The town is laid out after an effective plan of feus; its streets are wide, intersecting one another at regular intervals. From being a mere straggling row of humble houses in the beginning of the century, mostly situated on the shores of the shallow bay, the town has assumed the extensive proportions it now displays. Along the shore, in front of the main street there extends a sort of esplanade walk, with a break where the Established church, and the street beyond intervene to vary its uniformity. From this esplanade the various streets run far up the ascending ground, and ranges of fine villas, some of a highly ornate style of architecture, adorn either side. Handsome church spires arise from amidst the verdant flowering gardens and clumps of trees, and, in other parts of the town, the public buildings are worthy of the prosperity of this popular place. While, from every coign of vantage in the streets and terraces of the upper portion of the town, there are gained delightful views of the Rosneath peninsula, with its lordly castle, or palace, amidst stately fir trees, the long stretch of purple moor, and clusters of plantations round the shores of the Gareloch, the swelling forms of the noble Argyllshire mountains in the background, and the winding, wooded slopes of Row and Shandon towards the north. Helensburgh, from its position, enjoys a great deal of sunshine in summer, and sometimes, the fervent heat is rather too much at the height of the season, unless tempered with the refreshing sea breeze. It is a favourite place of resort for those who wish to combine the pleasures of the town along with rural scenery, as they can take the steamers which sail to some of the romantic and beautiful islands and lochs in the West Highlands. In summer also, the railway brings down thousands of visitors, for the day, who throng the streets and esplanade, or wend their way to Cairndhu park, from whence a prospect of the Gareloch and opposite shores of Rosneath is obtained.

Very little of old Helensburgh remains, namely, the row of humble, thatched, or red tiled, cottages that used to run along the shore road in what is now known as Clyde Street. In those days there were no steamers to transport their motley company of pleasure seekers from the dingy and smoky purlieus of Glasgow, into the heart of the West Highland scenery, enjoying a constantly changing series of panoramic views of mountain, moor, and pebbly strand, as they swiftly glided along. No railway invaded the secluded valleys, down whose heath and bracken clad braes the sparkling burns leapt in headlong race to the brawling stream rustling amidst the rocks of its wave-worn channel. Not even the well appointed coach, with its cheery driver urging his rapid team of horses along the highway, and the guard sounding his " echoing horn " to the delight of ruddy faced village children, was ever seen by the peaceful waters of the Gareloch. Those passengers who sought to reach the great capital of the West of Scotland, from the outlying towns down the Clyde, or in its vicinity, had to hire a post-chaise, or to trudge on foot their weary way to purchase, perchance, some of the "luxuries o' the Saut Market." And if they wished to make their way across to Greenock, or Port-Glasgow, they had to take the ferry boat from Drumfork ferry house, long kept by Walter Bain, and brave the often stormy passage, with the possibility of being storm-staid for one or more days, ere the return voyage could be made.

Helensburgh is spoken of in Chalmers' "Caledonia," as follows:

" This village was founded by the proprietor, Sir James Colquhoun
of Luss, about 1775, but during twenty years it made very slow
progress.   Since 1795, it has increased rapidly, having become a
regular fashionable sea bathing place, for the merchants and manu-
facturers of Glasgow and Paisley, who have regular and easy con-
veyances to it by means of steamboats.   It is built on a regular plan,
has a theatre, several inns, a large Hotel, extensive hot and cold baths,
with every accommodation for invalids.   It has been created a burgh
of barony, with a regular establishment of magistrates, and a small
harbour for coasting vessels and pleasure boats has been constructed
at it.   This rising town already contains a permanent population of
1,000, and in the summer season it has more than three times that
number of people."

A number of years later, in 1839, it is thus described by the Rev.
Mr. Laurie of Row in the Statistical Account.   " The only town
in the parish is Helensburgh, a rapidly increasing watering place.   It
was founded by the first Sir James Colquhoun, and was named in
honour of his wife, Lady Helen Sutherland.   It was created a burgh
of barony by charter in the year 1802, and has a provost, two bailies,
and four councillors.   It has the privilege of holding a weekly market
and four annual fairs.   There is a small and incommodious pier,
principally used by the steamboats, of which several sail daily to
Glasgow.   There is also a daily post from Dunbarton and Greenock."
There are not very many living who can remember the town as it
was seventy years ago, and therefore it is interesting to read what
an intelligent visitor, the Rev. W. M. Wade, says of Helensburgh, in
his work on the *Watering Places in Scotland*, published at Paisley in
the year 1822.   In this pleasantly written book we read, " As a
watering place Helensburgh is well and genteely frequented.   Houses
and lodgings are often engaged months before they are required, and
yet disappointments are not uncommon.   The houses already built
accommodate a resident population of more than about 900 or 1000
persons.   Many of the bathers lodge in the hotel, a large edifice ; or
in the inns, of which there are, or were, lately three.   Of the private
lodgings, some are well, and even elegantly fitted up, and furnished.

The baths, of which there are both hot and cold, with every necessary convenience, are in a handsome and commodious edifice, a little apart from the town. Near them are some handsome dwelling houses. Helensburgh contains a theatre and a post-office, at which the arrival from Glasgow is daily, as is the despatch thither. A small harbour for coasting and pleasure vessels is an agreeable appendage to the place. Towards improving it a Government grant of £1500 has been made." The author goes on to speak of communications between different towns on the Frith of Clyde, by means of steamers, and in summer a daily coach runs to Dunbarton and Glasgow. He also gives various routes for excursions along the Gareloch. Mentions the "Inn of South Cairndow, opposite the mouth of Loch Gare." Speaks of "Rosneath Castle as yet unfinished," and mentions a "ruined chapel," near the beautiful bay of Camsail, on Rosneath side of the Loch. Also alludes to Faslane house, on the Gareloch, as "a pleasant villa that was wont to be let during the bathing season, and in the neighbourhood of which is a bowery chapel ruin."

Yet another description is given of Helensburgh in the *Road Book of Scotland*, published in London, 1829. "Helensburgh in Dunbartonshire is pleasantly situated on the north bank of the Frith of Clyde, and is much frequented as a watering place. It was founded towards the close of the last century by Sir James Colquhoun of Luss, and laid out on a uniform plan. Government granted £1500 towards the construction of a harbour, on condition that Sir James should expend an equal sum. Hence there is a ferry to Greenock. About 500 yards to the east are the Helensburgh hot and cold baths, fitted up on an elegant plan. Ardencaple Inn, in Dunbartonshire, is situated on Gair Loch, on the opposite shore of which is seen Rosneath House."

The contrast is striking between the old and the handsomely appointed modern town, with its fine Gothic churches, ornate municipal buildings, large and commodious post-office, public halls, streets squares and terraces of variegated freestone, and well arranged shops full of all the most attractive wares, and a broad esplanade and sea wall thronged in summer with crowds of visitors enjoying their breezy

promenade. The broad streets run up the hill from the main terrace
on the sea front, some of them planted with strips of turf on either
side, and trees at intervals, like the boulevards of Paris. There is a
delightful combination of grass plots, umbrageous hedges, and green
shrubs, mingled with the decorated villas, giving an air of opulent
prosperity to the town, and these are gradually extending to the
upper slopes, which afford beautiful vistas of the Cowal mountains
and reaches of the Clyde. No doubt, Helensburgh was a considerable time in arriving at its present condition, since January 1776,
when the lands of Maligs were first advertised by the superior, Sir
James Colquhoun, who had acquired them from Sir John Shaw of
Greenock. An elaborate feuing plan was prepared in 1803 by Mr.
Peter Fleming of Glasgow, regular rectangular blocks for building
sites being laid down, the streets leading from the shore and the
cross streets being all of a uniform breadth of sixty feet.* The
quantity of land allotted for the proposed burgh was 175 acres, 3
roods, " exclusive of the high road from Glasgow to Inveraray leading through these lands." There were, at that date, 82 feus taken
off, the first one being at the foot of William Street, where the old
red-tiled house, which still stands, is an undoubted relic of the
Helensburgh of that period. There was also planned a good large
harbour, with two breakwater walls on either side, and a consider-

---

* The following list of original feuars will be of interest :—

William Stewart, -	-	£0	6	8	Malcolm Taylor,	-	-	£1	0	0
Donald M'Kinlay, -		0	13	4	David Reoch,	-	-	0	6	8
Andrew M'Lachlan,	-	0	6	8	Robert Colquhoun, -	-	1	0	0
Robert Watson,	-	-	0	6	8	Angus Ferguson,	-	-	0	13	4
James Walker,	-	0	13	4	Archd. M'Auslane,	-	0	14	0
Donald Smith,	-	-	0	6	8	John Govan,	-	-	0	6	8
John M'Naughten,	-	0	8	0	Patrick Gray,	-	-	0	8	0
William Bruce,	-	-	0	6	8	John M'Auslane,	-	-	0	6	8
John M'Aulay,	-	-	0	13	4						

The whole village at that time consisted of a dozen or more small red-tiled or
thatched cottages, on the side of the road leading to Row and Garelochhead.
In 1812, from the list in Robert Colquhoun's rental book, there were 61 feuars,
who paid, in all, £142 6s. 8d. A number of these paid 6s. 8d. per acre, but one
large feu was £48.

able space of wharfage, although this was only partially carried out. This proved a great drawback to the prosperity of the town for a number of years, for, although the Government granted £1500 conditionally, the amount raised locally never got beyond £1100, and thus the scheme of a harbour fell to the ground. The original pier was a mere stone dyke for landing goods and passengers, but it was gradually improved and lengthened, being under the management of a committee of subscribers till 1834. In that year it came under the control of the provost and council as well, a piece of ground was purchased on which to erect a bazaar, or market place, but this plan was superseded by Sir James Colquhoun granting all the vacant ground, eastward to the old granary, in front of the Established Church, on condition of this being kept vacant for future improvements of the pier and harbour. Having no actual rights of property in the pier, the original subscribers transferred their control over it to the town council, in the expectation of a large and commodious harbour being constructed, worthy of the rising importance of the town.

Under the first charter, the bounds of the burgh of Helensburgh extended from the Glenan Burn to the old road leading to Luss at Drumfork on the east, and about as far to the north as the existing line of King Street. Owing to the discontinuance of the ancient custom of perambulating the marches, and the boundary stones having been removed, it is not now easy to determine the exact limits of the burgh on the north. The curious old ceremony used to be annually observed known as the "riding of the marches," when the magistrates and council officially assembled, accompanied by a crowd of boys, and the march stones or dykes were duly pointed out to all present. When the new Act of Parliament was got, these old boundaries were extended, and the burgh ran from the East Toll to Ardencaple wood, a distance of over a mile, and up the hill more than a quarter of a mile from the shore. One great advantage that Helensburgh enjoys is from being situated on a natural slope of ground, and the feuing lots are in rectangular squares of two acres each, the number of houses on each acre being restricted to four, and in many instances to two, except in the two principal streets to the front. Many of the houses are of the cottage description, though a number of modern villa residences of considerable size have been erected in the last few years. Nowhere along the coast are there to be seen more tastefully laid out pleasure grounds, gay with spring and summer flowers, and many varieties of plants, elsewhere only seen under glass, grow in the open air owing to the southern exposure they enjoy away from the blighting effects of the east wind.

It is curious to read the first public notice regarding Helensburgh, which then had not yet acquired its name, in the old *Glasgow Journal*, of date 11th January, 1776, twenty years after the purchase of the Barony of Maligs by Sir James Colquhoun.

"NOTICE. To be feued immediately, for building upon, at a very reasonable rate, a considerable piece of ground, upon the shores of Malig, opposite Greenock. The land lies on both sides of the road leading from Dunbarton to the kirk of Row. The ground will be regularly laid out for houses and gardens, to be built according to a plan. There is a freestone quarry on the ground.

"For the accommodation of the feuars the proprietor is to enclose a large field for grazing their milk cows, etc.

"N.B. Bonnet-makers, stocking, linen and woollen weavers, will meet with proper encouragement. There is a large boat building at the place for ferrying men and horses with chaises."

In the old charter of 1802, the town was created a burgh of barony, for the purpose "encouraging industry and promoting manufacture in the village of Helensburgh." The boundaries are described as on the south by the river Clyde, on the north by the march dyke of the farm of Stucklcekie, and by the march dyke of the farms of Two Maligs and of Glenan, on the west by the burn of Glenan, and on the east by the road leading from Clyde to Loch Lomond, commonly called the "Duke's road."

There is no doubt that Sir James Colquhoun was correct in his surmise that Helensburgh would prove an attractive place of resort for visitors, and it has now come to be recognised, by medical men of high reputation, as especially favourable for invalids. Certainly

it is since the opening of the railway in 1857 that the great prosperity of the town may be said to commence, and the introduction
of gas in 1844 was another vast improvement over the old system of
lighting by oil and candles.   This was simultaneous with the new
Police Act of 1846, when the powers of the governing authorities
were enlarged, in accordance with the efficient maintenance of law
and order.   And the fine water supply, gained from the reservoir on
the Mains-Hill above the town, has been a permanent blessing to the
community, since the town council carried out this great improvement in March 1868.

   There are still living natives of Helensburgh who can perfectly
recall the old features of the town as it was before the epoch of
water supply, gas, railway, police acts, boulevards, banks, and other
of the institutions of modern society.   One of these, Mr. M'Aulay,
fisherman, whose familiar form has long been known to passengers,
as he sits at the head of the pier in summer, has kindly furnished
the author some interesting reminiscences.   The oldest houses in the
town he considers to be the red tiled ones at the foot of Maitland
Street, which used to be occupied by John Gray, while a cooperage
was situated on the shore, nearly opposite; but in one of the great
storms, more than sixty years ago, this building was entirely washed
away.   There was a carved stone over the door, with the cooper's
coat of arms, consisting of the letters, P. G. M. D. G., a pair of compasses, and some implements, with the date 1778, which is now to be
seen built into the wall of the house at the foot of the street next
the shore.

   The Helensburgh of those days consisted of Clyde Street and
a few houses in Princes Street.   Mr. M'Aulay, when a boy, remembered there was a broad stretch of green grass all the way from the
pier to Cairndhu point, with whins, brambles and sloes, growing in
abundance.   In his early days there was a sort of rude harbour,
formed by the pier, which ran out in breadth over twenty feet at
first, then became a sort of rough dyke, a few feet wide, with an arm
striking off nearly at right angles.   There were generally two or
three wherries and coal gabbards in the harbour, as all the coals came

by this means to the town, and on being taken ashore were carted
over the beach near the granary into Sinclair Street for distribution. A shed, in those days, rested against the walls of the old
granary, and outside of all was the road, but these outlying sheds
were subsequently all swept away by the sea. When the tides
suited, three of these wherries would start from the harbour; and
smacks with grain, farm produce, and often passengers, traded with
the various coast towns down the Clyde.

Steamers regularly made the voyage from Glasgow to Helensburgh
and the Gareloch, touching all intermediate points in the river. One
of these, the *Helensburgh*, Captain Macleod, was in her day a notable
vessel, with a gross tonnage of 125 tons. Her side lever engine, of
52 horse power, was constructed by the eminent Robert Napier, at
his foundry at Camlachie, and she was the first single engined
steamer which had two eccentric rods, one for going ahead, and one
for going astern, while her mast was of iron. She was sold in 1835,
and ran between Liverpool and Woodside, till she was broken up in
1845. The *Clarence*, Captain Turner, the *Caledonia*, Captain White,
the *Waverley*, Captain Douglas, the *Sultan*, *James Oswald*, and the
steamers of the Helensburgh Steamship Company, *Monarch*,
Emperor, *Sovereign*, were all well known to summer visitors of the
period. The *Waverley* used to leave Glasgow every day at 10 A.M.
for Helensburgh, and the *Caledonia* at 3 P.M., and three times a week
the former sailed to Garelochhead. The latter, in the days before
there were piers on the loch-side, made the run every day to the
Gareloch, and towed a small boat from Helensburgh pier, in which
the passengers landed at Row and at Rosneath. The *Clarence* and
Helensburgh also made runs to the Row and Rosneath ferries, and the
passengers at the old pier of Helensburgh had often great difficulty
in landing on the narrow plank extending from the vessel to the
wave-washed stone pier, if the wind was high and a heavy sea on.
In those days there were no piers at Renfrew, Dunbarton, or any of
the river-side towns, until you reached Port-Glasgow. Row was the
first pier built on the Gareloch, and steamers were glad to land their
passengers there, when it was impossible to take the ruinous stone

dyke at Helensburgh. The wherries sailed thrice a week from Helensburgh to Rosneath, and sometimes to Shandon and Rahane, taking loaves of bread, which old "Gibbie" Macleod used to distribute at the Clachan village, and at the Parkhead, in Rosneath policies. Although there were often abundant shoals of herring in the Gareloch, the fishing latterly was not much carried on, while there were salmon stake nets on the shore in front of where Ferniegair now stands, as also at Craigendoran. There were large quantities of fish of the usual varieties to be had by line fishing from boats, also excellent sea trout, sometimes four and five pounds in weight, were often caught.

Education in the landward part of the parish, and in Helensburgh, was of the usual excellent description, so well known as forming a special feature in Scottish rural life since the days of John Knox. Truly our country owes a debt of gratitude to the hard working, and often self-denying, men who for so many years upon miserably inadequate emoluments, imparted admirable tuition to the youth of Scotland. By the Act of 1696 it was decreed that the heritors in each parish should supply a suitable school-house, with a salary for the master of not less than a 100 merks, £5 11s. 0½d., nor over 200 merks, £11 2s. 3d., payable half-yearly, besides the casual fees, which formerly belonged to the readers and clerks of the Kirk Session. By the subsequent Act of 1803, a dwelling house and garden was further provided, and adequate school buildings for the district. These village schoolmasters were frequently men of capacity and learning, who often had been educated for the ministry, but failed in attaining to the dignity of a parish minister, and were content to seek to bring into play the latent qualities of intellect and scholarship which might be found amongst the children of the humble cottars. He generally also acted as registrar, session clerk, and precentor in the church, besides being secretary or manager of the various charitable and other village associations. Mr. Battison of this town was a man of varied occupations, and in addition to being an instructor of the ingenuous youth of Helensburgh, he was town clerk and collector of statute labour money for the burgh. His school in

1834 was incorporated with the session school of Row, which was built by public subscription, and enjoyed the government grant, being kept up by the Free Church until the passing of the Scotch Education Act of 1872.

In many respects a teacher of exceptional merits, Mr. Battison was sometimes assisted by his nephew James Walker. There was another school, attended by some sixty scholars, in Mr. M'Aulay's time, established by Mr. Hunter, who used to keep a similar one at Cardross. He built the schoolhouse in what was then called Sir William Wallace Street, at the corner of Princes Street, and his fees were from 3s. to 4s. per quarter for each scholar, the instruction imparted being chiefly writing and arithmetic. There was also a third school, the teacher's name being Mr. John Oatts, which for a time occupied a room in the old municipal building, that was built at first for a theatre. Mr. Hunter managed to combine the two offices of teacher in Princes Street, and grocer in Clyde Street, and is still remembered by some as of a gentle and genial disposition, unlike the stern, conventional pedagogue of fiction. In those days the Church used to superintend much of the instruction given, and her ministers took an active part in the inspection of schools. In 1847, when the *quoad sacra* Church of Scotland was opened, there was a flourishing school in connection with it, under the charge of Mr. John Fraser. Old Mr. Story from Rosneath, Mr. Laurie from Row, and Mr. John Anderson, all used to assemble in the schools at the examination time, and see that the boys and girls were properly instructed in religious as well as secular knowledge. Mr. Hunter used to fill the office of precentor in the Original Seceders Church (which then stood in Colquhoun Square), along with his work of imparting tuition to the young.

A school which proved of great use to the community was established in the year 1851 in the room above the old town hall, chiefly through the interest and liberality of several public spirited ladies and gentlemen. Mr. George Mair was appointed as teacher, and about fifty children, in the first instance, were enrolled, chiefly from amongst the poorer classes of the community, the fees being reduced

to a minimum.   Two years afterwards, a government loan was
obtained, and was the nucleus of the present large Grant Street
School, and Mr. Mair, happily, is still spared in the post he has so
long and faithfully filled.   The Hermitage Public School, under the
able guidance of Mr. David Buchanan, is very successful in imparting secondary education, and also the widely known Larchfield
Academy, under the superintendence of Mr. Thomas Bayne, where so
many scholars have gained considerable distinction.   The Row School
Board has an extensive jurisdiction, embracing Helensburgh, Row,
Shandon, Garelochhead districts, and even extends as far as the peaceful region of Glenfruin ; while the Episcopal and Roman Catholic
Schools provide for the comparatively small number of children
embraced in these denominations.

    At the commencement of the present century the only place of
worship for the inhabitants of Helensburgh was the Parish Church
at Row, and a pleasant walk it was along the Gareloch side on a
calm summer morning.   The oldest place of worship in the town was
the square building, known as the "Tabernacle," which was erected
on the site of the present Congregational Chapel in James Street as
far back as 1802.   For many years this remained the only chapel in
Helensburgh, although a very small Episcopal congregation was
founded in 1814.   Towards the close of last century, the early
Scottish Congregationalists made Helensburgh a preaching station in
summer, and conducted their services, either in or out of doors,
according to the state of the weather.   Thus a small flock was
formed, and, in 1800, an application was made to the Rev. Greville
Ewing, of Glasgow, to send down some of the young men then
studying for the University under his training.   In 1801, Mr. Ewing
was prevailed on to visit the small congregation, and, shortly afterwards, subscriptions were gathered to defray the expense of a
humble place of worship.   This was of very rude description, without
any flooring, but with a foot-board laid on the earth within each
pew.   The following sketch of this primitive building was furnished
to Mr. Macleod by a friend, and gives us a glimpse of what Helensburgh was in these early days of its existence.   "Our early recollec-

tion of the building itself is that it stood in the middle of a field
where a number of sheep grazed in summer, which afforded to us
youngsters, who were within the walls on Sundays, as we looked
out at them through the old-fashioned windows, more suitable illustrations of the restoration of the wanderer of the flock, and of inno-
cence and pastoral life, than what the 'secondly' or 'thirdly' of the
discourse often gave us.   In wet weather, the approach to the building was somewhat critical, for the ground was mossy and undrained,
and a row of stepping-stones led across the line of the then unformed
street near which it stood, and these stepping-stones were by no
means reliable to those who were not to the manner born.   Inside,
the building was bleak and bare, seated with high, stiff pews, all
overlooked by an enormous pulpit, with a wooden canopy." Another
small congregation was that of the few Original Seceders from the
Church of Scotland, who met for worship in 1824, in the old
Granary, which is such a conspicuous landmark near the shore.

In his book upon Helensburgh and the Gareloch, Mr. Macleod
gives some of his uncle's reminiscences of the town, as he knew it
shortly after the commencement of the century.   There was then no
doctor within its bounds, Dr. Hunter from Dunbarton, being chiefly
called into requisition in cases of emergency.   About 1809 the
magistrates and Council began to occupy the old theatre, which had
been put up mainly by the surrounding county gentlemen, but it had
a brief existence.   The Council held their courts in this building,
until the handsome new Town's House was built in 1878.   For a
number of years the municipal honours were not much coveted, for
those elected to office often preferred rather to pay the small fines of
ten or five shillings, exacted from such as declined to serve as bailie
or councillor.   At first the magistrates might be seen dispensing
justice seated on a log on the shore, perhaps with their coats off in
warm weather.   At other times they would prefer the seclusion of a
public-house kept by one of the bailies.   The more important class
of offences consisted in members of the corporation neglecting to
attend the Parish Kirk, which were punished by fine and admonition,
and the minor charges were chiefly disturbances in the public-houses.

Those of the bailies and councillors who adhered to the Church of
Scotland had a seat set apart in the Row Church, a fine of one
shilling being imposed when any member failed to attend worship
with the Council. On occasions of special importance, the two town's
officers, with their halberts, accompanied the whole Council to church.
One of the officers, a very worthy man, old James Lennox, survived
to within a few years ago as assistant harbour-master, and his familiar
and , weather-beaten visage must be still well remembered. For a
time he acted as burgh-officer, fiscal, constable, harbour-master, town-
crier, and pursued his avocation of fisherman, his services being
remunerated by means of a collecting box, which annually went the
round of the various householders.

Fowler's "Helensburgh Directory, for 1834-5," gives the population
of the burgh as about 1200, the qualified voters for the county being
stated as 69 within the burgh, and in the suburbs 24.   The municipal
constituency consisted of 56, who were all the male inhabitants,
having right to a house and garden ground within the burgh by feu
or lease of 100 years, and, as such, entitled to choose annually on
the 11th day of September, at eleven o'clock forenoon, the magistrates and town council out of their number. The householders
names, as given in the directory, numbered 217 within, and about 12
more outside the burgh. No less than 126 householders offered
lodging accommodation for summer visitors, the number of apart-
ments ranging from 1 up to 14.   There was a Public Subscription
Library, which had been established by means of £4 shares, owned
by householders connected with the town.   It was located within the
walls of the old theatre, then doing duty as the municipal buildings,
and the pit and boxes forming the court hall.   Inside this building
where once the actors were wont to " strut and fret their hour upon
the stage," there were a grocery store, the library, and the police
cells.   The Subscription Library proprietors used every year to dine
together in the Baths Hotel, but it was broken up in the year 1850,
and the books divided by lot among the shareholders.

In Fowler's Directory, the beauty of Helensburgh is referred to in
glowing terms.   " Readily accessible by land and water—close to a

fine beach, open to the soft and salubrious marine breeze, celebrated
for its fresh water springs, sheltered by hill and wood from the keen
blasts of the north and east, plentifully furnished by the sea with
wholesome, palatable and nutritious food, at a short distance from a
complete depot of every necessary, and almost even every luxury of
civilised life, in the immediate neighbourhood of charming and varied
scenery, of the safe and pleasant ride, and of the romantic walk—
what can be awanting to render Helensburgh a most attractive spot
to all who resort to the sea-shore in quest of health."

There were, in the older days of the burgh, two annual fairs held,
which were kept up for a number of years, servants being hired at
them, and a good many cattle bought and sold. At these fairs,
there figured the usual concomitants of travelling circuses, wild beast
shows, jugglers and acrobats, wandering minstrels, shooting galleries,
wheel of fortune men, and, along with all these attractions, the public-houses did a large business to the grievous detriment of the
neighbourhood. Smuggling used to be carried on with more or less
impunity, in those days, and plenty of contraband whisky could be
had in the licensed houses in the burgh. The wherries brought over
the malt from Greenock, and it was taken to the various well-known
haunts of the smugglers on the Garelochside under cover of night.
It was wonderful how cleverly those engaged in these evil practices
managed to evade the Revenue .officers, but occasionally they were
captured, and lodged in comfortable quarters in the old jail in the
High Street of Dunbarton, opposite the Elephant Hotel.

To one visiting Helensburgh about the year 1830, the town would
present a very different appearance from what it now does. It would
then have only the one long front row of houses, in Clyde Street,
small two-storied buildings, hardly one of which is now to be seen,
and about half-a-dozen newly built ones in Princes Street. There
was no esplanade, or sea-wall, the old crumbling pier jutted out into
the waters of the Frith, and a considerable expanse of grass land lay
between the road and the beach at the east bay, on which the school-
boys played their favourite game of shinty. A similar field lay in
front of the west bay, and this was usually selected by the itinerant

Punch and Judy shows, and others of the travelling showmen for their novel entertainments. The tide has gradually swept away these two verdant strips of ground, but the old Granary still rears its unadorned walls where it has stood so long. The West, or Glenan, burn flowed into the sea close to where William Street now is, a limpid stream, with grassy banks and mossy stones, brambles and ferns beautifying its course, and it ran into the sea under the stone bridge over which the road went. In those days the Ardencaple woods, which extended to the end of Clyde Street, were full of fine, lofty trees and sweet hazel dells, and the avenue to the old castle entered by the gateway which now leads to Ferniegair. There used to be a singularly picturesque old gate lodge, with thatched roof and rustic wooden pillars, which the late Mr. Kidston reluctantly had to pull down, some years after he built his new house. But the old gate remains, exactly as it was, with the grey granite posts, which were said to have been brought from Inveraray, encased in iron. There were several villas at this end of Clyde Street ; the one next Ferniegair, now the property of Dr. Douglas Reid, so long and so honourably known in Helensburgh, having formerly been occupied by Lord John Campbell. The next but one was built by Mr. Kerr, the founder of a well-known firm of accountants in Glasgow, and Lady Augusta Clavering occupied the one next the burn. This is a plain, substantial house, with a grass plot in front, and a strong iron railing next the street. It was built about the year 1804, by Dr. Gardiner, and is now so far altered that there are two tenements in it, the upper storey being entered by a stair at the back. Immediately across the burn there was the old ferry-house, Samuel M'Kinlay's public-house, a small red-tiled building, with two massive iron rings, on either side of the door, to which the ferry-boat could be attached.

At the other end of Clyde Street, not far from where Craigendoran pier now stands, there were, close to the shore, several ornate villas, amongst them Provost Dixon's residence of Rockbank, Rockfort, and the adjoining Baths Hotel, a square castellated building, which had been started as far back as 1808, by the enterprising

genius Henry Bell.* There was another hotel at that time, now
known as the Imperial, but then called the Tontine, and afterwards the George, and was first kept by Mr. Napier, afterwards,
about 1840, by Mrs. Aberdeen. Several of the houses in Clyde
Street had been built about 1830, Mr. M'Callum's well known drapery
store, Mr. M'Lachlan's shop, and the one adjoining, which was
known as the Caledonian Hotel, and kept by James Lamb. In
Maitland Street, and in Sinclair Street, there were several two storey
houses, and the one in Colquhoun Street, now number 21, had
recently been built, and was then considered a handsome house. In
Princes Street there were a few houses, and in John Street some
cottages, and one two-storey house built by Mr. M'Hutcheon. The
three-storey building in Princes Street, so long the old Post Office,
was one of the early dwelling houses of the town. The adjoining
long single storeyed cottage, with red-tile roof, was always known as
the " Bog house," probably from the marshy character of the ground
there, and was taken down twenty years ago. The site of Colquhoun
Square was formerly a disused red-stone quarry, which had been
first excavated for making a common sewer in 1843, and a pool of
water gradually accumulated in which a poor old woman was drowned.
This woman was a noted hawker, who owned a pony and cart, and
sold herrings and oysters, which had been got in Loch Long, all the
way between Garelochhead and Dunbarton. In Mr. M'Aulay's early
recollection, the Post Office used to be at Mrs. M'Kinlay's, in Clyde
Street ; there the first Provost Breingan was Postmaster. Afterwards
Mr. Hunter in Clyde Street kept it, and latterly it was beside the
familiar " Bog house," from whence the office was removed to its
present amplified and decorated home in Colquhoun Square.

Seventy years ago the green fields extended all the way down the
slopes to Clyde Street, excepting the portion of Princes Street above
alluded to, and the burns, apart from the two stone bridges in Clyde

---

* The ground for Henry Bell's Baths was feued by him in 1806, and the hotel
was afterwards built, the whole property being acquired by James Smith of
Jordanhill, in 1823, and held, till 1883, by his representatives.

Street, were either spanned by small wooden structures or crossed by stepping stones. Even at a later period the streets now running up from Clyde Street, with houses and villas on both sides, were merely indicated by incipient side walks and rows of trees, at intervals, on which the village boys delighted to hang swings of ropes. Seven farms existed on what now constitutes modern Helensburgh, and the schoolboys could play to their hearts content all along the verges of the east and west burns, within whose borders the infant town was comprised. Woodend farm to the east was close to the Ardencaple policies, then came Easterton, next Glenan, then Malligs, Stuck, Townhead and Kirkmichael. Several of the old farm houses are still standing, and the Malig Mill close beside the Luss road is worth a visit. It is a plain building, with the inscription on a stone inserted in the front wall, "Malig Mill, 1834," and the Malig burn runs beside it, under a rocky bank, well clothed with hazel and brushwood in summer. In former times there were three public wells on what is now the Luss road, but only one remains, built of massive old slabs of stone, and the venerable iron spout and handle are still quite fit for duty. Two similar wells existed farther down the road, one at the corner of Princes Street, beside the hedge, which forty years ago bordered the road there, opposite the railway station, and the other at the Established Church.

Some of the announcements in Fowler's Directory are curious in their way, as shewing the changes sixty years have wrought. There were then two inns, the Baths Hotel, kept by Mrs. Henry Bell, with superior accommodation, and with hot and cold baths, also " chaises, noddies and curricles." The Tontine Inn, also in Clyde Street, announced the same useful vehicles for hire. There are two places of worship in the town besides the Row church, several Sabbath schools, and the Helensburgh Infant School instituted in 1833, supported by voluntary contributions. The ministers are the Rev. John Laurie, Row, Rev. John Anderson, and Rev. John Arthur. The Provost, James Smith of Jordanhill, eminent in many ways as an author and scientific man. There is a Reading Room, Library, and Post Office, shops of every description, and " what they do not afford

L

can easily be procured from Greenock." It is also noted that steamboats call nearly every hour in going to Rosneath and Garelochhead. "A small harbour for steam and coasting and pleasure vessels is an agreeable appendage to the place." Henry Bell's labours are eulogised as from the man who had "opened up new channels of national happiness and universal benefits—to whom we owe floating bridges upon the ocean." There are various wine and spirit merchants, some of them combining other occupations, as John Bain, boot and shoe maker, with the sale of spirits, "James Breingan, grocer, wine and spirit merchant, Postmaster, and Procurator Fiscal, Clyde Street," and "J. Glen, flesher and spirit dealer." Two carriers:—John Glen, for Dunbarton and Glasgow, starts Tuesday, arrives Wednesday, and John Bain, Maitland Street, for Garelochhead twice a week. Steamers *Clarence, Sultan, Helensburgh, Waverley*, besides three ferryboats to Greenock.*

Old Ferries in Cardross and Helensburgh.

	Master.	Departures.	Boats.	Tons.	Men.
Craigend Ferry	John Menzies	Hourly	5	1 to 5	3
Cardross Ferry	John Frazer	do.	5	1 to 5	3
Hill of Ardmore	Charles Buntin	do.	3	1 to 5	3
Muir's Ferry	John M'Crae	do.	4	1 to 5	2

The above Ferry boats cross hourly every day to Port-Glasgow, and when hired, will go to Greenock, Tail of the Bank, Gourock, or off to steamboats, passing up and down channel for or with goods and passengers. Goods, parcels, etc., for the Ferry boats to be left with Richard Gooding, Elephant Tavern, Fore Street. N.B.—Craigend Ferry is nearest to Dunbarton, Cardross Ferry is opposite Port-Glasgow, Muir's Ferry is lower down towards Helensburgh. The Ferry Hill of Ardmore is distant from Helensburgh three miles on same side.

Steamers from Port-Glasgow to Helensburgh, Garelochhead and Glasgow.

Vessel.	Master.	Departure.	Tons.	Men.
James Oswald	James Whyte	daily	68	7
Waverley	Robert Douglas	do.	· 55	7

To Helensburgh, Rosneath, and Glasgow.

Caledonia	James Wallace	daily	57	7
Clarence	John Turner	do.	70	8
Greenock	James Henderson	do.	70	8
Helensburgh	Alex. Macleod	do.	81	8
Sultan	Alex. M'Kellar	do.	68	8

Various ancient Scottish customs used to be kept up by the Helensburgh people in the days when steamboat and railway communications had brought the town into more immediate contact with the more prosaic and utilitarian centres of civilisation. Before regular steamers ran to Greenock and Glasgow, coaches took passengers several days in the week to Dunbarton and Glasgow, and James Stewart used to drive his carrier's cart for light goods, with accommodation also for two or three passengers, three times a week to Glasgow. Donald M'Callum also made the journey thrice a week, with his one-horse van, with groceries and sundry light ware. The following extracts from the Glasgow Directory for 1806 give the coaching and carrying accommodation to Dunbarton and Helensburgh :—

"Dunbarton. A Coach from Mr. Burns' Bull Inn, every Monday, Wednesday, and Friday, at 5 o'clock ; fare 5s.

"Helensburgh. From the Star Inn, at 4 afternoon, every lawful day ; fare 6s., outside 4s.; and from Gow's, Queen Street, at 11 forenoon, every lawful day ; fare 5s.

"CARRIERS' CARTS.

"Dunbarton. At Provan's, 64 Ingram Street ; at Gow's, Queen Street ; and at Ronald's, 73 New-Wynd ; arrive on Tuesday and Friday, and depart on Wednesday and Saturday.

"Helensburgh. At Nelson's, 45, and M'Farlane's, 148 Stockwell, and at Bryson's, Argyll Street ; on Thursday once a week."

New Year's day was welcomed by old and young as the statutory outlet for frolic, and the various Scottish dainties, in the shape of cakes, puddings, and their accompanying potent beverages, were liberally set out for the parties of merry-makers who perambulated the town. A variety of sports were provided for the athletic youth —shinty matches, football, quoits, foot-races, jumping matches, and, if frost prevailed, the "roaring game" of curling—all were indulged in, and the utmost good humour prevailed. Cock-fighting amongst the school-boys was one of those cruel pastimes which lingered on long into the present century, and this so-called "sport" was actually encouraged by the schoolmaster, and the unseemly spectacle was

thus presented of pupils and dominie exhibiting what would now be
termed an "object lesson" of cruelty to animals.

The vicinity of the Gareloch afforded ample opportunity to all who
enjoyed the pursuit of fishing for indulging their fancy, while, with
a good many, it partook more of a business than a recreation. Bait
could easily be procured by digging in the sand, at low tide, when
quantities of log-worms would be got, with mussels and other shell-
fish. It is requisite, at the present day, towards success that the
fisherman should be well acquainted with the haunts of the fish at
special seasons and conditions of the tide. Formerly there was
abundance of sea-fish of all sorts, but now the supply is much
diminished. Much of the diminution of the fish may be set down
to the bad practice of trawling on the banks in the spawning season.
Still there are quantities of cod, whiting, flounders, and lythe, while
the saithe, a coarse-grained, dark-fleshed fish, will be found in abundance amongst the shallow currents of the loch. Great numbers of
this fish are to be got about the Mill Bay, and above the "Narrows"
of Rosneath ferry, in the mornings and evenings, with a white
feather on the hook, and the indications of the fish are obtained from
the surface agitation of the water. As a rule, saithe are about the
size of herrings, but eight or nine pounds is no uncommon weight for
specimens to be got near the mouth of the Gareloch. The boat should
be moored in the run of a current, where the water is about twelve
feet deep, and the bait allowed to play below the surface, by dipping
the point of the rod under water. The following practical hints
from an experienced angler will be found serviceable and interesting. Sea-trout are to be got at the various creeks, and near the
mouths of the burns that flow into the loch, but not in deep water.
In the early spring they are to be caught on shore-lines, baited with
common earth-worms, but later in the season they are found to be
indifferent to this species of bait. Trawling from a boat is the favourite mode of trout-fishing on the loch, with sand-eels, minnows, and
sprats for bait, and it is necessary to have a very long line, especially
if the day is calm. After hooking the fish, it is best to keep out in
deep water, for there is much chance of losing him amongst the

tangle and sea ware nearer the shore.   Sea-trout are to be found varying from half a pound up to six pounds, and even more.   Trout are got in all the small burns in the vicinity of Helensburgh, but they are of such insignificant size as hardly to reward the trouble of catching them.   Salmon, that in former years used to be so plentiful in the loch, are now rarely to be caught.   Cod-fishing is still very successful at times, and with the line and mussel bait, cod of ten, twelve, and sixteen pounds weight will be got.   One old fisherman on the Gareloch, who still prosecutes his calling, took with the line, some years ago, a cod of twenty-three pounds weight in the Strouel Bay.   Mussel bait is now difficult to get in any quantity, whereas in former years there were immense deposits of mussels in Strouel Bay, and near the "Narrows."   There is still abundance of small, immature mussels on the Row point at low water, but so little is done to protect the spawn that, every year, this valuable bivalve is becoming more difficult to procure.

Helensburgh at present enjoys the advertising medium of two weekly newspapers, which chronicle all passing local events, and circulate in the district.   As far back as July 1856, there was a modest sheet, published under the title of the *Helensburgh Telegraph*, printed and edited by the then local bookseller, who gave as his address, Robert Oliphant, West Bay, Helensburgh.   On the first page was a woodcut representing Clyde Street, as it then appeared, with its humble unadorned edifices, the rough sea beach close to the street, and no broad esplanade and graceful Henry Bell monument to give dignity to the principal thoroughfare of the "Brighton of Scotland." The last page of the *Telegraph*, which was a monthly organ, was entirely occupied with the local steamboat and coach announcements. The coach started for Dunbarton at a quarter-past seven a.m., and half-past two p.m., returning at nine a.m., and twenty minutes past five p.m.   The first steamer left Garelochhead at a quarter before seven a.m., and the last at four p.m., there being seven runs down the loch.   A few of the well known inhabitants and tradesmen of the time appear in the advertisement sheet, amongst them those two greatly esteemed veterans, Ex-Bailie Finlay Campbell, and Mr.

George M'Lachlan, who delights both young and old with his pawky humour, and mellow words of wisdom. Mr. Peter Campbell, the popular auctioneer of to-day, then followed the useful calling of a maker of cabinets, but hardly another of the advertisers will be found in the present Directory of Messrs M'Neur & Bryden.

A large portion of the August issue is taken up with the account of the visit to Helensburgh of the celebrated preacher, Mr. Spurgeon, and with a summary of his fine discourse, from the solemn text, " He shall see of the travail of His soul and shall be satisfied," from that chapter in Isaiah, which is the Christian's great charter and title deed to glory hereafter. Owing to the immense crowd which gathered on the occasion, in place of having the service, as was proposed, in the Free Church, the worshippers assembled in the Manse grounds, when by seven o'clock an audience of over 2,500 were present, including twenty ministers of various denominations. Great as were the expectations raised, those assembled were not disappointed with the fervent oratory of the devoted Baptist preacher, whose sermons have stirred the world as none others have during this century.

The *Telegraph*, in the same number, devoted its leading article to some exceedingly plain-spoken comments upon the state of Helensburgh ten years before, when it emerged from a straggling row or two of houses into a rapidly extending and populous burgh. Then it was ill lighted, ill drained, and streetless. Behind the first row of houses was a chaos of half feued fields and quarry holes, amidst which a few cottages had sprung up here and there. During the day, the streets afforded good pasturage to a number of the feuars' cows and horses, and to occasional troops of black cattle from the hills. The corporation kept one officer, John Campbell, who united, according to tradition, the occupation of ginger-beer trader along with his more onerous public duties, and against whom the baron bailie vindicated the majesty of the law by several times imposing upon him a fine for non-attendance at the parish kirk. Its native population was lazy, ignorant and disorderly, addicted to habits and vices of the lowest order, and few efforts were made to reform them.

It was prolific of small public houses, and the manners of the inhabitants were such as to have acquired for the village an evil and unenviable cognomen.   This is certainly not a flattering picture of the morals and manners of the natives of Helensburgh, and the physical deformities which abounded came in for sarcastic comment. In more than one issue of the paper, violent denunciations were expressed of the old "granary," which then, as now, occupied the foremost site in the front street, right before the Established Church, with its ambitious Italian tower.   Years come and go, bailies and provosts fulminate in vain against its hideous deformity, but this old relic of Helensburgh, in the past century, asserts its existence as of yore.   The architecture of the neighbouring church is, to a certain extent, enhanced by the vicinity of the ancient receptacle for grain, but it has been much eclipsed by several of the ornate ecclesiastical edifices which have been reared in different parts of the town. Within the walls of the parish church, its late genial and popular minister faithfully proclaimed the everlasting Gospel for close upon fifty years, and constituted nearly the sole remaining link between his brethren in the Presbytery of Dunbarton, and those who filled their places two generations ago.   The other clergymen of Helensburgh are diligent in their Master's work, and the large congregations who attend their ministrations, and the numerous admirable Christian agencies at work, amply prove that the pure teaching of the Word of God will be followed by abounding blessing.

The village, as has been stated, was, in July 1802, created a Burgh of Barony, with the view "of encouraging industry and promoting manufactures in the village of Helensburgh."   For regulating the civic administration of the burgh, the charter declares that the Magistracy shall consist of one Provost, two Bailies, and four Councillors, to act along with them, all inhabitants within the burgh, having right, by feu or lease, of one hundred years to a house and garden, should have the privilege of burgesses.   The powers of the Councillors were limited, consisting chiefly of holding a weekly market, and four annual fairs, the levying of tolls and customs at markets, and the preservation of good order.   The old statute of George II., regulating the privileges of Burghs of Barony, only conferred the power of awarding payments of rents and feu duties to the baron, with trifling jurisdiction in civil actions, and in criminal actions, extended to ordinary assaults and minor offences. In November 1807, the magistrates purchased from James Smith a feu of ground opposite David Colquhoun's house, for the purpose of erecting a Town's House, and subsequently the plans and specifications were approved of, the building to be proceeded with at all convenient speed. Shortly afterwards this scheme was abandoned, and the ground feued was surrendered to the superior. For many years the duties of the municipal authorities were very light, and, among their records, there may be read the dutiful address which the Council presented to King George IV., on the occasion of his visit to Edinburgh in 1822. The place of meeting for the Council was the old Town Hall, a building of humble dimensions, which no longer exists, and of which no representation remains, and subsequently in the Theatre, which had, early in the century, been built for the patrons of the drama in Helensburgh. This edifice was transformed, by a dividing wall separating the stage from the auditorium, and the conversion of pit and boxes into the Council chambers and Court house,—the police office taking the place of the stage. Concerts and other entertainments were also held in the new hall, and on the Sundays it was utilised for public worship. Henry Bell enjoyed the honour of being the first Provost of Helensburgh, in the year 1807, and his term of office was distinguished by various improvements which suggested themselves to this inventive genius,—such as the introduction of water, the laying out of new streets and squares, and the starting of industrial enterprises. From that time down to the present day the civic chair has been filled by a succession of practical men, who carried out the numerous schemes of public utility which have made Helensburgh what it now is,—an important and thriving town. Another notable man, who was twice Provost, was the well known James Smith of Jordanhill, who, before he succeeded to the estate, lived a good deal in Helensburgh. As a scientific discoverer, and a diligent student in botany, geology, meteorology, and other physical

sciences, Mr. Smith achieved very high distinction, and as an author
of several works showing much erudition, his name adorns the ranks
of literature.   The work on which his fame chiefly rests is *The
Voyages and Shipwreck of St. Paul*, which has gone through many editions, and has been received with unqualified approval, not only in
this country, but in America, and on the Continent of Europe.   Mr.
Smith wrote other valuable books and scientific treatises, and formed
at Jordanhill a fine library, enriched with works of discoveries by
sea and land.   He lived to an advanced age, dying in 1867, and for
upwards of sixty years was an enthusiastic owner of yachts, some of
them, such as the *Orion*, being notable in their day.   His son, the
lamented Archibald Smith of Jordanhill, a man of singular beauty
and nobility of character, while pursuing a laborious professional
career, found time for those deep mathematical and magnetical researches that gained him European fame, and from which nautical
science received benefits, whose practical importance can hardly be
overstated.

ROSNEATH.

CHAPTER I.

History of the Clan Campbell, and its connection with Rosneath.

THE Clan Campbell was not originally designated by its present surname of Campbell, but in remote ages was known as Sliochd Dhiarmid MacDhuibhn. In the time of Malcolm Canmore, who ascended the throne in the year 1057, the Clan Dhuibhn assumed the surname of Campbell upon the marriage of Eva, the heiress of the lands of Argyll, then called Lochow, with Gillespie Campbus-bellus, a Norman by birth. In the Gaelic language the family of Argyll and their posterity are known as Siol Diarmid, the offspring of Diarmid. The crest of the boar's head erased, which is carried in the arms of the Argyll family, was gained through an achievement of Diarmid o' Dwine while hunting the wild boar at Glenshie, in Perthshire, when he killed a boar of monstrous size which had already caused the death of several persons.

In the *House of Argyll and Clan Campbell* is the following regarding the Argyll family :—

"Some writers have endeavoured to trace the name as well as lineage of the Campbells up to Diarmid O'Duine, they say: 'It is personal, like some others of the Highland names, being composed of the words *Cam*, bent or arched, and *beal*, mouth, this having been the most prominent feature of the great ancestor of the Clan Diarmid, a brave warrior, celebrated in traditional story, and contemporary with the heroes of Ossian.' But this theory is highly improbable, as we do not find, in other cases, that the affix to the names of any of the chiefs, to denote their personal qualities, was transmitted even to their grandsons, much less to a whole clan.   Pinkerton, who has devoted some attention to this subject, while deriving it from *Campo bello*, wishes to give it a Gothic rather than a Celtic origin, but fails to produce proof in support of his theory.

"In the matter of spelling we may notice the fact that many old writers call the head of the house Arigil, and many of the present day still write it Argyle, though the Argylls themselves have always used the two ll's.   Perhaps one of the most convincing proofs of the correct derivation of the name is the record of the Parliament held by Robert Bruce in 1314, where the name of the then head of the house, 'Neil or Nigel M'Cailen More Na Sringe,' is entered as 'Sir Nigel de Campo Bello;' he was the eighth from Gilespie Campus Bellus, which tends to show the gradual shortening of the name. We also find that, in a charter of the Monks of Newbattle, Sir Colin, known as Mac Cailen More, is thus described, 'Dominus Colinus Camp-bell, Miles fillius Dominus Gileuspec Camp-bell."

The following is an extract from " The Argyle Papers " 1834 :—

" The Campbells, according to Chalmers, are undoubtedly of an Anglo-Norman lineage.   It has been contended they were genuine Celts, and Lords of Lochow, as early as 404.—Wood's *Peerage*.   To reconcile these conflicting theories matters are thus accommodated. The Lordship of Lochow is conferred on Paul O'Dwbin, or O'Dwin, commonly called Paul Inspuran, a genuine Celt, whose daughter Eva married Gillespie Campbell, a gentleman of Anglo-Norman lineage."

Another extract as to the origin of the family may be given from R. Campbell's *Life of John Duke of Argyll and Greenwich* :—

"The Bards derive the original of the family from one Diarmid Odwin, who came with Fergus the Second from Ireland to assist the Scots against the Picts in 404.   This D. Odwin settled in Argyllshire, and he and his successors were styled Knights of Lochow for ages.   One of his descendants went to Normandy and settled on a small estate which his heirs enjoy to this day and changed his name to Le Camile, which his progeny in that country still retain.   Two brothers, his sons, came to England with William the Conqueror ; one of them went to Scotland and married Eva, heiress of Lochow, who was his relation.   He retained his own name Le-Camile, which was used for 300 years."

Colonel Robertson, F.S.A., in his learned work upon the Clans of Scotland, traces the rise of the powerful Clan Campbell. It appears that the earliest spelling of the name is *Cambel*, in the Ragman Rolls of 1292 to 1296, and also *Kambel*. The author considers that the idea of the derivation of the name from the Gaelic cam-beul or crooked mouth, cannot be maintained. The first Crown charter of the Argyll, or Mac Cailean Mor branch of the name, for lands in Argyllshire, was one by Robert the Bruce to his nephew Sir Colin Cambel, dated at Arbroath, February 1316. The other designation of the Clan in Gaelic is, "Clan Diarmid na'n Torc," or Diarmid of the wild boar, an ancient and celebrated Pictish hero. The Mac Cailean Mor family rose to great influence, and obliged several small clans to assume the name of Campbell. In 1420 to 1423 the ancestor of this branch of the family was designated "of Lochawe," and became first Lord Campbell. He was reputed one of the wealthiest of the barons of Scotland, his revenue, a very large one in those times, being stated to be 1500 merks.

Sir Colin Campbell of Lochow distinguished himself by his warlike actions and was knighted by King Alexander III. in 1280 ; he added greatly to the possessions of the family, and from him the chief of the Clan is styled in Gaelic, Mac Chaillan Mor. Sir Colin, who was slain in 1294 in a battle with the Lord of Lorn, and his son, Sir Neil, fought with King Robert the Bruce in most of his great battles. His eldest son, Sir Colin, accompanied the King to Ireland, and married a daughter of the house of Lennox. Passing by his son, Sir Archibald, we come to Sir Duncan Campbell of Lochow, who first assumed the designation of Argyll, and became a lord of Parliament in 1445, under the title of Lord Campbell, and was buried at Kilmun. His grandson, Colin, was first created Earl of Argyll in 1457, and acquired the lands of Rosneath in 1489. He was one of the Commissioners for negotiating a truce with King Edward the Fourth of England in 1463, was one of the Commissioners sent to France to renew the treaty with that Crown in 1484, and became Lord High Chancellor of Scotland. The Earl died in 1493, and shortly afterwards Archibald, his son, the second Earl, acquired the fine property of Castle Campbell, near Dollar, in 1497 by grant of confirmation by James IV., which remained in the family till 1808, when it was sold. At the fatal battle of Flodden, 9th September, 1513, the Earl of Argyll was killed along with his brother-in-law, the Earl of Lennox, and the flower of the Scottish nobility. Passing by Colin, the third Earl, we come to Archibald, fourth Earl of Argyll, who distinguished himself at the disastrous battle of Pinkie, in September 1547, and who was the first of the Scottish nobility who embraced the principles of the Reformation. Archibald, the fifth Earl, was famous as one of the most able of the Lords of the Congregation. His name appears in the bond subscribed by some of the nobility in favour of Queen Mary's marriage with Bothwell, in which affair he seems to have played a double part. He carried the Sword of State at the coronation of James the Sixth, 29th July 1567, and was appointed Lord High Chancellor in 1572.

The first of the Argyll family who took a commanding part in Scottish history and affairs was Archibald, eighth Earl, and first Marquis of Argyll, who was born in 1598, son of Archibald, seventh Earl, and Lady Anne Douglas, daughter of the Earl of Morton. He attended the famous General Assembly of the Church of Scotland held in Glasgow in 1638, and in 1641, when Charles I. came to Scotland, he was created first Marquis of Argyll. In 1644 Argyll was commissioned by the Convention in Edinburgh to raise an army to oppose the Marquis of Huntly, who had hoisted the standard of rebellion. This he did, and throughout the year was engaged in various hostilities in different parts, reaching Inverurie, in Aberdeenshire in October, with an army of 2500 foot and 1200 horsemen, when he found himself close to the camp of Montrose. With a much inferior force, Argyll attacked the army of Montrose, and threw the followers of the latter into confusion, but after a time they were rallied and assailed their foes with success, forcing Argyll to draw off his men. In February 1645, Argyll's troops were totally defeated, at the battle of Inverlochy, by his powerful rival Montrose, when some 1500 of his family and name were killed. Shortly afterwards, at the battle of Kilsyth, his counsel was disadvantageous to the

Covenanters, who were signally defeated by Montrose. It, however,
was not so much as a *warrior* that Argyll achieved distinction, but as
a statesman and as a patriot. Very strongly attached to the Presbyterian party, the Marquis sought to bind Charles II., when he came
as a fugitive to Scotland, to support that form of religious observance.
At the coronation of the King at Scone, in January 1651, Argyll
placed the crown on Charles's head, and was the first to swear
allegiance to him.

On the Restoration of the King in 1660, the Marquis was accused
of a multitude of crimes by his great enemy, the Earl of Middleton,
who was sent purposely to be present at his trial, as Lord Commissioner to the Parliament of Scotland, in February, 1661. Notwithstanding the fullest and most searching investigation to blacken his
character, and to bring in a conviction, the only species of treason
which could really be charged against him was that common to all
his judges—that they submitted to and acknowledged the Government established in Scotland under the Protectorate of Oliver Cromwell. The Marquis, in his reply, successfully vindicated his position
in the judgment of every impartial person. " That what he did, he
did with a good intention, with a desire to serve His Majesty, and to
preserve his subjects ; and that he blessed God he had succeeded in
both. That, however, he had done no more than others did, even
those who were now his prosecutors and his judges. He advised
them, therefore, to consider how fatal a precedent they were about
to establish, with respect to themselves and to their posterity." It
is said that the King wrote his Commissioner, the Earl of Middleton,
to press no acts of treason but such as happened after 1651, and not
to proceed to sentence before his Majesty had revised the proceedings. Lord Middleton complied with the first instruction, but
pretended that the latter showed such a distrust of Parliament that
he could not bring it forward. Accordingly sentence was pronounced
on 25th May, 1661, "That he should be beheaded on Monday
following, at the Cross of Edinburgh, his head set up where the
~Marquis of Montrose's formerly stood, and his coat-of-arms torn
before the Parliament and at the Cross." The noble Marquis

received the sentence with great firmness, and with calm dignity, and raising up his eyes to Heaven, thus addressed his judges : " I had the honour to set the crown upon the King's head, and he now hastens me to a better Crown than his own.   You have the indemnity of an earthly King in your hands, and have denied me a share in that, but you cannot hinder me from the indemnity of the King of Kings, and shortly you must come before His tribunal.   I pray He mete not out such measure to you, as you have done to me, when you are called to an account for all your actions, and this among the rest."

The last words of the great Marquis of Argyll were : " I desire you gentlemen, and all that hear me, again to take notice, and remember that now, when I am entering on eternity, and am to appear before my Judge, and as I desire salvation and expect eternal happiness from Him, I am free from any accession by knowledge, contriving, counsel, or any other, to his late Majesty's death ; and I pray the Lord to preserve the present King, his Majesty, and to pour His best blessings upon his person and Government, and the Lord give him good and faithful councillors."   On the scaffold his behaviour was calm and heroic.   After affectionately taking leave of all his friends, he gave away his watch and other small articles of jewellery to his sons-in-law and others, not omitting some money to the executioner, and gave the signal for his death by holding up his hand.   His head was struck from his body by the instrument called the Maiden, and fixed on the west-end of the Tolbooth as a monument of the iniquity and injustice of Parliament.   His friends placed his body in a coffin, and it was conveyed with all respect and honour, accompanied by a number of attendants, through Linlithgow and Falkirk, to Glasgow, and thence to Kilpatrick, where it was placed in a vessel, and buried in the family vault in the church of Kilmun.*

---

* The Parish Church of Kilmun.   This burying-place of the Argyll family took its name from St. Mund, a native of Ireland, who, after a life of devotion, came to Scotland, and took up his abode on the Holy Loch, where he founded a monastery and church, in which he was buried, and which was hence called by his name.   The church of Kilmun was erected into a Collegiate Church,

Though the head of Montrose was exposed for ten years on the Tolbooth, that of his rival was more tenderly dealt with, and on the 8th
June, 1664, by a warrant from King Charles II., it was taken down,
and interred along with his body in the tomb of his ancestors at
Kilmun. Such was the end of the Marquis of Argyll, "the true
portrait of whose character," says Wodrow, "cannot be drawn."
His enemies allow that he was a man of great piety, remarkable
wisdom and prudence, of singular gravity and authority, and who
had rendered inestimable services to his country. He was the head
of the noble band of the Covenanters of Scotland, and had much to
do in building up the majestic structure of civil and religious liberty
in his distracted country, and upheld the principles of the Reformation when many of his contemporaries of less foresight had forsaken
the glorious cause in which he found a patriot's and a martyr's
death.

Archibald, the eldest son of the Marquis, succeeded to the family
honours, with the exception of the Marquisate, and had been
educated by his father in the true principles of loyalty to the Crown
and the Protestant religion. In 1654 he received a commission as
Lieutenant-General from Charles II., and joined the Earl of Glencairn
with the view of taking arms on behalf of the royal cause. In 1657
he was thrown into prison by order of General Monk, and kept in
confinement until the restoration of Charles to the throne. During
the troubles which befel his father, Lord Lorne endeavoured to save
his life, and incurred the displeasure of the Earl of Middleton, Lord
High Commissioner, and the sworn foe of the Marquis of Argyll, and

---

with a provost and six canons or prebendaries, in the year 1442 by Sir Duncan
Campbell of Lochow, the first peer of the family. The foundation bears to be
made "For the soul's repose of Marjory, his deceased wife, of his wife that now
is, and of the deceased Celestine, his first-born son." The Knight of Lochow
died in the year 1453, and was buried in the church which he had thus founded,
where a stately monument was raised to his memory, with an inscription in
Latin, which, as translated, runs: "Here lies Sir Duncan, the Lord Campbell,
Knight of Lochow," and from thence forward this has become the burying-place
of the great house of Mac Chaillan Mor.

afterwards again underwent a long term of imprisonment in the Castle of Edinburgh. Charles, becoming sensible of the services which Lord Lorne had rendered him, at last, in 1663, restored him the estates of his father, and the title of Earl of Argyll. In 1681, when the Duke of York, afterwards James II., went to Scotland, a Parliament was summoned at Edinburgh, which established certain oaths and tests to be subscribed by those who possessed offices— civil, military, and ecclesiastical—and this test was taken by Argyll. Soon after this he was committed to prison on a charge of high treason, but contrived to make his escape, and fled to Holland, where he resided during the remainder of Charles' reign. On the King's death in 1685 he came over to Scotland with the view of trying to preserve the civil and religious liberties of his country, in concert with the King's nephew, the unfortunate Duke of Monmouth.

This expedition proved disastrous in the extreme, and after trying in vain to rouse the country in the extreme North of Scotland, Argyll sought his own territory, but even the fiery cross failed to bring men to his standard, and at Tarbert, on Loch Fyne, his whole force was found to be under 1800 men. He thought of dislodging Atholl from Inveraray, but did not attempt this, and was obliged, by the appearance of some English frigates, to land his troops and fortify the castle of Ellengreg in the Kyles of Bute. More re-cruiting was tried at Glendaruel and Loch Striven, but so few were induced to join, that Argyll made for the low country by crossing Loch Long. Hearing on the Gareloch that Atholl and Huntly were intending to effect a junction with the Earl of Dunbarton in the neighbourhood of Glasgow, Argyll, after considerable marching to and fro, crossed the country to Rosneath, with the object of engaging the royal troops. From Rosneath he marched his men round the Gareloch, and then, by way of Glenfruin, to the Leven, which river he crossed at Balloch at the foot of Loch Lomond. Next day the king's forces were discovered near Kilmaronock, and Argyll was anxious to engage them, but Sir Patrick Hume opposed it, and it was agreed to pass the enemy in the night, and try for Glasgow. Large fires of peat were kindled, and the rebels escaped in the darkness,

M

but were misled by their guides, and wandered through bogs and
morasses, and utter confusion ensued, officers and men getting mixed
up together, until order and discipline were at an end. Next morning, when the scattered remains of the army were gathered together
at Kilpatrick, there were scarcely 500 worn out and dispirited men.
Most of the men now made for the hills, and Argyll, forced to shift
for himself, sought shelter in the house of an old retainer near Kilpatrick, but was refused, and disguised as a common yeoman, crossed
the Clyde and tried to elude his pursuers. At the ford on the river
Cart near Inchinnan, he was assailed by two mounted militiamen and
was nearly overcoming them, when some soldiers came up and the
Earl was overpowered and knocked over, falling to the ground with
the exclamation " Alas ! unfortunate Argyll."

Very soon he was tried in Edinburgh, and his sentence was that
he should be beheaded at the Tolbooth on 30th June, 1685. His
behaviour during his confinement and on the scaffold was worthy
his noble Christian character. Addressing the spectators he said,
"I hope by God's strength to join with Job, and the Psalmist, and
to trust and pray, and hope as they did. I freely forgive all men
their wrongs and injuries done against me, as I desire to be forgiven
of God." Mr. Annand, the Episcopal clergyman who attended him,
for he was denied the consolation of any Presbyterian minister, repeated his words louder to the people, and said " this nobleman dies
a Protestant." The Earl then stepped forward and said, "I die not
only a Protestant, but with a heart hatred of Popery, Prelacy and
all superstition whatsoever." Having taken leave of his friends,
he at last kneeled down, and embracing the maiden, said, "This is
the sweetest maiden I ever kissed, it being the means to finish my
sin and misery, and my inlet to glory, for which I long." Then he
prayed a little within himself, thrice uttering these words "Lord
Jesus, receive me into thy glory," and giving the signal to the
executioner by lifting his hand, his head was struck off, and the
martyr's crown was gained.

The following extract from the Council Record gives the particulars
regarding the execution of the Earl of Argyll.

"Edinburgh, 29th June, 1685.

"The same day Bailie Robertson and Bailie Spence produced an order from the Lords of Justiciary for executing the late Earl of Argyle; which being read, the Council appoints the same to be recorded in the Council Books, whereof the tenor followed—'Forswameikle as Archibald Campbell, lait Earle of Argyle, as being found guilty of the cryme of treasone, is, by warand of his Majestie's prive counsell, founded on a letter from his sacred Majestie, adjudged by us to be taken to ye mercate-cross of Edinburgh, on the threttie day of this instant month of June 1685 years, and ther, betwixt two and five of the clock in the afternoon, to be beheaded; and thereafter his head to be affixed on the tolbuith of Edinburgh, on ane high piece of irone : These therefor require and command the magistrates of Edinburgh to see the s^d sentence and dome put to due execution in all poynts, as they will be answerable, and for that end, to receive the person of the s^d Archibald Campbell, lait Earle of Argyle, at the Castle-gate of Edinburgh the s^d threttie day of June, at twelve of the clock precisely, from which they are to carie him down to the laich town Counsell house of Edinburgh, with a strong guard, where they are to keep him till the ordinary tyme of execution, and for the doing of all which, thir presents are to be to them ane sufficient warand.' "

From a curious publication entitled *Account of the Depredations committed on the Clan Campbell and their Followers*, printed in Edinburgh in 1816, and taken from a lately discovered manuscript, there occurs the following details of the burial of the bodies of three members of the Argyll family. Andrew Brown, a near relative of the writer of the letter, John Brown, was nearly 100 years old when he died, having been born in the parish of Inverchaollan, on Easter day, 1674, and buried at Dunoon in 1774. Andrew Brown also stated that, on the 27th day of June, 1703, he attended at Dunglas, along with the numerous vassals, or military tenantry of Argyll, who had been summoned, according to the common form used on such occasions, to assemble there, in order to accompany the remains of Archibald, first Duke of Argyll, and those of his father and grandfather to the place of interment at Kilmun.

"Archibald was created Duke by King William III. in 1701, and died at Newcastle, on his way to Scotland in 1703. On his remains

being brought to Edinburgh, they were joined by those of his two
predecessors, Archibald, Marquis of Argyll, and Archibald, ninth
Earl, who had been deposited in the family vault of the Marquis of
Lothian at Newbattle, since their execution in 1661 and 1685. From
Edinburgh they were carried to Dunglas, a place situated on the
banks of the river Clyde, about two miles east from Dunbarton.
Here a suitable entertainment was provided for the numerous company who attended. After which the remains of the Marquis and
Earl were shown; their heads properly disposed in their places in
the coffins. This ceremony having ended, the remains of these three
illustrious personages were put on board of the principal barge decorated with suitable devices. They sailed down the Clyde, the 27th
June, 1703, with the numerous attendants arranged under their
various chieftains; and the procession was closed by a band of
national musicians playing high martial airs. The Highlanders were
at this period an unmixed people, attired in their native garb, all
using the same language, and having uniformity in dress. As they
passed Dunbarton Castle, the fortress saluted with minute guns.

  " The day was fine, and the declining western sun shone beautifully
on the numerous whole. Having at length arrived at Kilmun, the
burying place of the family of Argyll, and having performed the
usual ceremonies on such occasions, with all due solemnity, the
three were interred in the mausoleum of their ancestors. Archibald,
the third Duke of Argyll, who died at London in 1761, and deposited
here, is the first coffin to be seen above ground."

  This account, though curious, is however at variance as regards the
burial of the famous Marquis, with the usually accepted belief that
his body, shortly after his execution, was interred at Kilmun, and
the head, upon being removed from the Tolbooth at Edinburgh, was
also placed in the family mausoleum.

  The next holder of the title was Archibald, son of the preceding
nobleman, who, for certain services performed, but probably more on
account of what his father and grandfather had done for the cause of
civil and religious liberty, was created, in 1701, Duke of Argyll and
Marquis of Lorne. His son was the celebrated John, Duke of Argyll

and Greenwich, a distinguished soldier, who served under Marlborough, and contributed to the victories of Ramillies and Malplaquet.
In January, 1711, he was sent to Spain as ambassador, at the same
time being appointed Commander-in-Chief of the English forces in
that kingdom.　His conduct as regards the Union between Scotland
and England was peculiar, for in 1713, though only four years previously he had forwarded that great measure, he supported a motion
in the House of Lords for its repeal.　In the year 1715 the Duke,
while Commander-in-chief in Scotland, was largely instrumental in
suppressing the rebellion, and totally defeated the Pretender's army
at the Battle of Sheriffmuir, although at the head of much inferior
forces.　Famous alike in the Cabinet as in the field, he was a Privy
Councillor, an Extraordinary Lord of Session, and a Knight of the
Thistle, and was appointed by Queen Anne as Lord High Commissioner, to represent her in the Scottish Parliament in 1705 ; on his
return to Court he was created a Peer of England by the title of
Baron Chatham and Earl of Greenwich.　In 1710, when Ambassador
Extraordinary and Plenipotentiary to Charles the Third of Spain, he
was created a Knight of the Garter.　At the battles of Ramilies,
Oudenarde, and Malplaquet ; at the sieges of Menin, Ostend, and
Tournay, he greatly distinguished himself, and completely defeated
the rebel army at Dunblane in November, 1715.　In addition to
various high offices which, under King George II., he enjoyed, such
as Governor of Portsmouth, Colonel of the Royal Regiment of Horse
Guards, Master General of the Ordinance, and Field Marshal of
Great Britain, he was Lord Steward of the King's Household, and
created Duke of Greenwich in 1718.

For a number of years the Duke held a high position as a patriotic
nobleman and a soldier of renown, and the lines of Pope indicate his
character—

> " Argyll, the State's whole thunder born to wield
> And shake alike the Senate and the field."

On his death, without male issue, in 1743, a fine monument was
erected in his honour in Westminster Abbey, and he was succeeded

in his Scotch title by his brother Archibald, third Duke of Argyll.* This Duke also entered the army, and served under Marlborough, being present at the battle of Sheriffmuir, when his elder brother, who was commander of the King's forces, defeated the followers of the Earl of Mar, at the Jacobite rising in 1715. He held various important civil appointments, was a Lord of Session and Privy Councillor for Scotland, Keeper of the Privy Seal, and Chancellor of the University of Aberdeen. He rebuilt the family seat at Inveraray, and was the confidential friend of Sir Robert Walpole. He had the chief management of Scottish national affairs, besides being most attentive in assisting the trade and manufactures of his country. John, fourth Duke, was the son of the Honourable John Campbell of Mamore, on the Gareloch, and also was an officer in the British army. He was active on the Royal side in the rebellion of 1715, and served in the war in Germany in 1744, besides being commander of the forces in the West of Scotland when the rebellion of 1745 broke out. John, fifth Duke, was eldest son of the preceding, and became General in the army in 1778, and Field Marshall in 1796, and was first President of the Highland Society of Scotland. He married the widow of the Duke of Hamilton, who was one of the three beautiful Miss Gunnings, and their son, George William, became sixth Duke in 1806. Duke George was an amiable, highly esteemed nobleman, and a good landlord, and dying in 1839, was succeeded by his brother, Lord John Campbell, who long resided at Ardencaple Castle, Row.

---

* In the special vote of both Houses of Parliament the Duke was characterised as "A truly noble and magnificent prince, the true father of his own people, and one who had most largely contributed to the prosperity of England, by elevating the House of Hanover; thus securing a firm succession to the British throne." On the base of the monument is this inscription:—"In memory of an honest man, a constant friend, John, the great Duke of Argyll and Greenwich; a general and orator exceeded by none in the age he lived. Sir Henry Farmer, Bart., by his last will left the sum of five hundred pounds towards erecting this monument, and recommended the above inscription."

The motto of John, Duke of Argyll and Greenwich was "Vix ea nostra voco," which has been rendered, "I scarce can call these things mine own." The best known motto of the Argyll family is "Ne obliviscaris"—"Forget me not."

He was thrice married, his second wife, Joan, heiress of John Glassel of Long Niddry, being the mother of the present Duke, George John Douglas Campbell, born in 1823. The Duke married in 1844 Lady Elizabeth, eldest daughter of the Duke of Sutherland, and their son, the Marquis of Lorne, born in 1845, is the heir to the ancient title of Mac Chaillan Mor and head of the house of Argyll.

The present holder of this title is well-known to his fellow-countrymen. He is the thirty-second Knight of Lochow, and the thirtieth Campbell in the direct line of descent. From his exalted position as head of the great Clan Campbell, from his extensive territorial possessions, and, above all, from his talents, he is well worthy of taking the highest place in the councils of the nation. From his earliest years he has diligently applied himself to acquire knowledge, and to study the varied and intricate political, social and scientific problems of the day. He is eminent as an author, and has written various volumes of learning and merit, his best known work, perhaps, being the *Reign of Law*, which has gone through many editions. More recently, in the *Unity of Nature*, in *Scotland as it Was and as it Is*, in the *Unseen Foundations of Society*, and in his last work, the *Philosophy of Belief*, he has shown what a clear grasp he can take of great social and political and religious problems. The Duke of Argyll's political career has been long and distinguished. He first accepted office as Lord Privy Seal, under the administration of the Earl of Aberdeen, in December 1852. After Lord Palmerston assumed the office of Prime Minister, he was continued in the same office, until, in 1855, he exchanged it for the office of Postmaster General. In 1859 he again became Lord Privy Seal till 1866 ; in 1868 he was Secretary of State for India till 1874, under Mr. Gladstone's administration. Again, in 1880, he was appointed to his old office of Lord Privy Seal, which he retained till 1881, when he resigned office, and since then has held no place in the Gladstone administration. In addition to his various hereditary titles, such as Duke and Earl of Argyll, Marquis of Lorne, Earl of Campbell, and Viscount of Lochow, and others, the Duke is Knight of the Thistle and of the Garter, and Lord Lieutenant of Argyllshire. In 1854 he was elected Lord Rector of

Glasgow University, and in 1855 he presided over the meeting of
the British Association held in Glasgow.

The heir to the high honours of the house of Argyll is the
Honourable John George Edward Henry Douglas Sutherland Campbell, by courtesy, Marquis of Lorne, K.T. He was born August 6th,
1845, was educated at Eton, and Trinity College, Cambridge, and
for some years was member of Parliament for Argyllshire. He has
been a diligent reader, and has travelled extensively, and for five
years occupied the high position of Governor-General of Canada,
where he gained great popularity by his genial charm of manner and
attention to business. Like his father, the Marquis of Lorne possesses
considerable literary abilities, and has written several volumes, both
in prose and in poetry, which have obtained wide circulation ; he
is also a diligent man of business. While filling the post of
private secretary to his father, it was publicly remarked that Lord
Lorne had carried out with assiduity and success, a much larger
amount of business than is usually attempted by a private secretary.
The Marquis was married on 21st March, 1871, to Her Royal Highness the Princess Louise, fourth daughter of Her Gracious Majesty,
Queen Victoria.* In the Queen's "Journal of our Life in the Highlands," there is noted the following in the account of the royal visit to
Inveraray. "The pipers walked before the carriage, and the Highlanders on either side, as we approached the house. Outside stood
the Marquis of Lorne, just two years old, a dear, white, fat, fair
little fellow, with reddish hair, but very delicate features, like both

---

* On the occasion of the marriage the designation of the "91st Argyllshire
Highlanders," or "91st Foot," was changed to the "Princess Louise's Argyllshire Highlanders," with the crest and motto of the Argyll family, in addition,
inscribed on the regimental colours. This distinguished regiment received its
letter of service from King George III. on the 10th February, 1794, being then
numbered the 98th, until it became known as above. The complete Highland
uniform, so greatly prized, which was lost soon after the regiment was raised on
proceeding to join the British expedition against the Dutch, in Cape Colony, was
granted in 1881, when affiliation took place with the 93rd Sutherland Highlanders, of which the 91st became the 1st Battalion Princess Louise's (Argyll
and Sutherland) Highlanders, when the honoured numeral "91st" was dropped.

his father and mother ; he is such a merry, independent little child. He had a black velvet dress and jacket, with a ' sporran,' scarf, and Highland bonnet."

The *Court Journal* thus speaks of the Princess Louise, now Marchioness of Lorne.—" Fourth daughter of the Queen, and was born at Buckingham Palace on the 18th May, 1848. The Princess is a lady of a very graceful presence and—if a word so familiar may be used—of most gracious and engaging manner. She is, of course, as accomplished as the highest culture could render her ; and she has besides developed something more than artistic tendencies in regard to drawing, painting, and sculpture. It is understood that Her Royal Highness has also decided literary tastes, and is so assiduous a reader as to be in some sense a student. Her amiability of disposition is well-known in the circle of the Court, and is proved by her popularity with every member of the Royal Family ; while possibly no better proof of her excellence and singleness of character could be given than the fact of her having, in the bestowal of her affections, stepped out of the narrow bounds of choice to which our princesses are usually limited, and being willing to honour a subject of the Queen with her hand in marriage. On several occasions of State ceremony Her Royal Highness has officiated for Her Majesty, and has always called forth remark for a combination of dignity and kindly graciousness which was considered to be the perfection of the art of Royal reception."

The Marquis and his Royal bride visited Rosneath the year after their marriage, and were welcomed on arriving at the Castle by the principal tenants, the magistrates of Kilcreggan, and others. On more than one occasion they stayed at the Castle, and greatly enjoyed the quiet life, rambling through the woods and along the shore, sketching many of the lovely views, or frequently calling upon some of the old cottagers on the estate. Every one who met the Marchioness was charmed with her pleasant and unassuming manners, and she and her husband won golden opinions from both high and low for their invariable kindliness of demeanour. An enthusiastic lover of Nature, with a keen eye for its beauties, the Marquis can use his pencil to advantage, while he has long wielded the pen. Amongst the works which he has published are, a *Trip to the Tropics*, *The Psalms of David in Verse*, *Guido and Lita*, *Life of Lord Palmerston*, and an excellent *Guide to Windsor Castle*. In 1895 the Marquis was elected to represent one of the divisions of Manchester, thus returning to the House of Commons, in which he formerly represented the County of Argyll. He has acquired the fine estate of Rosneath by purchase from his father, and often visits the property, taking a deep interest in its management and successful development.

CHAPTER II.

Topography of Rosneath ; Sir William Wallace; the "Heart of Midlothian" and Sir Walter Scott.

THE beautiful peninsula of Rosneath has long been a favourite place of resort for those who are in search of romantic and salubrious summer quarters.   There is a wondrous charm about the sinuous shores and winding bays of the Firth of Clyde, overlooked as they are by many a heathery mountain slope, across whose breezy heights flit the ever-changing shadows of a summer day.   Last century the scenery of the valley and estuary of the Clyde presented an aspect very different from their now luxuriant clothing of well-tilled lands and spreading plantations.   Any one then sailing along the Clyde saw the heather and brackén-clad slopes of the hills, interspersed with glens, in which the indigenous birch and alder trees grew in profusion, but none of the great plantations of larch, spruce and silver firs, which are now such a feature in the landscape.

The name of the peninsula has been fruitful of controversy, being claimed by English and Gaelic writers as derived from divergent sources. Undoubtedly the true orthography of the name is *Rossniath*, a Gaelic term, not the modernised and more euphonious *Roseneath*. No doubt the latter mode of spelling is the accepted version by compilers of guide-books and railway time-tables, but it is repudiated by natives of the " island," as the name is written in old title-deeds, as an unworthy concession to ignorant outsiders.   One Gaelic deriva-tion of the word is *Rhosnoeth*, the "bare or unwooded promontory," another *Ros-na-choich*, the " virgin's promontory,"—these being the two generally accepted terms which have gradually been corrupted

into Rosneath. The latter is more generally adopted, but still another
reading gives it as *Rossneveth*, the "promontory of the sanctuary."
Now, from time immemorial there has been both a place of worship and
of burial in the peninsula, in the immediate vicinity of the present
church at the Clachan village. Thus the "promontory of the sanctuary" would be an appropriate name for the now populous and frequented parish of Rosneath.

It is believed that Rosneath church was dedicated to St. Modan,
who lived in the sixth century, and who set out from Iona on a mission of Christianity, dwelling for a time on Loch Etive, then at the
Kyles of Bute, and ending his days at Rosneath. The following
quotation from the beautiful poem entitled the "Bell of S. Modan's
Chapel," by Lady Elisabeth Clough Taylor, of the Argyll family,
may be given here :—

> " In good St. Modan's ruined shrine
>   Once hung a golden bell,
> And still Loch Etive's fishers gray
>   Its strange, sweet story tell—
> How in the days of other years
>   Its healing powers were blest,
> And many thronged from distant isles
>   In simple, trustful quest ;
> And none unanswered turn'd away,
>   But all found health and rest.
>
>   .   .   .   .   .   .
>
> " Fair is the spot St. Modan chose
>   Wherein to work and pray—
> The slumbrous gloom of purple hills
>   O'ershadow creek and bay,
> And far and wide, from yon green glen
>   Upon the wanderer's right,
> Rises the mountain range of Mull
>   In ever-changing light ;
> While fierce and free, by Brander's Pass,
>   In eddying rapids wild,
> The foaming Awe leaps headlong forth
>   From waters many isl'd.

" And at his feet the ancient well—
　　Awaking tender thought
Of all the weary, suffering souls
　　Its healing charm that sought—
Still feeds from never-failing depths
　　The murmuring mountain burn,
That low-voic'd woos to fleeting kiss
　　The drooping sprays of fern.
But greener woods, more smiling shores,
　　Wash'd by a gentler tide,
Where Cruachash and his brethren guard
　　The fertile vale of Clyde,
Welcom'd the aged Saint's worn feet
　　To haven of repose.

" And there, in memory of his name
　　And long life's peaceful close,
His followers rais'd the cloister'd aisles
　　That Fancy's feet alone
May tread again, with rapt delight,
　　In day dreams all her own.
Her eyes alone see 'neath sad years,
　　With measur'd footsteps walk,
Rossneveth's cowled monks of yore
　　In grave and earnest talk."

Little more than fifty years ago, along the strand of the peninsula, there was an almost unbroken verge of grass, or undergrowth of brushwood, the natural woods spreading close upon the shore about Rahane, Mambeg and Gareloch-head. At Clynder there were one or two villas and some thatched houses, the shore green and grassy, where now there is a continuous row of modern mansions, trim gardens, shops, a bowling green, a pier, and other indications of a teeming summer population. At that time there were no piers on the Gareloch for disembarking passengers, and when the steamers sailed up the loch, those on board had to be landed at their destinations by means of the various ferry-boats at Row, Rosneath, Shandon and Gareloch-head.

At this period, on landing from the old *Duchess of Argyle*, at Rosneath Ferry, the visitor would find himself on a point of land

opposite Row, where the tide forms a rapid race at certain periods of
its rise and fall.   Often, when there is a south-west wind meeting
the full force of the ebb-tide, the channel is very rough, and
full of breakers.   This narrow strip of water constantly changes its
aspect, and according to the atmospheric phases and irridescence of
the sky, the colouring of the waves is strangely varied.   At the calm
hour of midnight, sometimes, the rushing and gurgling of the great
body of water as it races and swirls on its passage through the
" Narrows," can be heard a long way off, like the sound of a cataract,
even though the loch is in perfect repose.   On disembarking from
the steamer, fifty years ago, the only house visible was the little
Rosneath Inn, which has stood in its present situation for about one
hundred years.   Most of the stones of which the inn is built were
brought from the remains of the old mansion belonging to the Campbells of Carrick, which stood close to the celebrated " Big Trees,"
within the Campsail woods.   The former hostelry, a humble,
thatched, single storeyed cottage, stood a little further up, facing the
bay, and the ancient road to the ferry followed the bend of the shore
from Strouel bay, bordered by a row of venerable ash trees.

   A short distance up the road is the Clachan of Rosneath, which,
even now, is a picturesque-looking row of houses, and has interesting
features fast passing away.   Before the erection of the new school-
house and grocer's shop adjoining, the row of cottages were white-
washed, old structures, with thatched or red-tiled roofs, mellow with
age, and overgrown with moss and lichens.   The end cottage was
long known as M'Wattie's public-house, one of the six which were in
the parish in the days of the Rev. Robert Story.   The old house,
with its gable to the road, and facing the churchyard, was long used
as the village school, and the schoolmaster occupied the upper storey.
It was for many years tenanted by the worthy schoolmaster, the late
Mr. John Dodds, who, for fifty years, taught the youth of the parish,
and died in 1870.   In addition to the ordinary branches of knowledge
imparted in Scottish parish schools, Mr. Dodds taught the higher
departments of mathematics, land surveying and navigation, and
many of his pupils (one of whom was the late distinguished Archibald
Smith, of Jordanhill) achieved eminence in various walks in life.

His successor, the present schoolmaster, Mr. William Stewart, has fully maintained the high character of the school. He has fulfilled his onerous and responsible duties to the entire satisfaction of the heritors, the School Board, and community of Rosneath. Mr. Stewart is of a modest and retiring disposition, but his conscientious character has gained him the respect of all, and the great success which his scholars have achieved in the Bursary competitions of the county is a sure proof that the high eulogiums officially pronounced over the Clachan school are thoroughly deserved.

One of the admired features of Rosneath is the fine avenue of yew trees, which extends, from the little wooden bridge over the Clachan burn, up to the old mansion at the other end, long used as a dower-house of the Argyll family. It is not easy to ascertain the exact age of these stately yews, but it certainly must be well on to two hundred years. In the very hottest day in summer there is ever a grateful shade under their mantling boughs, which are, at many points, interlaced together, and form an appropriate avenue to the ancient resting-place of the dead. Sometimes the light breezes play amidst their sombre sprays, with a subdued murmuring sound, like the hollow voice of the ocean. Many generations of Clachan children have gambolled under the branches of these venerable trees, their merry voices resounding through the bosky glade. This is a favourite subject for artists, and in summer they may often be observed depicting this rich sylvan scene. When the moon is full, and shining right down on the hoary yews, the soft shadows lie sleeping on the sward below, the vista is one full of impressive beauty. Beyond the yews are two rows of spreading lime trees, which give shelter to the avenue, and whose boughs in summer resound with the hum of many bees, as they gather their fragrant harvest, and " flee hame wi' lades o' treasure." *

---

* The yew avenue was a favourite walk with the late Dean Stanley when he visited at the Manse. The fine sycamore tree at the end, near the burn, is 120 feet in height, and girths 14 feet 4 inches at three feet from the ground. One of the old yews has twenty-eight flutings in the stem, is 11 feet 3 inches in girth, and has a spread of branches 57 feet in width. There is an outer row of fine limes and Spanish chestnuts.

Conjecture has been busy as to the meaning of this yew avenue
and the moss-grown mansion house. It would seem that two massive
stone pillars once formed the entrance, at the spot where the wooden
bridge over the Clachan now stands. Their foundations were seen,
not long ago, by the village joiner when making some repairs. There
was a tradition that a monastery had once existed where the Clachan
House is placed, and when the tenant of the farm was making a drain,
he came upon a quantity of massive stones, all solidly located, and
forming a firm foundation for a large building. The existing house
has been erected at different dates, the oldest portion being next the
avenue, and it was once of much greater extent—a large wing having
been pulled down about forty years ago. A little distance from the
old house, along the road, you come to the Strouel Well, a running
stream of water that has only been known to fail on very rare
occasions of extreme drought. The old road to the ferry used to run
along the shore, between the beach and the row of venerable ash trees
which now overhang the strand, and are, one by one, succumbing to
the fury of the wintry blasts. Early in this century the road had
diminished to a mere track, and has long been wholly obliterated.
No doubt this was the ancient road from Glasgow to the West Highlands, by which pilgrims journeyed to Iona. It went along the loch
side until Hattonburn, near Barremman, was reached when it ran up
the hillside and along the ridge of the moor for some distance, then
striking down the shores of Loch Long to Coulport, from whence
there has long been a royal ferry to Ardentinny.

We are now at the commencement of the various feus which have
been taken off the Barremman estate, which marches with the Argyll
property at the small burn beyond the Strouel well. Feuing commenced in the year 1825, previously to which date the shore from
this point to Gareloch-head presented an unbroken slope of green
fields and bracken-clad braes, with the exception of some thatched
cottages at rare intervals. The first feu taken, in the year 1825, from
Barremman estate, and subsequently entirely bought up, was the
villa, now know as Achnashie, "Field of Peace," where the Rev. Dr.
Macleod Campbell lived and died. It is an unpretending solid stone

structure, with heavy overhanging eaves, and beautifully arranged pleasure grounds, adorned with a great variety of fine shrubs and trees. Nearly opposite is the small rocky island, entirely submerged at high water, known as *Carrick-na-raon*, or "Rock of the Seal," shewing that, before the advent of the steamers, seals used to frequent the Gareloch. Passing along the shore we arrive at Clynder, where are a few shops and a small hotel, where there used to be some rough stone houses with thatched roofs, their gables to the loch. Also at Crossowen, near where Barremman pier is placed, there was a small, old thatched farm house and buildings, and another similar cottage at Hattonburn. Barremman House, a plain mansion of moderate size, facing the loch, is now passed ; the estate for more than a century and a half was in possession of the Cumming family, and is now owned by Mr. R. Thom of Canna.

A little to the north of the present house, the old mansion stands where the Cummings resided in former days, a very simple, rough cast house of two storeys. Part of the house is of ancient build, the lower portion constructed with unhewn stones taken from the shore, interspersed with clay, and it had a thatched roof. An extra storey of more substantial architecture was added and a slated roof sub-stituted. Over the door the names, "Patrick Cuming 1730, Mary M'Farlane," are cut in the stone, and the whole has a venerable aspect, corresponding with the old ash and plane trees overhanging the wimpling burn which rushes down to the loch in small sparkling cascades. From the windows of the new mansion there is a fine prospect of the entire Gareloch, and, towards the south-east, the long peculiar stretch of the Row point sometimes bare grey shingle, at other times merely indicated by a curved crest of broken water, while the head lands of Cairndhu, aud the dark promontory of Ardmore close in the view. Towards the northern end of the loch, there is the lofty outline of the Loch Long range of mountains, the "Argyll Bowling Green," and those on the Row and Shandon shores, with the ridges of Glenfruin just seen peering over the lesser heights.

On the left, up on the hillside, are seen the two farms of Little Rahane, and Meikle Rahane, with their dwelling houses and steadings

N

some way above the loch.   It needs all the patience and energy
which the farmers possess to enable them to overcome the
unremunerative nature of their working in such exposed positions.
But it is interesting to note what has been done to develop the
natural capabilities of the bare hillside, and good stock has been
reared on these Gareloch farms.   The old farm-house of Little
Rahane, only a small part of which is now standing, used to be a
favourite subject for artists, on account of its picturesque aspect, the
walls of very rough stones plastered with clay.   On the shore will be
noticed the small village of Rahane, consisting of a few humble
cottages, and some villas, the first of which, Aikenshaw, was built in
1851.   It is a primitive looking spot, access from the steamers being
gained by the ferry-boat, but its secluded situation gives it a charm
in the eyes of many.   The ferry house, built half a century ago,
occupies the site of two older thatched structures, which faced the
wood, and three contiguous cottages were pulled down a few years
ago.   These were originally malt houses for the distillery which,
many years ago, stood about a hundred yards back, and of which
only the faintest trace can be observed.   The malt mill was a little
nearer the shore, on the border of the burn into which the water
wheel projected, and used to delight the village boys with its gyra-
tions.   From this to Gareloch-head the road is well shaded by the trees
which grow to the very water's edge, and shed their leaves in autumn
into the sea, many of them fine specimens of oaks and ashes.   In
spring, these woods, and all the fields which slope down to the road,
are thickly covered with a luxuriant, beautiful growth of primroses,
while the pale yellow flower also decks the mossy banks of the burns
which bound down to the loch past many a shady nook.   A plantation
of young birch, rowan, hazel, beech, fir, and other varieties of trees,
clothes the hill-side near Mambeg, and at intervals of a few years, it
is thinned for the bark.   A mile beyond this, the houses of Garelochhead open to view, and the end of the parish is reached, at the burn
which flows down the hill from the heights above Whistlefield.

   Returning to the Clachan of Rosneath, and proceeding in the
direction of the Castle, the visitor will notice the fine old trees,

chiefly of the plane and ash species, which adorn the landscape. The Mill, or, as it is also called, Campsail Bay, is now seen gleaming through the trees, one of the most beautiful inlets of water in all the Frith of Clyde, and a favourite place of anchorage for yachts of various sizes, when laid up for the winter. Near the middle of the bay, an old-looking avenue gate points the way to where Campsail House once stood, formerly possessed by the Campbells of Carrick. The gate posts are covered with delicate grey lichens, and one of them has an ornamented top in the form of an acorn, but its fellow has long since disappeared. The wood beyond is a sylvan nook of rare beauty, many of the trees being old, and casting a sombre shade from their mantling branches. Oaks, beeches, walnuts, Spanish chestnuts, planes, and straight, lofty silver firs, all combine to impress the spectator with a feeling of peace and solitude, as in some lonely forest far from the haunts of men. The bracken and ferns which clothe the ground, mingled with periwinkle, wild sorrel, honeysuckle, and other creepers, harmonise with the verdant retreat, and the shining leaves of holly, hawthorn, sloe, and ivy, thickly clustering round the rugged trunks, gleam amid the slanting sun-rays. A short walk from the old avenue gate brings the visitor in front of the two peerless silver firs, which are the special glory of Rosneath, whose fame has endured for many generations. These are two grand specimens of the fir tribe, their huge trunks, gnarled and massive, bearing all the solidity and seeming indestructibility of the granite rock, and their great roots are deeply fixed in the mossy soil. Probably not in Europe are there to be seen two such magnificent and venerable silver firs, as these celebrated "big trees" of Rosneath. Multitudes of visitors have been attracted to the peninsula, many from America and the Colonies, to behold these two monarchs of the forest, which, for centuries, have flourished in the secluded woods of Campsail. Nearly twenty-five feet in circumference, and one hundred and thirty in height, with immense branches, themselves respectable trees, springing from the great, grey, seamed stem, hoar

with age, and clad with lichen as the rock,—these twin giants lift
their verdant crests above their companions of the grove.*

In winter, when the whole sylvan scene is dazzling white with
snow, only patches of bracken or thorns peering over the fleecy mass,
while long streaks of snow lie on the stems of trees, or cluster in
thick wreaths on their pendent boughs, the twin giants stand out
with grand effect in the wintry landscape. The yews, and the other
dark firs beyond, seem to bring out the great trees, whose strange
grouping of mighty, grey, twisted boughs, bulge and twine round
one another, as though in deadly conflict they seek to rise above
their fellows, and dark hollows and caverns are formed by their fan-
tastic formation, when they leave the parent stem. All is still and
quiet, the roar of the storm is hushed, the boughs are bent with the
accumulated masses of snowflakes, and, glancing below the drooping
branches, the eye sees the swelling uplands in their silvery shroud,
crowned with distant woods, arrayed in frosty garb, and overhead,
the misty, faintly crimsoned sky, suffused with the light of a brief
winter's day. And a little way off may be seen the cold, leaden-
hued, calm waters of the bay, on the oozy sand of which are gathered
some sea-gulls, whose screaming, querulous cries break upon the
silence of the grove, and the sudden screech of the heron, in his
measured flight far above, adds harsh music to the scene.

---

* The following notice of these firs appeared in *Gardening Illustrated*, in February 1891. "On the Duke of Argyll's property at Rosneath are many fine old
trees of the silver fir species, from 100 to 130 feet in height, with clean stems,
and girth 20 feet, a yard from the ground. Especially there are two fine old
silvers, called Adam and Eve, the first named has few equals in this or any
other country. They were planted over 200 years ago, and are now respectively
130 and 124 feet high, and Eve girths at 3 and 5 feet, 22 feet 8 inches and 21 feet
8 inches respectively. At 1 foot from the ground Adam girths 28 feet 10 inches
size of stem, and is 130 feet high." These trees were measured in 1817 by Sir
Thomas Dick Lauder and Lord John Campbell. The uppermost one, "Eve,"
at five feet from the ground, girthed 15 feet 9 inches, and at one foot from the
ground 19 feet 8 inches. In 1833, when the tree was again measured, the proportions were 17 feet 7 inches, and 22 feet at the same distances from ground.
The other tree, "Adam," in 1833, was found by Sir T. D. Lauder and Lord
John to be, at the root, 24 feet 9 inches, and five feet up, 18 feet 2 inches.

Close beside the great silver firs may be observed the foundations of the old mansion of Campsail, which once belonged to the Campbells of Carrick, and where their representative, the sister of John Duke of Argyll, known as Lady Carrick by the Rosneath people, long lived, and was beloved for her good deeds. A sweet spot it must have been, with fine mossy sward around the ancient pile, which, in the spring, is thickly carpeted with wild hyacinths and primroses, with a lovely peep through the opening branches of the bay, and Helensburgh in the distance. Even now, the terraced formation of the sward indicates where the pleasure grounds had been, the old well still offers a cool draught of limpid water, and the worn flagstones of the courtyard speak of "auld lang syne." In the earlier part of the century, the stones of the ruinous dwelling were partly removed to build the inn at Ardencaple, near Row, and to add to the Ferry inn at Rosneath.

Emerging from the wood by a wicket gate, between two very lofty and straight old silver firs, the road by the shore is regained, and the visitor sees before him the entrance, over a low bridge, to the grounds round the Castle. Lifting their dark bushy heads above the surrounding trees, are several picturesque great Scotch firs, with red, rugged bark, which glows warmly in the rays of the setting sun, and harmonises well with the prevailing colour around. Beautiful peeps of the loch and distant hills are gained as the visitor skirts the winding reaches of the rocky strand, and some specially venerable beech trees are seen, near the old sea wall of conglomerate rock, at the spot known as "Wallace's Leap." It was here that the hero leaped down with his gallant steed from the summit of the rock, and though the horse was killed, Wallace succeeded in swimming across the loch to Cairndhu point. This was somewhere about the year 1297, when Wallace was contending against King Edward of England.

There is every reason to believe that the renowned warrior of Scotland did once visit Rosneath in the course of his remarkable adventures. William Hamilton of Gilbertfield, in 1721, wrote a poetic account of the hero's achievements, which was dedicated to James, Duke of Hamilton. Wallace had been engaged in one of his numerous struggles with the English, in the neighbourhood of Cathcart, and was on his way to visit his friend and supporter, Malcolm, Earl of Lennox. He seems to have sacked the town of Dunbarton, and burnt the castle of Rosneath, which was occupied by the English, after which exploits he made his way into the strongholds of Lennox. Apparently he had been guided by one well affected to his cause who,

> " Directed Wallace where the Southron lay
> Who set their lodgings all in a fair low,
> About their ears and burnt them stub and stow.
> Then to Dunbarton cave, with merry speed,
> March'd long ere day, a quick exploit indeed.
> Toward Rosneath next night they past along,
> Where Englishmen possest that castle strong,
> Who that same day unto a wedding go,
> Fourscore in number, at the least, or moe.
> In their return, the Scots upon them set,
> Where forty did their death-wounds fairly get ;
> The rest scour'd off, and to the castle fled ;
> But Wallace, who in war was nicely bred,
> He did the entry to the castle win,
> And slew the South'ron all were found therein.
> After the fliers did pursue with speed,
> None did escape him, all were cut down dead.
> On their purveyance seven days lodged there,
> At their own ease, and merrily did fare.
> Some South'ron came to visit their good kin,
> But none went out, be sure, that once came in,
> After he had set fire unto the place,
> March'd straight to Falkland in a little space."

Such is the account of the taking of Rosneath Castle given by Hamilton of Gilbertfield. On another of his raids against Dunbarton, Wallace was very nearly being made prisoner by his relentless foes, the English. Being in a hostelry in the town, an officer and twenty-four men were sent to apprehend him, but he leapt out of the window and proceeded to assault the soldiers outside. With one or two sweeps of his terrible two-handed sword, our hero cut down the commander of the party and a dozen of his men, while the rest fled precipitately to the castle for refuge. Wallace's favourite weapon was a ponderous, long, two-handed sword, which, from his great strength, he wielded with ease, and until the last few years, a rusty weapon, known as "Wallace's Sword" was preserved in the armoury at Dunbarton Castle, and considerable indignation was aroused at its removal to the Wallace Monument at Stirling, where it now rests.*

Blind Harry gives his account also of the taking and sacking of Rosneath Castle by Wallace.

---

* Respecting the armour and sword of Wallace, Dr. Jamieson in his notes on "Blind Harry" has the following remarks. "In the Castle of Dunbarton they pretend to show the mail and, if I mistake not, also the sword of Wallace. If he was confined in that fortress by Menteith before being sent into England, as some have supposed, it is not improbable that his armour might be left there. The popular belief on this head, however, is very strong." Carrick, the author of a *Life of Sir William Wallace*, has the following note on the subject of the hero's armour. "Certain it is, if such armour was in Dunbarton Castle at the time, it is unknown to those connected with the garrison, at present (1830); and we cannot conceive that a relic, so valuable in the estimation of the public, would have totally disappeared, without its being known what had become of it. All that they pretend to show in the Castle of Dunbarton, as having belonged to Wallace, is a sword of very antique fashion, intended to be used with both hands, but by no means of a weight that would prevent men of ordinary strength of the present day from wielding it. There is no proof, however, that it belonged to the Deliverer of Scotland; and if we may credit the account given by old people, of its having been dragged up from the bottom of the Clyde by the anchor of a vessel, about sixty years ago, its identity becomes more than doubtful. Such, however, is the prevalence of the report in its favour, that it was some time since sent to London, for the inspection of certain official characters connected with the Board of Ordnance. At the time it was sent off, it wanted several inches of its length which, it seems, had been broken off by some accident."

The sword measures from point to point four feet eleven and a half inches, the handle is one foot two inches long, and the blade three feet nine inches in length. It varies in breadth from two and a quarter inches at the guard, to three quarters of an inch at the point, is six pounds in weight, and has been welded at two different places. The following item occurs in the books of the Lord Treasurer under date 8th December, 1505, when King James IV. visited Dunbarton. "For bynding of ane riding sword rappyer, and binding of *Wallas* sword with cordis of silk, and new hilt and plomet, new skabbard, and new belt to the said sword, xxvjsh."

A short distance from Wallace's leap there stands the present castle, or rather palace of Rosneath, a noble building of massive construction, the work of an Italian architect, Bonomi of London, which was begun in 1803. The site is a fine one, at a greater distance from the shore than the old castle, and is said to have been selected by the famous landscape painter, Alexander Nasmyth. The former residence of the Argyll family long rested upon the point of land opposite Ardencaple. It does not seem to have been a building of any special importance, or architectural merit, but, about the year 1630, it was enlarged and embellished by the famous Marquis of Argyll. This mansion remained until about the beginning of the present century, when it was nearly all burnt to the ground. Upon this occasion, the old Duke of Argyll, a pious man, calmly viewed the conflagration from his castle of Ardencaple, opposite, and expressed his gratitude by saying, " I thank my God, I have another house to go to." An old stone, with the date 1634, carved with the cypher of the famous Marquis, and his wife Margaret Douglas, is now at Inveraray castle, one of the few remains of the ancient structure. The architecture of the new castle is a mixture of Italian and Greek, massive and imposing, the splendid Ionic portico, with its lofty stone pillars, is almost unequalled in Scotland. The castle is 184 feet long, and 121 in breadth, with two very handsome fronts, each adorned with fine Ionic columns, the stone of the finest freestone from the famous Garscube quarry, near Glasgow, and is hewn into ponderous blocks. From the high circular tower in the centre of the building there is a grand panorama of wood, water, lawn and moor, affording endless pleasure to the spectator. Each door and window is of stately dimensions, though a large portion, both of the interior and exterior, is quite unfinished, many of the pillars with their noble capitals, and finely moulded balustrade above, never having been placed in position. Inside, the rooms are lofty and finely proportioned, one of them, the circular library under the tower, being exceedingly elegant, with decorated friezes, and classic ceiling ornaments. Several family portraits, one of the most recently added, the Marquis of Lorne, in full Highland costume, and an engraving of the beautiful

Miss Gunning, afterwards Duchess of Argyll, adorn the public rooms.

There is an interesting old plan of the Rosneath estate dated 1731 in the castle, which shows the houses, roads, and woods as they existed at that date. In this plan the castle stands back from the shore, in front of it being the "Little Green," and to the side the "Meikle Green," and garden at the back, all bounded by what is called the "new avenue." Various crofts are marked at "Little Ross," "Middle Ross," and "Meikle Ross," and at Portkill several small cottages are situated. Near Old Kilcreggan, on the opposite side of the road, "Ruins of an old cell" is marked, which locally is known as the "Broken castle," though no trace of the ruins can be seen. Near Campsail Mill there are entered an "Upper" and "Nether" pond, no doubt for water supply. The old house of Campsail is noted with the avenue leading straight up from the bay. Three small cottages are marked on Campsail hill, and they remained till a few years ago, when the new Clachan farm house was built. At the Clachan, the cruciform Kirk is put down, and the road from the castle and Campsail bay is noted as coming to an end at the Clachan village. A brick yard is situated near the present schoolmaster's house, and there are two cottages at the ferry which is called "Clachan point." Going along the shore the "Strall" spring is noted, with a cottage beside it, and at "The Clynders," there are three cottages. No houses are marked as existing on the Kilcreggan or Cove shores, but there is a pier not far from the present one. The farms of Aiden, Ailey, Knockderry, and others, are indicated, and a good many cottages near them, but hardly any plantations, except on the Gallowhill, and near the castle and Campsail bay.

One delightful feature is the pleasant, old-fashioned garden at the back of the castle, with its long stretches of mossy turf, and quaint arrangement of laurel and heath plants, groups of flowering shrubs, and graceful, drooping bushes, trimly kept walks with heavy box borders, all vastly superior to the formal parterres now so much in vogue. The soft, mossy walks seem to allure you to stroll along, and to enjoy the scent of wallflowers, sweet peas, and mignonette. There

are quiet, retired nooks, in which you may repose, quite secluded
from observation, and listen to the cooing of the wood pigeons, the
lively strains of the chaffinch, or whitethroat, and the rich warbling
of the mavis and blackbird, from the surrounding groves,—while the
songs of infancy steal over the senses, or the day dreams of youth
enrapture the mind with the languor of thrilling remembrance. The
shrill cry of the welcome and friendly peesweep, as he lightly skims
over the adjoining fields, falls upon the ear, and, as you advance, his
graceful evolutions, as he turns on the wing, bringing his white breast
into view, are pleasing to witness. And the long drawn, peculiar
wail of the curlew, which frequents all the shores near the " Green
Isle," is heard amidst the sharper notes of the various descriptions of
sea fowl which abound. Going along past Culwatty bay, on the left,
the dark thick wood is approached, in which is situated the heronry
of Rosneath, chiefly in the midst of a number of lofty Scotch and
silver firs, surrounded by a thick belt of plantation. This is a scene
of sylvan repose, forming a still retreat, which the visitor would
scarcely expect to meet. The screen of spruce, larch, and silver firs,
with rowans and beeches at intervals, is crossed by grassy glades of
turf, decked in spring with rich profusion of wild hyacinths. Only
a little distance beyond is the busy, seething world of toil and commerce, with the manifold wheels of industry, in ceaseless hum, while
here is all the loneliness of the grove. In the spring, however, the
woods resound with the harsh clamour of the herons, who are engaged in the important work of rearing their young. The nests are
great unshapely masses of dried twigs, with a few tufts of coarse
grass inside, and there are generally four eggs in each, of a pale
green colour. Sometimes the bird will courageously defend itself, if
surprised by an intruder, while sitting on its eggs, and a blow from
the long sharp, horny bill is sufficiently severe. There were last
year over eighty nests, and as you walk below the lofty trees, when
the breeding season is in full swing, there is much stir and commotion
overhead. The herons fly to and fro, crashing amidst the boughs
with their long bodies, and spreading wings, many of them carrying
fish in their bills to satisfy the cravings of their nestlings.

Proceeding across the fields at the back of the castle, the visitor sees the extensive pile of buildings, known locally as "The Steeple," facing the range of steadings of the Home Farm. There is here an old threshing mill, worked by a water-wheel supplied by water brought chiefly through an underground channel all the way from Lindowan reservoir, on the moor above Kilcreggan. The buildings are about 280 feet in length, of massive construction, and semi-Gothic architecture, and once were ornamented by a tower, 90 feet in height, designed by Nasmyth of Edinburgh, but which, after the great fire, nearly fifty years ago, was curtailed of its lofty proportions. Originally this whole structure was intended to have been the castle stables, but, for some reason or other, this was found impracticable. In front of the Home Farm rises the Gallowhill, 414 feet above the sea, once completely covered with a fine plantation of fir trees, but these, forty years ago, were cut down by the proprietor. The view from the summit of the hill is extensive, and gives a striking idea of the diversified scenery of the Frith of Clyde. Looking towards the north the whole of the upper part of the peninsula is seen, an undulation of purple heather and bushy bracken, while the dark mass of mountains above Loch Long, and their distant peaks, are faintly shrouded in blue haze. Many burns seam the sides of the hills round the Gareloch, whose waters reflect the fringe of trees along its shore, amid which nestle numerous villas, and the green fields above join on to the moorland ridge. The russet brown of autumn spreads its mantle over the uplands, and the plantations on both sides are glowing with yellow and roseate tints. In the full blaze of mellow sunshine which, on an autumn day, bathes the whole loch and surrounding mountains, beautiful effects are gained by the delicate blending of the warm tints of moor, glen, and sloping braes. While the edge of the nearer rugged mountain outline is sharply defined against the sides of receding peaks, which reflect the sun with brilliant lustre—a lovely soft haze envelopes the horizon, although the immediate foreground is strongly coloured with the purple water and the dark green of the pine forest. A white line of strand marks the upper reaches of the loch, and the tawny coloured streaks of spreading brushwood give

variety of tints to the picture. Some of the old beech trees are seen
in the castle woods, their foliage flaming with yellow and crimson,
with their shining, grey trunks intervening between the red Scotch
firs and lordly oaks—all presenting a sylvan picture of rare beauty.
Your solitude is undisturbed, for there is a considerable extent of
moor round the summit of the Gallowhill, and it is difficult to realise,
at certain points of the landscape, that you are so near the great
bustling world of commercial enterprise of which Glasgow is the
centre.*

Descending the hill, and rejoining the road leading over to Kilcreggan, the small hamlet of Mill of Campsail is reached. The old
meal mill is a picturesque building of rubble work, "harled" over,
but has long since lost its pristine whiteness, and is, in many places,
thickly covered over with a soft mossy growth like green velvet. A
rich mantle of lichens covers the roof, and thick layers of downy
moss overspread the stone work and eaves, while ferns have obtained
a lodgment in many parts, and hang their graceful fronds over the
old walls. There is a date, 1752, on the lintel stone of the door, low
down, and another date, 1777, is cut on the stone projection at the
gable, probably indicating when it was enlarged. The old wheel,
with its water trough, and the wooden shoot down which there
trickles a tiny rivulet of water, is a favourite subject for artists.
Peter M'Neilage, the present miller, is a member of a family who
have tenanted the mill and croft adjoining for many generations, and
he finds it very different from what it used to be in his father's lifetime, when the farmers in the district all used to bring in their grain
to be ground. His father made the first cart with wheels which came
to the mill, for, before that time, the grain was brought on horses'
backs in bags. The road past the mill was made about a century ago,
and the miller's cottage was built in 1827 ; a few years before, the

---

* In the month of May, in taking a walk along the shore, the following wild
flowers may be gathered :—Daisy, buttercup, cowslip, whin, broom, hyacinth,
lesser celandine, goat weed, *stillaria religinosa*, primrose, star of Bethlehem,
pink campion, dog's mercury, blue borage, violet, speedwell, cuckoo flower,
wood sorrel, forget-me-not, and a few more.

old cottages, which used to stand in the field opposite the mill across the burn, were all pulled down. In these primitive days the farmers used to dry their oats with peat fires before coming to the mill, for coals were unknown in the district. At that time there were no fanners for separating the chaff from the grain, and this operation was done on the summit of the mound at the side of the miller's house, known as the "Shelling hill," where, on a breezy day, the grain and chaff were thrown into the air from bags and basket till the required result was got. His father and Donald Turner, the smith at the Clachan, were both baptised one Sabbath afternoon about 1792, in the open air, on the "Shelling-hill," by the Burgher minister, Mr. Henderson of Kilmalcolm.

Just beyond the Mill is the Free Church, a plain building, erected over the quarry from whence the stones used were extracted, but some notable men have preached within its walls, including many of those worthies who guided the fortunes of that Church after the Disruption. On the hillside, beside the plantation surrounding the church, sixty years ago, there was a sweetly secluded hamlet, called the Millbrae, access to which was gained by a path across the whin clad, rocky brae, where the sheep wandered at will. Several pretty cottages were there, with gardens, fruit trees, and many wild roses, some of which still remain, with broken stems and torn branches, to tell of the happy, ruddy-faced children, whose joyous voices resounded in this now silent spot. A romantic and suggestive scene, from which the spectator could survey the opening of the Gareloch, with the villas of Row beyond, looking almost like a picture on the Italian lakes, richly bowered amid trees, and the verdant crest of hills overhanging the sorrowful Glenfruin bounding the view.

Returning to the road, the traveller opens up the broad estuary of the Clyde, with its rippling waters ploughed by many a passing vessel, and turning back, the calm land-locked Mill bay lies embosomed in trees. This bay has a charm of its own, and, on a summer day, presents effects of colour, light and shade, subtle and full of beauty. The water near the shore may be dark sapphire, out in the open loch a shimmering opal, the green turf touching the strand, and the perfume breathing beeches and oaks reflected in the waves, the sloping hills round the Gareloch closing in one side of the picture, with gleaming patches of sunshine bringing into contrast the lowering and frowning mountains beyond Loch Long. Suddenly, a change comes, the colours on the mobile surface of the loch are reversed, smooth bright folds seem to agitate the waters near the shore, while, further out, the depths look unnaturally calm and dark, ominous of a coming storm. Yet here and there tender streaks of sunshine lovingly linger between the silvery boughs of the lofty silver firs, towering above the grove. Looking round upon the broad frith, the various sea-side resorts, so popular in summer, are seen on the right, dominated by the fine range of the Cowal mountains, and the rugged peaks of Arran looming grandly in the far off haze. A little way down the road on the left is the row of old cottages known as Old Kilcreggan, the primitive hamlet remaining much as it was fifty years ago. In former years the tiled and thatched cottages had a picturesque appearance, as they faced the rustling burn, which falls into the sea near the original pier, a massive structure, whose great stones still give shelter to the humble sailing craft. Before the present farm of Portkill, so long occupied by the Duke's chamberlain, Mr. Lorne Campbell, was built, there was an old farm house at Old Kilcreggan that, for many generations, had been tenanted by a family, Chalmers by name, the last of whom died a number of years ago at Gourock. There was a small farm house at Portkill, a thatched building, which stood near where the present factor's house is built. Two other cottages were at the top of the brae, near Portkill House, but, in the various changes brought about by time, they have passed away.

At the foot of the steep brae leading to Kilcreggan pier, there stands the pretty, white cottage, embowered in flowers, where the M'Farlanes, who for nearly a century worked the ferry over to Gourock, long resided, and where the venerable widow of the last ferryman still lives in a serene old age. Her father and grandfather were in the Duke's service, and from the old pier, her husband's commodious wherry daily set forth for Greenock and Gourock, laden with passengers, and all sorts of farm produce, besides cattle, and sheep, and brought back a miscellaneous cargo. Often great risk was run, from the violent gales which would suddenly arise, and the compass had to be used when thick banks of fog enveloped the channel. It is difficult to realise that, where there is now a continuous row of handsome villas all along the shore for four miles, sixty years ago there was nothing but a silent strand, laved by the clear waters of the Clyde, and the rough cart track at the foot of the heath clad braes, all over-grown with whins, brambles, and wild briar roses. One small cottage there was, situated in a beautiful alcove of rocks and rowan trees, to which the builder, whose name was Coll Turner, member of a family long resident at the farm of Duchlage, gave the appropriate designation of Craigrownie. This expressive name has since been localised by being adopted in the nomenclature of the district and *quoad sacra* parish.*

One old cottage was then standing below the rocky face of the cliff above Cove pier, a humble, thatched building, long occupied as a public house by the father of the late Mr. John M'Lean, Clachan of Rosneath, who also acted as ferryman to the opposite village of Blairmore. Going past this, and crossing the Dhualt burn, which falls into the small bay of the same name, there was no dwelling on the shore road, until Peatoun mansion house, and one or two cottages beyond, were reached ; an unbroken stretch extending from Letter farm, until you came to Coulport ferry. On the high road there were the various farms of Meikle and Little Aiden, near Kilcreggan,

---

* Craigrownie.—The author has been favoured with a letter from Mr. Archibald M'Neilage, Clerk to Rosneath School Board, a native of the parish, from which the following is given :--" The only house between Mrs. M'Farlane's and the head of Cove pier, sixty years ago, was Craigrownie cottage, a slated house, built by the late Coll Turner, who afterwards went to reside in Greenock. Mr. Turner built this cottage about 65 years ago ; it still stands among the trees immediately below Baron Cliff villa. To it the name of Craigrownie was originally given. Mr. John M'Lean, postmaster, Rosneath, says he was a little boy running about when it was building, and interesting himself in the various parts of the work as they proceeded."

North and South Ailey, Knockderry, and Barbour, besides some others now no longer existing. About this time the Duke of Argyll caused a carriage drive to be made along the shore, taking the place of the old cart track, rudely constructed, and dangerous from large portions of the rock protruding above the ground. Here he would drive in his stately old barouche with its mighty C. springs, and panels emblazoned with the Argyll coat of arms, which, for many years had done duty, both in this country and on the Continent.

Proceeding along the shore road past Cove pier, a fine prospect is opened up of Loch Long, with the dark swelling forms of the mountains rising from its deep waters, prominent amongst them being Cruachash, above the retired village of Ardentinny. Presently more of the purple waters of Loch Long come into view, with the Holy Loch, and mountains beyond. Fields and plantations stretch down to the shore, and ascending to the moor above with its slopes of fragrant heather, the harsh cry of the grouse or black cock may be heard from the moss hag, or he may be seen skimming away in his rapid flight.

As you approach Barbour farm, the new cemetery, made for those families resident in the peninsula who have no right of burial at Rosneath churchyard, is seen occupying a fine site, and already there are a good many graves. It is a sequestered and peaceful spot, where nature has put forth her gentle hand to soothe the sorrows of those who mourn departed friends, whose place on earth now knows them no more. Looking back, the bold headland of Knockderry stands out above the sea, an interesting spot, from its being the site of an ancient Danish or Norwegian fort, hardly any trace of which now remains. As Barbour is neared, the view grows wilder, while Loch Long assumes the appearance of an inland lake, seemingly surrounded with hills ; those in the foreground bearing signs of cultivation, while the mountains on the opposite shores of the loch rise steep and rugged, clothed with bracken and birchwood near the water's edge. Ascending the hill, after crossing the Camloch burn, there is a broad expanse of moor, the distant swelling outlines of the ridges beyond Loch Goil now coming into view, and the serrated

peaks of the Argyll Bowling Green forming an appropriate background.

The highest point in the peninsula is easily climbed from either
Peatoun or Mambeg on the Gareloch side.   Its Gaelic name is
Knoch-na-Airidhe, which, in English, may be rendered " Hill of
Shieling," and is now corrupted into Tomnahara.   From this
moderate elevation of 717 feet, it is surprising what a varied expanse
of mountain, moor, craggy fell, and glittering sea can be gained, and,
on a clear day, the noble crest of Ben Cruachan may be seen.   Rising
above Garelochhead are the swelling outlines of the grassy mountains
at the head of Glenfruin, from whence the eye ranges on to Helensburgh, and to the distant braes above Kilpatrick.   Opposite are the
uplands of Renfrewshire, the busy ports of Greenock, Gourock, and
Port-Glasgow, the Cloch Lighthouse, and the craggy reaches of the
Ayrshire coast, and following on, you gain fine views of the Cumbraes, Bute, Arran, and the nearer mountains of Argyllshire.   To
any one fond of studying the varied atmospheric effects visible from
such a spot, according to the changes of weather, the scene from any
of the higher points on the moor is full of interest.   On a warm
summer afternoon in June, when the sky is of a faint blue colour,
and light fleecy clouds move slowly over its face, delicate changes in
the aspect of the landscape will be seen.   Towards the summit of the
moor, the ridge of fir trees in the middle distance stands clear against
the filmy sky, the gathering mist growing more dense over Loch
Long and its mountains.   While the outline of the peninsula behind
Garelochhead is clear against the background, a thick blue haze
nearly conceals the intervening glens and hollows.   The fine rugged
mountains about the middle of the Argyll Bowling Green, loom
out in solid grandeur, but those beyond Loch Goil seem very faint,
until they blend with the misty haze.   Cruachash, above Ardentinny, looms out by itself in rounded proportions, like a well defined
blue cloud emerging from the horizon, and about to overspread the
sky.   The distant Ben Im, and the Cobbler above Arrochar, can
faintly be traced in the nebulous haze, while a tinge of yellow suffuses the lesser heights over Glenfruin, shading away into purple all

o

the subtle gradations of tint so impossible to depict, even by the
most cunning brush. As the fleecy clouds steal over the hidden
ravines, the most delicate phases of colour are observed, the fields on
the loch side being of a lighter green than the pasture lands above,
and the woods darker in hue where the fir trees predominate. The
heather is of a brown hue, with stretches of green moss and bracken
intervening, streaked with the yellow blossom of the whins. The
sun's rays strike upon the beech or oak trees, scattered here and
there, casting their shadows upon the turf, which is decked with
wild flowers. Grey walls and rocks gleam in the sunlight, and the
villages and houses on the loch are seen clearly amidst their verdant surroundings, the white line of strand fringing the water. In
the still depths of the purple loch the peaceful landscape is reflected,
a light zeyphr ever and anon causing a faint streak of ripple to
appear, with a white-winged gull skimming over the tide.

When the russet hues of Autumn cast their mantle over the scene,
fresh beauties appear. The mellow sunshine bathes the moor with a
deep golden tint, which seems to glow amid the silvery sheen of the
fir trees, and sparkles on the glistening faces of rock beside the
mountain streamlets. The heather is in full bloom, and the green,
mossy sward is seen in patches between the masses of abounding
bracken, which has began to assume its rich brown colour. Many
are the richly variegated tints of the woods which clothe the slopes
of the hills, and the corn fields gleam yellow where the grain has yet
to be gathered. A vapoury haze seems partially to envelope the
higher mountains, and the lesser heights assume soft and rounded
outlines against the blue depths of the intervening valleys. As the
shades of evening steal over the still landscape, all is hushed in
repose, unless the harsh, whirring cry of the grouse falls upon the
ear, or long drawn, quavering, piping of the curlew is echoed on the
sides of the ravine, and when night darkens the scene,

> " The crisping rays, that on the waters lie,
> Depict a paler moon, a fainter sky ;
> While through the inverted alder boughs below,
> The twinkling stars with greener lustre glow."

At all seasons, and at all times of the day, there is to be seen much that will repay the closest inspection. So constantly changing is the sky, and so correspondingly varied is the colour of the Gareloch, that a series of beautiful panoramic effects reward the patient student of nature. Whether it be in summer, when not a cloud rests on the blue ether of the sky, or is embosomed in the calm loch, with all nature quivering in the hot, impalpable haze,—or in winter, with a soft shroud of snow enveloping mountain, field, and garden alike,—the picture is radiant with loveliness. Spring has its own peculiar elements of beauty, the first suffusion of the glow of mingling colour, which afterwards pervades the spot. Autumn's rich mosaic flames over wood and brake, and the deep crimson of the setting sun flushes over sky and strand. At times, the sun's horizontal rays, just before the luminary is sinking behind the Loch Long hills, catch upon the upper ranges of fir trees, investing them with an exquisite pearly grey hue. And, in winter, while all the ground is robed in snow, there is a solemn stillness that awes the feelings of the solitary wayfarer. The loch is chill and leaden in aspect, the fields and moors have all landmarks obliterated beneath the snowy mantle, the trees are powdered with the hoarfrost, their black branches are set off by silvery rime. If it is morning, as the early sun begins to suffuse the sky, then the graceful forms of the trees are traced out in fleecy indistinctness. As the sun rays grow warmer, a yellow tinge spreads on the woods above, but, lower down, all is coldly grey. Nearer to the beholder the pale frosted boughs are traced against the horizon in a delicate fret work, and showers of snow, like ocean spray, fall from the evergreens, as the startled wood pigeon rushes from his perch. By the moonlight, the scene is only deepened and intensified, the snow is more ethereal, the trees more ghostly, and the hills more unreal in their dusky outlines. Each far off peak gleams faintly against the wan firmament in the cold glitter of the stars.

Atmosphere and cloud effects of singular and varied beauty are to be observed at various seasons, some of the finest of them in the early hours of a summer morn, or about midnight when the days are long-

est. It would need all the word painting of a Ruskin to do justice
to such a scene. Sometimes great masses of billowy clouds are
heaped above the Loch Long mountains, and, as the early sun rays
play upon the shifting surface, subtle gradations of colour can be
marked. A bright patch of clear sky is opened up from time to
time, and it is difficult to distinguish the rugged outlines of the hills,
from the clearly developed lines of clouds traced against the horizon.
There is, in summer, sometimes a lovely effect of deep purple in
the colours of the cloud banks resting on the mountain ridges, and
innumerable islands seem to float in a golden sea. This cloud bank
becomes all the denser and darker as the clear border of sky is more
and more reflected in the still waters of the loch. Great mountain
precipices and vast crags seem toppling over in the moving cloudland
overhanging the waters. The pale green of the young bracken is in
strong contrast with the purple clouds, and light streamers of mist
curl themselves round the fir plantations.

At the height of summer, when there is hardly any night, and the
faint flush of a new day is fast tinging the sky, a still and impressive
scene of beauty is presented to the eye. A dark mass of clouds rests
on the highest ridges, while away at either end of the horizon light
is reflected in the placid loch. The foreground is of an indefinite
hue, the trees and moorlands ghostly and ill defined, the murky
atmosphere lending faint colour to the picture. The great and
dominant feature is the dark shroud overhanging the distant hills,
intensely gloomy, and seemingly charged with presaging woe. An
oppressive languor pervades the atmosphere, even at that hour of
early dawn, and all nature is hushed in preternatural repose.

Moonlight on the Gareloch has always a beautiful effect, owing to
the rugged outlines of the mountains against the canopy of heaven,
and the smooth unbroken surface of the water, which reflects the
stars in their lustrous sheen. To view the scene, in all its weird and
ghostly loveliness, a visit to the summit of the Gallowhill, the high
ground at the end of the Rosneath peninsula, will well repay the
walk. It is a lonely spot, but it commands the view far down the
Clyde, as well as the Gareloch, and the hills near Helensburgh and

Cardross. Immediately above the Loch Long mountains on such an evening the horizon is of pale green, against which the purple peaks are sharply outlined, and the trees on the crest of the nearer slopes are softly pencilled against the luminous sky, as if they were but shadows. The Arran mountains seem like dark clouds, but the contour of the hills on the Argyllshire coast is more clearly defined. The broad Frith glows in the moon's lustre, and the lights of the various towns twinkle along the dark line of strand. Ardmore Point, in deep shadow, reaches far into the sea, and faintly visible in the distance is the great mass of Dunbarton rock. In the near foreground are the woods round Rosneath Castle, and the lamps of Row are reflected in the calm waters of the bay. Hushed is the night breeze on the solitary moor, but the cry of an owl arises from the old fir trees, and sounds strangely in keeping with the solemn stillness around. Overhead, the blue, glittering stars scintillate with gem like effulgence in the opaque, purple firmament. An hour and a spot calling for reverent contemplation, as the musing spectator views the pale picture, so delicately lambent in the wan rays of the moon.

Standing on the hill on such a peaceful evening, watching the gleaming silver ripple on the broad estuary, and the long avenues of lights shining in stillness on the opposite strand,—a belt of fire beside the dimly purple water,—the mind of the lonely stranger must respond to the impressive associations of the spot. Yon steep rising town, with many a tall chimney pointing to the star spangled sky, is the place where the great but modest man of genius, who first guaged the gigantic power of steam, saw the light of day. He solved the problem of how to blend the two opposing forces of water and fire, and summoned into being the terrific energy of steam. The genius of Watt so regulated the mighty throbbings of the imprisoned giant within that iron cylinder, that the transmitted energy sufficed to drive the ponderous vessel through the mountainous billows of the Atlantic. At the summons of the magician's wand, the spirits which lay dormant in those antagonistic elements, brought together in auspicious union, have evolved a power far transcending the fabled Cyclops of the Grecian poet. Seated at his workshop, just

across the gently heaving water, the brain of the unknown mechani-
cian, solved the problem which was to add a new born motor to nature, and created novel possibilities in the scientific world whose
might would be felt throughout the succeeding ages.   Contrasting
the puny results of the dynamics of the past century with the marvellous achievements of the modern steam engine, it seems almost as
though one looked upon the feeble rushlight in some lonely midnight
cell, and next morning beheld all the rising effulgence of the rolling
sun in its glory, lighting up the firmament with approaching meridian
splendour.

Turning round in the moon's rays, the lights of Helensburgh shine
out against the opposite side of the estuary, and here comes up in
imagination the humble wheelwright, whose prophetic insight into
the future of steam navigation enabled him to conjure up a vision of
great transatlantic steamers ploughing their way through the green
and billowy ocean.   Henry Bell lived for many years in Helensburgh,
a man of fine inventive skill, and destined to adorn a niche in the
temple of science.   He patiently matured his schemes for using the
infant force of the steam engine, and impelling his vessel against the
solid impact of the ocean waves.   Nor did he seek to enlist the
favouring gale in guiding his ship over the waste of waters, the
opposing blast had to yield to the overmastering strength of steam,
and the mariner could face even the raging tempest with the assured
hope of success.   The crested Atlantic rollers would no longer daunt
the aspiring traveller searching for the far-off parts of the world, and
the anxious merchant could send away his argosies, freighted with
the rarest products of the loom, to swell the stream of commerce on
the banks of the swift rolling Ganges, or amidst the palm girt islands
of the Malay Archipelago.

Where the heavy timbered, painted, galleys, with the rude warriors
from the North Sea, slowly and cumbrously made their way up the
waters of the Clyde, their carved prows and long bending oars toiling
through the waves, now may be seen the mighty iron-clads, bearing
aloft those guns whose discharge shakes the adamantine rocks, with
self-impelled, resistless way, moving majestically to their appointed

place. Their shadows fall athwart the watery channel, and they lie each one at anchor, destined, perchance, to destroy the fell usurper's power, or bear the "meteor flag" of Britain to victory in a far-off conflict, whose echoes shall one day reverberate amidst the "cloud cap'd towers" and sun-girt palaces of some hostile fortress. All these now sleeping shores, when dawn begins to steal over the mountain brow, will awake to the busy hum of toiling masses, and the whirring wheels of commerce, and how vast is the debt of gratitude which they owe to that illustrious man, whose discovery was fraught with incalculable blessings to the human race.

Down these waters had sailed, from yonder nearly isolated lofty rocky fortress, whose rounded outline is faintly indicated amidst the misty exhalations from the Vale of Leven, some of Scotland's monarchs on their voyages in quest of glory and success in love and war. Amongst them yon hapless queen, around whom gathers an environment of crime and woe, while warriors and statesmen, famed in the annals of their country, swelled the ranks of her attendants. Here, too, was wont to sail in his galleys of pleasure, reclined amidst the companions he loved, and who stood by him on many a field of gore, the warrior king of Scotland, who sought retirement in his declining years by the verdant banks of the smoothly flowing Leven. And up the winding Frith, in their humble sailing craft, there came from the shore of Ireland and the Western Isles, those pious and holy men bringing as their blessed evangel, "Peace on earth and goodwill towards men." A rich blending of ancient story, woven into one long drawn chain of mellowing reminiscences, over which the mind and fancy might well linger in pensive reverie.

> " 'Tis a picture in memory distinctly defined
> With the strong and imperishing colours of mind."

The never-dying interest which attaches to all that proceeded from the magic pen of Sir Walter Scott renders the latter portion of the *Heart of Midlothian* of special import to those who seek to connect the romantic incidents of each stirring narrative with the actual surroundings and history of the scene in which they were laid. In

almost all the tales of the "Wizard of the North," his descriptions of
scenery, and peculiarities of the people and territory of which he is
treating, prove that he himself had gone over the ground with the
view of giving graphic touches worthy of the master. But there is
good ground for believing that in the pathetic tale of the hapless
Effie Deans, and her noble sister Jeanie, Sir Walter trusted to
memory, or to information derived at second hand. To begin with,
in the story, Rosneath is throughout spoken of as an island, and
many of his readers rise from the perusal of the fortunes of the
Deans family, fired with the wish to inspect the beautiful isle, where
so much that is of thrilling interest is concentrated. Not that Sir
Walter is singular in the idea he had conceived of the insular form
of Rosneath, for in old title deeds of the local families it is sometimes
mentioned as the "isle," and, in former days, colloquially it was
spoken of as "the island."

Most readers are familiar with the beautiful story of the *Heart of
Midlothian*, which largely turns upon the powerful influence with the
King and Queen wielded by the great chief of the Clan Campbell,
the Duke of Argyll. Following the fortunes of the simple and
guileless Jeanie Deans who had, after surmounting many difficulties
reached London on foot, she is found in the library of his Grace, who
arranges that she should have a private interview with Queen
Caroline, in order that she may plead for a pardon for her sister
Effie. Sir Walter thus describes the character of John Duke of
Argyll and Greenwich :—"Soaring above the petty distinctions of
faction, his voice was raised, whether in office or opposition, for those
measures which were at once just and lenient. His high military
talents enabled him, during the memorable year 1715, to render such
services to the House of Hanover as, perhaps, were too great to be
either acknowledged or repaid. He had employed, too, his utmost
influence in softening the consequences of that insurrection to the
unfortunate gentlemen whom a mistaken sense of loyalty had engaged
in the affair, and was rewarded by the esteem and affection of his
country in an uncommon degree." This powerful nobleman's
influence with the Queen secured Effie's pardon, and the thread of

the story is soon after transferred to Scotland, and more particularly
to Rosneath. Having elicited from Jeanie in her open artless way
the information as to her own life and her own simple love passages,
in which the good Reuben Butler bore a part, the Duke sought to do
his best to bring to fruition the hopes which the lovers had ventured
to entertain in their own unsophisticated way. He also wished to
discharge the debt of gratitude under which his ancestor lay to the
grandfather of Reuben, who had been the means of saving his life on
one occasion in the Civil War, and he resolved to present Jeanie's
lover with the living of the Parish of Knocktarlitie, which was in his
Grace's gift. Jeanie's father, " Douce Davie Deans," had, unknown
to the former, been placed by the Duke, in charge of a new farm in
the Rosneath district of his ample possessions. It was therefore
arranged that she should travel to Scotland, under the charge of a
discreet attendant of the Argyll family, along with a somewhat
timorous and extremely voluble English dairy woman, by name Mrs.
Dolly Dutton. Readers of the novel know well how the party proceeded on their journey and finally reached their destination at the
Duke's residence in Dunbartonshire.

The following is the description which Sir Walter gives of the
district in which the lot of the Deans family was now cast. " The
islands in the Firth of Clyde," he writes, " are of exquisite, yet
varied beauty. Rosneath, a smaller isle, lies much higher up the
firth, and towards its western shore, near the opening of the lake
called the Gare-Loch, and not far from Loch Long and Loch Seant,
or the Holy Loch, which wind from the mountains of the Western
Highlands to join the estuary of the Clyde. In these isles the severe
frost winds which tyrannise over the vegetable creation during a
Scottish spring, are comparatively little felt. Accordingly the
weeping-willow, the weeping-birch, and other trees of early and
pendulous shoots, flourish in these favoured recesses in a degree unknown in our eastern districts. The picturesque beauty of the island
of Rosneath, in particular, had such recommendations, that the Earls
and Dukes of Argyll, from an early period made it their occasional
residence, and had their temporary accommodation in a fishing or

hunting lodge, which succeeding improvements have since transformed
into a palace."

The surprise of Jeanie was great when upon reaching the landing
place—which is described as "shrouded by some old low, but wide-
spreading, oak trees, intermixed with hazel bushes "—she was clasped
in the arms of her father.   Another personage of far greater importance, in his own estimation, was the worshipful gentleman, the
Laird of Knocktarlitie, Captain of Knockdunder, Bailie of the Lordship to the Duke of Argyll.   This wrathful and imperious Celt, who
reigned supreme in those regions, had made all the necessary arrange-
ments for the induction of good Reuben Butler to the vacant charge
of Knocktarlitie.   "The whole party being embarked, therefore, in a
large boat which the Captain called his coach and six, and attended
by a smaller one termed his gig, the gallant Duncan steered straight
upon the little tower of the old-fashioned church of Knocktarlitie,
and the exertions of six stout rowers sped them rapidly on their
voyage.   As they neared the land the hills appeared to recede from
them, and a little valley, formed by the descent of a small river from
the mountains, evolved itself, as it were, upon their approach.   The
style of the country on each side was simply pastoral, and resembled
in appearance and character the description of a forgotten Scottish
poet.   They landed in this Highland Arcadia, at the mouth of the
small stream which watered the delightful and peaceable valley.
Inhabitants of several descriptions came to pay their respects to the
Captain of Knockdunder, a homage which he was very peremptory
in exacting.   Besides these there were a wilder set of parishioners,
mountaineers from the upper glen and adjacent hill, who spoke
Gaelic, went about armed, and wore the Highland dress.   They first
visited the Manse, as the parsonage is termed in Scotland.   It was
old, but in good repair, and stood snugly embosomed in a grove of
sycamore, with a well stocked garden in front, bounded by the small
river, which was partly visible from the windows, partly concealed by
the bushes, trees, and boundary hedge."

When we try to trace the resemblance between this ideal glen
in which the church and manse of Knocktarlitie stood, and the same

structures as they are at the Clachan of Rosneath, it is evident that the great novelist had never visited the latter scene. Rosneath Church and manse cannot be said to be in a pastoral country, there are only two small fields between them and the sea shore, and the pretty, wimpling Clachan burn, which issues from the wooded glen running up from the cluster of old cottages until it reaches the loch on the moor from whence it takes its rise, can scarcely be dignified by the appellation of a "small river from the mountains." Tomna-hara, the extreme summit of the Rosneath peninsula, is but 714 feet above the loch, and the whole ridge of high lands can scarcely be said to rise above an ordinary hill in height. The Manse is prettily situated, partially sheltered at the back by the rising ground and a strip of wood, now sadly bared of its once luxuriant growth of trees. While there are one or two beautiful glens in the peninsula, rich in ferns, full of lovely shady nooks, resounding in the long summer days with the notes of the blackbird, mavis, and cushat dove, there is no "upper glen" in which "mountaineers" of stern aspect and warlike dress once resided. The whole peninsula consists mainly of one continuous ridge, and with the exception of the level grounds in the vicinity of Rosneath Castle and policies, and the fields of the Clachan Farm, the cultivated portions are the slopes on either side rising from the Gareloch and Loch Long.

Going on to describe the farm of Auchengower, which was hence-forth to be occupied by the staunch Cameronian, Deans, in lieu of his former holding at St. Leonard's Crags, Sir Walter writes as follows: "The situation was considerably higher than that of the Manse, and fronted to the west. The windows commanded an enchanting view of the little vale over which the mansion seemed to preside, the windings of the stream and the firth, with its associated lakes and romantic islands. The hills of Dunbartonshire, once possessed by the fierce clan of Macfarlanes, formed a crescent behind the valley, and far to the right were seen the dusky and more gigantic mountains of Argyllshire, with a sea-ward view of the shattered and thunder-splitten peaks of Arran." There is no site on the Gareloch side of Rosneath Peninsula from which such a view could have been obtained,

and if it were supposed to apply to the Kilcreggan side, then the
spectator is facing the west, and has the Argyllshire mountains
opposite him, while the rugged peaks of Dunbartonshire are at his
back, concealed from observation by the uplands of Rosneath.

We then come to the strange secret interview which Jeanie had
with her unfortunate and wayward sister, Effie—now the lawful wife
of the reckless and abandoned Sir George Staunton, formerly known
as Robertson, who had so long set the authorities of the law at defiance. It was a lovely night, the pale moon shedding soft radiance,
and "flinging a trembling reflection on the broad and glittering
waves. The fine scene of headlands, and capes, and bays, around
them, with the broad blue chain of mountains, were dimly visible
in the moonlight; while every dash of the oars made the waters
glance and sparkle with the brilliant phenomenon called the sea-fire."
Jeanie springs lightly ashore at the "usual landing place, at a quarter
of a mile's distance from the Lodge, and although the tide did not
admit of the large boat coming quite close to the jetty of loose stones
which served as a pier." The sisters have an affectionate but very
hurried interview, interrupted by the sudden apparition of Effie's
wild husband, now handsomely dressed, and with the assured mien
of a person of rank. Ere long Effie "tore herself from her sister's
arms, rejoined her husband—they plunged into the copsewood, and
she saw them no more." Presently she heard the distant sound of
oars, "and a skiff was seen on the Firth, pulling swiftly towards the
small smuggling sloop which lay in the offing."

Years roll on after the happy union of Jeanie and Reuben Butler,
which was graced by the puissant presence of the Captain of Knockdunder, who was full of wrath that David Deans had rigidly stood
out against the "iniquities of pipes, fiddles, and promiscuous
dancing." The captain had many disputations with old David,
whose notions of politics and church government were stigmatised
by the Duke's irascible and bibulous henchman as "nonsense, whilk
it is not worth while of a shentleman to knock out of an auld silly
head, either by force of reason or otherwise." The patron and friend
of the Butlers, John, Duke of Argyll and Greenwich, died in the

year 1743, universally lamented, and admitted to be a true friend of his country, and one who would never stoop to any act of undue subserviency to court royal favour. In time the stern, worthy, David Deans also was gathered to his fathers, expiring in the arms of his affectionate daughter, after earnest prayers for the welfare of the noble house of Argyll, and Duncan of Knockdunder, when his own immediate family circle had been remembered at the Throne of Grace.

Then came the last eventful visit of poor Effie, now Lady Staunton, who came to see her sister, and for a short time partook of the hospitalities of the manse. During this sojourn the remarkable interview took place, in a wild glen a few miles from Reuben Butler's home, between Effie and her unhappy boy, who, after various strange adventures, had been sold to a lawless ruffian, by name Donacha Dhu, a sort of ferocious freebooter, well known to the Captain of Knockdunder. The boy was little removed from a mere savage, and the place where he dwelt was known as "The Whistler's Glen," a terrible and wild scene of tangled desolation. The place where this young savage found his lair is thus described :—"A single shoot carried a considerable stream over the face of a black rock, which contrasted strongly in colour with the white foam of the cascade, and at the depth of about twenty feet another rock interrupted the view of the bottom of the fall. The water, wheeling out far beneath, swept round the crag, which thus bounded their view, and tumbled down the rocky glen in a torrent of foam." At length Lady Staunton and Jeanie's two boys "came full in front of the fall, which here had a most tremendous aspect, boiling, roaring, and thundering with unceasing din into a black cauldron, a hundred feet at least below them, which resembled the crater of a volcano."

There is no fall of water or defile in Rosneath district to which this description would be at all applicable, but on the Row side of the Gareloch, not far from the old mansion of Ardenconnel, there is what is known as the "Whistler's Glen." In this glen there are one or two considerable falls of water, and in some parts its tangled gorge might be said to resemble the aspect of the defile where Effie

encountered her boy.   Then there comes the last eventful scene in
the tale, when Effie's husband and Reuben Butler are being rowed to
Rosneath in an open boat, and are in danger of being caught by a
gathering storm.   "They approached the little cove, which, concealed behind crags, and defended on every point by shallows and
sunken rocks, could scarce be discovered or approached except by
those intimate with the navigation."   Soon after the Captain of
Knockdunder and his followers, who had been scouring the close,
entangled wood and little glen near Caird's Cove in their search for
Donacha and the smugglers, heard a shot in the vicinity of the spot
where Staunton and Reuben Butler effected their landing.   In the
skirmish which ensued, poor Effie's dissolute husband received his
death-wound, and the novel is brought to a close with the account of
Effie's return for a season to the vortex of London society, in which
she had shone for a brief period, and her eventual retirement to the
seclusion of a convent on the Continent, where she died.

   Some of the natives of Rosneath who are proud of the great
" Wizard of the North " selecting their territory for the closing scenes
of his fine romance, are inclined to place " Caird's Cove " below
some steep rocks not far from the pier at Cove on Loch Long.   The
commanding rock known as Knockderry, further along the loch side,
has been named by others as the site of the dwelling occupied by
the redoubtable Captain of Knockdunder.   Another site has been
assigned to it on the grassy plateau opposite the range of buildings
near Rosneath Castle, known as the Parkhead, and an old house
which was pulled down over forty years ago, may have once sheltered
the distinguished representative of the might and privileges of Mac
Chaillan Mor.

CHAPTER III.

Rosneath Estates; Old Families; Agriculture; Folk Lore;
Eminent Men.

ROSNEATH peninsula, or the "Island of Rosneath," as it used to be
styled in some of the old title deeds, from its beautiful situation, and
salubrious climate, possesses advantages which enhance the value of
the properties comprised within its bounds. The air is pure and
healthy, and the refreshing rainfall encourages the profusion of ferns,
mosses, and the perennial verdure so grateful to the eye. It is not
easy to trace back the various owners of the lands, which seem frequently to have changed hands. They were possessed in 1264 by
Alexander Dunon, who became indebted to the King, and his
property was burdened until he could deliver over 600 cows at one
time. Afterwards they became the property of the Drummonds,
ancestors of the noble house of Perth, who agreed to assign over to
Alexander de Menteith the whole lands of Rosneath as an "assyth-
ment" for the murder of his brothers. Part of the peninsula at one
time was in the possession of the ancient Scottish family, the Earls
of Lennox, who owned so much of the territory on the opposite
shores of the Gareloch. But about the year 1425, the head of that
family, and various of his near relations, were put to death at
Stirling. And, in 1489, the Earl of Lennox, having been engaged
in treasonable undertakings, his lands were confiscated, although, as
appears from the records of the Scottish Parliament, he was pardoned
for the offence. Still the forfeiture of his lands was not withdrawn,
for, in 1489, the property of Rosneath was awarded to Colin, first
Earl of Argyll. Thus the greatest part of the southern half of the

peninsula was conveyed to the Argyll family, whose genius has so
strongly·impressed itself upon the history of their country and clan.
There were several other properties in Rosneath, such as those of
Campbell of Peatoun, Campbell of Rachean, Campbell of Mamore,
Campbell of Carrick, Cumming of Barremman, some of which only
came into possession of the Argylls well in to the eighteenth century.

Beginning at the upper end of the peninsula, near Gareloch-head,
the estate of Fernicarry, known in early days as Feorling breck, or
Fernicarr, was, in 1545, held by the Colquhouns of Luss, as were
also the adjoining lands of Mamore and Mambeg. They passed to
the family of Campbell of Ardkinlass, who, at that time, were considerable proprietors in "the island." Mamore afterwards became
the territorial designation of John Campbell of Mamore, second son
of Archibald, ninth Earl of Argyll, who succeeded to the Dukedom
in 1762. The estates of Meikle and Little Rachean, with the lands
of Altermonyth, or as it came to be known, Peatoun, were given by
King Robert I. to Duncan, son of Mathew of the Lecky family.
This grant included that of the office of hereditary sergeant of Dunbartonshire, and was long enjoyed by the family of Lecky or Leckie.
The Rachean estate was subsequently acquired by Robert, the
younger son of Campbell of Ardkinlass, and afterwards by John
Campbell of Mamore. Peatoun, a beautifully situated property on
the shores of Loch Long, was purchased by John Campbell, son of
the proprietor of Rachean, from Campbell of Skipness. He was one
of the Commissioners of Supply in 1715, and died without lawful
issue, but his illegitimate daughter, Margaret, married in 1721 John
Smith, a son of his wife by a former marriage. This man was concerned in the notorious Peatoun murder, for John Smith was
convicted of killing both his wife, and his own sister, and was hanged
in Dunbarton for the crime in 1727. The Peatoun estate is now
owned by Lorne Campbell, who chiefly resides in Canada, it having
come into this branch of the family in virtue of the disposition, in
1810, by Donald Campbell of Peitoun, or Peatoun, in favour of the
heirs of the Rev. William Campbell, minister of Kilchrenan in
Argyllshire. The Peatoun family are the representatives of the

Campbells of Rachean, and, according to the genealogical tree of Ardkinlass, and to the belief of the last baronet of the family, Peatoun might establish his claim to the title, and also head of that ancient and powerful branch of the house of Argyll. Peatoun was, for a short time in the sixteenth century, in the possession of Campbell of Ardentinny; the name Altermonyth, or Alt-na-mona, signifies "stream of the moss."

Adjoining Peatoun is the small property of Douchass, or as it is now called, Duchlage, which belonged to Stewart of Baldarran in 1465, but, in the middle of next century, it was purchased by Campbell of Carrick, from whose possession it passed into that of the Argyll family. Still keeping to the Loch Long side we come to the lands of Knock Barbour, granted to the church of Dunbarton by the widowed Countess Isabel of Lennox; at the Reformation it was acquired by the Cunninghams of Drumquhassil, and then by the Ardkinlass family. Knockderrie belonged in the sixteenth century to a Mackinnie, extending in those days to five lib. land. On the rocky headland once stood what was said to be a Danish, or more probably a Norwegian fort, erected at the time,

> " When Norse and Danish gallies plied
> Their oars within the Firth of Clyde,
> Then floated Haco's banner trim,
> Above Norwegian warriors grim,
> Threatening both continent and isle."

The contiguous farms of Blairnachtra, Cursnoch, Ailey, Aiden, Portkill, and Kilcreggan, formed part of the possessions of the Campbells of Ardkinlass, and from them went partly to their cadet the Captain of Carrick, and partly to the Earl of Argyll. Portkill at one time attained to the importance of being a burgh of barony.

Returning to the Gareloch side of the peninsula, we come to the compact property of Barremman. This estate at one time was owned by Campbell of Ardentinny, and, in 1871, was sold by its then proprietor, the late Robert Crawford Cumming, to Mr. Robert Thom, of the Isle of Canna. It was acquired by Walter Cumming, styled "indweller in the Clachan of Rosneath," of date 13th March, 1706, from

Daniel Campbell, Collector of Newport, in return for a "certaine soume of money, as the full and adequate pryce of the lands aforesaid." These comprised "all and haill the lands of Clandearg (Clynder) and Boreman, extending to a seven merk land of old extent, with the yards, houses, orchards, parts, pendicles, and universell pertinents of the same lying in the Isle and Baronie of Rosneath, and Sheriffdom of Dumbrittaine." Proceeding along to what is known as the Kirkton, or Clachan, of Rosneath, close to the old church there, is the family mansion house, which was added to by the Honourable John Campbell, of Mamore, when he acquired the estate, with the much-admired famous yew tree avenue with its sheltered walk of sombre shade. In the 16th century these lands were owned by another family of Campbells, and by a branch of the Macfarlanes in the following century. Beyond this, again, is Campsail, which for generations was the property of the Campbells of Carrick, who built here an old mansion, traces of which still remain near the celebrated silver firs, the great botanical glory of Rosneath. On the shores of the lovely Bay of Campsail, one of the most admired in all the beautiful Frith of Clyde, was heard, in 1662, a most remarkable echo, and described by Sir Robert Murray in the transactions of the Royal Society. He got a trumpeter to sound a tune of eight semi-briefs, and then to stop, as the trumpet ceased, the whole notes were repeated, completely, in a rather lower tone; when these stopped, another echo took up the cadence in a still fainter tone, and finally a third echo resounded the notes once more, with wonderful softness and distinctness. The Campsail property was added to the Argyll estate at the death of John Campbell of Carrick, who married Jean, the daughter of the Duke of Argyll, and fell fighting gloriously at the battle of Fontenoy, in 1745. Beyond this are the policies of Rosneath Castle, the fine building itself forming a conspicuous object on the land-locked bay. The old castle, which was destroyed by fire, was described by George Campbell, a century ago, in an old manuscript, as a "good house most pleasantly situated upon a point called 'The Ross,' where they have good planting and abundance of convenience for good gardens and orchards."

From the statistical account of Scotland of 1792, some details may
be gleaned regarding the parish of Rosneath which were furnished,
at the time, by the Rev. George Drummond. Apparently the parish
could sufficiently supply its inhabitants with provisions, if they were
not obliged to sell their produce for ready money in order to pay
their rents. The population of the peninsula, according to Dr.
Webster, was 521; amongst whom were 7 weavers, 3 smiths, 4
shoemakers, 5 tailors, 96 herring fishermen, 5 seceders, and 14
Cameronians. The annual rent of a cottage and yard was from ten
to twenty shillings. The fish commonly caught were cod, mackerel,
skate, flounders, herring and salmon,—the latter fish sold from 1d.
to 3d. per pound. One salmon fishery, with price of ground attached,
let for £30 a year.

There were no villages in the peninsula, but 98 dwelling-houses,
all detached, scattered over its surface. The average stipend of the
parish, including the glebe, was £110, which, as now, was paid by
the three heritors, the Duke, Campbell of Peatoun, and Cuming of
Barremman. The educational wants of the population were met by
a schoolmaster who enjoyed the modest salary of £8 9s., while, in
addition, other fees and perquisites amounted to £8 7s. In winter
the number of scholars was 38, and £18 was the annual amount
raised for support of the poor. The provisions in use in the parish
were of the usual kind, customary in rural districts of Scotland.
The cost was small, compared with prices of the present day; beef
and veal, 5d., mutton, 4d. to 6d. the pound. A good hen cost 1s., a
chicken, 4d.; butter was 9d. to 1s. the pound; oats sold for 13s. the
boll. The wages of a common labourer, without victuals, were 10d.
to 1s.; joiner, 2s. a day; mason, 2s.; and a tailor 8d. a day, and his
meat. The common fuel used by the cottagers was peat, only a few
families burning coal, which cost 5s. per cart.

Prices had somewhat advanced when the Rev. Robert Story drew
up his account of the parish in May 1839. It appeared there were
then over 3000 acres of uncultivated moorland, of which 500 were
considered capable of profitable culture, 520 were under valuable
wood plantations of various sizes, and 720 were of old and natural

copse wood. At that time the average value of land under the
plough might be about £1 5s. per acre, the charge for grazing a cow
£2 10s., and a sheep 5s., the total rental of the peninsula being estimated somewhat under £3,500.   In 1792 the amount of land rent
was given as £1000.   In 1839 the agricultural labourer received
1s. 10d. and artisans 2s. 6d. per day, farm servants being hired at
£7 and £8 for the half-year, with bed, board and washing.   The
average yearly value of all sorts of produce was then about £5,820,
which was arrived at as follows :—

Value of all kinds of grain, .	£2000
Potatoes and Turnips, . . .	1500
Hay cultivated, ...	400
Flax, ...	20
Land in pasture, ...	1200
Annual thinnings from plantation grounds,	600
Salmon fishing, ...	100

Together, £5820

In former years there were many more farms on the Rosneath
peninsula than now, where there are about fifteen, and the remains
of the steadings may be seen on the high road between Kilcreggan
and Peatoun.   At Barbour farm, near Peatoun, there used to be two
rows of thatched cottages, near the road-side, and about fifty families
altogether lived on the farm, which was let in four parts to different
tenants, and amongst them were twenty cows and four horses.   The
farm of Cursnoch was formerly let by itself, though now part of the
large holding of Knockderry.   Cursnoch was long occupied by Mr.
William Chalmers, the name being often pronounced and also written
as Chambers.   His rent for a number of years from 1800 was £76,
and at that time the tenant paid a portion of the minister's stipend,
road-money, and land cess.   The following receipt by the old
minister, Dr. Drummond, shows how he drew his stipend direct
from the farmers :—

"Roseneath, 22 Feby., 1797.   Received six shillings and three
pence the Vicarage Teind, furth of Cursnoch, for cropt and year
seventeen hundred and ninety-six.

"GEO. DRUMMOND."

The "horse and house duty" for year for Whitsunday 1798 to 1799 was 15s. 4d.   In 1808 the farmer pays 4s. for window-duty, and 12s. 6d. for a draught horse.   In 1811 the duty on a draught horse was 14s.   In 1813 the farmer had to pay 3s. a gallon for his "ail" in Greenock, and a few years later his candles cost him 9d. the pound; ordinary sugar, 9d. the pound, and loaf-sugar 1s. 3d. the pound; while for his tea he had to pay no less than 8s. per pound. In the year 1800 the local smith at the clachan of Rosneath charged Mr. Chalmers 1s. 4d. for a "potato hoe;" a "hoop," 7½d.; for one " horse shoe of my iron," 9d.; for four shoes "made of your iron," 1s. 4d.; "2 removes," 6d.   Coals in the year 1829 were only six shillings the cart, less than half what is now charged.   In 1831 the price of a pound of tea was 6s.; brown soap, 7d. the pound; sugar, 7d.; soda, 4d.   The practice seems to have been for the tailor to come to the farmer's house and make clothes for the family. Accordingly, in July, 1817, Duncan "Chambers" charges "William Chambers" for a "suit to your son, 16s.," and "coat to your self, 8s. 6d."   Teaching, however, is very moderate, for Andrew M'Farlane only charges for "teaching James 3 months 4s. 3d." The family doctor's account is to "John Reid, Surgeon, four visits to family, bleedings and medicines, £2 5s. 8d."   So that it can be seen that the cost of living was, in most respects, considerably dearer to the farmer seventy years ago.

In Irving's *History* there is given the rental of the parish of Rosneath, taken from a copy of the old Valuation Roll, which was subscribed by the Commissioners of Supply in the year 1657, as follows :—

Marquess of Argyll,	...	...	£640	0	0
Captain of Carruk, ...	...	...	340	0	4
Clachane, ...	...	...	83	6	8
Ayllie, ...	...	...	80	0	0
Ardintanie, ...	...	...	143	6	8
Luss fourteen merk land,	...	...	80	0	0
Robert Douglass, ...	...	...	150	0	0
Baillie of Rosneath,...	...	...	180	0	0
	Summed,		£1696	13	0

This may be contrasted with the former rental for the year 1766 :—

Rental Rosneath—Crop 1766—Feu-duties, ...			£2 5 6
Rental of lands in Proprietor's hands, ...	£75 2 8		
Portkill farm, ...			37 14 9
Little Aiden, ...			24 16 11
Meikle Aiden, ...			32 10 8
Knockderry, ...			29 16 3
Kilcraigan, ...			21 14 8
Hill of Campsail, ...			20 0 9
Parks, &c., Campsail, as possessed by Lady Carrick, ...			12 0 0
Ailie, ...			47 14 10
Mamore, Mambeg, and salmon fishing, ...			66 0 0
Feornicarrie, ...			12 11 4
Duchlaze—superiority, ...			2 4 5
Meal Mill—Campsail, poultry and "linnen,"...			0 13 4
Clachan Farm, ...			49 7 2

Together, ...	£359 10 7
Lands in my Lord's hands, ...	75 2 8
Total, ...	£434 13 3

This is from an old rental, and would be in Sterling money. In the *Blue Book of the Heritages of Scotland*, published a quarter of a century ago, the agricultural rental value of Rosneath estate was stated at £5,170. At the present time, including feu-duties, the rental of the estate is over £8000 per annum.

Upwards of a century ago the herring-fishing was a source of much profit and occupation to many who resided on the shores of the Gareloch and Loch Long. The owners of the fishing-boats resided all along the loch side, from Row on to Faslane Bay, Garelochhead, Rahane, Mamore, Crossowen, Clynder, Campsail, and the Mill Bay, thence over to Kilcreggan, Cove, and as far as Coulport on Loch Long, where the Marquis family, notable as fishers and ferrymen, resided for nearly one hundred years. The late Mr. James Campbell of Strouel, himself an experienced fishery man, widely known and greatly esteemed, told the author that he could remember well when over 100 fishing-boats would be in the loch at one time, a good number hailing from ports on the east coast and elsewhere. The

boats were large two-masted ones, half-decked, and they went to all
the lochs on the west coast in the season, three men to each boat.
The herrings were so plentiful, that it was no unusual thing for one
boat to get as many as ten thousand herrings in one night, and the
fish sometimes sold as low as sixpence for a hundred. Quantities of
herrings were shipped by the *Alma* from Garelochhead for Glasgow,
which left at half-past five in the morning, loaded to the water's edge
with fish. The buyers came from Greenock, and often their custom
was to go from boat to boat in the evening, before fishing commenced,
and distribute bottles of whisky to the crews, a bottle to each boat,
on the understanding that they got the night's take at a reasonable
price, which was to be made up amongst the buyers. However,
about 1827, the herring-fishing began to fall off with the advent of
steamers up the loch, and very few boats went out, as the fish ceased
to frequent the lochs in anything like the former quantity. Still,
every few years there are great shoals of herring which come up the
Gareloch to their favourite waters at its head. Salmon, also, were
tolerably abundant, and there were stake-nets at different stations on
the Gareloch and Loch Long, where many fish were got. A very
pleasing feature in former years was the Sabbath morning worship,
which was regularly conducted on board the herring-boats, the strains
of praise and the solemn accents of prayer arising from the simple
fishermen, and were wafted across the placid waters of the loch.

Steamers began regularly to appear in the Gareloch and adjoining
waters before 1830, but the open packet-boat, or wherry, still made
the passage from Rosneath Inn and Kilcreggan old pier to the surrounding ports. The wherry would take a good quantity of farm-
produce—sheep, cattle, horses, and other animals—to Greenock and
Gourock, with probably a considerable number of passengers in
addition, and generally used sailing power in preference to oars,
while in the fogs which occasionally prevailed they had to be steered
by compass. For the conveyance of the Duke of Argyll and his
friends on the occasion of their visits to the district, his Grace's
emblazoned six-oared barge plied between Cairndhu point and the
castle. The barge was signalled from Cairndhu by means of three

fires or smokes if the Duke and Duchess were to be transported across the channel; two smokes for relatives and friends; and one smoke for those in a humbler position in life—flashes of flame regulating the traffic after dark.

Smuggling was quite an occupation in Rosneath in the early part of the century, and many are the stirring reminiscences of some very old natives with reference to this violation of the excise laws, which in those days was considered a venial offence. The formation of the parish rendered it highly suitable for such operations, which were carried on by some of the younger fishermen, who found a ready market for their illicit produce at Dunbarton, Greenock, Port-Glasgow, and other towns. Several of the burns on the Rosneath side, near Strouel and Clynder, were haunts of the smugglers, the one running into Strouel bay in particular. It was the practice for the revenue cutters to keep a sharp look out for smugglers, although they were, as a rule, much more lenient in their operations than the regular Dunbarton excisemen. On one occasion the crew of a revenue cutter landed on the Peatoun shore, and all but took red-handed a number of smugglers engaged at their trade. Soon the news spread, and the natives emerged from their crofts—men, women, and boys—and a goodly array confronted the revenue men as they were triumphantly carrying off the spoil. Thus emboldened, they encountered the revenue officials, who demanded that they should not be molested in the discharge of their duty, but, owing to the force of numbers, were compelled to yield up the booty they had. Shortly after the latter reached the cutter, the exulting array of Rosneath natives were defiantly surveying the offending vessel, when all of a sudden the latter sent two or three cannon shots amongst the astonished crowd of spectators. Fortunately no one was hurt, but they beat a rapid retreat, and kept discreetly in seclusion the next time the cutter made her appearance on a voyage of investigation.

At Rosneath, in former days, marriage ceremonies were attended by somewhat boisterous crowds, and on the intermediate days before the "kirking," the young couple and their jubilant attendants, preceded by a bagpiper, perambulated the parish from house to house, visiting their friends. The nuptial rejoicings were closed by the whole party, after divine service on the Sabbath, adjourning for refreshments to the nearest tavern, and a scene of unseemly mirth and riotous festivity too often ensued. Baptisms were frequently desecrated by the accompanying conviviality, and, after the service in church, the friends and relatives proceeded to the inn, and indulged in copious libations of the national beverage. Even funerals sometimes partook of the character of orgies, and it was considered that becoming honour to the departed necessitated at least four different distributions of spirits. On the farms round the Gareloch, also, some curious customs lingered on till about "sixty years since." One of these was the cutting of the last sheaf of corn—the "maiden," as it was called here and elsewhere in Scotland—and this sheaf, usually adorned with parti-coloured ribbons, was hung up in the farmhouse, and allowed to remain for months, even sometimes for years, the momento of a prosperous harvest.

Miss Macdougal, one of the old natives of the parish, who still resides in the cottage in the Clachan village built by her father, remembers a good many of the old inhabitants and their primitive ways. Her father used to describe the former pre-Reformation church, which stood almost on the site of the existing ruined fabric. It was a handsomely decorated building, of cruciform shape, with a row of images round the pulpit, a finely carved font for holy water, and the staircase leading up to the family pew of the Duke of Argyll. Old Mr. Macdougal was of an hospitable turn of mind, and was fond of entertaining the natives on their holiday occasions, when they assembled for their favourite shinty sports. On New Year's day there was generally a great shinty match played in the "barn" park, when Mr. Lorne Campbell and his men came with a piper, the laird of Barremman and his piper, and Archibald Marquis, of the Ferry-house at Coulport, accompanied by a piper, and the company indulged in various games. After the sports were over, Lorne Campbell, Barremman, and others, came to Macdougal's and got refreshments of whisky and oat-cakes. On the first day of the year

there was always a dinner at the old Clachan house, where the
Campbells of Peatoun lived for many years as tenants of the farm,
and sometimes the attractions at Macdougal's and at the Ferry Inn
kept the company so long that the dinner would suffer.   The shinty
match was the great festival of the year, and hundreds assembled,
old and young, with music and banners, to see the play ; and a dance
at the inn, which was prolonged till dawn of the following day,
finished the proceedings.

   Both Dr. Story and Dr. James Dodds, formerly of Glasgow, now
minister of Corstorphine, and natives of the parish, can recall some
of the primitive ways of the inhabitants.   They remembered the old
" tent," as it was called, used on sacramental occasions, and the
curious box where the watchers remained all night on the look out
for " resurrection men," as they were termed in those days.   On the
Sabbath mornings, fifty years ago, the workers and families from the
farms on the Loch Long side would cross the moor, and descend the
braes above the Clachan, the women stopping to bathe their feet in
the burn before entering the church.   In those days only three
houses on the loch side regularly took in loaf-bread, which was
carried from Helensburgh, and across the ferry from Row, by the
well-known "Gibbie" Macleod.   In some of the farm-labourers
cottages, bread only was known, perhaps, three or four times in the
year, being brought from the Clachan at the half-yearly "preach-
ings," and at the New Year's holiday.   Half an ox side of beef was
salted and laid in at Martinmas, and an occasional joint of pork, with
abundance of salted herrings, constituted the larder of the cottagers.
Porridge was then the main stay of the diet of both children and their
elders ; such a luxury as tea was only known, very sparingly, on
Sunday mornings, and coals were rarely used, peat being the
universal article provided for fires.

   Seventy years ago the farms were, in many cases, but indifferently
cultivated, and only a short time previously there were no dykes or
fences on the ground, and the cattle were herded by children.   One
venerable native of Rosneath, the widow of Archibald Marquis of the
Coulport Ferry, can remember the building of most of the walls on

the Duke's farms. There were then very few sheep in the peninsula, and the farmers twice in the year attended the Dunbarton and Balloch markets, while drovers came to Rosneath from time to time and bought cattle for transport both to the Highlands and low country. The father of Mrs. Marquis put up a small thatched house for the purpose of a school at Letter farm, and in this humble edifice, which had four small windows, and a hole in the roof to serve for a chimney, the schoolmaster, John Chalmers, taught the children. The master came for a fixed period, and generally stayed with one of the farmers, getting his board and very small fees for remuneration. On the Barbour farm there was a similar old school, even humbler in its furnishings, for the boys and the master, Andrew M'Farlane, who had lost an arm, used to sit round the peat-fire, piled up in the middle of the floor, on stormy winter days. The seats were one or two planks placed on lumps of turf, and there was a long form at one end at which the boys wrote, each scholar being expected to bring a contribution every day in the shape of a large peat for the common good. The good old implement of flagellation, known as the " tawse," was in frequent use, for the former school of teachers had implicit confidence in this gentle art of persuasion. Later on there was rather an original character, James Campbell, from the Ardentinny side, who acted as teacher, and he would enjoy his pipe while imparting instruction, and one of his pupils remembered how the master, when finished with his smoke, would pass the pipe to the nearest boy, from whom it circulated through the class. In 1834 there was yet another school, a well-built, small, stone house, close beside the Dhualt burn, on what was formerly Blairnachter farm, erected by the Duke of Argyll and his tenants for the benefit of the children on that side of the peninsula, and frequently used as a place for public worship by the Rev. Robert Story, before the church at Craigrownie was built.*

---

* Kilcreggan school. This school, which was largely endowed by the late Lorne Campbell, the Duke's Chamberlain, serves for the children of this side of the peninsula. Mr. William M'Cracken, the able and efficient teacher for over thirty years, fills other responsible offices in the district.

Clothing in those days was supplied to the farmers and cottagers by the tailor and shoemaker coming with their cloth and leather, and remaining until they had made the needful garments and shoes for the family.   Weavers also would come from Greenock to get the home-spun cloth, to be finished and dyed.   All the lights used in the farm-houses were the old-fashioned cruizie ; and the children, on the bright moonlight nights, would amuse themselves gathering rushes to furnish wicks for the home-made tallow candles.   Letters were but seldom received, the postage from Glasgow, sevenpence half-penny, being prohibitory, and in early days they used to lie for weeks at the old Ferry Inn at Rosneath.   Later on, however, Donald Brodie, the postman, walked from Dunbarton to Row and crossed to Rosneath, leaving at 3 p.m. for Dunbarton again.   This feat was eclipsed, however, by Brodie when he contracted to deliver letters all the way to Garelochhead, walking there and back to Dunbarton six days in the week.

In the days when the Marquis family kept the Coulport Ferry, in the early part of the century, the old ferry-house was in what is now part of the Milnavoullin feu, and it is still used as a dwelling-house. The new house is beside the modern pier put up by the Duke, and has not the same amount of accommodation as the former, which was also an inn, where belated travellers could remain all night when the crossing was dangerous.   There were four different farmers on what is now the Barbour farm, and others of the existing holdings were then subdivided.   At Barbour farm and at Peatoun there were various thatched cottages, and at Rahane a row of red-tiled ones, all of which have long ago been pulled down.   On Ailey farm there were eight families of crofters, where none now are, and there was a regular settlement of crofters on Blairnachter.   At one time, it is said, there was a small hamlet of thatched cottages on the edge of the moor above the Clachan braes, but no trace of these can now be discovered.   At the farm of Mamore there is a substantial house, which was built by the father of Mrs. Bain, who resides at Cove, and she recollects, as a child, the then factor of the Duke coming to her father, who was intending to repair the old farm-house, and telling him that he would supply stones, slates, and windows from the old castle of Rosneath. Robert Campbell of Mamore, the grandfather of Mrs. Bain, knew the far-famed Rob Roy, so dear to all lovers of romance in history, and encountered the hero on Loch Long side once, when the military were in search of him. As the danger seemed imminent, it was agreed that an exchange of clothing should be made, and, shortly afterwards, the soldiers came up, and were greatly enraged at finding they had run down the wrong man, for by this time Rob was well on his way to one of the glens leading to Loch Lomond. One morning after this a fine cow was found on the farm, and not claimed by any of the neighbours, and this was understood to be Rob's mode of showing his gratitude. Her grandfather remembered of an unwelcome visit from the "Athole raiders," as they were known, who searched the country for cattle, but as they had all been driven away to a remote hiding-place under the cliffs beyond Portkill, the invaders were baffled. It was also matter of tradition that a fight once took place between a body of raiders and the natives of the "Island," near a green knoll at the march dyke bounding Knockderry farm, and this spot, probably from the dead buried beneath the turf, came to be known as the "Highlandman's Knowe."

It was no unusual matter, even in this remote part of the county, for attempts at robbery and "hereship" to be made. From the Burgh of Dunbarton Criminal Records we learn that Duncan Glass M'Allum was convicted in August, 1687, of going to Rosneath in company with a party, "that he got his shaire, three young kyne and a stirk, confesses that there were uplifted at the foirsaide time about a hundred kyne and horse, and some sheep; and confessed that he was in Patrick Cummin's house with the rest, when it was robbed, but denyes he midled with anything himself that was therein, and that those who robbed it were the personnes that took away with him the foresaide herschip." Proof being led, it was found that the accused had threatened one of the witnesses, and compelled him to swear that he would not give information, and the unfortunate M'Allum was

sentenced to be hanged on the 26th of August, in the afternoon betwixt the hours of two and four.

The "Peatoun murder" was a dreadful tragedy, perpetrated by
John Smith, who had married the daughter of the laird of Peatoun,
and thereafter assumed the name of Campbell.   The marriage took
place in 1721, and, on 15th December, 1725, his sister's dead body
was found in a pool of water, not far from the mansion house of
Peatoun, near a place she was often in the habit of passing over the
moor.   The body was carried to Mamore, her brother John's house,
and on the day of her funeral he consulted a lawyer about the recovery of a sum of money which was to fall to him in event of her
death without issue.   As yet there was no suspicion of her having
met with her death by foul means.   On 3rd September, 1726, after
John Smith had taken breakfast with his wife, they were seen to go
together towards the Mill of Rahane, but on different sides of the
glen.   She was never seen alive again, and the husband helped in the
search, and, when her dead body was discovered near Mamore, his
residence, he seemed in a distracted state, although he directed the
servants to attend family worship as usual in the evening, shewing
great agitation when he read in the Psalms at worship threatenings
against violent and bloody men.   Some days afterwards, suspicion
was directed against John Smith, or Campbell, and he was apprehended in the churchyard of Rosneath, where he was attending a
funeral.   Certain papers were found at Peatoun gravely incriminat-
ing Smith, and ultimately he confessed his awful crimes, admitting
that he had premeditated both the murders a considerable time before he accomplished them.   His sister he threw into the pool of
water, and on her recovering herself, and crying out, "Lord preserve
me," he deliberately kept her head under water until she died.   The
unfortunate wife was thrown into the pool with such force that she
received some cuts on the head from the rocky side, but thinking
that it would not favour his design of concealing the murder to leave
her in the water, he took the body in his arms, and carried it some
little way off to the place where it was afterwards found.   The murderer was executed at Dunbarton on 20th January, 1727, and made

an edifying profession of penitence on the scaffold, entreating the spectators not to encourage themselves in secret sins, in the hope of their not being discovered, for he had no peace of mind after the murder of his sister. His motive for the double murder was in consequence of a guilty passion which he had formed for one of his wife's bridesmaids, at the time of the marriage, and an oath which he had taken to her to give her 1000 merks if she would agree to marry him in event of the death of his wife within a certain time. John Smith was attended to the place of his execution by several ministers of surrounding parishes, and, after they had suitably exhorted him, all present prayed most fervently for the murderer, and it was believed that the solemn scene had a most powerful effect upon all.

Mention has been made of some of the eminent men, chiefly belonging to the Argyll family, who resided in Rosneath. During the persecuting times of the later Stewart kings, some notable lowland Presbyterians, such as Balfour of Burley, Chalmers of Gadgirth, and others, found their way to the peninsula, as the names and traditional histories of several families indicate. One who must be always held in honour was John Anderson, the well known founder of the Andersonian Institution of Glasgow. This distinguished man was born at Rosneath manse in the year 1726. He was the eldest son of the Rev. James Anderson, the parish minister. While residing in the town of Stirling he received the rudiments of learning, but the more advanced portion of his education at the college of Glasgow, and he was chosen to be professor of oriental languages in that institution while just thirty years of age. In 1760 he was appointed to the chair of natural philosophy, and entered upon its duties with an enthusiasm rarely equalled, for he visited all the workshops of the artificers in town for the purpose of gaining experience in the details of manufactures. He was elegant in his style as a lecturer, with a great command of language, and the skill and success with which his manifold experiments were performed could not be surpassed. Nothing delighted him more than hearing of any of his pupils distinguishing themselves in the world. The only distinct work which

Mr. Anderson published in connection with the science of natural philosophy was the *Institutes of Physics*, a valuable contribution, which appeared in 1786, and went through five editions in the next ten years.

Mr. Anderson's sympathies were on the side of the people at the beginning of the French Revolution, and he had invented a gun, the recoil of which was stopped by the condensation of common air within the body of the carriage. His model of the gun he took to Paris in 1791, and presented it to the National Convention. The Government, seeing the benefit to be gained from the invention, ordered Mr. Anderson's model to be hung up in the public Hall, with the following inscription over it: "The gift of Science to Liberty." He made numerous experiments near Paris with a six-pounder gun, and amongst those who witnessed them was the celebrated Paul Jones, who gave his strong approbation of the gun as likely to be very useful in landing troops from boats, or firing from the decks of vessels. He assisted with his advice the Government in devising measures to evade the military cordon which the Germans had drawn round the frontiers of France, and was present when the unfortunate King, Louis XVI., took the oath to the Constitution in Notre Dame Cathedral.

Mr. Anderson died on 13th January, 1796, in the 70th year of his age, and directed by his will that the whole of his effects should be devoted to the establishment of an educational institution in Glasgow to be called *Anderson's University*. According to the design of the founder there were to be four colleges, for arts, medicine, law, and theology, besides an initiatory school. Each college was to consist of nine professors, the senior professor being the president or dean. The funds, however, being inadequate to carry out Mr. Anderson's design, the college was commenced with only a single course of lectures on natural philosophy and chemistry by Dr. Thomas Garnett, known as an author of scientific and medical works. This course was attended for the first year by nearly a thousand persons of both sexes. In 1798 a professor of mathematics and geography was appointed. In 1799 Dr. Garnett was succeeded by the eminent

Dr. Birkbeck, who, in addition to the branches of instruction taught by his predecessor, introduced a familiar system of philosophical and mechanical information to five hundred operative mechanics, free of expense, thus giving rise to mechanics institutes. The Andersonian institution was placed under the inspection and control of the Lord Provost, and other influential citizens, as ordinary visitors, and under the more immediate superintendence of eighty-one trustees, who were elected by ballot, and held office for life. This admirable institution, which has only within the last two years been incorporated with the Technical College, Glasgow, for nearly a century gave instruction, on very reasonable terms, to thousands of students. There was a staff of professors who taught surgery, institutes of medicine, chemistry, practical chemistry, midwifery, practice of medicine, anatomy, materia medica, pharmacy, medical jurisprudence, mathematics, natural philosophy, botany, logic, geography, modern languages, English literature, drawing, painting, and other branches. The institution possessed a large and handsome building belonging to the Corporation, also an extensive museum, and was a striking example of what can be done by one man of no very great resources for the benefit of his fellow-creatures. The name of the founder has now dropped from the old building in George Street, so dear to the memory of thousands of grateful hearts, who recall their happy hours of generous emulation with those who have long passed away. But the medical branch of this useful institution is perpetuated under the name of "Anderson's Medical School" at Partick, so that succeeding generations of students will yet have cause to cherish the honoured name of John Anderson.

Matthew Stewart, one of the most distinguished of Scotch mathematical scholars, and father of the famous Dugald Stewart, was for some years minister of Rosneath. He was a man of eccentric habits, and was wont to perambulate for hours, in absorbed meditation, in the old yew-tree avenue. The well-known Dr. Alexander Carlyle, the minister of Inveresk, visited the parish on his way to Inveraray in the month of August, 1758. In his journal he relates :—" From Glasgow I went all night to Rosneath, where, in a small house near

Q

the castle, lived my friend, Miss Jean Campbell of Carrick, with her
mother, who was a sister of General John Campbell of Mamore,
afterwards Duke of Argyll, and father of the present Duke. Next
day, after passing Loch Long, I went over Argyll's Bowling Green,
called so on account of the roughness of the road." Another
Carlyle, still more renowned than the imposing and eloquent leader
of the "Moderates" in the Church of Scotland, seems to have visited
Rosneath in August, 1817. In Froude's *Reminiscences* the visit is
thus recorded : "Brown and I did very well on our separate branch
of pilgrimage ; pleasant walk and talk down to the west margin of
the Loch incomparable among lakes or lochs yet known to me ; past
Smollett's pillar ; emerge on the view of Greenock, on Helensburgh,
and across to Rosneath manse, where with a Rev. Mr. Story, not yet
quite inducted, whose life has since been published, and who was an
acquaintance of Brown's, we were warmly welcomed and were
entertained for a couple of days. Story I never saw again, but he
acquainted in Haddington neighbourhood some time after, incident-
ally, a certain bright figure, to whom I am obliged to him at this
moment for speaking favourably of me. Talent plenty, fine vein of
satire in him, something like this. I suppose they had been talk-
ing of Irving, whom both of them knew and liked well. Her, probably, at that time I had still never seen, but she told me long
afterwards. Those old three days at Rosneath are all very vivid to
me, and marked in white. The quiet, blue mountain masses, giant
Cobbler overhanging bright seas, bright skies. Rosneath new
mansion (still unfinished and standing as it did), its grand old oaks,
and a certain hand-fast, middle-aged, practical, and most polite
Mr. Campbell (the Argyll factor then), and his two sisters, excellent
lean old ladies, with their wild Highland accent, wire drawn, but
genuine good manners and good principles, and not least, their
astonishment and shrill interjections at once of love and fear over the
talk they contrived to get out of me one evening, and perhaps
another when we went across to tea ; all this is still pretty to me to
remember. They are all dead, the good souls. Campbell himself,

the Duke told me, died only lately, very old; but they were to my rustic eyes of a superior furnished stratum of society."

Dr. Thomas Chalmers was an intimate friend of Mr. Story's, the latter having been introduced to his charge by that eminent divine. On one occasion, when Dr. Chalmers, accompanied by Edward Irving, then his assistant, visited Rosneath, an entertainment was given in their honour by Miss Helen Campbell at her bower, or sylvan retreat, above the little fall known as "Helen's Linn" in the Clachan glen, and on this occasion Irving astonished the company by dancing with marvellous vigour the Highland fling. The rustic bower is now gone, a retired and sweet spot it was in the shady glen, where, even in hottest summer day, the visitor felt in a "cool grot," the overhanging old oak and beech trees twined round with clinging woodbine, scenting the air, and the mossy rocks glistening with ivy leaves. The gifted Irving was a frequent visitor to the manse, and he tried hard to persuade his friend Mr. Story to join the Catholic apostolic body. "Oh, Story," he wrote in 1832, "thou hast grievously sinned in standing afar off from the work of the Lord, scorning it like a sceptic instead of proving it like a spiritual man." Sometimes on sacramental occasions at Rosneath he used to address the large congregations assembled in the churchyard, speaking from the wooden "tent" which stood near the manse, and astonishing those present by his weird and dramatic oratory. He warmly espoused the claims of Mary Campbell to supernatural gifts and to manifestations of "tongues," and the series of extraordinary scenes and blasphemous utterances of the excited spiritualists which occurred in Regent Square Church, resulted in his deposition from the Church of Scotland. Of those who sought a retired residence on the shores of the Gareloch in later years, the most notable was the amiable and talented Dr. John Macleod Campbell, whose writings have had so deep an influence on the theology of the present day. After his deposition from the Church of Scotland, Dr. Macleod left the Gareloch, but a few years before his death he purchased the pleasant residence at Strouel, to which he gave the Gaelic name of *Achnashie*, "Field of Peace," and there he died in 1872. His

honoured remains rest in the ancient churchyard of Rosneath, near
the beloved friend with whom he was so long associated in the
Master's work.

The geological structure of the peninsula does not require much
notice, nearly the whole strata belonging to the primitive class of
rocks.   The prevailing formation is clay slate, which, in certain
places, passes into chlorite slate, and occasionally into mica slate.
Here and there beds of conglomerate may be met, as at the old sea-
cliff near Rosneath Castle, and in one or two parts of the shore.   On
the high ground above Clynder will be observed good examples of
chloride slate, in the quarries which have been opened up, the
direction being from north-west to south-east.   On the shore of Loch
Long, not far from Knockderry, there appears a large mass of greenstone, lying interposed between the strata.   The greenstone is like a
dyke, from twenty to thirty feet thick, and close to it is more of the
chlorite slate rock.   Another bed of greenstone is found nearly half-
a-mile further south.   The south-western extremity of the parish is
pervaded by conglomerate, and coarse sandstone rock, which occurs
in beds of considerable thickness.   This rock is of similar description
to the great sandstone formation which extends along the Renfrew
and Ayrshire coasts, and embraces the Cumbraes and a portion of the
southern half of Bute.   The line of formation between the sandstone
and primitive rock of the parish runs along the valley stretching
from Campsail Bay to Kilcreggan.   In the slate formation on the
Loch Long shore, as well as in the quartz, iron pyrites is found in
considerable abundance.   It is crystallised in the slate and in the
quartz appears in large irregular masses.   In the colour of the slate
there is much variety, due to the quantity of oxide of iron pervading
the deposits.

In Rosneath are to be found many birds which are more or less
familiar in the west of Scotland.   The extensive woods in the vicinity
of the castle, and elsewhere throughout the peninsula, offer good
cover for the feathered songsters, and the range of moorland insures
an ample stock of game birds for the purpose of sporting.   Both
grouse and black game are tolerably plentiful, and these birds may

be seen in considerable numbers in the early morning, when the fields of corn in the vicinity of the moors are about ready for the reaper, enjoying their repast off the mellow grain.   In autumn and winter, many woodcocks are found, having arrived in numbers from other countries in their annual migrations.   In recent years, also, there have been several instances of woodcocks nesting near the "Green Isle" point, amongst the rhododendron bushes and in the bracken. Snipe will be found to a fair extent in the marshy ground in the moors, and also about the drains in the higher fields.   Pheasants and partridges are tolerably plentiful, the former bird frequenting the Campsail and Gallowhill woods, and the familiar chirp of the partridge is heard amidst the ample fields of turnips.   Plovers and curlews are also common, their pleasant cheery notes salute the visitor wandering along the unfrequented moor, or over the fields near the Home Farm.

The birds of prey are not so numerous of late years, as they are looked upon with dire aversion by the keepers, in their zeal for game preservation.   Sparrow-hawks may be seen sometimes flying around the farm-yards, ready to pounce upon any unwary chicken, and sometimes they will even dart upon a covey of partridges, and carry off their prey.   This hawk breeds in the high fir-trees in the castle woods, and also in some of the precipitous faces of rock near Portkill. The kestrel also is met with, and constructs its nest in the cliffs and rocky banks, sometimes even at the foot of a rowan tree, where the ground falls away near a secluded burn.   There are plenty of owls in the old woods about Campsail and the Clachan glen, and their melancholy cry may be heard, especially on moonlight nights, with weird effect.   That destructive bird of prey the hooded crow, is met with on the upper moors, its nest being found in some retired glen, on a tall fir, or sometimes even a rowan tree, an unshapely mass of sticks lined with heather and wool.   Although the rook skims over the fields on Rosneath, sometimes in considerable numbers, it does not seem to fancy the spot for nesting operations, for the only place where there are a few nests is in the neighbourhood of Knockderry. A good many of that pert and lively species the jackdaw will be seen

in the tall trees near the Mill Bay, their quick cries resounding amid
the firs overhead.   Magpies are not very numerous, but their shrill
notes will be heard in the fir plantations, and their plundering propensities draw down the vengeance of the gamekeepers.

THE SILVER FIRS, ROSNEATH.

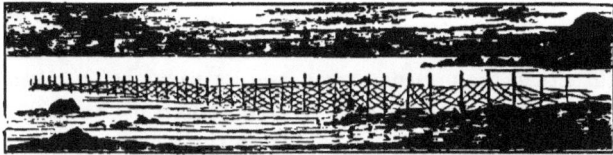

CHAPTER IV.

*Parochial Records ; Succession of Ministers ; The Story Family ;
Ecclesiastical.*

FROM the *Origines Parochiales* we are informed that the ancient parish
of Rosneath contained the present parishes of Rosneath and Row,
with a small part of Cardross and Luss, on the east, but exclusive of
Glenfruin, and a part of the coast of the Gareloch which formerly
belonged to Cardross. The modern and existing parish of Rosneath
consists of the Rosneath peninsula, lying between the two arms of
the sea, Loch Long and the Gareloch. It is bounded on the south
by the broader and more troubled estuary of the Clyde, and it
stretches for about eight and a half miles in length from the "Green
Isle" point, opposite to Greenock, to Portincaple on Loch Long side.
Within these limits is embraced a wonderful variety of scenery, in
some places all the silence and seclusion of a Highland moor, with its
robe of purple heather, feathery bracken, and yielding cushions of
velvet moss, in others the sylvan greenery and rich pasture of an
agricultural country. The parish consists mainly of one continuous
ridge, rising from the wooded point opposite Greenock, in gradually
increasing lines of elevation to the hill of Knock-na-Airidhe, or as it
is more commonly called—Tomnahara, near Mambeg farm, at a height
of 717 feet above the sea. All the upper table-land of the ridge is
covered with heather or marsh, with many a clear mountain streamlet pursuing its rock-impeded course down to the loch.

The date of erection of the first church of Rosneath is not known,
but the ancient church of Neueth, which was dedicated to St. Modan,
was situated on the Ros, or promontory, in the district of Neueth. At
a short distance from the castle of Rosneath, it stood near the shore

upon the site of the present church, and its name being taken from its situation was sometimes styled the church of Neueth, or the church of Rosneth. It is uncertain when the church of Neueth was founded, but the earliest notice of it occurs in the grant which Alwyn, Earl of Lennox, made to the church of Kilpatrik before 1199, and which was witnessed by Michael Gilmodyn, pastor of Neueth. Amelec, also called Auleth, a younger son of Alwyn, and who seems to have had this district as his inheritance, granted the church of Rosneth, with all its just pertinents, in pure and perpetual alms, to the Monks of Paisley, to be held by them as freely as their other churches, acquired by gift of the patrons. This grant was confirmed by Amelec's brother, Earl Maldoven, and subsequently by King Alexander at Trefquer on the 12th March, 1225. About the same time, Amelec granted a salt pan in his land of Rosneth to the Monks of Paisley, and to this gift Nevinus, parson of Neueth, and Gilmothan, son of the sacristan of Neueth, are witnesses. In the settlement of a dispute which arose between Walter, bishop of Glasgow, and William, Abbot of Paisley, regarding vicarial churches held by the Monks in the diocese of Glasgow, and which the bishop was grievously oppressing, it was appointed by amicable compositors in the church of Peblis in 1227 "that the church of. Neueth should be ceded to the Monks *in proprios usus*, and exempted from the payment of procurations, on condition that they should present to the church a fit secular chaplain, who should answer to the bishop *de Episcopalibus*." *

---

* In *Origines Parochiales* it is stated, "The Church of Rosneath was dedicated not to St. Nicholas but to St. Modan, abbot and confessor, who withdrew from the monastery at Falkirk, where he had converted the surrounding tribes, to the western coasts of Scotland, not far from Dunbertane and Loch Gareloch in a lovely spot sequestered from men by waves and mountains; there is the parish church of Rosneath dedicated in honour of him, and there do his relics rest in honour in a chapel of the cemetery of that church." Spottiswoode gives it as the belief of some that Rosneath was a Priory of canons regular, belonging to the Abbey of Cambuskenneth, of the order of St. Augustine, founded by the Earls of Lennox.

At a later period Rosneath was known as "the parochine without and within the isle." About 1620, Parliament was petitioned to transport the kirk of Rosneath to the lands of Ardenconnel, on the mainland; and, between 1643 and 1648, the boundaries between it and Cardross were settled, and the new parish of Row was erected. Much difficulty was experienced in erecting the new parish of Row, but in time a presentee was inducted, with the proviso that, when the measure was matured, it should receive his sanction, and that he would be willing to alienate a portion of the tiends to provide a competent living for the minister. The Laird of Ardencaple only agreed to his admission on condition of his preaching alternately in the new church of Row. Upon quite insufficient evidence, for no trace of the building remains, it was supposed that the Earls of Lennox founded at Rosneath a religious house of canons regular, and dedicated it to the Virgin Mary. The church continued in the possession of the Monks of Paisley, who drew all the revenues till the Reformation, a curate being employed in preaching and performing divine service. At the Reformation the revenue was let by the Abbot for £146 13s. 4d., and in 1587 the patronage and titles, which were then held for life by Lord Claud Hamilton, were granted to him and his heirs for ever. Subsequently the patronage of the church was acquired by the Argyll family, who retained it till the abolition of patronage in the Church of Scotland. It is certain that the rectory of Rosneath long continued an appanage of the Abbey of Paisley. In 1591 when the Regality of Paisley was erected, Rosneath was worth 3 chalders of oatmeal, besides vicarage and small tithes, a great diminution from the revenue of 1545. In 1635 the stipend was· fixed at 7 chalders of oatmeal, and one of bear, besides communion elements, which was converted into 4 bolls of bear.

There is reason to believe that the castle of Rosneath existed as a royal castle before the end of the twelfth century; it was said to have been burnt by Sir William Wallace. In the reign of Robert II. the lands of Rosneath were granted by Mary, the widowed Countess of Monteith, to John de Drommond, and by him given to Alexander de Menteth. They were legally annexed to the Crown, along with the castle of Dunbarton in 1455, but Colin, first Earl of Argyll, Chancellor of Scotland, had a charter of the lands of Rosneath, under the Great Seal in 1489. *

The following may be given as the succession of ministers of the parish of Rosneath, commencing from the early, and perhaps doubtful, records of pre-Reformation times. First we have St. Modan, who lived in the sixth century, and is supposed to have set out from Iona on a mission of Christianity, towards Loch Etive, near which he dwelt for a considerable time, and subsequently on the shores of the Kyles of Bute. From thence he crossed the mountainous district of Cowal until he reached the shores of Loch Long, where he found himself opposite Rosneath, in which secluded spot he took up his

---

* The following note is from the *Helensburgh Guide*, published in 1871. "It appears from the ecclesiastical records that the kirk of Row was at first an ease, or subordinate, place of worship for local accommodation, served by the minister of Rosneath. An Act of General Assembly, of date 27th August, 1639, empowered the Presbytery to take measures for settling both parishes of Rosneath and Cardross, with *Ease*. When the Presbytery began their proceedings on 4th February, 1640, the 'Kirk upon the Row of Connel' existed, and M'Aulay of Ardencaple required the ease to be there. At another meeting held the same month, Mr. George Lindsay, minister of Rosneath, offered security to maintain a helper ; but Mr. Robert Walton, minister of Cardross, rather than that any part of his parish should be united to Rosneath, made a large offer for building a church and maintaining a helper for Glenfruin. There ensued a long and keen conflict between contending parties. The minister of Rosneath, instead of being disburdened of the part of his charge east of Gareloch, was charged with having to preach every second Sabbath at the kirk of Row. At length (3rd July, 1643) the Lords Commissioners for the plantation of kirks decreed the disjunction so long contended for. As much of Rosneath lying to the east of Kirkmichael was annexed to Cardross, as was disjoined from Cardross to be annexed to the kirk of Row. The part of Cardross taken to make up the new parish embraced the Bannachras, Glenfruin, and lands about Garelochhead. The compensation received by Cardross, from Rosneath, lay between Kirkmichael and the present church. Till then, that church stood on Cardross Point, at the influx of the Leven with Clyde. Row continued to be without a settled ministry till the Presbytery, on 27th September, 1648, appointed the admission of Mr. Archibald MacLeane, of Kingarth, as its first minister."

abode, making occasional missionary tours to the surrounding districts of Dunbarton and Stirling shires.

1200. Michaele Gilmodyne, Parson of Renyt.

1225. Nevinus, Parson of Rosneath.

1350. Sir Richard Small, Rector in time of David II.

1458. William, Chaplain.

1515. Sir John Clerk, Curate.

"Rosneith, 20 February, 1515.—William Lyndsay of Bunnill by virtue of a precept from the Lord of Lennox deliverit the halie water stoup to John Buntyn of the priests clerkship of Rosneith. Sir John Clerk, Curate of Kirk, deliverit the said stoup to the said John Buntyn as the gift of the Abbot of Paisley as parson and vicar of the said Church after the tenor of the Lord's gift." (Camstradden writs).

1545. Dean John Sclater and Mr. John Wood had a nineteen years' tack of the vicarage and parsonage of Rosneath, with the glebe and house, from John, Abbot of Paisley, they paying 220 merks and 2 chalders of meal as rent, besides paying the curate and keeping the Kirk in repair.

1565-76. Malcolm Steinson was exhorter here, with stipend of 40 lib, and, about same time, Ninian Galt was reader, perhaps at the chapel of Kilmahew. M. Steinson translated to Luss before 1585.

1566. David Colquhoun, Minister.

1585. George M'Gleis, Reader at Kilmaronock.

1574 to 1580. George Lyndsay, A.M., 1614. Translated from Bunnill. Was member of Court of High Commission, 21 October, 1634, of General Assembly in 1638, died 1644, aged 69. Becoming old, got an assistant with 500 merks of salary in 1640.

1639. Robert Lyndsay, A.M. Son of preceding. Ordained to preach and catechise at Row, 19 March, 1644, on a stipend provided by his father, died 1647.

1646. Ewen Cameron, A.M.   Translated from Dunoon—called 29
       March, admitted 4 August.   Member of Assembly, 1647,
       was opposed to the erection of Row, and returned again
       to Dunoon before October, 1648.   During his incumbency
       Row parish was formed, and he was compelled to give up
       one chalder of the parsonage teinds, and all vicarage east
       of the Gareloch, in support of the new charge, which he
       was to supply, as well as his own, till a regular minister
       was obtained.

1651. Ninian Campbell, A.M.   Translated from Kilmalcolm, called
       in November, 1650, admitted 12 March, died 1657 aged
       58.   In his time Gaelic found to be unnecessary, as only
       30 persons found who could speak it.   Published a
       treatise upon Death.

1659. Adam Gattie, A.M.   Educated at Edinburgh University.
       Licensed by Presbytery June 1659, admitted November
       same year.   Deprived by Act of Parliament 1662.   Be-
       fore the Presbytery of Paisley 1666 for living so near
       his former charge without licence, but reported in follow-
       ing March as having gone to Ireland.

1665. Alexander Cameron, translated from Balfron, admitted
       April, 1680, and demitted in June.

1682. James Gordon, A.M., son of Mr. Hugh Gordon, minister of
       Row ; had his degree from University of Glasgow, July
       1673 ; passed trials and received testimonials from
       Presbytery 1680 ; recommended by Archbishop St.
       Andrews for Port of Monteith 1681, presented to Ros-
       neath in July and installed October, 1682 ; deprived by
       Privy Council September, 1689, for not reading Pro-
       clamation of Estates, and not praying for their Majesties,
       William and Mary ; died 1694, aged 40 ; left a son,
       William.

1689. Robert Campbell, ordained minister of Presbyterian con-
       gregation in Ireland, 1671.   August called, and accepted

December ; got testimonial of his having served to Whitsunday, 1691.   Married Margaret Kelso.

1691. Duncan Campbell, A.M.   Translated from Inverkip, admitted July, died November, 1707, at age of 72.

1709. Neil Campbell, translated from Kilmalie; admitted July;
translated to Renfrew June, 1716.   In 1728 was chosen
Principal of Glasgow College.

1719. Daniel M'Laurin, translated from Kilfinan, admitted June,
died February, 1720. " A man of rare parts and honest."
Only 26 Gaelic families in parish.

1722. James Anderson, son of Mr. John Anderson, one of the
ministers of Glasgow, ordained July ; died June, 1744.
Married Margaret Turner, who survived him 40 years.
Became senior annuitant on Ministers Widow's Fund,
died 1784.   One of their sons was John Anderson, Professor of Natural Philosophy in University of Glasgow,
and founder of the Andersonian Institution.

1745. Matthew Stewart, son of Dugald Stewart, minister of
Rothesay ; born 1717; educated at Grammar School,
Rothesay; studied at University of Glasgow and Edinburgh; favourite pupil of professors of mathematics in
both cities; licensed by Presbytery of Dunoon, May,
1744; presented to Rosneath by Archibald, Duke of
Argyll, and ordained May, 1745.   Elected Professor of
Mathematics in Edinburgh University, and resigned
parish in October, 1747.   Wrote various abstruse works
on mathematical problems ; and his son, Dugald Stewart,
who afterwards attained such eminence as a professor of
moral philosophy, was elected jointly with his father to
the chair in 1775.   Died January, 1785 ; 68 years old.

1749. Andrew Duncanson ; translated from Kilcalmonell ; presented by Archibald, Duke of Argyll in 1748 ; admitted
January, 1749 ; demitted, on getting an allowance, in
1763, and died April, 1772.

1764. John Kennedy ; licensed by Presbytery of Haddington,

1763; presented to parish by John, Duke of Argyll, June, 1764, and died a year after.

1766. George Drummond; descended from a representative of the family of Hawthornden; licensed by the Presbytery of Stirling in 1761; presented by John, Duke of Argyll, August, 1765. Got the church rebuilt in 1780; received degree of D.D. from University of Edinburgh in June, 1800; died in 1819 in his 82nd year, and in the 53rd of his ministry. "A gentleman of high respectability, deep erudition, and eminent worth." Married Catharine Buchanan, widow of Mr. M'Gowan of Mains of Kilmaronock.

The ministry of Dr. Drummond brings us to a period, within the memory of one or two aged natives of the parish, who can recall the church of those days. Dr. Drummond seems to have been one of the old "Moderate" ministers of the Church of Scotland, and he added to his modest stipend by farming the Strouel farm, with the aid of two men and horses. For some time he had been tutor to the laird of Luss, and through his influence with the Duke of Argyll, the tutor became minister of Rosneath. He married a widow possessed of some property on the water of Endrick, who appears to have been of a managing turn.

On one occasion, at a rent-collection at Luss, Dr. Drummond happened to be present along with Sir Humphrey Colquhoun and the Sheriff of Dunbarton. The party were at dinner when, on a sudden, three men, with blackened faces, having overcome the resistance of the servants, rushed into the room and attacked the astonished gentlemen. Evidently they hoped, in the excitement following this unwelcome intrusion, to secure the rent-money, which lay loose in a paper inside the press. However, the minister of Rosneath made a valiant defence, first laying hold of a chair, and then the poker, with which he struck one of the robbers violently on the head. The wound was the means of identifying the man, John Gray by name, and he was subsequently convicted for his crime at Dunbarton. Owing to loss of blood from a wound he received in the struggle, Dr. Drummond was long an invalid, and in the closing years of his ministry the duties of parish minister were almost entirely performed by assistants. Allusion is thus made in a letter from Mr. Robert Campbell, long factor on the Argyll property, to Lord John Campbell in 1815, who writes : " The poor infirm body Brown, who assisted Dr. Drummond, died on Friday last. The old doctor, whose mind is almost gone, has entered into some engagement with our idiotical schoolmaster, Graham, to make him his assistant, although he wants two years of his divinity studies, and was, on that account, refused a license by the Presbytery of Dunbarton." In the autumn of 1815 an offer was made to the Rev. Robert Story, who had recently received license as a preacher from the Presbytery of Haddington, to become assistant to old Dr. Drummond, which was accepted.

Robert Story, for over forty years minister of Rosneath, was born in the village of Yetholm, a few miles from Kelso, in March, 1790. His father, George Story, taught the Parish school, besides acting as factor or agent for Mr. Wauchope of Niddrie, his mother being Margaret Herbert, of a Northumbrian family. He was educated at the University of Edinburgh, and, amongst others, had for one of his instructors the eminent Dugald Stewart, son of the former minister of Rosneath. For the next two or three years he acted as tutor in the families of Mr. Macpherson Grant at Ballindalloch, the Earl of Dalhousie, and others, and then was appointed assistant to old Dr. Drummond at Rosneath, after having been licensed in 1815. At that time the spiritual condition of the parish was at a very low ebb. Where there are now seven places of worship belonging to the different denominations, there was then the old church at the Clachan of Rosneath. None of the numerous villas, extending for more than four miles on the Loch Long side of the peninsula, which now form such a feature in the landscape, were then in existence. On a Sabbath morning the farmers and their servants, and the humble cottagers, might be seen crossing the moor by the various pathways which led to the House of God from the different farmhouses. And in simple rustic attire, the women would be seen sitting beside

the Clachan burn, washing their feet in the limpid water, and
donning their stockings and shoes which had, up to that point, been
carried in their hands.

Mr. Story was introduced to his charge by Dr. Thomas Chalmers,
who was his warm friend, and a frequent visitor at the manse, and
soon proved that he was a minister of ardent piety and enthusiastic
temperament.   At the same time he was a favourite in society, and
his exceedingly handsome and striking appearance, his cultured mind,
and agreeable manners, made the young minister to be courted by
the wealthy, and even the titled, in the land.   In the year 1827 he
was in indifferent health, and sought relief by a change of residence
in England, visiting, amongst others, the celebrated but erratic
Edward Irving.   Some time after his return from England Mr. Story
was happily united in marriage to Miss Helen Boyle Dunlop, one of
a numerous family, her father Mr. Dunlop of Keppoch, near Helensburgh, being a well known banker in Greenock.   One of his sons
was the greatly esteemed John Dunlop, the father of the temperance
cause in Scotland, whose name is held in high honour amongst the
friends of that great movement.   Mrs. Story, a clever, practical, and
energetic lady, was long spared to be a comfort to her husband, and
soothed him in his last lingering illness, and died at Rosneath in
1882, greatly regretted by her many friends.   Mr. Story cultivated
intimate relations with his near neighbour the Rev. John Macleod
Campbell of Row, and stood by his side during the painful controversy in the Church courts which issued in the deposition of the
latter from his ministry, on the ground of certain views which he
held regarding the Atonement.

During the time of his peaceful ministry in his quiet vineyard at
Rosneath, Mr. Story ever kept a watchful eye upon the movements
and ecclesiastical controversies of the period, though he was never
very prominent in Church courts.   After the Disruption of the
Church of Scotland, and when he had returned home from the
General Assembly of 1843, he found his hitherto happy, and un-
divided, parish in the full throes of the painful excitement of that
memorable time.   Party spirit in the district ran very high, angry

controversy ensued, but the good minister of Rosneath wrote: "If the agitation shall lead to the conversion of any from the error of their ways, I shall be thankful for it all." One worthy man, the coachman of a local gentleman of great influence, who drew with him not a few of those who looked up to him as a guide and friend, gave probably a unique reason for his joining the ranks of the Secessionists. A friend meeting the wavering charioteer, said to him, "And what will you do John?" to which query came the ready response, "I'll gang whar the horse gangs."

Towards the close of the year 1849, symptoms of failing health began to manifest themselves in Mr. Story, whose upright form, dark kindling eye, and long, flowing, white hair, attracted observation wherever he moved. He consulted two doctors in Edinburgh, and was advised not to preach out of his own pulpit, as he was evidently suffering from heart disease. Thus stricken, though seemingly in the prime of life, with all his faculties unimpaired, he meekly submitted to the Will of his Heavenly Father. He undertook the labour of raising funds for the new place of worship in the summer resort of Cove, on the shores of Loch Long, which it was considered desirable to erect. For the next few years Mr. Story was obliged to have the aid of assistants in the carrying on of his ministerial work, though he rarely delegated to them his beloved duties of visiting the sick, or such occupations as demanded but little exertion of voice or strength. As the years of 1858 and 1859 gradually passed away it was evident that the days of the much loved pastor of Rosneath were drawing to a close. Many of his dearest friends came to the manse in order once more to see its honoured head, and have a few farewell words of communion and fellowship. For friends and parishioners alike he ever had the same winning smile and kindly welcome, and the blessing, though sometimes well nigh inaudible, was hardly ever omitted. His son and successor in the ministry, who was doing work in a church at Montreal, was hurriedly summoned across the Atlantic, but arrived too late to take farewell of his beloved father, who died on 22nd November, 1859. To the end his spirit was calm, and his intellect unclouded, though the body was wasted and en-

feebled. A chaste and simple monument, with a medallion, all the
work of William Brodie, the well known sculptor, was erected to his
memory inside the parish church. The inscription bore that it was
"dedicated by his parishioners and friends to the revered memory of
Robert Story, for forty-two years the faithful and beloved minister
of the church and parish of Rosneath."

The Rev. Professor Story, his son, received the presentation to the
parish of Rosneath, from the Duke of Argyll, when quite a young
man, in the year 1860. The patron knew that the parishioners would
approve of the appointment, for indeed the presentee had been
brought up amongst them, and his abilities were early recognised.
His career at Edinburgh University had been a successful one, and
he had gained both credit and experience in Montreal, where he had
officiated for eighteen months as assistant minister in the Presbyterian Church of St. Andrew. After being inducted to the parish
of Rosneath, Mr. Robert Herbert Story diligently laboured in the
spirit of his father, and although, in many respects, the externals of
church worship had changed, he sought ever to maintain a high
standard of service and preaching. From an interesting volume
about the ministers and churches in 1889 of Helensburgh and neighbourhood, the following particulars are taken. "Even those who
esteemed the father most, recognised in the son if not a more faithful
and earnest, a more effective preacher. His preaching from the first
was fresh in thought, devout in tone; graceful and poetic in diction.
As he grew in knowledge and experience, it became richer, wiser,
and more spiritual. The high-toned preaching of the young minister,
and the orderly and dignified devotional service which he conducted,
soon made the parish church of Rosneath a centre of spiritual attrac-
tion to the surrounding district. In the summer season the church
was overcrowded, and it became necessary to add transepts, containing nearly two hundred sittings, to the original building. By
this time, about 1867, the battle of the organ had been fought and
won, and an organ with the unanimous, or all but unanimous, assent
of the parishioners was placed in the north transept of the enlarged
parish church. Not long afterwards the Scottish Hymnal received

the sanction of the General Assembly, and was of course adopted by the congregation of Rosneath."

Mr. R. Herbert Story, while faithfully attending to his parochial duties, began to contribute in various ways, to literature, and published in 1862 the much admired biography of his father, which had a good circulation. Besides writing in magazines and publishing occasional pamphlets on subjects connected with Church history, he wrote in 1870 the *Life and Remains of Dr. Robert Lee*, with whom he had long been in terms of intimate friendship. Being fully in sympathy with Dr. Lee in his views regarding a more elaborate system of Church service, he narrated, with much fulness of detail, the ecclesiastical controversies in which for a long time the minister of Greyfriars was engaged. Again in 1874, Mr. Story gave to the world a book, the preparation of which involved him in considerable labour, the *Life of Principal Carstares*, from whom, through his mother's family of the Dunlops, he was collaterally descended. There is much valuable matter in this book, with reference to the story of the "Resolutioners and Protesters," and of the period after the Revolution Settlement of 1688. Carstares was in many respects a powerful personage. Macaulay writes of him in his History as follows:—"William had, however, one Scottish adviser who deserved and possessed more influence than any of the ostensible ministers. This was Carstares, one of the most remarkable men of that age. He united great scholastic attainments, with great aptitude for civil business, and the firm faith and ardent zeal of a martyr with the shrewdness and suppleness of a consummate politician." Sketches of the policy and characters of many of the notable men of that eventful period, the Prince of Orange, Shaftesbury, Monmouth, James the Second, Argyll, Russell, Sidney and others, appear in the volume, which enhanced its author's literary reputation. These volumes and the solid work which he had done on behalf of the Church of Scotland were recognised by the University of Edinburgh conferring the degree of D.D. upon Mr. Story, whose diligent pen was frequently enlisted also in the literature of Church defence. A volume of sermons, entitled *Creed and Conduct*, a little book on the *Health*

Haunts of the Riviera, a monograph on *Saint Modan of Rosneath*, and
one or two minor works were also brought out by Dr. Story, and he
was mainly instrumental in starting the Church Service Society,
whose objects were to vary and improve the form of worship in the
Church of Scotland.   He also edited for a time, a magazine with the
title of the *Scottish Church*, which was published mainly in the
cause of Church defence, though containing much matter of general
interest, and more recently has edited, and contributed to, a new
history of the Church of Scotland in five volumes.   The same volume
from which an extract has been given further remarks, "Dr. Story
for the last fifteen years has taken an active part in the work of
Church courts.   The Presbytery of Dunbarton, recognising his power
as a debater, and his ability as a man of business, has elected him
annually as one of its representatives in the venerable Assembly.
The wisdom of this departure from custom, in the matter of representation, has been proved by the position to which Dr. Story has
risen in the great Council of the Church. . . .   Of late years,
thanks to the attacks of the Liberationists, party distinctions in the
Church of Scotland have been well nigh obliterated.   The Church is
now of one party, that which exists for the defence of an institution,
with the continued existence of which she believes that much that is
best in the nation's life is bound up.   Of this great party Dr. Story
is recognised as one of the most able and influential members."   Dr.
Story is one of Her Majesty's Chaplains, and a number of years ago
was appointed to the office of Junior Clerk of the General Assembly
of the Church of Scotland.   On the lamented death of the late Rev.
Professor Milligan of Aberdeen, he was promoted to the post of
principal Clerk of Assembly, and in 1894 the crowning honour was
conferred upon him by his election to the high and responsible office
of Moderator of the Church of Scotland.   Several handsome presen-
tations were made to Dr. Story on this occasion, from the congregation of St. Andrews Church, Montreal, from his old parish of
Rosneath, from his students in Glasgow University, and the sum of
five hundred guineas, from friends in Glasgow and the West of
Scotland.   Sir James King, of Glasgow, in making the latter presen-

THE STORY FAMILY. 229

tation, said, "they recognised in Dr. Story a faithful pastor, an eloquent preacher, a learned teacher, a brilliant debater, and an accomplished man of letters." In his reply Dr. Story stated "he came behind none of his predecessors in the Moderator's chair in his desire to do justice to the high office, and to try to preserve its traditions unbroken and untarnished—the traditions of the chair of the oldest and most venerable legislative body in the British Empire."

Having been appointed to the chair of Church History in the University of Glasgow, Dr. Story had reluctantly to resign the parish of Rosneath, and took leave of the congregation to whom he had so long ministered on Sunday 5th June 1887. The parish church was crowded at the noon-day service, many visitors having come long distances to hear the farewell discourse, which was from the text, Joshua vii. 10. In concluding his sermon the preacher said, "the thought that the tie which has connected you and me for so many years is now broken, and that I shall never again stand here as minister of this parish touches me too deeply to be spoken about, all the more that I know it is not a matter of indifference to you—to some of you a matter of much concern and regret. The years that have passed over us have seen many a wonderful change. How many have been taken from us—the beloved! the unforgotten! They have brought, too, much happiness, and many a good and perfect gift. May the coming years be yet fuller to you of outward prosperity and inward peace. Forsake not the assembling of yourselves together. Maintain the beauty of God's house, and the reverence and seemliness of its services. Keep His commandments, and be always mindful of His poor. With this I say farewell. When in the days to come you assemble here for worship, think sometimes not unkindly of one whose thoughts, on the Lord's Day at the house of prayer, will never be far from this dear and familiar place. I commend you all unto God, and to the word of His grace, which is able to build you up and to give you an inheritance among them all which are sanctified, and to whom be all glory in the Church, world without end. Amen."

During Dr. Story's ministry the Kirk-Session had lost several of

its old and valued members, who had officiated as elders in his
father's lifetime.   On the vacancy being declared, a congregational
committee was formed, the Rev. J. Webster of Row being moderator,
and in August a new minister was elected, the Rev. Alfred Warr,
M.A., who was educated at Edinburgh University, and had for some
time acted as assistant in St. Cuthbert's Church.   Mr. Warr took
high honours at the University, gaining the first place in Professor
Flint's classes of Divinity in the two sessions of 1882-83 and 1884.
He also took a high place in the class of Church History in the sessions of 1883-84.   He was also awarded the first Gray prize for an
essay on "The supremacy of conscience in man's moral nature," and .
the Hepburn prize open to all students of the Faculty of Divinity.
His carefully prepared discourses indicate a well-cultured mind.   He
is a member of the School Board, and takes an appreciative interest
in all that is for the benefit of the children of the parish.   He
entered with great energy into the scheme for enlarging the church
at Rosneath, for which a considerable sum of money was raised.   At
its re-opening, the well-known- Dr. M'Gregor of St. Cuthbert's, who
had testified to Mr. Warr's ability and zeal, preached an eloquent
sermon to a large congregation.   During the agitation in defence of
the Church of Scotland, Mr. Warr's services were often availed of in
addressing meetings throughout the country.   His arguments and
illustrations were telling and forcible, and he threw himself into the
defence movement with much enthusiasm.

The Kirk-Session at present consists of Mr. William Stewart, the
much esteemed parish schoolmaster, Surgeon-General Bidic, C.I.E.,
Mr. Alexander Airth, Mr. David Silver, and Mr. Finlay M'Callum.

The various storms which, from time to time, agitated the ecclesiastical atmosphere in the west of Scotland had but a small effect in
a secluded parish like Rosneath.   It was not till about the period of
the long ministry of Dr. Drummond that the beautiful peninsula
became much known to the outer world.   During his uneventful
rule, the affairs of the parish were conducted in the quiet way usual
in rural districts, and the Session records afford an insight into the
morals and manners of the neighbourhood.   In 1766 the sum paid

for support of the poor was £59 8s. The following inventory of utensils was taken as the property of the Session : "Two silver cups for the Communion; four Communion tablecloths, big and small; two pewter flagons; a big pewter plate; a pewter basin for baptism; two mortcloths, one large, one small.* The Session appoints that the large mortcloth be let out within the parish for 2s. 6d., and the small one for 1s. 6d. Sterling."

The school fees were appointed as follows :—"For such as read English only, 1s. 6d. for each quarter. For those who read and write only, 1s. 6d. for each quarter. For those who learn English, writing, and arithmetic, 2s. 6d. for each quarter. For Latin, 2s. 6d." There were frequent cases of discipline in connection with members of the church, and the offenders had to submit to a solemn rebuke administered to them before the congregation, in addition to being fined. One of the heritors seems, more than once, to have given cause for rebuke, whose fine was sometimes four and five guineas, but those lower in the social state were let off with a payment of five shillings. The school was long held in the church, but, in October 1766, it was reported that " the school could not be kept longer in the Kirk on account of the coldness of the weather, and the Session appoint the house formerly possessed by David Guthrie to be cleaned and the school kept there." On 10th November, 1773, it is stated that " the bason made use of in baptisms almost wore out, Treasurer to get it exchanged, and pay the balance." The Duke of Argyll had ordered gates to be made for different entries into the churchyard. On 8th

---

* Rosneath old Communion cups. The author is indebted to the Rev. Thomas Burns, M.A., who has written a valuable work on old Scottish Communion plate, for the following :—" They are about the oldest in Scotland, and it would be interesting to know who was the donor of them. Their type is thoroughly characteristic of the age. They were made in Edinburgh by a famous goldsmith, John Mosman, who was admitted to the Incorporation of Goldsmiths in 1575. The cups were made in 1585-6. Mosman was Deacon in that year, and they bear his Deacon's punch. They stand 8¾ inches high, and have a depth of bowl of 3¾ inches. There are most valuable on account of their antiquity, apart from their historical associations."

May, 1776, "The Session, considering that they have more of the poor's money on hand than they choose to keep by them without bearing interest, and as no private person of good security can be found to take it, they therefore unanimously resolve to put £120 into any one of the banks of Glasgow, and for that purpose they now lodge the money with their Moderator, hereby appointing him to lay it out as above as soon as convenient."

Time rolled on, and the aged Dr. Drummond pursued "the even tenour of his way," and was succeeded, in 1815, by the Rev. Robert Story, both of whom ministered in the old church, whose ivy clad ruins now stand in the churchyard, beside the Clachan burn. It is by no means a venerable structure, having been built about the year 1770, on the site of a much older and more ornate edifice. The latter was of a more uniform and cruciform shape, with a row of stone images round the pulpit, and the ornamental basin for holy water was at one side of the entrance door. Also, on the right-hand side of the doorway were five or six "jougs," as they were termed, iron manacles for detaining wrong doers by the neck. It is believed that old Dr. Drummond, who must have had severely Protestant proclivities, persuaded the Duke of Argyll to pull down the edifice dedicated to the Virgin Mary, although for his Grace's convenience there was a special gallery and staircase in the church, However, one relic of the old church still survives in the shape of the interesting and peculiar belfry, which surmounts the existing ruin in the church-yard, the bell having been transferred to the present parish church, where it does duty every Sabbath. A considerable portion of the wall, on the side of the church near the manse, with the west gable wall, surmounted by the picturesque old belfry, still stands in the centre of the church-yard, the outside overgrown with clustering masses of ivy. The two windows in the wall, and the door in the gable are all of the simplest style, and the architecture of the plainest and least ornate description. Still, there is a charm about the relic of a byegone century, whose roofless walls and ivy-mantled stones speak with thrilling, though inaudible, accents to those who can recall the happy days when the old church rang with the soul-moving strains of many a grand and pathetic psalm or paraphrase. Mute they are now, save when of a soft summer's evening from the summit of the old belfry the mavis may be heard pouring forth its liquid, trilling notes, until the warm air is resonant of song, as the strain is echoed by his fellows from their sylvan retreat.

Inside the church, when it was used for public worship, everything was of the plainest description. The seats were of rough deals, and the floor was long only of earth, while a gallery ran round three sides of the interior—the pulpit standing between the two windows next the manse. The walls of the building were plain and white-washed, and grew green through damp and mould, and altogether the church had a forlorn appearance, although it was regarded with affection by many of the old forefathers of the parish. When the sacrament was dispensed, there was one long table running down the passage, from door to door, the minister and elders occupying one end. The crowds who assembled to hear celebrated preachers, such as Edward Irving, were fain to fill the church-yard, and listen to the great pulpit orator, who declaimed from the " tent."

The new church was commenced in 1853, and finished in the end of that year—a plain building, in the early English style, from the plans of Mr. Cousin, architect, Edinburgh. Since then two additions have been made to the edifice, and in 1895 a new vestry and an organ chamber have been erected, and the wings have afforded a considerable increase to the accommodation for seat-holders. The interior has a handsome appearance, though it is rather dark, owing to the introduction of several stained-glass windows—one erected many years ago by Mrs. Oliphant, the distinguished authoress, a frequent visitor to the parish and manse, in memory of a beloved young daughter, and another, at the opposite end, to the memory of Dr. Macleod Campbell. There are a number of mural monuments on the walls of the church, the chaste one in Ayrshire stone and white marble to the revered memory of old Mr. Story, and the space on the chancel wall below Mrs. Oliphant's window is occupied by a finely illuminated table of the commandments, the Lord's prayer being on the east wall—all drawn and designed in mediæval pattern by Mr.

W. A. Muirhead of Edinburgh. The new marble font and ornate oak pulpit, resting on a marble pedestal, were both gifts to the church, the former from Dr. Carnachan, and the latter from Mr. William Donaldson.

Rosneath churchyard is beautifully situated, with the Clachan burn running past its wall. At one time there was a low, half-ruined dyke surrounding the spot, and some fine old plane trees grew at intervals within the turf-covered wall. It was thought better to remove these, though many mourned their destruction, the dyke was rebuilt, and the old church put into more decent condition, while ivy was carefully trained up its mouldering walls. The old enclosed grave of Dr. Drummond, the minister, with very high railings, was altered by the removal of the railings, the two large gravestones being taken from their position against the wall of the church and laid flat upon the ground. Inside the ruin, and fixed with rivets into the window, is an interesting memorial stone, with curious scroll work, similar to what is seen on the ancient town crosses in many parts of Scotland. This stone, some years ago, was dug up in the church-yard, and is, doubtless, of great antiquity. The editor of the pro-ceedings of the Society of Antiquaries thus describes the stone. "The monument is a shaped slab about 5 feet long, 20 inches wide, and 5 inches thick, ornamented on both faces, and on both edges with patterns of interlaced work. On the obverse it presents a cross of the whole length of the slab, the centre filled with a spiral pattern, and the shaft and summit with patterns of interlaced work. The reverse also bears a cross of the whole length of the slab; the orna-ment is much more defaced, but seems to consist entirely of inter-laced work and fret. The edge of the stone has its ornaments also of interlaced work. The monument thus differs entirely in the character of its ornaments from the crosses and slabs decorated with foliagenous scrolls which are so common in the West Highlands. Its style is earlier, and corresponds with the purely Celtic ornamentation of the erect and shaped slabs of the western area of Scotland."

The mantling ivy has covered a good part of the ruined walls of the old church, giving it a more venerable appearance than its actual age, and it forms a decided addition to the picturesqueness of the spot. On being removed from the old belfry, the church bell was fixed in its appropriate place in the new edifice, and its soft, pleasing tone is heard every Lord's day, and also, according to an old custom, at midnight on the last day of the year. The old bell is now getting considerably worn, as it was cast towards the close of the seventeenth century in Holland. It bears the appropriate inscription "Soli Dei Gloria—Johannes Burgerhuys me fecit." As the soft, mellow tones of the old bell, indicating the birth of a new year, are wafted across the peaceful waters of the Gareloch, the response is heard from the steeple of the Row church, but with a more resonant sound, the omen, as it were, of a year of joyous anticipation.

Although the Rosneath churchyard is undoubtedly of great antiquity, for it must be remembered that, even in the charter of the twelfth century, the building was designated the Church of St. Nicholas,—and the whole peninsula was styled the Virgin's promontory,—with one or two exceptions there can hardly be said to be any ancient monuments. There are two or three old grey, lichen covered stones, one, with slightly bevelled edges, lying flat on the ground, which are, probably, of a great age, and on one of them what seems like the tracing of a sword or cross may be discerned. Another which is broken in two has three heads roughly carved on it, and part of the Colquhoun coat of arms. Most of the older head stones bear Celtic names inscribed on them, indicating the large number of Highland families formerly located in the district. Campbells, M'Arthurs, M'Farlanes, M'Colls, M'Kellars, M'Lellans, M'Aulays, and others, form the majority of the names on the stones, though Turners, Chalmers, and Ritchies seem to have lived long in Rosneath. An ancient looking stone bears to be in memory of Janet Liston, "Spouis" to John Ramsay, servant to John, Duke of "Argyel," 1744,—a little way off is a small slab, with the initials P.W.—H.M. 1721. Another venerable looking stone is evidently in memory of a shoemaker, for plainly delineated on its face are a boot, an old-fashioned, high-heeled shoe, and the curved knife used in cutting leather. The grave of the Rev. Robert Story, and his widow, is

close to the wall of the churchyard next the manse, and is marked
by a marble Iona cross, with an appropriate inscription. A white rose
bush grows on the grave, and sheds its leaves over the resting place
of the beloved pastor, whose voice so long sounded in the mouldering
ruin close by. Two other ministers of Rosneath are buried not far
off, their flat monumental stones greatly decayed, the Rev. James
Anderson died in 1744, and Rev. J. Kennedy in 1765. Near the
wall round the churchyard, on the west, is the slab, rudely sculptured
with a cherub's head and wings, two human figures, a coffin, a coat
of arms, and weighing scales, to the memory of Archibald Niven, who
sailed ferry boats to Greenock, and did all sorts of work, including
teaching, in the olden times, and died 1735. Tradition speaks of the
famous John Balfour of Burley, one of the murderers of Archbishop
Sharp, being buried in Rosneath churchyard. It is affirmed that he
found an asylum at Rosneath under the assumed name of Andrew
Salter, and that his descendants continued there for generations, and
were always considered of more gentle degree than the farmers of
the district. The last of the race died about the year 1810, and two
small, moss grown, stones, only a little elevated above the grass in the
south-east corner of the churchyard, are pointed out as the spot
where rest the bones of the dauntless Covenanter.

During Mr. Story's ministry at Rosneath, and up to the memorable
period of the Disruption of the Church of Scotland, in May 1843,
there was little overt expression of dissent in the parish. The wave
of ecclesiastical excitement which passed over Scotland at that time
stirred up to unwonted agitation the placid waters of the Gareloch
district, with the result that, in due time, a Free Church was established at Rosneath. The congregation assembled for the first time
for worship in the schoolhouse at Knockderry, and on alternate Sabbaths there, and at the old saw mill, a little way up from the Mill
Bay near Campsail. The Rev. John Grant of Pettie was inducted
to the charge on 7th November, 1843, and the Rev. Dr. M'Farlane
of Greenock, at the close of the service, laid the foundation of the
existing edifice. It is a commodious unpretending church, situated
at the rise of the brae above Mill of Campsail, and two wings were

added to the main building in 1858.   The success which attended
the Free Church of Rosneath, especially in its early days, was largely
due to the commanding influence, and strong personality of Mr.
Lorne Campbell, the Duke of Argyll's chamberlain.   He was a man
of fine presence, of much benevolence and kindliness of heart, of powerful will, and could sway men in an eminent degree.   He was held in
the highest esteem by the Argyll family, and his word was law throughout the peninsula.   In 1855, owing to ill health, Mr. Grant, the
minister had to employ an assistant, and soon after the present in-
cumbent of the church, the Rev. John M'Ewan, was appointed to the
post.   Mr. M'Ewan was born in Glasgow, and educated at the High
School there, and for a time was a clerk in Laird's shipping office.
During his long occupancy of the pastorate of the church Mr.
M'Ewan has laboured with the greatest zeal and faithfulness, his
earlier discourses having attracted the favourable attention of the
Rev. Dr. Candlish, who for several summers resided at Kilcreggan.
He is a diligent student, a vigorous defender of the faith, orthodox,
and evangelical, and, in all weathers, may be encountered in remote
corners of his parish, attending to the duties of his sacred calling.

For the accommodation of the summer population in Kilcreggan
and Cove, on the Loch Long side of the peninsula, there was erected
at Craigrownie the present commodious *quoad sacra* parish church.
The foundation stone was laid on July 31, 1852, and the church was
completed the same year at a cost of over £1100.   The architecture
is of early English Gothic, with chancel, nave, and transepts, and the
church was originally seated for 350, but increased accommodation
was gained by an addition in 1889.   It has a fine commanding situation on the high ground overlooking the waters of Loch Long and
the Frith of Clyde, and an excellent manse stands in the vicinity of
the church.   For thirty-four years the late Rev. Dr. David Shanks
filled its pulpit,—an able minister, an eminent master of Oriental
languages, and one who was sincerely mourned by his attached congregation.   His successor, the present minister, is the Rev. Kenneth
A. Macleay, B.D., a student of St. Andrews, who at that time was
assistant at Wallacetown near Ayr.   The late Principal Cunning-

ham of St. Andrews, in introducing Mr. Macleay to the congregation, spoke of the eminence which he had gained in his philosophical
studies. Of a more retiring and studious temperament is the Rev.
John Stevenson, who is minister of the iron chapel near Kilcreggan
pier, erected in 1869, for the use of worshippers of the Church of
Scotland in that part of Rosneath. Those who appreciate a quiet,
reverent, thoughtful discourse, find such in the pulpit utterances of
Mr. Stevenson, who has laboured in his sphere of duty for over
twenty-three years. The only other regular place of worship on the
Loch Long side of the peninsula, apart from the small iron chapel at
Peatoun, which is occasionally open in summer, is the United Presbyterian Church at Kilcreggan. This is a handsome structure, and
was built in 1869, holding over 600 persons, and there is an excellent manse on the adjacent ground. The present minister is the
Rev. Armstrong Black, who was for some years in charge of a large
church in the West-end of Edinburgh, but which, through ill health,
he resigned. Culture, breadth of thought, poetic fervour, and
earnestness of tone, characterise his discourses. He has recently
accepted a call to Egremont, Cheshire.

Any account of the ecclesiastical features of Rosneath would be
incomplete, without referring to the so-called miraculous manifestations of a member of the family of Campbells of Fernicarry, in the
gift of "tongues," which are associated with the famous Edward
Irving. This erratic divine and marvellous preacher fully believed
in the pentecostal gifts of one, at least, of the family, Mary Campbell.
Her elder sister, Isabella, who was of a saintly nature, had a brief
and blameless life, and her early death was brought into prominence in
the beautiful memoir of this devoted Christian, written by the Rev.
Robert Story, and widely circulated both in this country and America.
The quiet, secluded spot is shown at the back of Fernicarry where
the pious Isabella was wont to resort for prayer, an inscription upon
a stone marking the holy place. She had been so much in communion with her Heavenly Father, that many stories were repeated
of the marvellous spiritual insight which she possessed, and her influence was profound over those who had been in attendance on the

sufferer, or were admitted to her friendship. Her sister Mary became known about this time in connection with those who really believed that some strange 'gifts had been vouchsafed to men. Mary was young and beautiful, and being in delicate health she had a highly susceptible nervous temperament, and numbers of visitors, attracted by the fame of her pious sister, came to Fernicarry. One Sabbath evening, in March 1830, Mary Campbell, in the presence of a few friends, begun to utter strange sounds which she believed to have resemblance to the tongues spoken by the disciples in Jerusalem on the day of Pentecost. This language she affirmed to be that spoken in a group of islands in the Southern Pacific Ocean, and imagined it was a manifestation of the power of the Holy Spirit, and an invitation to her to proceed as a missionary to these remote parts of the earth. Soon after this Mary Campbell, after a surprising, or, as she affirmed, "miraculous" recovery, was married to a young man of the name of Caird, who had been attracted to Fernicarry by reading her sister's memoir. She was taken up by Edward Irving, who had full confidence in her manifestations of the spirit and her strange "tongues," and was introduced through him to various people of some position in the fashionable religious world. But in their society her piety and fervour began rapidly to deteriorate, her missionary zeal cooled, and the transient excitement caused by her reputed "gifts," soon passed away.

CARDROSS.

CHAPTER I.

Topography; Succession of Ministers; Ecclesiastical State.

THERE is considerable beauty of scenery, and much that is of great historical interest in the parish of Cardross, which is partly bounded by the waters of the Frith of Clyde, and by the river Leven issuing from Loch Lomond. No doubt the name is derived from "Ross," a point or headland, and "Car," a moorland ridge, and the church formerly stood on the high ground above the Leven, near its confluence with the Clyde. It is bounded on the south by the Clyde, on the west by the Parish of Row, and on the north it marches with Luss and Bonhill parishes. Its extreme length may be about eight miles, and its breadth varies from one and a half to three miles. In former times the parish appears not to have extended much farther along the shores of the Frith of Clyde than the site of the present church. Some lands in Glenfruin, and on the Gareloch, and even as far as Loch Long, then belonged to it, although these were detached from it in 1643, when the parish received an addition on its western boundary.

Cardross was part of the lordship of the old Earls of Lennox, but portions of it were held by their vassals before the wars of the suc-

cession. In the middle of the thirteenth century Earl Maldoven of
Lennox granted to Donald Macynel a land in Glenfreone called Keal-
bride, which is held on a fourth part of a "harathor," bounded by
the Lavaran and the burn called Crosc, as they run from the hill and
fall into the Freone; the reddendo, the twentieth part of the service
of a man-at-arms. The grant is witnessed by the Earl's brother,
Amelec, of whose large appanage Glenfruin formed a part. Before
1294, John Napier held Kilmahew of the Earl, giving three suits at
his head court, and paying what is exigible for a quarter of land in
Lennox.

Malcolm, Earl of Lennox, resigned into the hands of the King,
Robert I., a plough of land of Cardross, getting in compensation the
half of the lands of Lekkie in Stirlingshire. The King, about 1322,
gave over the lands of Moyden, within the Barony of Cardross, to
Adam son of Alan, and he had a specific object in view in acquiring
land in the parish. For upon a bank overhanging the river Leven,
near its junction with the Clyde, the hero of Bannockburn built a
castle, and surrounded it with a park, which was called the King's
Park of Cardross. At the first milestone out of Dunbarton, along
the Cardross road, there is a wooded knoll which bears the name of
Castlehill, although there are no traces of any ruined buildings to be
seen. Having divested himself of the cares and vexations of government, the monarch found relief in the chase, and indulged in hunting
excursions, and made short voyages along the neighbouring waters of
the Gareloch and Loch Long, and the broad estuary of the Clyde,
while he was kept in security by the neighbouring castle of Dunbarton. Within the walls of his residence, in view of the fine mountain
ranges which throw their dark shadows over the placid waters of
Loch Lomond, the patriot king breathed his last on 7th June, 1329.

An interesting account of the closing days of the heroic King is
given by Fraser Tytler, the historian, in his life of Robert Bruce.
"By the advice of his physicians he retired to Cardross, a beautiful
retreat situated upon the Clyde, about six miles from Dunbarton,
where, amid the intervals from pain and sickness, his time appears to
have been much occupied in making experiments in the construction

s

and sailing of vessels, with a view, probably, towards the establishment of a more effective naval force in Scotland. We learn this fact
from the accounts of his High Chamberlain, which are yet preserved,
and the same records acquaint us that in these kingly amusements
he often enjoyed the society of Randolph.* His lighter pleasures consisted in hunting and hawking, when his health permitted; in sailing
upon the Clyde, and superintending his mariners and shipwrights in
their occupations; in enlarging and enclosing his park, and making
additions to his palace. As even the most trivial circumstances are
interesting when they regard so eminent a man, it may be mentioned
that he kept a lion, the expense of whose maintenance forms an item
in the chamberlain's accounts; and that his active mind, even under
the pressure of increasing disease, seems to have taken an interest in
the labours of the architects, painters, goldsmiths, and inferior artists,
who belonged to his establishment. In compliance with the manners
of the times, he maintained a fool, for whose comfort he was solicit-
ous, and in whose society he took delight. He entertained his clergy
and his barons, who visited him from time to time, at his rural
palace, in a style of noble and abundant hospitality. The minutest
parts of his expenditure appear to have been arranged with the

---

* The King's expenses at Cardross. The following are a few of the entries
from the "Cardross Household Book," as given by Irving in *Dumbartonshire*—
"Item. To wood for the scaffolding of the new chalmer, 3s.; making a door
for do., 6d. To 100 large boards, 3s. 4d. To Giles the huntsman for his allowance for one year, six weeks, three days, 1 chalder 3½ bolls meal. Grant to do
by the King's command, 26s. 8d. To a net for taking large and small fish, 40s.
To two masts for the ship, 8s. To persons employed in raising the masts three
times, 3s. To working 80 tons of iron for the use of the ships and the castle at
4d. per stone, 26s. 8d. To bringing the King's great ship from the Frith into
the river near the castle, and carrying the rigging to the castle, 3s. To twelve
men sent from Dunbarton to the Tarbet to bring back the King's great ship,
28s. To thirty loads of firing to be used in the work of the windows, 22s. 6d.
To conveying Peter the fool to Tarbet (on Loch Fyne), 1s. 6d. The house for
the falcons cost 2s.; a fishing net, 40s.; seeds for the orchard, 1s. 6d.; green
olive oil for painting the royal chamber, 10s.; chalk for the same, 6d.; a chalder
of lime for whitewashing it, 8s.; and tin nails and glass for the windows,
3s. 4d."

greatest order, and his lowest officers and servants, his huntsmen, falconers, dog-keepers, gardeners, and park-stewards, provided for in rude but regular abundance. His gifts and largesses to the officers of his household, to his nurse and other old servants, and to the most favourite amongst his nobles, were frequent and ample; his charity in the support of many indigent persons, by small annual salaries or regular allowances of meat and flour, was extensive, and well directed; whilst a pleasing view of his generosity, combined with his love of letters, is presented by his presents to 'poor clerks' for the purpose of enabling them to carry on their education 'at the schools.'"

The scene has been often described when the King, feeling his last hour drawing near, charged his old friend and companion in arms, Sir James Douglas, to take, as soon as he was dead, his embalmed heart and deposit it in the Church of the Holy Sepulchre at Jerusalem. This was done, and Sir James Douglas duly set out with a body of chosen companions for the Holy Land, with his precious charge enclosed in a silver casket, but being attacked by the Saracens, and surrounded by overwhelming numbers, he flung the casket before him, exclaiming, "Pass onward as thou was wont, and Douglas will follow thee or die."

In addition to the Parish Church near Dunbarton, there was a chapel at Kilmahew, dedicated to St. Mahew, probably Macceus, one of the companions of St. Patrick, which gave its name to the lands. Both the Chapel and lands of Kilmahew belonged to the Cochrans in the time of David II., but in the fifteenth century they had reverted to the Napiers. Between the years 1208 and 1233, Maldoven, Earl of Lennox, granted to Walter, Bishop of Glasgow, as mensal to the bishoprick, the Church of Cardross, along with its lands and fishings, reserving the right of his brother, Dungal, who was also in orders, and may likely have held this benefice as well as that of Kilpatrick. Before 1432 this parish had been erected into a prebend for a canon of the cathedral. The rectory of Cardross is taxed in Baiamond's Tax Roll at £61 13s. 4d., and in the Libellus Taxationum at £66 13s. 4d., and the Vicar pensionar gave up his living at the Reformation as of £10 yearly value. In the year 1467 the chapel of Kilmahew was rebuilt, and on the 10th May, George, Bishop of Argyll, with license from the Bishop of Glasgow, clad in his mitre and pontifical robes, consecrated the chapel and cemetery, dedicated to St. Mahew. He also granted, in name and by consent of Duncan Napare of Kilmahew, and James Napare his heir, to God and St. Mahew, and a chaplain to celebrate in the newly consecrated chapel, forty shillings and tenpence yearly, out of tenements in the Burgh of Dunbarton, with a croft adjoining the chapel.

From these particulars chiefly gathered from *Origines Parochiales*, it will be seen that the ecclesiastical history of the parish extends to a very early period. As far back as 1225 mention is made of the Kirk of Cardross, and for three centuries the Bishops of Glasgow and their Deans and Chapters held it. The old church was a small oblong building, forty feet in length and twenty in breadth, with a tower at one end. All that now remains of that ancient building is the eastern gable, in which is a small pointed doorway, and also some remains of the lower parts of the side walls. Near it was the manse, and the Clachan of Under Kirkton of Cardross. The church stood on the side of the public road which ran along the shore and thence to Ardmore and Row, and it did service as the parish kirk until the year 1644. When the old church ceased to be used for worship, it gradually fell into decay until the year 1805, when the Levengrove estate passed from the possession of Richard Dennistoun of Kelvingrove into the hands of the Dixons, and the churchyard was despoiled of its monuments, ploughed over, and actually included in the grounds of the new proprietor of the estate. Two venerable flat gravestones are still to be seen near the walls of the church, the one outside ornamented with a shield and cross bones, and the other, inside the church, with a large cross on its face, and, at one end, the words, "The xii. Aprel," at the other, "Heir Lyes 17." Inside the ruins rest the remains of a number of the Dixon family, but the old mansion house of Levengrove, where Robert Burns the poet on his second Highland tour in 1787, travelling on horseback from Arrochar along Loch Lomondside, was welcomed by Mr. M'Aulay, the lawyer, and his family, is now entirely obliterated from the scene. The whole of these grounds, the ruins of the old kirk, the site of the mansion, and the holy well of St. Serf, are all included in the fine park of Levengrove, which was the handsome gift to their native town of the eminent shipbuilders John M'Millan and Peter Denny, LL.D.

In the year 1644, the next church of Cardross was built, on the site which it at present occupies near the village, and is thus much nearer the centre of the parish. It was a small unadorned structure, capable only of holding about 400 persons, and, after being used down to the year 1826, was pulled down, and the present existing edifice was erected. The situation is a commanding one, with a beautiful view across the broad estuary of the Clyde down to the mountains of Argyllshire, and a belt of old trees shelters the sacred structure. Its architecture is Gothic, of a similar character to many churches built about that period, the solid square tower over the entrance being its main feature. The church is seated for 800, and within the last few years received considerable renovations through the liberality of the late Mr. Donaldson, of Keppoch ; there are also four stained glass memorial windows representing Matthew, Mark, Luke, and John, given by the representatives of heritors of Cardross. The glebe consists of 9½ acres of good arable ground, and there is a large and commodious manse embowered in old trees.

There is nothing of special interest about the Communion vessels of the parish church. The cups which are in use at present are dated February 1867. Metal tokens of the usual type in Scottish country churches dated 2nd December, 1858, were used until recently. Much older ones used to exist stamped Car on one side, and on the other Mr. E., 1767—no doubt in the ministry of Mr. Edmonstone,— but of these there are none now to be found. There are also two very old-fashioned ladles for collections. From an old document it appears that on 21st September, 1727, Mrs. Wallace, the widow of the previous minister, handed over the following articles which were used in the service of the church. Two silver communion cups, two large flagons, one "bason," Acts of Assembly 1690-1723, a table-

cloth used at the Sacrament of the Lord's Supper, with four towels,
a pulpit cloth and brass plate given by Mr. Wallace to the Session.
Up till the summer of 1895 the good old custom of the Fast day was
kept up in Cardross Parish, but following the easy-going tendencies
of modern ecclesiastical authorities, the preliminary day of worship
has been abrogated.   As one of the respected old elders of the
church sorrowfully remarked to the author, he remembered when the
Fast day services were even more fully attended than those of the
Sabbath.

The boundaries of the Parish of Cardross have been considerably
altered, as we learn from the pages of *Old Cardross*. From it we are
informed, "until 1643 the parish of Cardross was bounded on the
west by the Auchenfroe Burn, which divided it from Rosneath, but
on the other hand it included Bennachra, and the lands in Glenfruin,
and on the shore of the upper part of the Gareloch.   In that year
Glenfruin was disjoined from Cardross to make part of the parish of
Row, which was then being formed ; and in lieu of this the lands
lying eastward from Meikle Kirkmichael, and also Dalquharn, in the
Vale of Leven, were detached from Rosneath and added to Cardross.
In 1659 the lands of Bennachra were disjoined from Cardross and
annexed to the parish of Luss."

The following is the succession of ministers of Cardross as given in
Irving's *History of the County.*

1480. Robert Blackadder, son of Sir Patrick Blackadder of Tulli-
        allan and Elizabeth, daughter and co-heiress of Sir James
        Edmonstone of that ilk, was rector of Cardross in 1480.
        He was employed by James III. on a mission to the
        Papal Court.   While at Rome, the bishopric of Aberdeen
        fell vacant, and having ingratiated himself into the favour
        of Pope Sixtus IV., he was consecrated to that See.   In
        1484 an opportunity occurred for preferment to which
        his abilities gave him a claim, and he was translated to
        Glasgow.   In his person that See was advanced to
        Archiepiscopal rank ; and he continued to perform its

functions and to execute various important charges in the domain of politics until 1508, when he undertook a pilgrimage to the Holy Land, from which he did not return, dying on the 28th July of that year.

1512. James Stewart, rector. Promoted in 1518 to the Provostry of Dunbarton ; at this time Peter Fleming was curate, and Thomas Ald, vicar pensionar.

1529. Patrick Shaw, succeeded as rector, and is mentioned as such in 1529.

1558. Symon Shaw was parson of Cardross, and rector of Kilbarchan in 1558.

———. John Bell filled this benefice soon after the Reformation, and about this time William Cuik was reader, with 20 merks salary.

1569. John Flattisburry was exhorter, with 40 merks and the vicarage pension, manse and glebe.

1572. Thomas Archibald, rector, and was succeeded some time after in 1592 by

1592. James Cunningham died 1603.

1603. James Cunningham similar in name to last was presented, but died same year.

1603. John Blackburn was appointed rector. He was Dean of the Faculty of Glasgow College, and was translated to the Laigh Kirk of that city.

1616. Robert Watson was appointed, and continued to exercise the functions of the ministry till 1650, when falling into ill-health, he resigned his office and benefice into the hands of the Presbytery, reserving, however, the manse and glebe during his life, and also all the teinds above seven chalders, which he gave as a provision for his successor. The Right of Patronage having been abolished by Statute the parishioners gave a call to his son.

1651. Robert Watson, who was ordained in 1651. He conformed to the restored order of things in 1663, and died in 1671. He was married to a daughter of Principal Baillie.

1672. James Gartshore was next presented to the charge, and
     eleven years afterwards, was translated to Tranent.

1683. Hugh Gordon. A brief entry in the Wodrow MS. in the
     Advocates' Library, states that he was "ousted at the
     Revolution."

1689. Neill Gillies, who in 1679 had been chaplain to Archibald,
     Earl of Argyll, was minister at Cardross at the re-erection
     of Presbyterianism in 1689. He was translated to Glas-
     gow in 1690.

1690. James Gordon, "ane Ireland minister," had a popular call.
     He died in 1693.

1695. Archibald Wallace was admitted in 1695. Dying in 1725,
     the Crown presented John Smith, but the parishioners
     refused to receive him, and gave a call to John Edmon-
     stone.

1726. John Edmonstone was appointed by the Crown, and
     ordained in 1726. He was minister of the parish for
     forty-four years. A Latin inscription on his tombstone
     in the churchyard records his many high qualities. On
     his death, John Davidson, minister of Old Kilpatrick,
     was nominated to the parish, but declined.

1774. John M'Aulay was inducted minister of the parish in 1774.
     He was born at Harris, where his father was minister, in
     1720. Graduated as M.A. at King's College, Aberdeen.
     He was ordained minister of South Uist in 1745, and in
     the course of the same year acquired some notoriety in
     his district by furnishing information, through his father,
     which nearly led to the capture of the Pretender, Prince
     Charles. In 1756 Mr. M'Aulay removed to Lismore, and
     nine years afterwards made a second change to Inveraray,
     where he was minister when Dr. Johnson made his
     famous journey to the Hebrides. He married Margaret,
     daughter of Colin Campbell of Inversregan, and twelve
     children were born of the marriage. One of them was

the well-known Zachary M'Aulay, the father of the celebrated historian, Lord Macaulay.

1790. Alexander M'Aulay was presented to Cardross by the Crown
in 1790, but a counter-presentation was given to Abraham
Forrest by Sir James Colquhoun, who claimed the right
of patronage. The Civil Courts decided in favour of Mr.
M'Aulay.

1801. Archibald Wilson, for a good many years before his death,
was unfit for much parochial work.

1838. William Dunn, who was born in 1811 in the parish of
Doune, Perthshire, where his father held a small farm.
Educated at Glasgow and Edinburgh Universities, and
after leaving college held a tutorship for some time. His
first appointment after being licensed was that of missionary to the district of Stockbridge, in Edinburgh, and
then was elected first minister of St. Peter's Church,
Glasgow, in July, 1836. After two years of assiduous
work in this field, he was offered, and accepted the
appointment of assistant and successor to the Rev. Mr.
Wilson of Cardross. In 1839 he succeeded to the full
charge on Mr. Wilson's death, and for forty years gave
most earnest and faithful service in this parish, leaving
behind him a name greatly honoured and beloved.
Although he sympathised with the views of the "non-
intrusion " party, yet in 1843 he felt constrained to cast
in his lot with those who remained in the church of their
fathers, and the great bulk of his congregation stood by
their loved minister. Mr. Dunn was a model pastor of
a flock, and went in and out amongst his people with
disinterested and affectionate zeal. In 1845 he married
Miss Croil, the step-daughter of Mr. Donaldson of Keppoch, one of his own heritors, who worthily assisted her
husband in his parochial duties, and who still survives.
In 1877 Mr. Dunn appointed as his assistant the Rev.
William Maxwell, M.A., recently licensed, and four years

afterwards the latter was ordained assistant and successor.
Mr. Dunn died on 8th December, 1885, aged 74 years,
and his funeral sermon was preached by one, whose
father had been for over forty years his intimate and
beloved friend, the Rev. Professor Story, long minister
of Rosneath, and now Professor of Church History in
Glasgow University.   He was a man of striking simplicity and gentleness of manner, full of devotion to His
Master's work, exuberant in large-hearted benevolence,
and intense in his sympathies for those in anguish or
sorrow.

1885. William Maxwell, M.A., a native of Hamilton, and received
his early education at the academy of that town, and
afterwards attended Glasgow University.   Mr. Maxwell
always had the pleasantest relations with Mr. Dunn, and
very soon acquired the complete confidence and esteem
of the congregation of the Parish Church.   In parochial
and educational matters he takes a warm interest, being
an active member of the School Board, and his scholarly
tastes and general culture, with his faithful discharge of
his ministerial duties, have ever been appreciated by his
attached congregation.   He adheres to the good old lines
in worship and doctrine which have so long prevailed in
the parish, retaining the Fast day before the Sacrament
till a few months ago, and worthily maintains the honoured position held by the ministers of Cardross.   Mr.
Maxwell has kindly allowed the author to give his trans-
lations of the Latin inscriptions on several of the ancient
tombs in the churchyard, as well as furnished information regarding the parish.

The situation of Cardross church is a remarkably fine one, placed as
it is on an eminence looking away down the noble Frith of Clyde and
its mountain background, and shaded by a few old beech and oak trees
which flourish in full luxuriance of summer foliage.   Of massive construction, and with fine lines of Gothic architecture, it is an ornament to

the district, and has many features of interest. The red sandstone of which it is built is hewn in solid blocks, and at the east end on the gable there is a stone Latin cross of uncommon form, a most unusual decoration in churches of the earlier part of the century. It stands nearly upon the foundation of the previous building, which was an unadorned structure of small dimensions. Few are left who worshipped in the old church, but one native of the parish, Alexander Ewing, who long was carrier between Dunbarton and Glasgow, still survives, in his 96th year, and distinctly remembers the old church and its minister, the Rev. Archibald Wilson. It was a narrow, barn-like structure, with the pulpit at the side wall, and opposite were the gallery seats of the Dennistouns, Smolletts, and the Bontines of Ardoch, and the Kilmahew family. A small room off the Dennistoun pew enabled the occupants to enjoy a little repose between the services, there being an hour's interval. There was a small bell tower from which the bell was suspended which summoned the inhabitants to worship, and on sacramental occasions there would be sometimes a contingent from the opposite shores of Port-Glasgow to hear some notable preacher in the " tent " in the churchyard.

Inside the churchyard are some interesting tombs, especially those of the old ministers at the corner of the enclosure nearest the road. The oldest is in memory of the Rev. Robert Watson, who died in 1671, and the translation of the Latin inscription runs as follows :

" Sacred to the memory of Master Robert Watson. Oh ! sad to tell, this humble tomb contains Watson, for twice ten years parish minister of Cardross, a brilliant. ornament in the mystic sciences, a helper of the wretched, and a distinguished athlete for the Lord ; eloquent, fluent, in piety second to none ; having fought a good fight, now encircled with the crown. He died 7th September, 1671, aged 42 years."

Adjoining this is the tomb of Rev. James Gordon who died in 1693, and his tombstone is well preserved, though the lettering is beginning to be obliterated.

" To the memory of Master James Gordon, minister of Cardross. Gordon fell by the stroke of all-conquering Death, and his distin-

guished frame lies by this tombstone. He proved by his cleverness
that the sublime parts comprehend more wonderful things than
belong to nature; high souled, in good things daring as the eagle, but
as to praises indifferent, nor did the highest wisdom lie hid from the
learned man. Too early did the joys of life above snatch him from
us."

The Rev. John Edmonstone's grave adjoins, quaintly adorned with
death head, cross bones, and hour glass, and the long Latin inscription is fairly legible. It concludes with the following eulogy:—
"From the commencement of his duties to the end of his days a firm
upholder of honest virtue, and an unswerving ally and champion of
Christian peace, tender and compassionate to the ignorant and erring,
patient and forbearing to the wayward, he died 21 March, 1771, in
his 80th year."

There are a good many old tombstones in the churchyard, but
there is nothing of special interest to record. On one of them, to
the memory of Mrs. Bruce, there is an extremely elegant Latin inscription by a former professor of Humanity in Glasgow, one sentence
of which contains a beautiful thought, " sat sibi, sed suis, eheu quam
breviter vixit," which may be rendered, " enough for herself, but for
her friends, alas, how brief she lived." Several of the former lords
of the soil have large enclosed tombs, regular walled structures,
pompously adorned with coats of arms, the Dennistoun tomb in
particular, which abuts on to the church wall, is a large building constructed of massive stones.

There existed in pre-Reformation times, in the parishes of Cardross
and Row, several chapels erected for the requirements of the scattered
population, such as Kilbride in Glenfruin, the chapel of St. Michael at
Faslane, that of Kirkmichael at Helensburgh, St. Blane at Camis-
Eskan, and the chapel of Kilmahew. The latter is situated on the
lands known as Kirkton of Kilmahew, on the road from Cardross to
Balloch. It was erected about 1467, and a little way off, shaded by
some fine trees, is the schoolmaster's house and garden, where stood
in former days the priest's house. Formerly, on the same site, there
was a chapel in the days of David II., but in May, 1467, a new

building, dedicated to St. Mochta or Mahew, confessor, was conse-crated by George, Bishop of Argyll and the Isles. The present ruin, with its moss grown gables and venerable aspect, is doubtless the same chapel, and, though small, would be sufficient for the sparse population of the period. It was of some architectural ˉpretentions, the mouldings and arches arc of good design, and the sombre shade cast by a spreading plane tree is in keeping with the old graveyard adjoining. This is the last resting place of the earlier Napiers of Kilmahew, Buchanans of Drumhead, whose descendants still own that property, and others. At the Reformation, a Reader under the minister of Rosneath was substituted for the Romish paraphernalia and relics of Popery, but owing to the church being removed to its present site at Cardross, there was no need of the old chapel, which thus fell into decay. The chapel for a time was used as a school-house, for in terms of an agreement between Robert Napier of Kilmahew and the general body of the heritors, Kilmahew bound himself " to give the use of the chapell, and to mortifie to the schule-maister annually five bolls ane firlot of teind bear, and also a house and a piece of land extending to about an acre, together with ane piece of land for pasture, which was of old possest by the priest of Kilmahew in time of superstitione and popery ; third, to entertain the schulemaister in meat, drink, and bedding in household with himself within the house of Kilmahew, so long as he shall discharge the duty of family exercise and prayer within the said family."

From the *Statistical Account of the Parish of Cardross*, published in 1796 under the auspices of Sir John Sinclair, Bart., of Ulbster, we learn the following. It was written by the Rev. Alexander Macaulay, minister of the parish, whose nephew was the illustrious historian, Lord Macaulay. Agriculture is stated to be in a somewhat backward condition, although the action of the proprietors in enclosing their farm lands is commended. Oats and bear are the common crops, but wheat, peas, and potatoes are much cultivated ; fields are being laid down in clover and rye-grass, but the culture of turnips is in its infancy. Limestone is used for manure, and much sea-ware is distri-buted over the fields, and street-manure imported from Greenock and

Port-Glasgow at a cost of 2s. per cart. Drainage is greatly required on account of the incessant rains which prevail and drench the fields with water. Formerly every farmer used to keep a few sheep, but now, except on three farms, this practice is entirely given over. Not much attention is given to the breed of milk-cows. The farm-houses are neat and well constructed, and every year increasing in numbers. Nearly 200 acres are planted with Scotch firs and larches, and are succeeding well. Coal is the principal fuel, 12 cwt. of which brought by water costs 5s. sterling, unloaded in Cardross bay. Land is rising in value, and the increase of manufactures on the river Leven occasions an influx of people, and consequently greater demand for whatever the farms produce. The printfields of Dalquhurn and Cordale are stated to be the most extensive of any in Scotland, the Stirlings being then, as now, the great dyers and bleachers in the Vale of Leven. This eminent firm, as far back as the year 1772, purchased the estate of Cordale, which was formed of a neck of land owing to the river forsaking its former channel, and thus being a suitable place for the erection of their bleaching works. In the summer of 1792 there were no less than 876 persons employed at the Dalquhurn and Cordale works. The goods manufactured are said to rival in the London market even the very best produced at the first English printfields.

An account is given of the foundation of the village of Renton by Mrs. Smollett of Bonhill in the year 1782. Her estate being contiguous to the rapidly increasing works set agoing by Messrs. Stirling, the site was favourable for the erection of dwellings for the numerous hands employed. The village was named by way of compliment to the wife of Mr. Smollett's son, Alexander, who had married Miss Cecilia Renton, one of the Edinburgh *belles* of the period. It consisted of three principal streets, which ran in a direction from north to south, parallel to one another. These were intersected by a number of other streets, all laid off at regular distances, and the houses were rapidly taken up. Other houses were being built in the vicinity of the Leven to accommodate the workers upon the lands of Mr. Dennistoun and Mr. Graham of Gartmore. Two houses in the village of Renton had been licensed by the Justices to sell spirits of home produce, and the number of public-houses had diminished.

The *yair* fishings are stated to be peculiar to this parish. The *yair* is a structure of rough stones gathered from the beach stretching out a considerable distance and forming three sides of a square, but not visible till the tide is more than half way out. As the tide retires a quantity of fish, herrings in abundance, and often salmon are caught in the enclosure, and secured with a hand net. The rights of the proprietors to these fishings are of high antiquity, being granted by crown charters more than 500 years ago, and they are carefully guarded. Education is provided for the 40 or 50 scholars who attend at the school, but the fees are paid direct to the master, who draws no salary from the heritors. The proprietor of Kilmahew gives £5 sterling annually out of a sum bequeathed for this purpose, and the teacher enjoys some other privileges, of pasture for a cow, and £5 for his office of session-clerk. The poor of the parish are well maintained by Mrs. Moore's mortification, which at that time produced a revenue of £70 per annum, in addition to the church door collections.

In this account of the parish there is but a very brief notice of the antiquities of Cardross. All that is said is in reference to the palace of King Robert the Bruce, as follows :—" A little west of the Leven, upon a small eminence called Castle-hill stood, it is said, a castle at times the residence of King Robert Bruce. In this castle, of which no vestige is now discernible, that favourite prince, as history and tradition informs us, breathed his last. A farm in the neighbourhood still pays to the superior a feu-duty called *dog meal*. This tax is supposed to have been originally imposed for the maintenance of his Majesty's hounds."

It would appear that at one time it was intended to erect saltworks at the peninsula of Ardmore, for a memorandum was addressed to the Court of Directors of the Company of Scotland trading to Africa and the Indies, dated 8th January, 1697, bearing upon this project. The report is by Mr. James Smyth, who had repaired to the river Clyde according to order to him and to Mr. Cragg by the

Court of Directors of the Company trading to Africa and the Indies,
to intimate the cost of enclosing ground for the said company's intended saltwork.   The spot selected extended to 100 acres of land
on the north side of the hill of Ardmore, the greater part belonging
to the laird of Fairholme. Details were given of the thickness of the
stone wall required, and the cost of the same, and it was added, "a
tunn of coal may be set on the shoar at the place for 3s. sterling per
tunn or thereby."

There is a further minute of agreement between Mr. William
Dunlop, Principal of the College of Glasgow in name of the Company
of Scotland trading to Africa and the Indies and Noble of Ferme.
This bears that the "said Company having design to set up salt
works and to enclose bayes of the sea, and two bayes seem to be convenient lying adjacent to the laird of Ferme, his lands of Ardmore
and Ardardan ; because several parts of said lands are benefitted by
the sea wrack, which groweth and cometh ashoar in said bayes,
which benefitte they lose by the Company enclosing of same, whereby
the said lands may come to be damaged and impaired as to their
yearly rent.   Therefore the Company oblige themselves and contract
to pay to the laird of Ferme the full rent which these lands doe and
have ordinarily payed these seven years byegone.   And because the
said laird of Ferme hath *ane zaire* in said deep baye for taking of
herrings the benefits of which will be lost by enclosing of said baye,
therefore the said Company doth agree to pay such sum of money in
all time coming as shall be determined and awarded by six or eight
discreet and knowing persons."   Provisions were made that the
Company should be able to cut stones from the craigs and quarries,
and have land on which to build the needful houses they required.
Care also was taken that the laird should be compensated for any
damage done by workmen and others to his " gress and orchards."

CHAPTER II.

Agriculture; Eminent Men; Smollett Family; Dennistouns of Colgrain.

A CLEAR idea will be gained of the general state of the parish of Cardross as it was sixty years ago, from a perusal of the short paper which Mr. Dennistoun drew up, at the request of the minister, the Rev. Archibald Wilson, for the new *Statistical Account of Scotland.* The geological character of the parish is of the secondary formation, the predominating rock being freestone, which is of a red colour, and friable in quality. On the north-west side of Killiter, an eminence at the eastern end of the parish, there is a considerable dyke of jasper, of a coarse, hard quality, interposed between the conglomerate and sandstone, and there are veins of limestone on the Camis Eskan estate, which however is more suitable for building than for fertilising purposes. Near the shores of the Clyde there are extensive banks of blue adhesive clay, covered with sand, intermingled with shingly stones, which are all submerged at high-water, and it might be possible to reclaim some of this surface by judicious embankments. One remarkable feature on the coast is Ardmore, "the great promontory," which is a conspicuous landmark on the estuary of the Clyde. At one time this would be an insular rock, from which, through the gradual recession of the shore, the waters have retired, and it is now united to the mainland by a flat neck of fertile soil. The rock, which is forty feet in height, is of the same formation as part of that on Killiter, half a mile distant, a conglomerate, in which rounded, quartzose pebbles are imbedded. In a sense the broad entrance to the Gareloch, comprising the bay in front of Helensburgh, may be said to extend from Ardmore point to

T

the extremity of the Rosneath peninsula, after which it is suddenly
contracted by the remarkable point at Row.

There were several families of considerable eminence, amongst
them those of Dennistoun of Dennistoun, Spreull of Dalquhurn,
Napier of Kilmahew, Bontine of Ardoch, Noble of Ardardan, and
Smollett of Bonhill.   Later on a few details will be given of some of
the members of these houses, and of one or two of the more recent
proprietors in the parish.   The family of Geils of Geilstoun settled
in Cardross in 1798, when General Thomas Geils of the Madras
Artillery bought the properties of Ardardan and Ardmore from his
brother-in-law, William Noble.   The Geils family were a warlike
race, and several of them served their country with distinction in the
army, and they still own property in this and the neighbouring
parish of Old Kilpatrick.   A still older family was that of Donald of
Lyleston, who acquired the property in the person of James Donald
from the Nobles of Ferme in the year 1708.   The latter owned it
from the year 1537, and they again gained possession of it in 1890,
when it was disposed of by the Rev. D. Macalister Donald to
Captain Noble, C.B., of the Royal Artillery, who also, about the
same time, again acquired the Ardmore estate from the Geils family,
after having been out of the possession of the Nobles for about a
century.   Colgrain, which long was owned by the Dennistoun family,
who first came into the district as proprietors in the fourteenth
century, was disposed of in 1836 by James Dennistoun, sixteenth in
descent from William Dennistoun, first of Colgrain.   The purchaser
was Colin Campbell, who also bought Camis Eskan, and whose family
claim to be descended from Colin Campbell of Glenurchy, ancestor
of the Breadalbane house.   His grandson, William Middleton
Campbell, is the present owner of the Colgrain and Camis Eskan
estates, a merchant in London, and Director of the Bank of England.
Kilmahew estate, so long the residence of the Napier family, who
were territorial lords in the parish for centuries, is now owned by
John William Burns, also proprietor of the fine estate of Cumber-
nauld, whose father, the late James Burns, one of the founders of
the famous Cunard Steam-Ship Company, bought the property in

1859. Keppoch estate, now the property of Alexander Crum Ewing, was for a number of years in the possession of Mr. Dunlop, a well-known banker in Greenock, several of whose sons achieved distinction in different walks in life. He was a lineal descendant of the celebrated Principal Carstares,* the trusted counsellor of King William the Third, of glorious Protestant memory, whose life, written by his relative, Dr. Story, Professor of Church History in Glasgow University, contains many stirring vicissitudes of an eventful period in our national history.

Agriculture in the parish, when Mr. Dennistoun drew up his account, was in a somewhat backward condition. A slight change for the better occurred amongst the crofter race, who largely peopled the lands after the rebellion of 1745, but until the end of last century the outlay of the proprietors extended little beyond the mains, or home farm, the small holdings being left alone. During the first forty years of the present century an improved state of matters had prevailed, and a large amount of money had been spent on roads, enclosures, buildings, and agriculture. Considerable tracts of waste lands had been reclaimed, and draining, levelling, and manuring had enhanced the value of the cultivated soil. Cottaries were turned into

---

* This eminent man had no direct descendants, and the thumbscrews with which he was tortured passed at his death to his favourite sister, Sarah, wife of William Dunlop, Principal of the University of Glasgow. They had been presented by the Privy Council to Carstares upon their public acknowledgment of the baseless charges which had been brought against the latter. He was in the confidence of the leaders of the Presbyterian party, Argyll and others, then exiled in Holland, and was a trusted agent of the Prince of Orange. When subjected to the torture, Sir George Mackenzie, who was one of his persecutors, was constrained afterwards to admit, "All had on that occasion admired Mr. Carstares' fortitude and generosity, who stood more in awe of his love to his friends than of the fear of torture, and hazarded rather to die for Jerviswoode than that Jerviswoode should die by him." The thumbscrews were inherited by the Dunlops, now of Gairbraid, and long remained at Keppoch, and Dr. Story wrote a description of them, which appears in the proceedings of the Scottish Society of Antiquaries on 11th May, 1891. He also had the honour of exhibiting them to the Queen at Balmoral in 1886.

farms, crofts into convenient fields, and the sea ware which used to manure the land was everywhere being superseded by fertilising stuff from the farm yard, or imported from Greenock. The ancient occupiers of the soil were being converted into day labourers or artisans, and earned a good living, while substantial steadings replaced the dry stone hovels they inhabited. In a few places small holdings and short leases prevailed, but in the enlarged farms new tacks for nineteen years, stipulating for an approved rotation of crops and a fixed money rent, were mostly adopted.

Though much of the parish consisted of moor pasture, it was largely employed in grazing cattle and sheep purchased from the West Highlands. The low country being well adapted for dairy husbandry, a number of animals of the finest breed had recently been introduced from Ayrshire. Also the race of horses had been improved by a cross with the Clydesdale stock, and cattle of all sorts were rapidly gaining in quality under the auspices of an association recently formed in the county in connection with the Highland Society of Scotland. Though the district is remarkably well adapted for the growth of oak, the extent of natural wood was not great, and yet the evidence of ancient charters proves that in the country west of the Leven were situated the principal forests of the Lennox. On the Dalquhurn, Camis Eskan, and Kilmahew estates there were considerable oak, birch, and fir plantations. The fisheries were of small account, and there were *yairs* only at Ardmore and Colgrain, but large supplies of salmon were taken by the recently introduced bagnets in the open Frith near Ardmore.

At that time the state of education was fairly good, and there was a parish school, of which the teacher drew £34 of salary and £24 of school fees, besides £15 as the average value of some grounds. The schoolmaster, in addition, acted as Session Clerk and to Mrs. Moore's Mortification, and this gave him £25 more. In addition there were five private schools, the emoluments derived from fees varying from £15 to £70. At these schools the usual branches were taught, the fees at the parish school being, for English reading 10s., writing 12s., arithmetic 14s., and for Latin 16s. There was also a good general subscription Library at Renton, containing 1000 volumes, and one at Geilston for the landward district with 400 volumes. The poor were well cared for, and the weekly collections from the parish church produced £120 a year, with £15 additional from various other sources for the support of the 70 paupers on the Session Roll. Mrs. Moore's Mortification produced £228 from the rent of the estate of Ballimenoch, in addition to the interest on £1000 obtained from the sale of the freehold superiority. There were no public charitable institutions, friendly societies, savings banks, prisons or fairs in the parish, and considerable exertions had been made to check the increase of public houses.

The following is the account of the origin of the Moore Mortification as given in the Dennistoun MS. :—

"A servant in the family of Whitehill of Keppoch, named Jane Watson, had been in the habit of bestowing on her aged mother, who lived in the neighbourhood, a small piece of beef taken from the barrel, in which every Scotch farmer used to preserve his winter's supply. Making her way to the barrel in the dark one winter morning, Jane, by mistake, took out and wrapped up a fine tongue which had been placed there exclusively for her master's use. As it was cut up and partly used before she was aware of her mistake, no way seemed open to her to avoid detection and disgrace, and she therefore secretly fled from the house, and continued her course eastward till a stop was for a time put to her flight by the swollen burn of Auchenfroe. Sitting down upon the bank, and reflecting, no doubt, upon her past and present position, she is then said to have vowed that if she ever became possessed of the necessary means she would erect a bridge over the burn as a useful token of her penitence. Jane Watson proceeded to Leith, where she married a shipbroker named Moore, who afterwards settled in London, and was so success-ful in business as to enable his widow to exhibit, in a manner more munificent than she at one time ever expected, her sympathy for the poor of her native parish."

In former years the mosses and uplands of Cardross were covered with birches, pine and oak trees, and in digging in the moors, roots

and trunks of trees are often encountered. Thick woods, amidst
which roamed the wild animals of the chase, clothed the lands of
Darlieth, Auchendcnnan and Bromley, intermingled with copse woods
of hazel, willow and birch. The very name of Darlieth, the "grey
oak wood," indicated the prevailing class of wood which was indigenous to the soil, and the name of the river which bounds the
eastern portion of the parish, Leven or Elm river, shows that the elm
tree once was a feature of the forest. At one period the whole of
Scotland was thickly wooded, and the ancient name of those who
dwelt to the north of the Forth, Caledonians, men of the Celyddon,
or woodland thickets, is proof of this fact. The valley of the Forth
from Balloch to Stirling, was once a continuous forest, and the
famous Flanders moss, near Aberfoyle, was said to have been formed
when the Roman invasion, under Severus, took place, by the vast
quantity of timber he caused to be cut down. The highest hill in
the parish, the Killiter, or "wood of the wet hillside," indicates that
both wood and water were more abundant than now, and near
Drumhead may be seen the site of an ancient lake which formerly
received the accumulated waters of the uplands of the district.

From the pages of Dr. David Murray's masterly survey of the
parish in *Old Cardross*, are gathered the following particulars regarding
the old Tribe Lands, and the conditions under which they were
granted according to ancient Celtic tenures. These charters also
show evidence of the mode of life, and customs of the people at a
byegone era. The lands were the property of the tribe or family,
held for behoof of all its members, the arable land being subdivided
at intervals of time amongst individuals—reverting to the community
after a certain fixed period—and the waste and pasture land being
common to all. From this custom arose the merklands, pennylands,
and quarter lands, into which the soil was divided, also the baneful
system of runrig, which so seriously hindered all improvements in
agriculture. The word "toun," "town," or "tun," is frequently
found in connection with the old tribe-land distribution of the soil,
not to describe a settlement of individuals, but merely a farm-
steading, or the centre round which a number of farm tenants dwelt.

In the district leases of no very remote date, the town was often mentioned, as the town and lands of Havock, the town and lands of Succoth. In the parish of Old Kilpatrick there are some farms described as the "fourteen towns of Kilpatrick," from which the singular old feu-duty, called the "Watch mail of Kilpatrick" is payable as part of the revenue of the Constabulary of the Castle of Dunbarton.

During the 13th century the great possessions of the Earls of Lennox were becoming sub-divided and alienated, and the lands became gradually concentrated in different families, who continued to hold them in many instances till within recent years. Without attempting to give a complete list of the lands in the parish, it will be of interest to summarise those mentioned by Dr. Murray. Commencing at the north-eastern end of the parish there are the two Dalquhurns, the Cordales, and Pillanflatt, part of which is now enclosed in the public park of Renton, and next Rosrivan and St. Sebastian. Beyond this on the low ground beside the Leven is the Mains of Cardross, and higher up Hill Acre, Greenhill, and the Cottary of Hillhead and Dalreoch, Sinkyholm and Henryshott on the high road leading to Dunbarton, and near the bridge on the Ferrylands of Cardross. Laigh and High Kirkton encircle the Ferrylands close to Cardross point and up to the high ground, on which are Kirkton lands and muir. Easter Hole or Foul Hole and Braehead succeed, with Sandybraes, Castlehill, and Muirhouses fronting them, and beyond are Upper Mains, Barbisland and Whiteleys. Near this we arrive at Blairshalloch (or Willow Plain) with its castellated tower, and then to the north is Succoth. Nearer to the Leven are High and Laigh Dalmoak, to the west of which are North and South Kipperminshoch and Kipperoch, with Ardochbeg to the south. West of Ardochbeg is Kellochy, and beyond this Hawthornhill, or as it was formerly called Latriehill—the wet hill slope. Looking down upon the estuary of the Clyde is Clerkhill, and below this at the foot of the old sea beach is the Havock with Tartan Perrays to the west. We now arrive at the farm of Clydebank, which at the close of last century was taken out of the surrounding land by Mr. Robert M'Kenzie, who was then factor on the Ardoch estate.

Beyond Clydebank is the Lee, then Burnfoot of Ardoch, and ascending the burn Ardochmore is reached, where formerly the old mansion house of Ardoch stood. Wester Ardoch, Craigend, and Walton lie beyond, and much of these were included in the old barony of Ardoch, long the property of the Bontine family. Bloomhill, Bainsfield and Burnfoot of Auchenfroe succeed, and higher up Mildovan and Asker, also formerly a portion 'of the Bontine estate. Crossing the Auchenfroe burn the estate of Kilmahew is entered, which extends to Geilston burn. For many generations this ancient estate belonged to the Napiers of Kilmahew, one of the oldest branches of the Napier family, who were by marriage connected with the old family of Maxwells of Newark on the opposite side of the Clyde. Between Geilston burn and the Keppoch burn are Geilston, Ballimenach, Ardardan Noble, Ardmore and Lyleston, and to the north is Drumhead, or Blairhennechan, as it was called until the name was changed about the end of the seventeenth century by Archibald Buchanan of Glenmaguire, on his marriage with Isobel Buchanan, the heiress of the property. To the west of Lyleston is Keppoch, and then comes Colgrain, the two Camis Eskans, Little and Meikle, Drumfork and Kirkmichael-Stirling, the latter of which was originally part of the estates of the Stirlings of Cadder, and was obtained from the rival house of Keir by a villainous plot.

The improvements in agriculture and in estate-management which were gradually set on foot about the latter end of the 18th century, were commenced early in Cardross parish. It was only in 1747 that sheep-rearing was introduced into the county by Mr. Campbell of Lagwyne, and yet in 1782, when the Ardoch leases were renewed, the tenants were prohibited from keeping sheep. So unremunerative was this industry that even in 1796 sheep were only raised on three farms in Cardross. The lairds had small rentals, and a number of poor cottars were settled on the lands who mostly paid their rents in kind. Some of the former proprietors increased their wealth from various incidental sources, and in other cases their estates were sold to those who had money at their command. Thus the farm-steadings, roads, enclosures, and fences, were greatly improved, and considerable sums of money circulated in the district, and the tenantry were enabled to co-operate with their landlords in enhancing the value of the soil. Large tracts of waste lands were thus brought into cultivation, while what was formerly tilled was rendered more productive through improved systems of drainage and manuring. In Cardross parish the building of dykes and fences commenced in 1766, when a march dyke was set up between Keppoch and Colgrain, and Geilston and Ballimenach improved similarly by enclosure in 1770. In 1773 and 1774 march dykes were erected in Walton, Kirkton, Drumhead, and Dalreoch. The sheep-park and other home-parks at Ardoch were enclosed about this period, and cross-fences within the farms were constructed, provisions to this effect being inserted in the tacks and leases.

The land of old was held a great deal in runrig, rig and rig about, according to the number of tenants on the farm—one ridge belonging to one tenant, the next to another, and so on. The ridges were unequal, perhaps forty feet in breadth, and the crown of the ridge above could be ploughed, and commons and common property were numerous. As far back as 1569, the Common of Ardardan was divided between the proprietors of Ballimenach, Drumhead, and Geilston, though even after the division the lands were dovetailed into one another, and the lands of Geilston are still conveyed with the pasturing and grazing of six cows and one mare with a foal in the commonty of the 12 merk land of Ardardan—Macaulay. In 1783 Mr. Robert M'Kenzie, for many years factor on Ardoch estate, took a lease of two small parks where Dennystown of Dunbarton now stands, for the purpose of experimental improvements. At that time they were soft and boggy, but Mr. M'Kenzie got them drained, cleared of stones, and, after ploughing the fields, succeeded in raising good crops of oats and wheat. In 1789 he formed the holding of Clydebank farm, although it seemed unfavourable for agricultural operations, being open and unenclosed, full of brushwood, stones, and water. After draining, levelling, and ploughing the ground, putting in good supplies of lime and manure, it was brought into a full and profitable state of cultivation. Similarly, in 1773, the lands of

Ardardan, under the energetic and skilful treatment of Mr. Walter
Brock, were reclaimed from a waste condition to produce abundant
crops.   Colgrain estate, then and long owned by the Dennistouns of
Dennistoun, was not reclaimed until the end of the last century, its
public-spirited owner being presented in 1801 with a medal on
account of his improvements.   Part of Ballimenach in 1784 was a
mass of stones, and Blartimore was of such poor soil that the tenant
could dig peats close to the dwelling-house, and on the high lands of
nearly all the farms in the parish were great tracts of waste, scrubby,
and uncultivated ground.   Kirkton and Drumsaddoch were, not
much over fifty years ago, covered with whins, heather, bracken, and
wood, with stretches of marshy soil and bogs, while now they present
all the appearance of prosperous farms.

Rents of farms in the parish were very low in former days as
compared with what are now drawn for the same holdings, and much
of them was paid in meal, poultry, and eggs, while the tenants also
were subject to "bondage," or services of various kinds which they
had to render to their landlords.   The rent of Hawthornhill, of fifty-
two acres in extent, was, in the reign of Alexander III., 20s. per
annum.   In 1629 the whole value of the land would be about £60,
or £5 sterling, and in 1657 its annual value under Oliver Cromwell's
Act was £45 Scots, equivalent to £3 15s. sterling money.   In 1806
the rent was £40 sterling, and the present tenant pays nearly as
much per acre as was given in 1657 for the farm.   The annual value
of the two holdings of Kipperminshochs in 1367 was 16s. ; in the
reign of James V. it was £10 13s. 4d. Scots and twelve poultries,
which afterwards became a feu-duty payable to the Crown.   In 1550
the whole estimated capital value of the entire farm might be
assumed to be about £33 5s. sterling ; in 1657 the valued rent was
£7 1s. 8d. sterling, and in 1880 the rent paid was £455.   Ballimenach was purchased in 1708 by the Trustees of Mrs. Moore's Mortification for 11,500 merks Scots, or in sterling money about £639, the
capital value of which is probably twenty times the original cost.

Keppoch, a compact and finely situated property in 1676 produced
£144 Scots, or £12 in sterling money, and one hundred years later

it was let on a 19 year's lease at 450 merks Scots or about £25 sterling. In 1820 Mr. Dunlop, a well-known banker in Greenock, who effected great improvements in the estate, purchased it for £12,820 sterling, and its annual value at the present time, is about £350, excluding the mansion house. Gilbert Graham of Knockdolian sold Ardochmore and Wallacetown about the year 1531 to Walter Colquhoun, the third son of the laird of Luss, for 278 merks Scots ; and in 1625 Ardochbeg, Hoill and Dalreoch were apprised from Thomas Fallasdaill for a debt of 1100 merks Scots and interest, and were not redeemed.

In 1721 the estate of Kilmahew proper—consisting of the two Auchensails, Kirkton, Kilmahew Mill, and Mill Lands of Kilmahew, Drumsaddoch, the Barrs, Auchenfroe, and the Spittal of Auchenfroe, was adjudged from George Napier by Sir James Smollett for two debts of £12,896 1s. 4d. Scots and £1295 12s. Scots. In order to redeem his ancestral domain, George Napier sold in 1735 to James, eldest son of Sir James Smollett, the Auchensails, Barrs, and Drumsaddoch, with Wallacetown and Walton at the price of £33,152 Scots or £2762 sterling, being about 28 years' purchase of the then rental of £1200 Scots.

Alexander Chalmers, who was the tenant of Succoth farm, died bankrupt in 1735, when, owing to the need of realising the stock for the benefit of the landlord, it was disposed of by public roup, with the following result :—

The whole growing crop, which consisted of bere and pease was purchased by Alexander Ewing in Kipperminshoch at		£27 0 0 Stg.	
A cow and stot produced ...	£18 0 0 Scots or	1 10 0 ,,	
A hawked cow ,, ...	14 10 0 ,,	1 4 2 ,,	
A black cow ,, ...	12 13 4 ,,	1 1 4 ,,	
A flecked cow ,, ...	14 6 8 ,,	1 3 10 ,,	
An old brown mare and colt, another mare, a black horse, and a "bawsant" horse, all ...	75 0 0 ,,	6 5 0 ,,	
Two ewes and a lamb ...	2 8 0 ,,	0 4 0 ,,	
In all amounting to ...		£38 8 4 Stg.	

The farmer of Succoth, John Leckie; a former tenant, died bankrupt in July 1661, leaving an estate worth £158 Scots.

The foregoing most interesting information from *Old Cardross* gives a good idea of the condition of agriculture in the parish during the past century. In the same work will be found many curious illustrations of the style of houses in which both the lairds and the farmers lived, the food of the farm servants, and the very small wages for which they gave their services. The cottages were just built of dry stone, cemented with mud or clay, a door so low that you needed to stoop before entering, windows with no glass, the fire on the floor, and the smoke found its way outside through a hole in the roof. The ordinary fuel was peat, sticks, and whins, and in summer the servants rose at four in the morning and toiled on to nine or ten o'clock at night. While the servants lived in such a condition of drudgery, the owners of the soil evidently had but a small share of worldly goods and chattels, and money was a scarce commodity. Even such a laird as William Dennistoun of Colgrain when he purchased, in 1683, ten bolls of bere from MacAulay of Laggarie, at the price of eight merks a boll, was obliged to grant a bond for the same of £4 8s. 10d. sterling. In 1676 John Semple of Fulwood, granted his bond to William M'Farlane of Drumfad for £1620 Scots, or £135 sterling, having as cautioners William Dennistoun of Colgrain, Thomas Fleming of Dalquhurn, William Semple of Dalmoak, and John Bontein, fiar of Geilston. In spite of all these securities the lender of the money had to go to the process of horning and poinding before he could get repayment. On 5th February, 1732, George Napier of Kilmahew granted to George Mitchell of Glasgow a bill for £6 5s. 3½d. sterling, payable on 1st June at Mr. Shiells' coffee-house, and the bill being dishonoured legal proceedings had to be instituted for its recovery. Another illustration of the slender resources of the Cardross lairds is thus recorded: "In a scheme of the income and expenditure of Captain James Smollett of Bonhill, in 1735, the sum of 400 merks, or £22 4s. 5d., is set aside for the support of his brother Archibald's two younger children, one of whom was the celebrated Tobias Smollett, 'until they are twelve years old.' Small though this sum may appear, the provision made at the same time for the widow of Sir James Smollett—Old Lady Bonhill, as she is termed in the scheme—stepmother of the novelist, was but twice the amount, £44 8s. 10d."

The old mansion of Dalquhurn at Renton, where the Smolletts of Bonhill long resided, and in which the novelist was born, is described by Mr. Macleod in his volume on the Leven district as follows :— " The site of the old house Dalquhurn, in which Tobias Smollett was born in 1721, is embraced within the bounds of a field at the south end of the village, over-looking the Leven. Dalquhurn House was a three storey, gaunt, prosaic building, of a severely plain style of architecture. Its northern front shewed unadorned walls, pierced with three oblong windows in each flat. It had a one-storey wing at its west end, the whole being surrounded by a low wall. The old mansion house stood on a commanding knoll, which dominated the river at one of its most beauteous links. Its northern windows commanded a fine view of the Leven valley, and from its southern ones prospects of the castle and town of Dunbarton, and their beautifully diversified surroundings, could be obtained, so that while the 'auld hoose' was itself unlovely, its position was most attractive." At that period the scenery of the Vale of Leven was rich and pastoral, the verdant meads laved by the clear waters of the rapidly flowing stream, and its uplands diversified by a blending together of arable lands, woods, and great stretches of heather. As yet there were none of the great Turkey-red works which have been such a source of wealth to the Vale of Leven, and the landscape presented a scene of Arcadian peacefulness and beauty which is alluded to in Smollett's fine *Ode to Leven Water.*

> " Pure stream, in whose translucent wave
> My youthful limbs I wont to lave ;
> No torrents stain thy limpid source,
> No rocks impede thy dimpling course,
> That sweetly warbles o'er its bed,
> With white, round, polished pebbles spread ;
> While, lightly poised, the scaly brood
> In myriads cleave the crystal flood."

The Smolletts of Bonhill, who long resided at Dalquhurn, and owned much of the land in the parish, are an old family who still possess the estate, and some of whose members achieved distinction. John Smollett, the first of the family, occupied a good position in the burgh of Dunbarton as a merchant and bailie about the year 1504. His son John was one of the commissioners appointed to negotiate with the burgh of Renfrew regarding the navigation of the Clyde. Tobias Smollett who was designated as of Over Kirkton, was bailie of Dunbarton, and was slain at the battle of Glenfruin in 1603. Another John Smollett was bailie depute of the Regality of Lennox, and provost of Dunbarton for a number of years, and died about 1680. Sir James Smollett his son was the first proprietor of Bonhill, which he purchased in 1684 from the Lindsays. He was educated at the University of Glasgow, and in 1665 was apprenticed to a Writer to the Signet in Edinburgh, but after his marriage to Jane Macaulay of Ardencaple, he commenced business on his own account as a writer in Dunbarton. In 1685 he was chosen as commissioner from the burgh to the Parliament, and this appointment was continued during twelve successive Parliaments. About the time of the Revolution of 1688 he came under the suspicion of the Jacobite party as one who favoured conventicles, and he felt it necessary to remove with his family to Edinburgh. In 1698 he was made a Judge of the Commissary Court of Edinburgh, and was knighted by King William III. Sir James was nominated as one of the commissioners who were empowered to treat regarding the Union between England and Scotland, a measure which he warmly supported, though his Dunbarton constituents were averse to its being passed. By a Minute of Council dated 4th October 1706, it was resolved that their representative "declare their dislike of and dissent from the articles of Union, as in their judgment inconsistent with and subversive of the fundamental laws and liberty of the nation," and a petition was also forwarded from the Burgh of Dunbarton to the same effect. Sir James, however, resolved to continue his support of the Union, as conducive to the best interests of the kingdom, and showed his constituents that their action interfered with his independence. He was created a

Deputy-Lieutenant of the county in 1715, when he received a letter from the Duke of Argyll, who wrote, "I am very sensible of the good affection of your shyre for his Majestie's person and government, and I don't at all doubt but you will exert yourselves upon this occasion, for supporting me in reducing the rebells now in arms against their Protestant King, in favour of a Popish .Pretender." Besides being elected as ruling elder to represent the burgh in the General Assembly of the Church, Sir James was nominated one of the Commissioners appointed to visit and report upon the Universities and Schools in Scotland. He died in 1731, and was succeeded by his grandson James, a lieutenant in Captain Paget's regiment, who largely increased the family estates by the purchase of Kilmahew from George Napier in 1735, and other properties. Upon his death in 1738 he was succeeded by his cousin James, who was Commissary of Edinburgh and Sheriff-Depute of Dunbartonshire. He was a man of enlightened views, and of a very charitable disposition. He purchased the beautiful estate of Cameron, where the Smollett family now live, in 1763, and he and his successors have since resided at this finely situated house on the banks of Loch Lomond. Here he entertained Dr. Johnson and James Boswell on their return from the adventurous journey in the Highlands.*

With James Smollett, the Commissary, the direct male line of Sir

---

* From Boswell's *Journal of a Tour to the Hebrides* the following is extracted : "Mr. Smollett was a man of considerable learning, with abundance of animal spirits, so that he was a very good companion for Dr. Johnson, who said to me, 'We have had more solid talk here than at any place where we have been.' I remember Dr. Johnson gave us this evening an able and eloquent discourse on the 'origin of evil,' and on the consistency of moral evil with the power and goodness of God. He showed us how it arose from our free agency, an extinction of which would be a still greater evil than any we experience. I know not that he said anything absolutely new, but he said a great deal wonderfully well ; and perceiving us to be delighted and satisfied, he concluded his harangue with an air of benevolent triumph over an objection which has distressed many worthy minds, 'This then is the answer to the question "Ποθεν το Κακον."' Mrs. Smollett whispered me that it was the best sermon she had ever heard. Much do I upbraid myself for having neglected to preserve it."

James's descendants ended, as he had no issue.   The estate reverted
to the heirs of Archibald Smollett, the fourth son of Sir James, who
had married Barbara Cuningham of Gilbertfield, and had two sons
and one daughter.   One of the sons was the novelist and historian,
Tobias Smollett, who was born in 1721, and died at Leghorn, in
Italy, in 1771, in the 51st year of his age.   He was apprenticed to a
surgeon in Glasgow, Gordon by name, and then went to London in
1739, and soon after entered the Royal Navy as surgeon's mate, but
after a short experience retired from the service.   About the year
1746 he returned to London, and tried to practice as a physician, in
which he had but small success.   From henceforth he devoted himself to literature, and wrote several novels which brought him fame
and money, and his most important work, the continuation of Hume's
History of England.   His cousin, James Smollett of Bonhill, who did
little to assist the impecunious author during his life, erected an
elegant column of Tuscan architecture to his memory, which may be
seen in the village of Renton, beside the public road.   The long
Latin inscription upon the pedestal, written chiefly by Dr. Stuart,
Professor of Humanity in Edinburgh University, records the claims
of Smollett to literary distinction.   On the death of James Smollett
without issue, the estate of Bonhill devolved upon his cousin Jane,
who married Alexander Telfer of Scotston, and assumed the name of
Smollett, and was succeeded by her son, Alexander Telfer Smollett,
who married Cecilia Renton, one of the beauties of Edinburgh, after
whom the village of Renton, built upon the Smollett property, was
named.   Alexander Smollett died in 1799, and had issue, Alexander,
a colonel in the army, and member for the county of Dunbarton,
who was killed at the battle of Alkmaer in Holland.   His brother
John succeeded, and married first Louisa, daughter of William Rouet
of Auchendennan, and secondly, Elizabeth, daughter of the Honourable Patrick Boyle of Shewalton, ~~Lord President of the Court of
Session.~~ *& sister of Rev. Honble David Boyle, Lord* †

Admiral John Rouet Smollett, who succeeded to Bonhill, was a
type of the naval officer of the last century, plain of speech and
somewhat eccentric in dress, but of a kindly disposition.   He died in

1842, in the 75th year of his age, and was succeeded in the family estates by his son, Alexander Smollett, who was born in 1801. The new laird of Bonhill was, in every respect, a true representative of a Scottish proprietor who continually resided on his estate, and whose earnest desire was to add to the happiness and prosperity of every one with whom he was brought in contact. He shewed great judgment in the management of his extensive property, and in 1866 rebuilt the family mansion at Cameron, which now presents a fine baronial aspect on the beautifully wooded banks of Lochlomond. The town of Alexandria may be said to owe its existence to Alexander Smollett, and at all county meetings his sound advice and intimate knowledge of public business made him a trusted counsellor. From 1841 to 1859 he represented Dunbartonshire in Parliament, in the Conservative interest, and he was a devoted adherent of the Church of Scotland, to whose schemes he was a liberal benefactor.

On Alexander Smollet's death in 1881, lamented and esteemed by all who knew him, his brother, the late Patrick Boyle Smollett of Bonhill, succeeded to the estate. Having, early in the present century, left his country to seek a career in India, it was only late in life that Patrick Smollett was much known in Bonhill. He was educated at the old High School of Edinburgh, where one of his schoolfellows was the eldest son of Sir Walter Scott, and another the late William Forbes of Medwyn. Young Smollett boarded with a clergyman who lived in Brown Square, and opposite was the house of Lord Glenlee, one of the judges, and he used to watch the old judge dressing in his robes in the morning, and marching with his cocked hat on across the Cowgate to the Parliament House. In his father's house in Queen Street, while attending the University, he often met Sir Walter Scott, and he remembered the sensation caused when Sir Alexander Boswell of Auchenleck was shot in a duel by Stuart of Dunearn. He used to see Sir Walter also at Ross Priory, on Loch Lomond, the seat of Mr. Macdonald Buchanan, and Sir Adam Ferguson used to visit his father at Cameron House. After leaving the University of Edinburgh, young Smollett went to the East India Company's College at Haileybury, where, among his instructors, were

U

Sir James Mackintosh and the famous Malthus. About the year
1824, when he was twenty years old, Patrick Smollett got an appointment in the Board of Revenue, Madras, and was afterwards made
Secretary to the Board. After a time the Governor of Madras, Lord
Elphinstone, offered him the post of Agent to Government at Vizaga-
patam in 1843, where he had great powers, both judicial and revenue,
and here he remained till 1857, when he quitted the service upon a
moderate pension. On his retirement Mr. Smollett carried with him
the respect and regard of the native gentry, and of the whole native
agricultural community.

Returning to London, Patrick Smollett began to employ his active
mind in political affairs, and in 1859 when his brother Alexander
retired from the representation of Dunbartonshire, he was invited to
contest the county, and was successful. He continued to represent
the county till 1868 when he resigned, rather than face an expensive
contest. Once more again he entered Parliament in 1874, this time
for Cambridge, and sat for the burgh till the year 1880. His
speeches in the House of Commons were vigorous and racy, and
shewed an intimate acquaintance with Indian affairs, and he mercilessly exposed any extravagance or abuses in the Indian Civil Service,
while his absolute independence made him dreaded by the officials,
whose ill-will he lightly esteemed. On several occasions he crossed
swords with Mr. Gladstone, and the House greatly enjoyed the
quaint and peculiar humour of the descendant of Tobias Smollett.
In 1881, on the death of his brother Alexander, Mr. Smollett
succeeded to Bonhill, where he constantly resided, and discharged his
various duties of Convener of the county, and chairman of different
local boards with exemplary fidelity. Recognising his self-denying
labours his friends and neighbours presented him, in September 1893,
with his portrait, and a copy was placed in the county buildings at
Dunbarton, beside that of his brother Alexander. In spite of his
great age Mr. Smollett was regularly found on the moors every 12th
of August, till within two years of his death, and to the very last he
retained his tenacious memory, and great mental activity, shewing an
intimate acquaintance with passing events. Like his brother, Patrick

Smollett was never married, and peacefully passed away from this earth on 11th February 1895, the last scion of that branch of the Smolletts of Bonhill. A very large concourse of mourning friends and neighbours followed in the funeral procession to the cemetery at Alexandria, the chief mourner being his cousin Captain James Drummond Telfer, of Glenview Hall, Hereford, who has succeeded to the estates of Cameron and Bonhill.

Thus died, in the 92nd year of his age, one who possessed mental gifts of no common order, and a politician who, although holding pronounced Conservative views, yet fully recognised the need of admitting all the respectable classes of the community to share in the electoral franchise. Having had the opportunity of hearing from Mr. Smollett, reminiscences of his early days at Cameron, and in Edinburgh, the author is able to give some details of that period. His father, the Admiral, was a regular old sailor, who went about shabbily dressed, and one day coming out of his avenue gate was accosted by a beggar, with the question, "did ye get onything there?" His mother was a kindly old lady, who regularly gave the deserving poor from the neighbouring villages a supply of meal and other articles, and they were allowed to warm themselves by the kitchen fire on these fortnightly visits. The village of Renton in those days was only a row of cottages, called the "Red Row" for the workers at Dalquhurn dye-works. What is now the flourishing town of Alexandria, was then only a cluster of thatched cottages, known locally as "the Grocery," from a shop kept by John Campbell for supplying such goods. A butcher, a shoemaker, and two public-houses ministered to the necessities of the neighbourhood, and the carrier went up to Glasgow on Monday, returning on Wednesday with the requisite goods. All the way from Renton to Alexandria, where now is a continuous row of houses and public works, in these days were green fields in which young Smollett used to shoot rabbits and hares. The old family mansion of the Smolletts, in Dunbarton, was then in existence on the south side of the High Street, but in a dilapidated condition, and was three storeys high, with an old-fashioned crow-stepped gable projecting on to the street. One or two of the stones of the mansion, which was built in 1661 by Margaret Smollett, may yet be seen, though the house itself no longer exists. In those days the old Elephant Inn was the great hostelry in Dunbarton, which was kept by Mrs. M'Nicol, and there was always a large number of post-horses for the use of the county families when they drove to Glasgow or Edinburgh. Patrick Smollett used to post with his father to Edinburgh, but afterwards he made the voyage in Henry Bell's small steamer, the *Comet*, from Dunbarton to Glasgow. He remembered how she sometimes went aground when off the mouth of the Cart, and the passengers would run rapidly from side to side with the view of moving the vessel.

Cameron House was built about 1790, and was a modest, old-fashioned building, but was enlarged in 1812 by Admiral Smollett, and only a small portion of the first house remains in the present mansion. His father brought the most of the estate into cultivation when Patrick Smollett was a boy, and spent a great deal in draining and building suitable farm-steadings. He used to shoot on the moor, which came down to the high road near Cameron, and got abundance of grouse, black game, and woodcocks, while there were various birds, not now to be seen which frequented the shores of the loch, such as owls, hawks, herons, kingfishers, etc. Capercailzies were encountered occasionally, but most of the winged game has well nigh disappeared, with the exception of pheasants. In those days only the Duke of Montrose and Sir James Colquhoun kept gamekeepers, and the modern system of battue shooting was unknown. The farmers came to Cameron house to pay their rents to the steward, and some of them brought live poultry with them as part of the rent. They were a primitive set, and Mr. Smollett remembered one old farmer, who had lived for sixty years on Auchensail, telling him that during that time he had only once been at Dunbarton. Smuggling was a great institution, and was openly pursued, and once he remembered seeing a party of twenty smugglers passing along the road near Cameron, with a piper at their head, taking a large supply of whisky to Dunbarton for sale. He knew where four illicit stills were at work on Cameron moor, and could see the smoke of five others rising

from the grounds of Balloch and Boturich on the opposite side of
Loch Lomond, and the gaugers were set at defiance by those engaged
in the contraband trade. Some of the Highland proprietors who
were in the way of dealing in cattle and sheep, used to stay at
Cameron on their way to the well-known Carman market, held on
the moor above Dunbarton, regular visitors being M'Neill of Colon-
say, and his brother of Oronsay. Their cattle and sheep were
pastured in the fields, and many dealers came all the way from Nor-
folk and Suffolk to purchase stock. Much kelp also was sold by the
M'Neills to the Dixons of Levengrove for their glass works, and after
a fortnight's stay in the hospitable house of Cameron, the brothers
would wend their way back to their island homes by way of Glencroe.
The Dunbartonshire lairds then were glad to increase their means
from sundry incidental sources, but several of them were obliged to
alienate their cherished family acres. Towards the close of last
century the farm-steadings, roads, enclosures, and fences, were much
improved, more money circulated in the district, and the tenants
were able to co-operate with the landlords in enhancing the value of
the soil. Considerable tracts of waste lands were thus brought under
cultivation, and what was tilled was rendered more productive
through improved systems of drainage.

A still older family, whose representatives long possessed extensive
lands in Cardross, is that of Dennistoun of Colgrain, the proud boast
of one of them being, " Kings have come of us, not we of kings."
Sir William Denzelstoun, the first of Colgrain, third son of Sir John
Denzelstoun of that ilk, is designed in a deed in favour of the church
of Glasgow, in 1377, as " Dominus de Colgrane et de Cambesescan,"
and was one of the household of the unfortunate Prince David, and
received a pension of 20 merks out of the great customs of the burgh
of Dunbar. In 1455 Charles Denzelstoun of Colgrain is mentioned
as witness to a deed, and in 1481 died, seized in the lands of Colgrain, two Camiseskans, Auchendennan, and Cameron. Passing by
several of the family, we come to Robert Denzelstoun, who seems to
have been concerned along with the Earl of Glencairn in treasonable
correspondence with Henry VIII. of England. He also sought to

protect his property from the lawless invasion of some of the Highland clans, and had a commission from the tenants and occupiers of
his lands to recover the goods spuilzied from them by John
Colquhoun of Luss, Duncan Macfarlane of Arrochar, and others.
In 1638 the family is represented by John Dennistoun of Colgrain,
a strong supporter of the royal cause, his many services being at last
crowned with the sacrifice of his life.   The Earl of Glencairn having
been appointed by Charles II., in 1653, Commander-in-Chief of the
Royalist troops in Scotland, granted commissions to Dennistoun in
November and December of that year.   Monk, Couper, Argyll, and
other Parliamentary leaders, came to Dunbarton in 1654 "advising
on a hard and sorrowful work, what houses and what corn to burn."
Very soon they apprehended John Dennistoun as one of the most
active Royalists in that part of the country.   He subsequently died,
after lingering for many months, of a wound he received in the
Highland expedition in 1655.   He left three daughters, failing whom
the property was to go to William Dennistoune of Dalquhurne, the
son of Archibald Dennistoune, minister of Campsie, who now came
into the direct line of succession to the estate.   William Dennistoune being unable to maintain his rights against various interested
parties, was obliged to live in retirement, although he was a strong
supporter of the Tory party.   He was nominated as Commissioner
for the County of Dunbarton in the Acts of Supply for the years
1678-1685 and for 1704.   He was succeeded by his son John, who,
during his occupancy, cleared the estate of debt, and left it to his
son much enhanced in value, and also was a warm supporter of the
Jacobite cause.   James Dennistoun in 1752 had a resignation from
his father of the family estates, reserving to the latter his life-rent of
the mansion-house.   He would have joined Prince Charles Edward
in 1745 had it not been for his father, and ultimately took the more
prudent and profitable course of devoting himself to commercial
pursuits.   He gave up the estate to his eldest son, and resided in
Glasgow, becoming one of the leading Virginian merchants in the
city.   His son James, who succeeded in 1796, on the other hand,
preferred a country life, though very successful in mercantile pursuits,

and was chosen Convener of the county, holding this office till his death. He was an enthusiastic supporter of the Militia and Volunteer forces, and long commanded the regiment of Dunbartonshire local Militia. Another James Dennistoun, son of the preceding, succeeded to the family honours in 1816, and in 1825 he acquired from Sir James Colquhoun of Luss the lands of Drumfork in excambion for those of Auchenvennal Mouling. He also established his right to the designation of Dennistoun of Dennistoun.

In 1834 there succeeded to the estate the man whose intellectual and literary acquirements shed lustre upon the name—James Dennistoun of Dennistoun. He was born in 1803 and lived a considerable part of his life at Scotstoun with his grandfather, Mr. Oswald. After having studied at Glasgow University, where he gave great promise of future scholarly eminence, he passed advocate in 1824, and very soon turned his attention to literary matters. He became a member and contributor to both the Bannatyne and Maitland Clubs, which had been started with the laudable intention of aiding archæological researches, and elucidating and tabulating recondite and abstruse subjects in connection with our Scottish history. Mr. Dennistoun presented to the Bannatyne Club an edition, drawn up by himself of Moysie's *Memoirs of the Affairs of Scotland from 1577 to 1603*, in addition to which he edited for the Club *The Cartularium Comitatus de Levenax*, *The Coltness Collection*, and *The Cochrane Correspondence*. He also contributed to the *Miscellany* of the Maitland Club "Letters from Henry II. King of France to his cousin, Mary, Queen Dowager of Scotland," and other valuable papers. In 1825 he made a long tour on the Continent, and met at Rome his future wife, Miss Wolfe Murray, daughter of Lord Cringletie, one of the Lords of Session, whom he married in 1835. Next year he was reluctantly obliged to sell the fine old family estate of Colgrain, and afterwards purchased Dennistoun Mains in Renfrewshire, the property from whence his family designation was derived. From this time his studies seemed directed more towards artistic subjects, while family genealogies and local topography appeared to be left in abeyance, and he contributed elaborate and scholarly articles to the *Edinburgh* and *Quarterly Re-*

views.　Released from his duties as a resident county gentleman and magistrate, Mr. Dennistoun devoted a considerable portion of his time to Continental travel, and he was thus enabled to pursue his researches into the fascinating field of foreign art.　His elegant work, published in 1852, the *Memoirs of the Duke of Urbino*, was a proof of his zeal in art investigation, and it received ample approval from those thoroughly qualified to treat the higher branches of artistic criticism.　The suggestions which Mr. Dennistoun threw out in the course of his examination in 1853 before the Select Committee to inquire into the constitution of the National Gallery, proved to be most practical and valuable.　The last work which came from his refined and fastidious pen was the *Memoirs of Sir Robert Strange, Engraver, and his Brother-in-law, Andrew Lumsden*, the finished copy of which, sad to say, was only delivered at his house on the day of its author's lamented death in 1855.

The works which, above all others, testify to Mr. Dennistoun's archæological skill, critical culture, and powers of intricate and laborious research, are the eleven manuscript volumes which, by his trust deed, he left to his friend, the late Mark Napier, Advocate, himself an author of some repute, though his writings are disfigured by one-sided and very extreme views.　After careful examination and selection, and being accurately catalogued and indexed, Mr. Napier, in accordance with his friend's bequest, presented the volumes to the Advocates' Library in Edinburgh.　On this occasion the learned Faculty adopted a minute in which they record their gratification " on becoming the possessors of these collections, which cannot fail to be of great interest and importance, as being the work of one whose eminent qualifications for researches of that kind were so well known and universally acknowledged."　While these manuscripts are rich in antiquarian and topographical information touching upon many Scottish families and places, the notes and chapters specially bearing upon a projected history of Dunbartonshire constitute a mass of details, elaborate and accurate, which have been of incalculable value to all who seek to investigate the county history. Mr. Dennistoun was an eminent agriculturist, who did much to develope the capabilities of his estate, and was a capable and judicious man of business, holding several prominent positions in connection with industrial enterprise, and his advice was eagerly sought as a trusted counsellor. By his express desire he was not buried in the family vault at Cardross, but in that of a former Sir Robert Dennistoun of Mountjoy, in the Greyfriars Churchyard at Edinburgh, so full of hallowed and pathetic historic associations. The epitaph on his tomb truthfully tells of Mr. Dennistoun as " Distinguished in literature, of cultivated mind, sound judgment and refined taste ; his Christian character, moral worth, and courteous manners, endeared him to many friends." The present representative of the ancient Colgrain family is James Dennistoun's nephew, James Wallis Dennistoun, formerly a lieutenant in the Royal Navy.

CHAPTER III.

Description of Parish; Kilmahew and Killiter; Ardmore Promontory.

THE lands of Cardross parish have, with one or two exceptions, frequently changed hands during the past century. Commencing at Kirkmichael Stirling, beside the town of Helensburgh, it would seem that in 1610 it was sold by the successors of John Wood of Geilston to Walter Dennistoun of Colgrain, in whose family it remained till the end of last century, when it was purchased by Sir James Colquhoun of Luss. Kirkmichael was, in 1825, once more united to Colgrain estate, in excambion for lands in Glenfruin. A small portion of the property, known as Drumfork, was feued in 1748 by John Dennistoun of Colgrain to his son-in-law, John Stevenson, who built a mansion-house there. Adjoining are the lands of Colgrain, which, with Meikle and Little Camis Eskan, belonged to the Dennistouns before 1377, but which were sold, as we have seen, in 1836. It was purchased by Colin Campbell, third son of John Campbell of Morreston, in Lanarkshire, who claimed kindred with the house of Breadalbane. Keppoch, the next estate, was in 1545 the property of Stirling of Glorat, and in the following century passed into the hands of the Ewings, and remained in their family till 1820, when it was bought by a banker in Greenock, Alexander Dunlop, one of whose ancestors was the famous counsellor of William of Orange, Principal Carstares. He built the present mansion-house, but after holding the estate for about thirty years, it was again sold by Mr. Dunlop to the late Mr. James Donaldson of Keppoch. A few years ago the estate was sold to its present proprietor, Alexander Crum Ewing of Strathleven, who has continuously resided there and done much to improve the property. The two Ardardans succeed; Ardardan Lyle (or Wester) was in 1466 owned by John Lyle of the family of Lord Lyle. In 1537 his successor conveyed it to James Noble of Ferme, in whose family it continued till 1708, when it was sold to James Donald of Lyleston. Ardardan-Noble, or Mid-Ardardan, was the property of Noble of Ferme about the year 1500, and remained, along with Ardmore, in the family till 1798, when William Noble sold both these properties to his brother-in-law, General Thomas Geils, whose younger son, Major Edward Geils, succeeded and built the house on the point of Ardmore. Ballimenoch, previous to 1630, was owned by Macaulay of Ardencaple, and then was sold to William Noble, whose grandson sold it to the Trustees of Mrs. Moore's Mortification. Blairhennechan or Drumhead, as it is now called, formed part of the estate of Macaulay of Ardencaple in the sixteenth century. In 1530, owing to the marriage of a daughter of that house to William Buchanan of Boturich, it passed to that family, in whose possession it has remained. The male line of the family terminated with Archibald Buchanan, and the estate passed to his sister, Janet, who had married Robert Dunlop, of the Garnkirk family, and by deed of entail the proprietor is obliged to assume the name of Buchanan of Drumhead.

We now come to Nether Ardardan and Geilston, the latter of which was acquired in the sixteenth century by John Wood, and since then was owned by Bontine of Milndovan, Buchanan of Little Tullichewan, and Donald of Lyleston. In 1805 it was bought by General Thomas Geils, in whose family it remains. Milndovan, part of the estate of John Wood of Geilston, after being possessed by Bontine of Ardoch, became part of Drumhead property. Next we come to the fine estate of Kilmahew, long possessed by an eminent family, the Napiers, who seem to have owned the lands from the close of the thirteenth century down to the year 1820, when William Napier, resident in America, made up titles to Kilmahew and Wallacetown, as heir of his uncle, and conveyed them to Alexander Sharp, brother of the husband of his sister Elizabeth. The Kilmahew estate was acquired in 1859 by James Burns.

Ardoch estate comes next, stretching along the shores of the Clyde ;
it was long possessed by the Bontines, and about the close of last
century was disposed of by Nicol Bontine to his cousin, Robert
Graham of Gartmore, whose descendant, the well known ex-member
of Parliament, and champion of the working-classes, now owns the
property.   The adjoining lands of Dalquhurn, Ardochbeg, Pillanflatt, and Kipperminshoch, according to Irving, were likely embraced
within the bounds of the royal park laid out by King Robert the
Bruce in connection with his residence at Castlehill, and they
continued to be royal property until the time of King James V.
Dalquhurn was conveyed, in the fourteenth century, by Malcolm,
Earl of Lennox, to his seneschal, Walter Spruell, in whose family
it remained until it was sold by James Spruell to his son-in-law, John
Dennistoun.   Afterwards it was bought by Thomas Fleming, and
purchased from his son in 1692 by Sir James Smollett of Bonhill.
Kipperminshoch for two centuries was owned by Woods of Geilston,
afterwards by Noble of Ardardan, Edmonstone of Duntreath, and
latterly by Barton Aiken.   Succoth was held in the sixteenth cen-
tury by a cadet of the family of Ardoch, from whom it passed in
1616 to Robert Campbell, whose family became eminent on the
Scottish bench in the persons of Lord President Campbell, and his
son, Lord Succoth.   It is now the property of James Aiken of
Dalmoak, which estate was long possessed by the Sempills of
Fulwood, latterly by Graham of Gartmore and Dixon of Levengrove.
Mr. Aiken is the principal partner in the legal firm of Burns, Aiken
& Co., founded by William Burns, author of the *Scottish War of
Independence*, a learned work pervaded by an enthusiastic spirit of
patriotism.   Rosruvan and Pillanflatt at one time were Church
properties, and passed into possession of the Lindsays of Bonhill, on
the breaking up of whose estates in 1666, the lands became part of
the lands of Smollett of Bonhill.   The estate of Kirkton of Cardross,
on which is the site of the old parish church, belonged in 1528 to
John Smollett, burgess of Dunbarton, and in 1654 the estate passed
into the hands of Bontine of Ardoch.   The old property of Ferrylands is in the extreme east of the parish, close to the river Leven,

and upon it is built the suburb of West Bridgend.   In 1512 the property was conveyed by Robert Ferrier to Andrew Dennistoun of the Colgrain family, and it subsequently was laid out for feuing purposes. Levengrove was acquired from Richard Dennistoun of Kelvingrove by John Dixon, Provost of Dunbarton.

On a fine summer day the walk from Dunbarton across the fine bridge over the Leven down to Cardross is interesting, and affords many views of the Clyde scenery.   Ascending from the Vale of Leven, on the right hand there is the round mound, covered with old trees, which is undoubtedly the site of Cardross Castle, where King Robert the Bruce spent his closing years.   No trace of any building is to be seen, and the name of the farm, Castlehill, is all that remains to support the tradition that once the hero lived in this spot. About a mile from this we pass the site of the ancient house of Ardoch —or, as it used to be written, Airdoch—the dwelling-place of the Bunteins.   The castle was succeeded by a tall, bare-looking structure, which stood empty for a number of years, until it was occupied as a velvet factory.   The road now makes a descent, until it is but little above the shore level, and presently the old mill and the houses near Cardross Church come into sight.   There is little in its present aspect to remind the visitor of the hamlet which, in the last century, occupied the vicinity of Cardross Church.   The meal mill, called Cardross Mill, used to stand further up from the present structure, built `by Robert Ferrier in 1818, and still in the family.   The smith's shop was near the church, and the neat cottage, in which the venerable Alexander Ewing now resides, used to be a shoemaker's shop.   On the opposite side of the road is the small house known as Bainfield, once possessed, with the land attached, by a family of that name, whose ancestors purchased it from the Napiers of Kilmahew. Part of it is old, and used to be occupied as a ferry-house by Robert Barr, whose family have long been connected with the parish.   The old houses which, in Mr. Ewing's early days, he recollected near the church, have mostly been pulled down, and a succession of modern ornate villas now constitutes the village of Cardross.   One of them, a two-storey building called Seafield, stood near the old bridge, and a family of Napiers resided in it, one of whom was afterwards the wife of Robert Napier of Shandon.

Beyond the church the end of Auchenfroe glen and burn of the same name is reached, and the road crosses the stream by the bridge erected, as before mentioned, by the grateful Mrs. Moore. Though over 200 years old, the bridge is in excellent preservation, but the introduction of a modern iron railing over the archway, in the parapet wall, somewhat takes away from its antiquity. On the north wall can be read the inscription—" Not we but God—Jean Watson, 1688," and alongside is another stone with the date 1690, and a shield with quarterings ; the motto on the lower part being obliterated. On entering the small gate, and proceeding up the glen some old trees are noticeable and the rocky sides are picturesquely covered with ferns and creeping plants. Above the side of the glen Bloomhill House is seen through the trees, finely situated, and of handsome architectural proportions.

Proceeding up the glen under the old trees which clothe both sides, the policies of Kilmahew are traversed for some time before the large and imposing residence is reached, which was commenced in 1865, and finished in 1868 by Mr. Burns. The house, beautifully embowered amidst trees, from its topmost storey enjoys an extensive prospect over the Clyde estuary, and is beside the brawling burn, which is spanned by Mrs. Moore's bridge. It stands on the estate of Milndovan, which was part of the old Ardoch Bontine property, sold by Graham of Gartmore to the granduncle of Mr. Burns, Thomas Yuill of Darleith, by him to Buchanan Dunlop, who disposed of it to James Burns. There was a small residence on the adjoining field, known as the Triangle of Milndovan, of which a few old stones may be seen below Kilmahew, bearing the inscriptions—R.B.M.B. 1738 on one stone, and on the other only the date 1732, that are understood to have come from that old house. The first two initials were those of Robert Bontein, and the latter those of his wife. Near this was the small croft known as Ladeside, probably from the mill lade, which can still be traced for a long way on that side of the glen.

The chief interest in Kilmahew lies in the semi-ruinous castle, which is situated near the upper end of the glen, with a few old trees, and the site of a large orchard in its vicinity. There is little of architectural interest in the lofty pile, which presents a solid square appearance, its walls being about one hundred feet in height. Probably it was erected about the period of Oliver Cromwell, and it may have given shelter to some of his adherents in the troubled times of Scottish history. On all sides the walls and windows have been closed up and it is thickly overgrown with ivy on the south wall. Owing to the strange idea of Mr. Sharp, who, for a brief term after 1820 owned the estate, and who thought of making the old castle habitable, it was a good deal altered externally. He knocked out several new windows in the ancient walls, affixed a wooden balustrade on the south wall, and partially built a new entrance, flanked with niches for columns on the south-west angle of the wall. The general outline of the castle measures 46 by 25 feet, and it was altered from being a four storey to a three storeyed building. The broad lintel over the door at the north-west angle bore the motto, "The peace of God be herein." Some of the corbels left are large and shapely, and there are smaller ones in good preservation. The staircase near the doorway probably was carried up, and the passage along the west wall would give access to the kitchen and cellars. Towards the end of the last century the castle was burnt, when it is likely that the upper part of the battlements was much destroyed.

On the high ground above Kilmahew, on Walton Moor, in the middle of a small plantation there is a curious monolith standing erect upon a rocky foundation, which may possibly be an ancient tomb, as there were some smaller stones like the sides of an old cist found at the foot of the monolith. Those interested, also, in boulder stones will find a good specimen about five and a half feet in height, and a little less in width, right in the middle of the stream of the Wallacetown glen, which joins the Kilmahew glen a little below the mansion house. A great deal of its surface is white quartz, and obviously it has been deposited by ice in its present position long centuries ago. A much smaller boulder with well' defined ice marks upon its surface is in the grounds close to the mansion.

From Kilmahew a wide prospect is gained of the Killiter range of hills, the highest in the parish, and it is a pleasant walk to the top of the principal peak, going past the mansion-house of Darleith. Leaving the Helensburgh road beside the Geilston burn, the tourist sees on his left many umbrageous trees surrounding the house of the Geils family, with the waters of the burn rustling unseen below. The road is a plain country track, leading across the moor to the upper part of the Vale of Leven. On the right is passed that burying-place, known as the Kirkton of Kilmahew, to which allusion has already been made. A few trees throw their sheltering shade over the fragment of the chapel, which still stands in excellent preservation, the roof and door being in good order. On gaining admission through the iron gate of the enclosure, a few moss-grown old tombstones can be seen, slabs lying on the ground, one of date 1735, and two others to members of the family of Buchanan of Drumhead, whose estate is adjacent. On one of these can be made out: "Archibald Buchanan of Drumhead, died 26th May, 1789," and the other is that of "Dorothy Buchanan, who died 21st July, 1780." The rippling stream below gives appropriate music to this retired and peaceful resting place of the dead.

Proceeding along the Balloch road, the woods around Darleith house are now entered, and passing by a small sheet of water, and along the avenue, bordered by ancient trees, the dwelling-place of the Yuills is reached. Around it are grassy parks, with some lofty trees scattered over the turf. The burn winds its course through the grounds, with masses of ivy in some parts overspreading its rocky banks, and overhanging canopy of ferns, while little rills of water trickle down the mossy rocks. Through the leafy vista of trees glimpses are gained of the dark, purple, heathery slopes of the hills. In those verdant glades are some noble specimens of the beech, the ash, and the oak, which long have flourished in this beautiful spot. Darleith house is partly modern, but the original fortalice stands between a former addition and the later one in front, and tall, solid stacks of chimneys dominate the whole. In the north gable is a stone, with the arms of Darleith of Darleith, the initials J. D., and the date 1616, while on the eastern side of the tower are the letters I. Z., A.F., 1676, representing John Yuille, the first of Darleith, and Agnes Fisher his wife. On the west side are the family arms of the Yuills, with the date 1678, and the motto,

"GOD'S PROVIDENCE,
IS MY INHERITANCE." *

Leaving the farm-road near Darleith, and striking across the grassy and bracken clad stretch of intervening ground, the steep side of Killiter is gained. Ascending the heather brae, it takes not much time to reach the summit, and from it will be enjoyed an extensive panoramic view. Looking over to the Clyde, the most prominent features are the towns of Port Glasgow, Greenock, and Gourock, with their chimneys, factories, and shipyards, from which, on a still day, there comes the iron resonance of an army of labourers. The trees and cultivated grounds are further down the river, with the varied outline of Bute and the Cumbraes, and afar off the mountains of Arran. Between Bute and the purple ridges of Arran a gleam of sea is seen, and the different lines of the upper reaches of the Cumbraes and adjoining land come into view. Patches of sunshine, here and there, lighten up the masses of trees and moorlands blending into the Renfrewshire hill country. The spires and church towers of the villages and towns on the opposite shore catch the sunbeams, and, if it is an autumn day, there is a misty exhalation from the land which gives a hazy aspect to the landscape. On the near shore the hill of Dumbuck, and the Kilpatrick braes crested with trees, stand in relief against the sky, and the strong, solid mass of Dunbarton rock, of a dusky green colour dominates the river. Nearer to Cardross the fields shew alternate layers of green and yellow, with white farm houses and red tiled cottages embowered in trees painted with the tints of autumn.

---

* The old mode of spelling the name of the estate was Darlieth.

W

Looking towards the Gareloch, there juts out into the Clyde the rounded point of Rosneath, well clad with woods, and the brow of the peninsula, defined against the higher Cowal mountains of Argyllshire. The Holy Loch, and the many mansions and garden-fringed villas all down that shore, are partly enveloped in haze. Mingling their swelling outlines are seen in the distance the Loch Long and Gareloch mountains, and glancing down the latter loch, the eye rests upon the straight streets and verdant surroundings of the Helensburgh villas, with the broad grassy slopes conducting to sequestered Glenfruin. Ardmore point from this view loses the long promontory look which it has from the shores of the Clyde, and has an ample rounded surface, diversified with many old trees. The summit of Killiter itself is a comparatively level mass of mantling heather, with turf march dykes crossing its surface; on the one side the hill sloping steeply down to Darleith, and declining on a more easy descent towards the Camis Eskan moors. The eye can follow the farm road past Darleith on to the high ground above the Vale of Leven, which is generally overhung with a dark canopy of smoke from the manufactories which have added so much wealth to that once beautiful valley.

Turning to the north the spectator sees the lower end of Loch Lomond, with its richly wooded banks, sleeping in peaceful beauty, its waters reflecting the sinuous strand. Ben Lomond itself, and other less lofty peaks, are prominent against the northern sky, their seamed sides in deep shade and clad in purple panoply of heather. Round by the Endrick Valley, and towards the distant hills of Campsie and Stirling, there is a variegated and smiling country, cultivated fields, yellow in the sunshine, green plantations, and plenished farm-yards, with the curious cone of Duncroin in relief against the pasture and corn lands. Alternate stretches of light and shade vary the landscape, while many a dark ravine and shady hollow introduce another and a pleasing feature to the picture. Quietly rippling away amidst green meadows, and by briar-scented hedges, are many glancing burns, whose streamlets swell the rivers and lochs, but from the vantage ground on which he stands the spectator hears no sound of cascade or rush of water. The twitter of a stray swallow, the guttural *tok tok* of a grouse, the quick note of a stonechat, or the tiny hum of a laden bee languishing amid the flowery sweets, may perchance lightly fall upon the ear, along with the far off clangour of the Clyde building yards. When there are so many visible features of interest for the visitor he may perchance indulge in thoughts taking him. back into reminiscences varied and stirring, for in this district were enacted scenes which have left deep traces on our Scottish history.

Returning to the public road from Dunbarton to Helensburgh, an inspection may be made of the modern village of Cardross, and what remains of the older hamlet of a past century. One or two of the older houses are seen beyond the Parish Church, and others in the vicinity of the Geilston burn and mansion, but there is nothing of special interest to be noted. A conspicuous feature amongst the modern villas is the Free Church, which edifice is due to the liberality of the family of Burns of Kilmahew. A number of years ago the " Cardross case " caused great stir throughout Scottish ecclesiastical circles, for it appeared as though the cherished immunity of the Free Church from civil jurisdiction was to receive a rude and awakening shock. A notable minister, the Rev. Robert Boag Watson, LL.D., since December 1879, has officiated in this charge, one whose career has been interesting and honourable.   When the Crimean War broke out in 1854 Dr. Watson was ordained chaplain to the Highland brigade, and he endured many of the terrible hardships incident to those who took part in that historic struggle. As chaplain to the troops in India also, Dr. Watson was an eye-witness of some of the dreadful atrocities of the Indian Mutiny, when the fabric of British power in India was shaken to its base.   Subsequently, in 1864, he was nominated to the post of chaplain to the Free Church in Madeira, where he remained for ten years, and his services were highly esteemed.   Dr. Watson, in addition to eminent gifts as a Christian minister, is a scholar and a scientist, and when the Challenger Exploring Expedition was despatched, he was one of the staff, his special duty being to prepare the official report on the Mollusca discovered.

Mention has already been made of Drumhead, long in possession of the Buchanan family, and the grey mansion house stands a little to the north of Geilston, not far from the small Kirkton burying-ground. The older portion of the house is to the back, and, from an inscription on the gable, seems to have been built in 1700. Geilston house is of much more recent date, but has an attractive and antiquated appearance from the old trees which surround it. For a considerable distance in front of Geilston, the public road is over-shadowed by a fine avenue of trees, from which glimpses of the shining firth, with the numerous steamers passing up and down, can be obtained. Many lovely and lonesome scenes for an artist can be found in the shady nooks and fern-clad banks up and down the Geilston burn, which takes its rise in the Killiter range of moors. At a turn of the burn there is a very picturesque mill which has long done duty in various ways, first as a wool mill, latterly for charcoal, and now, extended in size, is known as the Kilmahew saw-mill. It is occupied by a well-known native of Cardross, Major M'Intyre, V.D., who is noted as a crack rifle-shot, having, on Lanark Muir, per-formed the splendid feat of making thirteen "bull's eyes" in succession at 900 yards. A still older structure behind the saw-mill, was from time immemorial a meal mill.

Following the Auchenfroe or Cardross burn down to the shore the beacon, shaped like an Iona Cross and painted black and white, will be noticed on the shore, close to the burn's mouth. Several more beacons of similar form are placed at intervals across the firth, the last at Newark Castle on the opposite shore. This indicates the jurisdiction of the Clyde Trust, and the posts are very serviceable in fogs to guide the ferry-boat across the river. There used to be several ferries in former days, with good substantial "wherries" for conveying passengers and goods across the firth, but now they are little used for that purpose. Cardross ferry over the river Leven at Dunbarton, where now is the old bridge begun in 1765, and several times altered and enlarged Craigend ferry; Burnfoot ferry at mouth of Cardross burn; Geilston ferry; at The Murraghs, and others. There was an old-fashioned hotel, known as Fraser's Hotel, which did a good business in those days, especially on Sundays, when the farmers and their servants would adjourn to the hotel after morning service. Murraghs farm is a small house with its gable on to the shore, it used to be a red-tiled structure from whence the ferry boats use to start, and there can be seen the remains of a *yair* for fishing in front of the farm building. An old right to the *yair* fishing must have been enjoyed here, as at other places on the shore. The rude quay from whence passengers used to embark on the boats, is standing yet, not much the worse of the storms of generations, and is often used by excursionists from Port-Glasgow and other places. Close to the farm building is the modest single-storeyed dwelling Sea-bank, where lived the last of the Sharp family who owned Kilmahew estate for a time. These old ferry houses, which have a few trees and shrubs around them, were well patronised until the construction of the Helensburgh railway, brought their trade to an end.

Once more returning to the Helensburgh road the two properties of Brooks and Ardardan are passed on the left, and to the right is Mollandhu. The latter is owned by the Parochial Board of Cardross, which has the administration of Mrs. Moore's bequest. These all formed part of the old estate of the Nobles of Ferme, and now have returned to the possession of Sir Andrew Noble. Ardardan is a long, old-fashioned, commodious house, which was described in 1778 as "a new built, genteel, modern house, pleasantly situated, and fit to accommodate a large family." The eastern wing was added by Mr. Neilson, the main building having been erected by Mr. Andrew Buchanan, a tenant who held under a long lease, and recently large additions have been made. Where the estates of Ardmore, Lyleston, and Keppoch march with one another, there is a splendid view of the Clyde estuary, with its mountain banks, and all the wooded and moorland scenery in the vicinity of the Gareloch and Loch Long, with the numerous embowered villas of Helensburgh in the foreground. On the left hand is the Ardmore peninsula crowned with fine trees, the trap rock shining at intervals amid the encircling belt of verdure, and the heaving waters of the Clyde lave this curious point of land.

Ardmore has indeed many features of strange interest, and will

richly reward the geologist and the botanist, and it has a history and
tradition which will repay investigation. It means literally the
"great height" or promontory, and no doubt, ages ago, was a mere
rocky island. Tradition tells that formerly there was a stone castle
upon Ardmore, with deep dungeons hewn out of the solid rock, and
it is almost certain that the hill of Ardmore was occupied as a
camp by the Romans. These invaders left traces of their occupation,
so it is alleged, in a rude causeway which led inland towards Keppoch,
although there is no longer any remains of this to be found. Of
Celtic occupancy there are many evidences in the names of the
neighbouring places, such as Camis-Eskan, "curve of the waters,"
Drumfork, "ridge of the port," Keppoch, "the tilled land," Kipperminshoch, "field of ash stumps," and many others. The land on the
neck of Ardmore point is but little higher than the shore, but the
round mass of red puddingstone rock, in which are embedded pebbles
of quartz, rises to the height of over forty feet above sea level. On
the summit of this great mass of rock, which seems to stand as a
tower to mark where the narrower estuary of the river widens out
to the full breadth of the noble Frith of Clyde, there is a table land
of excellent soil. Many venerable trees, particularly some large
beeches, and several noble Spanish chestnuts, the latter over 200
years old, with numerous other varieties, form a leafy fringe of deep
verdure round this remarkable rocky barrier. But the chief interest
is in the round rampart of conglomerate, where Romans, Celts, Picts,
and other ancient dwellers, found an appropriate stronghold from
whence to issue on their despoiling forays.

It is well to make the round of the great circular sea wall, and at
some points it presents a singularly picturesque bit of scenery, the
red rugged rock overhung and festooned with many different creeping plants, and ivy of several varieties, wild briars, broom, and
whins, and ferns of delicate foliage, with interesting groups of wild
flowers nestling amidst the clefts and hollows of the rock. In some
places the ivy has grown into huge umbrageous masses of pendant
verdure, and at intervals there may be seen long bare faces of the
rock. Cracks, caves and fissures every few hundred yards, shew

how the action of the waves, long centuries ago, had told upon the mass of conglomerate, detaching the quartz pebbles from their sockets. On the lip of the precipice different trees have formed a resting place, and their waving boughs mingle their sighing and rushing wail, as the storm winds wrestle with the long pendant branches. And a little way off the hoarse surges of the Clyde, on the long winter's night, form an appropriate dirge in the brief intervals of the howling tempest. Almost at the extreme end of the precipice there is a curious old round tower, built right against the rocky face, and which seems to have been a sort of outwork of defence. It is entered from the ground by a large door, and inside the tower there are traces of two distinct floors, also loop holes in the wall, and small windows. The height of the whole is over 30 feet, and it is not easy to conjecture to what purpose the structure may have been put in former days. From this point the promontory runs out some distance into the firth being now a field of rough grass pasture, with traces of former cultivation, for it is evident that all over the hill of Ardmore there was good arable soil.

There is a grass-grown road running around the rock, and many varieties of shrubs and wild flowers cluster along the verge of this roadway, and at the foot of the rock. Numerous botanical specimens of some of the rarer plants, mosses, and ivies may be culled. General Geils, who acquired the estate in the end of last century, built several wells, where beautiful clear water trickled in a copious stream from the rock, and these remain to this day, yielding a refreshing draught in the hottest day of summer. On ascending to the plateau above, there are several good sized fields, and embowered amid some fine old lime trees is Ardmore house, a good substantial structure, built in the beginning of the present century, of plain architecture, and well sheltered by the belt of trees from the tremendous gales which prevail on that exposed point. At the back of the house a walk with thick hedges on either side leads up to a curious telescope-shaped structure, known as " The Tower," with an open gallery all round the lower storey, and one or two rooms in the upper part.

Near the garden of Ardmore a grassy road leads to the old ferry-house, in the middle of which stands a stone pedestal, once surmounted with a statue of Diana. The ferry-house at one time did a good business along with the others between Helensburgh and Dunbarton, but now it presents a rather ruinous aspect. Twenty years ago, in a violent winter storm, a great part of the building, and the ground on which it stood was washed away; though the rough pier still stands on the shore in fair preservation. On the opposite side of the promontory is seen the old *yair* house, where the man lived who gathered in the fish left by the receding tide in the rude enclosure of stones, the remains of which can distinctly be traced in the bay of Ardmore. There was another *yair* a little way down, opposite Camis Eskan, known formerly as the Colgrain *yair*. Even at the present day salmon are sometimes taken near Ardmore point, and the long flat shore, with patches of half submerged turf and mounds of sea weed observable at low water on either side of the promontory, is a great haunt of numbers of sea birds. In winter time, large flocks of red shanks, golden plovers, geese, and ducks, gather on this favourite feeding ground. Great flights of golden plovers come together in time of snow, and alight upon the long reaches of sandy and muddy shore. Woodcock, snipe, teal, moor hens, and other fresh water fowls congregate along these flats, and feed upon the innumerable marine insects, sandworms, and molluscs to be found in the pools. When winter approaches these birds, along with sandpipers, curlews, widgeons, teal, ducks, and others, leave their accustomed haunts, and flock together near the Cardross shores. Even barnacles, and other Norwegian geese, are found amongst our home birds feeding upon the marine grasses, or occasionally betaking themselves to the inland fields.

The following description of the wild fowl shooting as it used to be carried on, and still is, to a smaller extent, taken from the old Helensburgh guide before referred to, will be found of interest. "It is by no means an easy task to obtain a shot at a flight of ducks, and exercises a more thorough knowledge of the habits of this wary bird than seems at first necessary. The sportsman must make up his mind to fatigue, cold, and repeated disappointment, if he would earn

success. There are two methods of following them generally employed, which we will attempt to describe. The first is by a sailing
boat. A bright day, with a smart breeze blowing, is preferred. Armed
with guns of larger calibre than are generally used on the moor, and
using No. 1 shot, or B.B., the sportsman endeavours to manage his
boat so as to keep the sun betwixt him and the birds. The light
thus prevents his approach being noticed so easily as it would be if
it were behind him, and a sailing craft glides much more noiselessly
and rapidly down upon the object than under oars. If he can get
within ninety yards of the flock, success is almost certain. A few
outer birds rise first, the others are alarmed and swim rapidly off,
turning their heads every way, apparently planning the best mode of
escape from danger ; suddenly a rustle of a multitude of wings, a
rush of water, and the whole are under flight. Now is the moment.
Fairly risen from the water, with outspread pinions, the gunner
draws upon them once or twice, as their distance may admit, and a
successful shot shows half a dozen of them dropping with a helpless
flap into their native element. The slain are immediately picked up,
and chase given to those only wounded, who oftentimes are difficult
to recover, and afford a long hunt before all are captured. If not
carefully watched from the very first, they disperse about by swimming and diving in various directions, and the pursuit soon becomes
utterly hopeless. Few things require more careful watching than a
wounded duck in the water."

"The other, and perhaps more successful, mode of duck shooting
is followed by moonlight at low tide, upon those banks where the
birds feed. When the moon is full, or nearly so, with a gray sky
overhead, the sport may be pursued with some prospect of success,
varying, of course, according to the knowledge and practice of the
shooter. A blue sky is quite unsuitable, as, however near the birds
may be, you cannot see them with the distinctness necessary to a fair
shot. The mode of proceeding is thus. On arriving at the bank, the
shooter selects a stone in a likely spot—the drier the more comfortable—squats down upon it, and invokes patience to his aid. If the
ducks are in migratory mood—which they are not always—his re-

verie will be soon broken, and his congealing blood startled into circulation by the whistling of the teal, or the melodious quack of the
mallard approaching him.   Cocking his gun and rapidly scanning the
horizon, his eye catches sight of the birds.   If they are only within
doubtful range, an old hand will let them pass without risking a shot,
knowing that, in all probability, they may return again more closely
to him.   If a fair shot offers, the birds are allowed to pass beyond
the sitter, who should on no account fire at advancing birds, as the
chances against his killing any of them, no matter how near, are
twenty to one.   Once past, however, he selects a bird from the centre
of the group, and fires.   If they are anything compact, three, four,
or five birds may fall.   Now is the value of a good dog known.   If
the shooter rises to collect his birds, he will get the slain, but may
have a weary and difficult hunt after the wounded, and probably lose
some of them in the dark.   What is perhaps worse, the time he is
dancing about he is scaring other flights of birds, and losing chances
he may never again have.   The rule seems to be never to let him rise
from his seat if he can avoid it, and the dog saves any necessity for
running after wounded birds ; but if he have gone, let him regain his
post as soon as possible.   If the night is favourable, the sport may
be pursued as long as the shooter can endure the cold, and the tide
admits.   When once the water flows to his knees it is time for him,
at all hazards, to take himself off, and seek the shortest road to land.
This sport is chiefly followed at Cardross, and the bays at Hill Ardmore."

Returning to the Helensburgh road the estates of Lyleston and
Keppoch are passed, and then the extensive property of Colgrain so
long owned by the Dennistoun family.   From 1466 to 1537 Lyleston
was in the possession of the family of Lord Lyle, who conveyed it to
James Noble of Ferme, whose family held it till 1708, when it was
sold to James Donald.   In 1890 the estate was sold by the Rev.
Duncan Macalister Donald, now minister of Moulin, to Sir Andrew
Noble, the descendant of its former owner.   Keppoch estate which
adjoins was acquired by William Dunlop, banker in Greenock
in 1820, who built the present mansion near the site of the old

tower erected when the Ewings owned the property, which a few years ago passed into the hands of Alexander Crum Ewing of Strathleven. The Keppoch estate was formerly given by John, Earl of Lennox to William Stirling of Glorat, for special services in the taking of the castle of Dunbarton. Camis Eskan has a fine situation, embowered in woods which clothe that portion of the estate, and are carried well up the heather hills at the back of the house, which is an irregular pile, part of it as old as the year 1648. The house was begun by that devoted adherent of the crown, John Dennistoun, but not completed till a number of years after his death in 1655. Even in 1667 the mansion was yet unfinished, for in that year his daughter Margaret was married to William Dennistoun, younger of Dalquhurn, "in a barn at the Feddans of Colgrain." On the Colgrain estate there are some valuable farms, the soil in this neighbourhood being alluvial, of great fertilising power, and the improvements commenced by Mr. Dennistoun were continued by his successors the Campbells. A short distance from Camis Eskan brings the visitor to the Craigendoran station of the North British Railway, which only a few years ago was the site of a comfortable farm house with the clear burn running down from Drumfork and mingling its pellucid waters with the broad estuary of the Clyde.

CHAPTER IV.

Historical; Archaeological; and Miscellaneous.

THE WODROW ANECDOTES OF THE MARQUIS OF ARGYLL.

AT Edinburgh in 1834 a book was published for private circulation only, entitled *The Argyle Papers;* this work is extremely rare, only fifty copies having been printed, and it contains some passages tending to clear the character of the Marquis and that of his son from some of the calumnies thrown upon them by their political opponents. From these papers the following extracts are made :—

"May 9, 1701. This day Mr. Alexander Gordon, who was minister of Inveraray, and the only living member of the Assembly 1651 told me, that the Marquise of Argyle was very piouse ; he rose at 5, and was still in privat till 8. That besides family worship and privat prayer, morning and evening, he still prayed with his lady, morning and evening, his gentleman and her gentlewoman being present. That he never went abroad, though but one night, but he took his write-book, standish, and the English New Bible, and Newman's Concordance, with him.

"November 11. That after King Charles' Coronation, when he was in Stirling, the Marquise waited long for ane opportunity to deal freely with the King anent his going contrary to the Covenant, and favouring of Malignants, and other sins; and Sabbath night after supper, he went in with him to his closet, and ther used a great deal of freedom with him ; and the King was seemingly sensible ; and they came that length as to pray and mourn together till two or three in the morning, and when at time he came home to his lady she was surprised, and told him she never knew him so untimeouse ; he said he had never such a sweet night in the world, and told her all, what liberty they had in prayer, and how much convinced the

King was. She said plainly they were crocodile tears, and that night would cost him his head, which came to pass ; for after his restoration, he resented it to some, though outward, he still termed the Marquise father, and caused his son to write for him up to court, which he did again, but the Marquise would not come ; till at last the Earl wrote partly in threatening, and partly with the strongest assurances, which prevailed, and he was no sooner come to his lodgings in ane Inn in London, but he was there seized and carried to the tower, and I think never saw the King, for all his insinuating hypocrisy and fervent invitations.

" The day on which the Marquise of Argyle was execute, he was taken up some two hours or thereby in the forenoon in civil business, clearing and adjusting some accounts, and subscribing papers, there being a number of persons of quality in the room with him, and while he was thus employed, there came such a heavenly gale from the Spirit of God upon his soul, that he could not abstain from tearing, but least it should be discovered, he turned unto the fire, and took the tongues in his hand, making a fashion of stirring up the fire in the chimney, but then he was not able to contain himself, and turning about and melting down in tears, he burst out in these words, ' I see this will not doe, I must now declaire what the Lord has done for my soul ; he has just now at this very instant of time, sealed my chartour in these words, Son, be of good cheer, thy sins are forgiven thee ; ' and indeed it seems it was sealed with another remarkable witness, for at that very instant of time, Mr. John Carstairs was wrestling with God in prayer in his behalf in a chamber in the Canongate with his lady, the Marchioness of Argyle, pleading that the Lord would now seal his Charter, by saying unto him, ' Son, be of good cheer, thy sins be forgiven thee.' The Marquise hints at this in his speech. (I had this from my father J. C. Carstairs).

" The Marquise was naturally of a fearful temper, and recconed he wanted naturall courage, and he prayed most for it, and was answered. When he went to his execution he said, ' I would dye as a Roman, but I chuse to dye as a Christian.' When he went out, he cocked his hatt, and said, ' come away, Sirs, he that goes first goes cleanly off.' Ther was one of his friends in the prison with him, and after some silence, the gentleman broke out in tears. ' What's the matter,' said the Marquise, ' I am in pain,' says he, ' for your family, my Lord.' ' No fear,' said the Marquise, ' it's none of thir things will ruin my family.' ' I fear their greatness,' says he, ' will ruin them.' I wish this prophecy be not too evidently fulfilled in his posterity."

Particulars Relative to the Landing of Archibald, Earl of Argyle.

" Edinburgh, June the first, 1685.

"Since our last we have an account that the late Earl of Argyle did, on the twenty-sixth of the last month, march from Campbeltoun in Kintyre with two troops of horse, (such as would be had in that country), and seven hundred foot, to Tarbet, and met three hundred of the Ila men, and two hundred more were expected, when they were all to muster, the twenty-eight. His three ships came from Campbeltoun on Tuesday, and the next day went into Tarbet, the greatest carrying thirty-six guns, the other twelve, and the third six. He had another small vessel with him, which he took upon the coast loaden with corn. The twenty-ninth he loosed from the Tarbet, accompanied with Auchinbreck (who we have already told you had joyned him) and came into the town of Rosa (Rothesay) in the Isle of Boot, where he took a night's provision for himself and his men. The thirtieth, he sailed round the island with his three ships and twenty small boats, and came again to the town of Rosa, and fired seven guns at his landing, having with him, as we are informed, in all about two thousand and five hundred men. He endeavours to persuade and encourage the people to rise with him by assuring them that there are already great risings in England, as you will see by a letter, all written and signed by himself, directed for the laird of Lusse, which is herein sent, and is as follows :

" Campletoun, May 22, 1685.

"Loving Friend,—It hath pleased God to bring me safe to this place, where several of both nations doth appear with me for defence of the protestant religion, our lives and liberties, against popery and arbitrary government, whereof the particulars are in two declarations emitted by those noblemen, gentlemen and others, and by me for myself. Your father and I lived in great friendship, and I am glad to serve you, his son, in the protestant religion, and I will be ready to do it in your particular when there is occasion. I beseech you let not any, out of fear or other bad principles, persuade you to neglect your duty to God and your country, at this time, or to believe that D. York is not a papist, or that being one, he can be a righteous king. These know that all England is in arms in three several places, and the Duke of Monmouth appears, at the same time, upon the same grounds we do, and few places in Scotland but soon will joyne, and the South and West, wants but till they hear I am landed, for so we resolved before I left Holland. Now, I beseech you, make no delay to separate from those abuse you, and are carrying on a popish design, and come with all the men of your command to assist the cause of religion where you shall be most welcome.

Your loving friend to serve you,

ARGYLE.

"P.S.—Let this serve young Loigie, Skipnage and Charles M'Eachan."

THE BURYING PLACE OF THE ARGYLL FAMILY AT KILMUN.

Hugh Macdonald in his *Days at the Coast* gives the following information regarding the place where the Argyll family have so long been interred.

"The first authentic notice that we have of Kilmun is in a charter, dated 4th August, 1442, whereby Sir Colin Campbell of Lochaweside—ancestor of the Argyll family, engages to found a collegiate church at Kilmun. This establishment, which was duly erected for the ' soul's health ' of the donor and his family, accommodated a provost and six prebendries, and must have formed a handsome addition to the previously existing institution. The charter of the foundation was confirmed at Perth by James II., on the 12th of May, 1450. Nor was this the only grant of the Argyll family to the Abbey of Kilmun. From the chartulary of Paisley Abbey (with which the institution was ecclesiastically associated) we learn that Kilmun obtained from time to time a variety of valuable gifts from the family, and that ultimately it became a place of considerable importance. The plan, the size, and the architectural style of the church are lost. Only one crumbling fragment remains. This is the church tower, a dreary looking structure of a quadrangular form, immediately adjacent to the modern place of worship, which was erected so recently as 1816. From an early period the church of Kilmun has been the burial place of the now ducal family of Argyll. When yet the Lamonts were lords of Cowal, and the Campbells were simply lairds of Lochaweside, the first of the race was as a matter of favour, permitted a resting place at this spot. From an old Gaelic rhyme, it appears that a scion of the Lochawe family having died in the low country was, at the request of his sire, allowed the privilege of a grave in the churchyard. According to the composition alluded to ' the great Lamont of all Cowal,' in consideration of present necessity—a snow storm prevailing at the time, and preventing the transport of the body to its native district—conceded the boon de-

sired by the knight of Lochawe. Afterwards, when the Campbells
became lords of Dunoon, Kilmun became the family place of sepulture. The place of interment was for centuries within the ancient
church, and the only access to it was through the body of the edifice.
At length, in 1793 or 1794, the present vault—a plain, unostentatious structure, adjacent to the modern church—was erected. This
has ever since continued to be the favourite repository of the ducal
dust. The entrance to the vault is by a doorway entering from the
churchyard, on either side of which there is a small Gothic window.
The place has a weary and woe-begone look, and at the time of our
visit, it is securely boarded up. In former times the prying stranger
was occasionally permitted a peep into the interior, but this is now
strictly forbidden. The place has been described, however, by one
who was privileged to enter the mansion of the mighty dead. He
says—'On entering, there appears on either hand a broad dais,
covered with large stone slabs, and about three feet in height, which
extends the whole length of the sepulture, and on which are laid the
coffins, five in number, and containing the ashes of four dukes, and
one duchess. Upon a lower and narrower dais, formed by a niche in
the wall, that runs across between the church and the sepulture, repose side by side, the statues of a knight and a lady. The warrior
lies *cap-a-pie*, with a huge sword by his side, while above him is a
boar's head (the armorial emblem of the family) divided into two
parts, and also a number of pieces of rusty armour, such as iron
beavers, war gloves, swords, etc.' Such is the interior of the last
home of the proud dukes of Argyll."

PRINCIPAL CAMPBELL.

From *Wodrow's Analecta.* Notice of Neil Campbell, minister of
Rosneath, afterwards Principal of Glasgow University.

"1727, Novr. 8. Mr. Campbell's patent came to Edinburgh. We
see now that the two brothers (Duke of Argyll and Earl of Isla) carry
all before them. Mr. Dunlop and the masters on that side are not
pleased, and the other side are dissatisfied, so that I think Mr. Campbell's exchange will be neither as much for his outward emolument
or inward comfort. . . . Mr. C. has the advantage that on a
change of Court he will not be turned out, as the chaplains probably
will be." (The Principal had been translated from Rosneath to Renfrew about 1715,)

" 1728, February 8. Upon the 8th of February Mr. N. Campbell had his inaugurall oration, and was admitted Principal at Glasgow. He was transported by our Presbytery Jany. 17. No appearance was made for his continuance at Renfrew. *Vide* letters about that time. There is a very foolish advertisement given of this in the Edinburgh Newspaper, as if ther had been a generall concurrence of ministers and many present. There were but two of the town ministers present, Mr. M'Laurin and Mr. Wishart. The satisfaction of the audience, they say, was not what was then spoken of, and his own friends say but little of the discourse. Be these things as they will he is like to have a pretty uneasy life for some time."

" 1728, May 9. Mr. Neil Campbell our new principal made a very poor appearance this Assembly. He was pushed and required to protest in strong terms against the power of the General Assembly to judge members of Universitys. However he softened it and put it in the form which is in my letters. Now and then he spoke some few words and voted slump. But I am informed he committed a very gross scrape and blunder when he brought in his protest to the Assembly, though he pretended it was in favour of the Crown. He had not the consideration to acquaint the Commissioner with it before hand. Yea, I find he threatened Mr. Colin Campbell, brother to Aberuchle, with the displeasure of the D. of A. if he continoued to vote as he had votted."

" 1729, September. The principal carryes all in the Faculty as he pleases, and now begins to make those who differ from him know what they may expect. I believe I notticed Mr. Wishart's being continoued Dean of Faculty, and Mr. Wood made sole factor. This step is much wondered at in a minister to choice a man, a professed and knouen Jacobite, and one who hears no Presbiterian minister and doubts of the validity of our ministrations to be factor to the Colledge of Glasgow."

" 1730. " As to Glasgow vacancy it is said that Pr. C. is received to the Laigh Church, and the Provost would be for him but the town oppose it becaust it wd. bring a burden on them still to make Principal ministers in the town when a vacancy falls out."

" 1731. Principal C. proposed in Faculty whether he should teach or not. Masters not disposed to help him. The Pr. said he expected the College would consider his additional trouble in teaching, especially as some of the masters had received money for extraordinary teaching. They refused, and said he should consider if it was not his duty as Principal Primarius professor of Divinity to teach. The

meetings of students of Theology were but form.   Principal only
hears discourses.   Has not this session above two or three prelec-
tions, does not explain almost anything but only hears discourses,
none present but bursars and few Glasgow lads and few from neighbourhood."

THE CELEBRATED SILVER FIRS AND YEW TREE AVENUE AT
ROSNEATH.

THE author has been favoured with the following particulars of the
above from Sir Joseph D. Hooker, K.C.S.I., the eminent botanist,
and formerly Director of Kew Gardens ; they occur in a letter dated
24th June, 1896.

"I took the opportunity of going to the Kew Library and con-
sulting *Loudon's Arboretum*, where I knew that these trees are described, in the hope that I might find something that would interest
you.   There I find that there is a drawing of the finest of the
Campsail trees, published by Strutt in his *Sylva Britannica* (fig. 2239),
made in 1829, when the tree was 90 feet high and 7 ft. 7 in. in
diameter 1 foot from the ground.   Also that Mr. Loudon was informed by Lord Frederick Campbell in 1835 that the tree was then
200 years old.

"The really interesting point to ascertain is the date of planting ;
as to which there appears to be no information.   Such statements as
200 years are really worthless, except if substantiated.   I think it
may however be assumed that they were planted by the great Duke
who filled Whitton Park, Middlesex, with a magnificent collection of
rare trees and shrubs—rivalling Kew.   Now Loudon states that
there is in Whitton Park a silver fir planted about 1720, which, in
1837, was 97 feet high and 3 feet 9 in. in diameter.   Assuming that
the Campsail trees were planted about the same time, they would
now be 176 years old.   With regard to the miserable diameter of
the Whitton tree, I should tell you that the soil and climate of the
environs of London are totally unsuitable for the growth of silver
firs, and that at Kew I found it impossible to keep a single specimen,
so ragged and ill-favoured they became, losing all character after the
first few years.

"According to Loudon the average height of a full grown silver fir
is 100 to 150 feet, and diameter of trunk 5 to 7 feet.   This may

refer to the tree in its native forests. As may the following table
of the average date of growth as shown by diameter of trunk :—

40 years growth, diameter 3 feet to 3 feet 6 inches.
50   „   „   4 „ to 5 „
60   „   „   6 „ to 6 „
75   „   „   10 „ to 11 „   „

After 150 years the tree begins slowly to decay.

"Loudon also mentions a silver fir at Harefield Park, Middlesex, as
one of the first planted in England (in 1603), which was seen by
Evelyn, and described by him, in 1679, as being 81 feet high, but
forked at the top, and 13 feet in diameter a little above the ground.

"As to the yews, they are more likely to have dated from the days
of the monastery. The yew is a very slow growing tree and attains
an immense age. Lastly, as regards the report that had reached me
of the downward progress of the two silver firs, it is what I should
expect, that they are past their prime; but on this point you
really should get the opinion of an expert if your work is to have
value as to the history of these noble specimens."

THE TAKING OF ROSNEATH CASTLE.

The following is "Blind Harry's" account of the taking of
Rosneath Castle by Wallace, referred to in the description given of the
castle and grounds. It is from "Schir William Wallace, Knicht of
Ellerslie, by Henry the Minstrel." Edited by James Moir. Scottish
Text Society. 1889. Bk. 9, p. 281, line 1470.

" Quhen nycht was cummyn, in all the haist thai mocht,
Towart Rosneth full ernystfully thai gang ;
For Inglismen was in that castell strang.
On the Garlouch thai purpost thaim to bid,
Betwix the kyrk, that ner was thar besyd ;
And to the castell full prewaly thai draw.
Wndyr a bray thai buschyt thaim richt law,
Lang the wattyr, quhar comoun oyss had thai,
The castellis stuff, on to the kyrk ilk day.
A maryage als that day was to begyn.
All wschyt owt, and left na man with in,
At fens mycht mak, bot serwandis in that place ;
Thus to that tryst thai passyt wpon cace.
Wallace and his drew thaim full prewaly
Nerhaud the place, quhen thai war passyt by,

With in the hauld ; and thocht to kep that steid
Fra Sotheroun men, or ellys tharfor be deid.
Compleit was maid the mariage in to playn ;
On to Rosneth thai returnyt agayn.
Four scor and ma was in that cumpany,
But nocht arayit as was our chewalry ;
To the castell thai weynd to pass but let.
The worthy Scottis so hardly on thaim set,
Xlty at anys derffly to ground thai bar ;
The ramaynand affrayit was so sayr,
Langar in feild thai had no mycht to bid,
Bot fersly fled fra thaim on aither sid.
The Scottis thar has weyll the entre woun.
And slew the layff that in that hous was foun ;
Syn on the flearis folowid wondyr fast,
Na Inglisman thar fra thaim with lyff at past.
The wemen sone thai seysyt in to hand,
Kepyt thaim clos, for warnyng off the land.
The dede bodyes all out of sycht thai kest,
Than a gud es thai maid thaim for to rest.
Off purwians vii dayis thai lugyt thar
At rud costis, to spend thai wald nocht spar.
Quhat Sotheroun come, thai tuk all gladly in,
Bot owt agayn thai leit nane off that kyn.
Quha tithandis send to the captane off that steid,
Thai seruitouris the Scottis put to ded,
Spulzeid the place, and left na gudis thar,
Brak wallis doun, and maid that byggyng bar.
Quhen thai had spilt off stayne werk at thai mocht,
Syn kendillyt fyr, and fra Rosneth thai socht."

GAELIC PLACE-NAMES IN THE GARELOCH DISTRICT.

THE author has been kindly allowed by Mr. Donald Maclean, Post-master, Helensburgh, to give extracts from a most interesting address given in April 1896 to the members of the Helensburgh Naturalist and Antiquarian Society. So many of the names of the parishes have Gaelic derivations that it is of importance to consider their signification. Mr. Maclean says, " what we now call Rosneath village was known as Clachan—still its local name—Rosneath being regarded as the parish name ; and Clynder could scarcely be said to enjoy a separate corporate existence, even on a small scale, its extent being limited to a few thatched houses."

From this I conclude that very probably Clynder is *Cil'e an tir* *
—church on the shore—or perhaps, church of the district, *tir* standing sometimes for the one word and sometimes for the other, just as
we appositely find a place further down the same coast named Kilcreggan—"*Cille-na-creige*," denoting a church by, or beside, the rocks
there ; while Rosneath—in Gaelic, "*Ros 'n fhè*," the point of the
marsh, or swamp—corresponds well, if we accept tradition, with the
natural aspects of this place in earlier times.

The little I can learn regarding Kilcreggan is contained, along
with other items of interest, in an obliging note from Mr. Bain, our
sub-postmaster at Cove, which you will doubtless wish me to read :—

"Peaton.—By itself, and in compounded names, was written
early in the 18th century Peitoun—[Gaelic '*Bidean*' (?)—a point,
tip, or pinnacle.] '*Blarnachtra*'—the 'plain or dale of cultivation'
—which you suggest, reminds me that in the 'forties' that farm was
wrought by three or four farmers on the rig-about system, and was
the only farm so wrought in the parish, no doubt the survival of a
remote practice. Its sheltered crofts facing the south were likely
turned over ages before the bleak knowes of the adjoining farms.
Craigrownie is a modern compound, the 'rowan tree on the rock.'
My mother remembers its origination sometime about 1830. Cursnoch—['*Coire 's cnoc*,'] 'corrie on brow, or side of hill,' describes the
situation fairly. Letter.—Peaton estate consists of two farms of
which Letter is one, so that 'half' [as suggested] is correct."

ADDENDA, 15th May, 1896, on questions brought forward during
discussion of the paper, and one or two others not then dealt with :—

Rosneath, formerly Rosneth, now appearing in official lists as
Roseneath :—The interpolated "a" is, unfortunately, by usage too
firmly established to be now discarded, but, although the intrusive
"e" is said to have first appeared in the word nearly fifty years ago,
there is no certainty yet of its finding there a "fixed tenure," the
noble proprietor of Rosneath estate, and many others, I understand,
continuing to write the name without this vowel.

Row, barely recognisable in this shape as the Gaelic *Rudha*—point
or promontory,—may have been at first, when it was the practice to
represent our present "u" by "v," written Rvv ; but in course of
time these sharp "u's" would be replaced by the compound "w,"
and then the round vowel would come to be used, thus completely
disguising and disfiguring a name which, even in its simplest form,
Ru, is at once seen to be alike interesting and appropriate.

---

* Or, *An tir chili*—the left shore—shortened and transposed to *Cli 'n tir*,
would appropriately describe the position as approached from the south.

Gareloch—*Gearr loch* (Gaelic)—meaning in contradistinction, no doubt, to those on either side of it, the "short loch." These—Loch Long and Loch Lomond—are both, probably, from *lon* (Gaelic)—a marsh or morass—terms applicable at one time, it is believed, to the inlet of the sea loch, as well as to the outlet of the other loch. Formerly a like condition may also have been present in the lower portions of the Endrick Valley, whence, perhaps, the plural form observed in the Gaelic equivalent of Loch Lomond—*Loch lonean.*

Other place names are given by Mr. Maclean, as Camsail, *Camis aille,* or "beautiful bay;" *Duchlaye* is for *Achlais,* "hollow or armpit." "In *Bun-a-chaṛa,* as the name ought to be spelt and pronounced, we meet with a purely physiographical term, "foot of the turn," the turn here referred to—right opposite the old castle—being made by the river Fruin, which almost doubles itself at the spot indicated. As to the name *Glenfruin,* Mr. Maclean observes, to quote from Dr. Murray's admirable monograph on "Old Cardross,"—page 10—"From the chartulary of the great earldom of Lennox we learn that about the middle of the thirteenth century Maldouen, the third earl, granted to Donald Macynel a land in Glenfreone (Glenfruin) called Kilbride." This disposes effectually of the current myth that the glen takes its name from the comparatively recent encounter (1603) between the clans Gregor and Colquhoun, leaving us, however, with three possible sources whence the name may have been derived. These are—" *Fraon* " (Gaelic), shelter in a hill; " *Freumhean* " (Gaelic), roots; and " *Fodh shron* " (Gaelic), below the ridge, or "nose." The last appears to satisfy all requisite conditions, and, as a combination, fitting physiographically, may, I think, be accepted without hesitation. The " *sron* " is unmistakably there, and sufficiently prominent to claim attention as an outstanding feature in the landscape.

The author is also kindly favoured by Mr. Archibald Stewart, Porthill, a Perthshire Highlander, with a few jottings as to the Gaelic topography of some places in Rosneath. *Tom-nan-Sionnach,* on the upper bank of the Clachan burn, near the moor, might be rendered the "knoll of the fox," *Dhualt* burn, "Black burn," beyond Knockderry. The hill above Strouel known as *Clach Mackenny,* "Mackenzie's Stone." The stream below Barbour Farm, *Sughedh* burn, or "Pleasant burn." The *Camloch* burn, near Peatoun, that is,

"Crooked burn." The farm of *Duchlaye*, or "Dark gorge" or "hollow." A height on the moor above Barbour Farm known as *Creayan Breac*, the "spotted" or "speckled knoll." The bare rocky point beyond Coulport pier is known as *Carrich Mhaol*. The old ferry on Loch Long side between Coulport and Portincaple, *Port-an-Lochan*. *Mhaol*, a "promontory;" *Mam*, as in *Mamore* and *Mambeg*, a "low hill."

Spelling of Rosneath. Some curious particulars are gathered from a scarce book by William Robertson, one of the Deputies of the Lord Clerk-Register for keeping the Records of Scotland, published at the desire of the Right Honourable Lord Frederick Campbell, Lord Clerk-Register of Scotland : Edinburgh, MDCCXCVIII. The volume is entitled *An Index, drawn up about the year 1629, of many Records of Charters granted by the different Sovereigns of Scotland between the years 1309 and 1413, most of which Records have been long missing.* On page 134, giving index of charters by King Robert II., there occurs, "3, Carta confirming a grant by Mary Countess of Monteith to John de Drommond, of the lands of Rosenethe, in the Earldom of Lennox, disposed by said John de Drommond to Alexander de Meneteth." As Robert II. began to reign in 1370, it would look as if the *e* after Ros had been interpolated by scriveners in legal documents from an early period.

THE BATTLE OF GLENFRUIN.

The following account of the battle was given by the Marquis of Lorne recently at a meeting of the Greenock Philosophical Society. The details were furnished him by a friend who had gathered them from original Gælic sources and traditions more than thirty years ago :—

"The hostility between the Colquhouns and the Macgregors resulted on one occasion in the slaughter of two sons of the widow of a Macgregor residing at Trelach. The lads were hanged and their heads placed on stakes, one on each side of Rossdhu. Their mother carried home the heads on two pieces of cloth and showed them to

the chief of the clan, who knowing and loving the lads, was greatly
enraged with Sir Humphrey Colquhoun, and resolved to encounter
him.   The arrangement was that a meeting should take place with
one hundred men on each side, but the Macgregors had a reserve of
a hundred to act in case of treachery, these being in command of a
brother of the chief.   On the other side, Colquhoun collected a force
of four hundred men, marching forward with a hundred, and having
the remainder of his retainers in reserve.   At the place of conference
a parley was held, apparently without result.   The Macgregors
turned to march homewards by a different way, and were then pursued by the Colquhouns, who called up their reserves.   The clans
met in battle array by the banks of a burn, the Macgregors securing
the advantage in point of position, although they were fewer in number.   The Colquhouns tried to rush the ford but failed, and the
Macgregor reserves, emerging from their place of concealment, plied
their bows sharply, completely routing the lowlanders with heavy
slaughter, many onlookers falling in the pursuit—amongst them an
unfortunate minister, who was a preacher at the seminary of Dunbarton.   At the head of Glenfruin the Colquhouns did make a temporary rally, but being again hard pressed, turned and fled.

"When the rout reached the middle of the glen the victors,
who were slaying as they went, overtook the principal of the seminary, who, with nearly forty of his students, was shewing every sign
of terror. They were conducted to Macgregor, who ordered them to be
confined for safety in a barn guarded by a man named Black Hugh.
After the cessation of hostilities, Sir Humphrey's people becoming
widely scattered, the chief of the Macgregors enquired of Black Hugh
as to his charge.   "What have you done with the young lads whom
I entrusted to you ? "   Hugh, drawing a dirk from his belt and shaking it above his head, said, " Ask that dirk and God's mercy what
has become of them."   " May God look on us," said Macgregor.   " If
you have killed the lads no mention shall be made of a Macgregor
henceforth."   He hurried to the barn, and there were all the youths
lying where they had been butchered, cold in their blood.   The chief
turned angrily and called Black Hugh, saying, " Why have you done
this ? "   Hugh answered—"After the youths had been for a time in
the barn, they became turbulent, I do not know why.   But they
spoke a great deal of English, and I could not understand a word of
English, but I shook the dirk at them, and told them to keep quiet,
but they would not, and attempted to get out in spite of me.   It
seemed to me that I might just as well lose my own life as let a prisoner escape, and as they came forward one by one to get out, I

killed them as quickly as they got within reach. I do not know what it means, but every one as he was pierced with the dirk seemed to me to cry out a sound like 'God's mercy.'" "It was not to hurt or keep them prisoners, but to protect them from harm that I sent you to the barn," sternly replied Macgregor. It was only then that Hugh perceived that he had blundered. All the Macgregors were sorrowful at the event, and the chief himself greatly distressed. They continued their march in gloom, taking home with them the body of their chief's brother, whom they found where he had fallen on the hillside. The fight, although named after the glen, really began about four miles from the glen, the pursuit continuing in its direction. A much larger number of the Colquhouns were slain on the lands of Finnart than at the head of the glen. After the battle the lowland party became enraged. They went and buried the dead, and kept their bloody shirts that they might be shown to the King ; and Sir Humphrey and his friends got 220 women to ride to Edinburgh, each woman carrying on a spear as a banner a bloodstained shirt, which she said belonged to a man massacred by the Macgregors. The youths who had been killed by Hugh were of good parentage, and the indignation caused by their death was not allowed to sleep by their kinsfolk and tutors. The King was greatly enraged against the Macgregors, having had a hatred against them on account of old strifes. He appointed a day for a Court of Justice, and Macgregor was summoned, but durst not appear. Neither was there any one to speak for him, and in his absence he and his clan were sentenced to lose their lands and name."

THE TRIUMPHANT BOAT SONG GREETING RODERICK DHU IN THE
"LADY OF THE LAKE."

Proudly our pibroch has thrilled in Glenfruin
  And Bannachar's groans to our slogan replied
Glen Luss and Rossdhu, they are smoking in ruin
  And the best of Loch Lomond lie dead on her side.
    Widow and Saxon maid
    Long shall lament our raid,
  Think of Clan Alpine with fear and with woe
    Lennox and Leven glen
    Shake when they hear again
    Rodrigh-Vich-Alpine-Dhu-hoieroe.

—Lady of Lake.

Early Feus at Row and Shandon.

About the earliest of the feus, July 1830, taken from the Colquhoun lands of Row was by James Brown, parish schoolmaster, who took 1 rood and 21 perches of land, part of Ardenconnell, on which was raised the small one-storey house at corner of road leading past Row churchyard. Right was reserved to Sir J. Colquhoun to cut down and carry an ash tree growing on the site. In December 1830 the ground on which the two-storey house at the head of Row pier stands, 1 acre imperial, at feu-duty of £10, was taken by Peter M'Auslane, "Change Keeper at Row." In 1831 the feu known then as Laggarie, consisting of 1 acre imperial, feu-duty £10, was taken by Alexander Colquhoun, wright, Helensburgh. This feu, much enlarged, is now occupied by the residence of Mrs. Heywood Collins, called "Lagarie." In 1831 also Major R. A. Mackay feued a considerable piece of land on the loch side, on Letrualt farm, viz., 18 acres, 3 roods, 2 perches, the feu-duty being £140 14s. 4d., or £7 10s. per imperial acre. In 1833 Miss Hopkirk feued part of Ardenconnell estate, to extent of 5 acres, 2 roods, 20 perches, and upon a portion of this ground the villas known as Woodstone and Rowmore were subsequently built. The first, Woodstone, was but a small plain house, but after it was acquired by William Couper, writer, Glasgow, the mansion was entirely rebuilt in its present form. Isaac Spy, mason, Ardenconnell, took a feu near Rowmore in 1836. At Shandon the feuing began about 1831 when several small houses seem to have been erected, and subsequently pulled down or rebuilt. In this way Berriedale came to be built by Major the Hon. James Sinclair, who took a large feu of over 9 acres, which was subdivided, and other houses erected. The feuars were taken bound in all these cases to "bring in all grain growing on lands hereby feued or which shall suffer fire and water in the houses thereon to the Mill of Milligs and paying such multure as the tenants of the Barony of Milligs pay for grinding thereof." In almost all cases also the feus had to be enclosed by stone walls.

EARLY MINISTERS OF CARDROSS.

From the well written account of the parish of Cardross in the "Sketches of Churches and Clergy," from which extracts have been given, the following is taken :—

"The first of the parochial rectors is William de Glendynwyn, a faithful adherent of Robert Bruce, and a constant companion of James, Lord of Douglas, called the 'good Lord James.' Of his successor, Robert Blackader, 1480, there is much more to be said. He was a man of affairs, and deeply engaged in state matters, for he was sent on embassies to England, France, and Spain, and was one of those who arranged the marriage, the consequences of which were so important to both countries, between James IV. the victim of Flodden and Margaret eldest daughter of Henry VII. of England. He died in 1508 while on a journey to the Holy Land, 'going,' as John Knox superciliously remarks, 'in his superstitious devotioune to Hierusalem.' Of his personal habits we have several glimpses ; his costly vestments, and luxurious living astonishing even the wealthy Venetian nobles; and if we look into the Lord High Treasurer's accounts we find that this dashing ecclesiastic loved high play and good company, for on New Year's day, 1490, he supped and played cards with the King, the Earl of Bothwell, the Chamberlain and the Treasurer. Blackader, we know, paid at least one visit to Cardross, though not in the line of his priestly functions, for in 1489 he was present with King James at the surrender of Dunbarton castle.

"The next rector, Jaspar Cranstoun, did not do even as much as this, for not only did he leave Cardross unvisited, but he seems to have even been non-resident in Glasgow. On February, 1501, there was an official visitation of the Chapter of Glasgow, and from the report it appears that the 'Prebendary of Cardross did not make residence, the Archdeacon and the Bishop's vicar were boys,' while of another dignitary it is reported that 'he often left the choir during divine service,' from all which we must infer that discipline was pretty free and easy at that time in the Cathedral Church of Glasgow.

"We must not pass over a later rector, Master James Stuart. He is a credit to Cardross, having attained, on the feast of St. Crispin and St. Crispinian, 1522, to the dignity of Rector of the University of Glasgow, an honour which was conferred upon him on more than one subsequent occasion. The rector, churchman though he was, had a daughter who, in 1536, married one of the Haliburtons of

Mertroun. Their daughter, Agnes, became the wife of Alexander
Erskine, a brother of the laird of Balgoney, and from this marriage
sprang the Erskines of Shielfield, one of these was Ralph Erskine,
the ninth of whose twelve children was the Rev. Henry Erskine, a
notable sufferer during the persecution of the Presbyterians in Scotland, and in later life minister successively of Whitsome and Chirn-
side. By his second wife, Margaret Halcro, he was the father of
Ebenezer and Ralph Erskine, the founders of the Secession Church,
now merged in the U.P. Church, which thus connects itself with James
Stuart, the Rector of Cardross.

"The last Rector was Thomas Archibald. On the eve of the
Reformation he feued out the Kirklands and Rectory to John
Smollett, only reserving the Manse, garden and pasture for two cows,
to the Vicar of Cardross in all time to come. He was chamberlain
to James Beaton, the last Archbishop of Glasgow, beloved by all who
knew him, who took up his residence in Paris, and acted as ambassador for King James. After the Reformation Archibald continued to
reside in Glasgow, and corresponded with the Archbishop for many
years.

"And now let us see what we know of these Vicars of Cardross,
who up till now seem indeed to us but shadowy and unreal personages.
In 1518, however, both vicar and curate come before us and speak
for themselves. There was at this time a vacancy in the vicarage,
and one Sir Thomas Auld (that is Thomas Auld, *Dominus*, or Bachelor
of Arts) received from the rector letters of collation as vicar pensioner.
Armed with these, and supported by a notary public, and witnesses,
he proceeded to the church to be put in possession, but in the
churchyard was met by the curate Sir Peter Flemyng, who flatly refused to let him have the keys of the church. The discomfited vicar
thereupon made a formal complaint, which has come down to our
own time. Sir Peter Flemyng was one of these cross-grained
troublesome ecclesiastics, who are still to be met with, and who keep
every presbytery in hot water. On several occasions, too long to be
here recorded, but sufficiently amusing, he was at cross-purposes with
his brethren, and he seems to have driven Sir Andrew Watson,
chaplain of the Rood Altar, in the parish church of Dunbarton,
nearly crazy. The latter complains that 'Sir Peter Flemyng stole
his surplice, and his breviary furth of the church, and also that the
said Sir Peter stole his key furth of his yard-yett."

"And now, having rapidly glanced over the history of the parish
before the Reformation, let us for a moment try to picture the
parochial life of Cardross at the time at which we have arrived. The

parish, we have seen, was ruled by a rector or parson, a vicar and a curate. The duties of the parson were those of his canonry, and although in earlier times it was expected that he should devote himself to the care of his prebend when not in residence, this had long since fallen into desuetude, and he enjoyed the revenues, without concerning himself whence they came. To the vicar was entrusted the actual charge. He occupied the parish manse, and to him belonged the small tithes, but in Cardross there was a vicar pensioner, who was paid a fixed stipend, and received the altar dues and offerings of the parishioners, while the vicarage teinds went to the rector. The curate was the officiating temporary clergyman, representing the vicar and taking charge of divine service in his absence or during a vacancy."

"After the Reformation 'Readers' took the place of the priests of the Roman Catholics. His duty was simple, extending merely to reading prayers and a portion of Scripture morning and evening, and teaching the children of the parish. The first Reader of Cardross, John Cuick, was succeeded by John Fluttisbury, who held the higher rank of "Exhorter," the name given to a Reader more advanced in knowledge and able to preach.

CARDROSS KIRK SESSION RECORDS.

These Records seem to contain but little of general interest. They commence 23rd February, 1727, and end 19th May, 1734. A long interval follows till 15th April, 1810, when the Records are carried on till the present day. A good deal of consideration was evidently given to the affairs of Mrs. Moore's Trust.

EXTRACTS FROM WODROW'S ANALECTA, CARDROSS.

"March 1703. James Gordon, minister of Cardross. Licensed in Ireland and preached under license from King James near Derry, was very acceptable there. His house which the people built for him destroyed at siege of Derry—he had predicted it would not stand long. Preached that shortly Ireland would be a desolation. Preached from curious texts, at the ordination of minister from the text 'The priests' window shall be towards the North.' Preached on

occasion of a monthly fast about 1692, there had been a meeting of
Jacobites at Balamahaugh when King James' health had been drank.
Some of them came to hear him. He said, 'weel this is a fast day
say you, we should mind our poor abdicated prince. Poor prince,
my soul, my soul pities him—weel what shall we doe for our poor
prince.' When Derry was besieged he went to see it, took boat
from Greenock and got to Derry Lough, went on board one of the
English ships, and remonstrated with Captain Brauny for not going
up the Lough when the city was in such straits. An altercation between the Captain and Major Kirk who had provisions for taking to
the besieged. He abused Kirk and said he deserved hanging, Kirk
threatened to shoot Gordon. Finally Major Kirk agreed to commission both, Captain B. and Gordon, and they went at the boom
and broke it. Captain B. was killed, and the ship got in and relieved
the garrison. Gordon stayed two days and helped to lay cannon on
the walls and returned to Cardross. Had a presentiment of his
death. One day when meeting of session was at his house, Mr. G.
after the sermon walked pensively up and down his room and said,
'Gentlemen, you must think upon another minister,' said no more
but walked up and down. Elders talked about it, and asked two of
them, Ferms and Geilston, should in name of the Session ask him
to-morrow. He was in perfect health, and when spoken to wished
to dismiss the subject gently. They pressed him, when he said he
had nothing against parish or people, or thought of going elsewhere,
but at the moment had a strong impulse moving him to speak as he
did. At the end of the week fell ill of a disease and never preached
more." On his deathbed he spoke seriously to many of the parishioners, and " he also made some of the most graceless gentlemen in
the parish pray beside him, such as old Ardoch and Cougraine."

REPORT OF PROCEEDINGS IN CONNECTION WITH THE ERECTION OF
ROW PARISH AND TRANSPORTATION OF CARDROSS KIRK TO
PRESENT SITE. (SUPPLIED TO THE AUTHOR BY THE REV.
WILLIAM MAXWELL OF CARDROSS.)

IN 1639 the General Assembly granted authority to the Presbytery
to settle both parishes, i.e., Cardross and Rosneath, "with case " to
the parishioners "to attend the ministry of the word." In January
1640 this act of the Assembly was presented to the Presbytery by

Walter M'Aulay of Ardencaple and John Napier of Kilmahew. At the next meeting of Presbytery, 4th February, 1640, my Lord of Argyll appears by his letter consenting to whatever the Presbytery thought fit to decide. Mr. M'Aulay again appears "requiring the ease of the ministry to be given at the Kirk upon the Row of Connell." John Napier of Kilmahew, John Dennistoun of Dalquhurn, and others appear "requiring the foresaid ease to be at the Chapell of Kilmahew," and John Dennistoun of Dalquhurn "requires the Kirke of Cardross to be transported." On the 18th of February there was a large attendance of parishioners from Rosneath and Cardross, "and in special John and Daniel Evens, brother german in Keppoch, requiring ease at the Chapell of Kilmahew; while "John Semple and Archibald Bounten in Kirketown within the Parochin of Cardross required they should not be diseased of the service of the ministrations, but that it might remain still at the Kirke of Cardross" (*i.e.*, the old site). A committee of the Presbytery were appointed to meet at the Chapel of Glenfruin and go through the "haill twa parochins" to find the "most commodious place of service."

At the next meeting of Presbytery, Mr. Robert Watson, minister of Cardross, along with John Bounten of Ardoch, Robert Hoill of Fulbar, Younger, and William and Archibald Bounten in Over-Kirkton appears and opposes all that had been done. The dispute was at last referred to the General Assembly which met at Aberdeen iu July 1640, and the act of the Assembly was laid on the table of the Presbytery, but afterwards "the matter of Rosnaith and Cardross" appears to have gone to sleep for some time.

On the 20th December, 1642, the Presbytery again took up the division of the parishes of Rosneath and Cardross, and the Presbytery forwarded a letter to the Commissioners for the settlement of kirks, setting forth that "the lands of Glenfrnin within the Parish of Cardross and all the bounds upon the Gareloch be annexed to the new kirk of the Row, and that all the lands within the Parish of Rosnaith, lyand eastward frae Mivell Kirkmichall might be annexed to the Paroch of Cardross. And the Paroch Kirk of Cardross to be transported to the most commodious place." In April following, 1643, Mr. Harry Semple, minister of Killearn, was appointed by the Presbytery to proceed to Edinburgh to support before the Commissioners on Kirks the recommendations of the Presbytery. On the 3rd July, 1643, the Lords of Commission pronounced Decree, annexing to Cardross all the lands in Rosneath mentioned in the Presbytery's letter and ordaining the transportation of the Kirk of Cardross, leaving the new site to be determined by the Presbytery with advice of the Parishioners.

The Presbytery thereafter resolved to visit the Parish of Cardross on 12th September, and to summon the minister and the heritors of that parish to the meeting. " Upon the which day compeared in the Kirk of Cardross Mr. Andrew Cameron, Moderator, and divers members of the Presbytery, with the Heritors and Parishioners and minister of the Kirk of Cardross, for visitatione of the said kirk and designatione of the stance of the new kirk to be builded. And his visitors, having taken advyce of the Heritors and Minister, went upon the same day to the lands of Wallastoune, accompanied with the Heritors and Minister, and fand that place, with the consent of the Heritors and Minister, to be the most commodious place for the stances of the new kirk and of the minister's manse thairat. And therefore designed ten scoir foots in breed, and ten scoir foots in length, upon the croft that lies on the north side of the King's high-way at the back of the house and yaird possessed by Patrick Glen, and designed ane ruid of land for the minister's house and yaird lying contigue with the kirkyaird, with special advyce and consent of Sir Humphry Colquhoun of Balvie, being personally present as having full right to the said lands who mortifies the said bounds for that use in all time coming."

At the next meeting of Presbytery the minutes of visitation were approved, and very soon thereafter the erection of the new kirk was proceeded with, provided with accommodation for four hundred sitters. It was taken down in the year 1825, and the present church built, which was opened for public worship on the last Sunday of April, 1827.

COUNTY AFFAIRS—ACTS OF COMMISSIONERS OF SUPPLY.

Under the old county management the roads and bridges were kept in repair, and when the new bridge over the Fruin was ordered to be repaired in June 1748, the inhabitants of the adjacent country were ordered to work three days in assisting to fill up the ends of the " new bridge built over the water of ffrone." Each tenant yoking four horses in a plough, betwixt Arnburn and the mill burn of Bonnell. And each tenant in Glenfrone on both sides of the Chappell of Glenfrone, to repair with two horses and work three days of next

week.   They are to bring with them carts, such as have them, and
"cars, creels, coups and other proper materials for carrying gravel,
sand, etc.," to work six hours each day.   Constables to attend and
take an account of absent men, and to fine them 20 shillings Scots.

Decree of Justices, 21st August, 1750.   At Tolbooth of Dunbar-
tane no Justice of the Peace is to suffer himself to be treated or entertained by Excise Officers at Excise Courts, or by any parties who
have suits depending before them.

Decree of Justices, 14th May, 1751.   To mend the road leading
from ferry of Dunbarton to the kirk of Cardross, and on account of
the difficulty of wheeled machines to go thereon, the county to be
called out to work on said road after they are done with their bear
seed.

Meeting of Justices, 4th June, 1751.   Constables are to summon
all persons who are fit for service, whether man or woman, and are
not presently employed in service to appear before the Justices.
They have to give reasons for not being employed in service.

Meeting of Justices, 2nd June, 1753.   All the roads in the county
to be examined, and Justices appointed in each district for this work,
the tenants, cottars, and labourers to work six days, or to pay fines.
Intimation to be made of place and time of working at the parish
church on Sabbath before work to be done, as prescribed by law.
From Clachan of Rosneath to Portindorneck assessors were Colin
Campbell, bailie of Rosneath, Patrick Cuming of Barreman, and
Patrick M'Adam in Mamore.

Meeting 1st November, 1756.   The following were authorised to
retail ale and beer and other exciseable liquors :

In Row Parish.

John M'Neil in Ferry House of Portincaple.
Malcolm Colquhoun in Tayichladick.
William Cuming in Shandon.
Aitken M'Arthur at kirk of Row.
Donald Smith, ferrier at Row of Connell.
Aulay M'Aulay at Row.
Alexander Miller at Stuck.
Duncan M'Farlane in Auchinvennel more—Glenfrone.
James M'Neill in Chapel of Glenfrone.

In Rosneath Parish.

Peter Cuming, Ferry house of Rosneath.
Elizabeth Campbell at kirk of Rosneath.
Robert M'Farlane there.

FROM "DEPREDATIONS COMMITTED ON THE CLAN CAMPBELL."
—Edinburgh, 1816.

List of the Goods taken out of Rosneith, from John Campbell, Captain of Carrick, and his Tennents, yrs, be Stranaver and his partie ; Being directed and led on be Dougal M'Glashan, servitor to the Laird of Strachurr, in June 1685 ; after ye Rebellion was crushed.

	lib.	s.	d.
Imprimis, Fra the sd Captain himself, taken out of the lands of Douglas, 180 coues, at 25 M. per piece, all estimat to	3,000	0	0
Item, from John M'Inneron, yr, 15 coues, at 25 M. per piece, 3 stirks at 4 lib per piece, 40 sheep at 2 lib per piece—*Inde*........................	342	0	0
Fra Duncan Leckie, yr, 15 sheep,........................	30	0	0
Item, fra Patrick Galbraith, yr, 11 coues, 1 stirk, and horse and ane mare, estimat to........................	254	0	0
Fra Donald Tailyeour, yr, ane coue,....................	16	13	4
Fra Archibald Wilson, 4 horses, 5 sheep,..............	90	0	0
„ Duncan Campbell, in Cursnoch, 3 mares 9 coues,	240	0	0
„ Alexr. M'Auslan, yr, 7 coues at....................	116	0	0
„ Archibald Chalmers, yr, 18 coues and a horse,...	340	0	0
Patrick Hall, in Alie, 3 coues and mare,..............	90	0	0
Fra Archibald Chalmers, yr., 2 mares, 1 foal,..........	60	0	0
Item, fra the Captain of Carrick, 7 sheep and wedders pertaining to himself, 160 sheep at 40s. per piece,	320	0	0
	4,798	13	4

Followes the List of the Goods taken from ye sd Captain and his Tennents, in Rosneith, be Angus Cameron and Allan his brother, in Inveredden.

	lib.	s.	d.
Fra Jon M'Inneron, in Douglas, 3 coues, 2 horses, estimat to	116	13	4
Fra Duncan Leckie, yr, 1 coue, 4 sheep,..............	24	13	4
„ Jon Tailyeour, in Cainsail, 1 coue,..................	16	13	4
Archibald Wilson there, ane horse,....................	33	6	8
Fra Patrick Cumyng, elder, yr, of houshold plenishing and furnitor, beds, wearing cloaths and ready money, and victual to ye value........................	333	6	8
Fra Patrick Hall in the Alie, 10 coues, 1 bull, 1 stirk, 2 mares, ...	242	13	4

	lib.	s.	d.
Fra Wm. Chalmers, yr, 14 coues, 1 bull, a stirk, 140 elns of lining at...	319	6	8
Fra Alex. Chalmers, yr, 14 coues, 1 stot, 4 stirks,...	261	6	8
Inde,	1,348	0	0
Item, interest and profit, coast, skaith and damage be the want of these goods these two yeares bypast,	136	0	0
The sds 3 soumes extend in haill to.....................	6,282	13	4

Exact list of the Horses, Coues, Nolt, sheep and oyrs plundered be a partie of men under the Lord Stranavers command, out of John Campbell of Ardintennie his lands in the paroche of Rosneth and Shrefdome of Dumbartan, the 22 June 1685 ; Dugall M'Glashan in Succoth of Strathquhirr being guide to the foresd robberie.

	lib.	s.	d.
Imprimis, Taken from the sd John Campbell of Ardintennie, a ryding horse, worth............	66	13	4
Item, from him 40 coues at 20 lib. the piece is.........	1200	0	0
Item from John Gay in Littlelaheane 8 coues at 20 lib per piece, and 2 horses at 40 lib p. piece.........	240	0	0
Item from John M'ilvaine in Clandearge, two coues at 20 lib per piece, and a mare at 30 lib..................	70	0	0
Item from James Hunter yr., 10 coues at 20 lib p. piece, and a mare and a filly at 40 lib..............	240	0	0
Item from John M'ilvaine in Boraman, ane coue at 20 lib	20	0	0
Item from Archbald Mitchell, 9 coues at 20 lib. per piece, 16 sheep at 2 lib.	212	0	0
Item from Archbald M'ilvaine, 3 coues at............ ..	60	0	0
„ from Alex. Campbell, 2 coues at.....................	40	0	0
Summa,	2148	0	0

Inventor of Goods, Geir, Houshold plenishing and oyrs, taken and robbed from Donald Campbell of Knockderrie, and his tennents, out of the lands of Blariunecktara, in Rosneath, be the persones underwritten in June and July 1685.

		lib.	*s.*	*d.*
Imprimis, from Malcolm M'Inneran in Blariunecktara be Alex. Roy M'Donald, son to —— M'Donald in Pelidabeig in Glencoa, and Alex. M'Donald of Keillisnacome, tennents, and vassals to the tutor of Appyne, eight milk coues with yr calves, 6 yeld coues, and 1 stott, the coues and calves at 20 lib. a piece, and th yeld coues and stott to 20 mks.......		253	6	8
Item fra th sd Malcolm be th forenamed persones 17 sheep at 40s. a piece....................................		34	0	0
Item fra him be th sd persones, of cloaths and houshold plenishing to th value of...............		24	0	0
Item fra Duncan M'Inneran yr. be th forenamed persones, and yr accomplices, 14 milk coues, with 8 quhey calves, and ane yeld coue, each milk coue estimat to 20 lib. and the said yeld coue to 20 mks.		293	6	8
Item be them fra the sd Duncan 42 sheep at 40s. the sheep..		84	0	0
Item, 1 copper kettle and 2 pans, 26 lib., and of pleugh irons and houshold plenishing valued to 20 lib....		46	0	0
Item taken be the forenamed persones, from Patrick Leckie, yr., 6 milk coues, with yr calves, at 20 lib.		120	0	0
Item, 12 sheep, pryce forsd...............................		24	0	0
,, houshold plenishing, with abrilziements, valued		40	0	0
Item fra th sd Donald Campbel, 4 coues with yr calves taken be the forenamed persones, estimat 20 lib. piece		80	0	0
Summa,		998	13	4

Item, the profit and encrease with the cost, skaith and damage susteint be the forenamed persones, amounting to the soume of		600	0	0

The above written goods, geir, and oyrs foresd, were assigned, be the sds tennents, in favors of the sd Donald Campbel, yr., master, who, with them, was in his majesties service, the whole tyme of the troubles.

| Additional *Items*. Taken be the Lord Stranaver and his men, fra the foresd Donald Campbell and his tenents the goods following.............................. | | 733 | 19 | 8 |

RENTAL OF THE PARISH OF ROW, 1814.

1. Sir James Colquhoun.

Stronmallinoch,	£100
Letruailmore or West,	56
Letruail or Middle,	74
Stickiedow and Blairnan,	71
Auchintaal and Kirkmichael,	200
Stuck and pendicles,	150
Malligs and do.,	550
Easterton of Ardincaple and pendicles,	316
Gartcloth head,	57
Tombowie and Tenant,	200
Portincaple,	45
Feorlinbreck,	34
Durlin,	35
Balimenock and pendicles,	83
Tomaioulin,	22
Stuckengairth,	212
Part of Meikle and Little Balernay,	148
Remainder of said Land and Shandon,	100
Stronratan,	133
Auchinvennal,	77
Meikle Drumfad,	100
Mains Park,	180
Daligan,	40
Little Drumfad,	54
Share of Balevoulin and Balnock,	62
Easter Kilbride,	73
Faslane and Chapelston, Greenfield and Dunnvaird,	224
Aldounot Mill and Lands,	10
	£3,406

2. The Mortification Lands of the Chapel of Glenfroun.

Lands of Chapel and pendicles,	£30

3. Lord John Campbell.

Middle and Wester Ardincaple and pendicles,	550

4. James Buchanan, Esqr., of Ardinconnel.

High Laggrey and pendicles,	£178
Laigh Do., ,, do.,	90

Blarvatan,   -   -   -   -   -   -   -   50
Ardinconnel and pendicles,   -   -   -   -   250
Letruailvoulin and Barkhouse,   -   -   -   206
Stuckaluick and Blarvadig,   -   -   -   -   180
West Kilbride,   -   -   -   -   -   -   55
Stucknaduff, -   -   -   -   -   -   -   ` 56
                                                        ——— 1,065
5. Herbert Buchanan, Esq., of Arden Bennachra,-   -   -   420
6. The Heirs of —— M'Farlane of Blarnearns, Blarnearns, -   210
7. James Dennistoun, Esq., of Colgrain, Share of Balevoulin
   and Balnock, -   -   -   -   -   -   -   -   -   78
8. James Oswald, Esq., of Shieldhall, Garstane, -   -   -   100

                                        Total,   £5,849

     The fifth part whereof for Teind,   -   -   -   - £1,169 16s.

By a note appended to this rental dated Edinburgh, 24th January,
1815, the Lord Ordinary in the cause the minister of Row against
the Heritors finds that the Teinds, parsonage, and vicarage of the
several Heritors lands "amount to the particular sums of money
contained in the foregoing scheme extending in haill to £1,169 16s.
stg."

ARDENCONNELL ESTATE.

In 1747 the estate seemed to have belonged to Arthur M'Arthur
from an advertisement in the *Glasgow Journal*. In 1749 it is thus
advertised in that paper as for sale, "the lands of Arconnel and
Lettwalbeg holding feu from the Duke of Montrose £25 17s. 8d. for
Arconnel, and £8 5s. 4d. for Lettwalbeg, to be exposed for sale in
Court Hall of Tolbooth of Dunbarton."

Arconnel was said to pay rent £164 2s. 8d. Scots silver rent, 27
bolls bear, 25 bolls oatmeal, 3 wedders, 2½ dozen hens. Lettwalbeg
£31 13s. 4d. Scots silver rent, 27 bolls meal, 2 wedders, 2½ dozen
hens at 4s. Scots each.   The Feu-duties to be deducted, and
£82 14s. 6d. Scots to minister of Row, and Arconnel further pays
vicarage dues, etc. £8 4s. 6d. Scots.

z

THE END.

Taylor, Lady E. Clough, 156.
Thom, R., of Canna, 161.
Torphichen, 39.
Topography of Garelochside, 91-111.
Trail, Mr., 49.
Tullichewan, 35, 283.

Umphredus de Kilpatrick, 32.
Ure, Mr., 20.

Wade, Wm., 114.
Wallace, William, 4, 54 *passim*.
Wallace's Leap, 165.

Walpole, Sir Robert, 150.
Warr, Alfred, 230.
Watt, James, 48.
Webster, John M., 65.
William III., 147.
William, Conqueror, 25.
Winnoch, Loch, 16.
Wood, Sir Andrew, 28.
—— John, 42.
—— John and Charles, 41.
Woodend, 129.

York, Duke of, 145.

THE END.

www.ingramcontent.com/pod-product-compliance
Lightning Source LLC
Chambersburg PA
CBHW020240290326
41929CB00045B/877